Understanding Africa:
A Geographic Approach

United States Military Academy
West Point, New York

Center for Strategic Leadership
United States Army War College
Carlisle, Pennsylvania

January 2009

Published by Books Express Publishing
Copyright © Books Express, 2010
ISBN 978-1-907521-40-9
To purchase copies at discounted prices please contact
info@books-express.com

Editors

Amy Richmond Krakowka

Laurel J. Hummel

Copy Editor

Chris Fuhriman

Cover Design

Matthew P. Cuviello

Cartographer

Ian J. Irmischer

Composition

Arthur L. Bradshaw, Jr.

Acknowledgement

The editors are grateful to all the authors who contributed their time and expertise to this book. We would also like to thank Chris Fuhriman for his many hours of copy editing, and Ian Irmischer for producing the maps. We wish to acknowledge the inspiration and mentorship provided to us by Francis Galgano, who unfailingly models best practices in teaching, scholarship, and professionalism. Finally, we thank the Center for Strategic Leadership and specifically Kent Butts, for believing in the need for this book.

Table of Contents

Authors

Lieutenant Colonel (Retired) Brent Bankus is a member of the National Security Issues Group, U.S. Army War College. Mr. Bankus has worked in Eritrea and Benin and was previously Director of Joint Training and Exercises, U.S. Army Peacekeeping Institute, and has been widely published on peacekeeping, homeland security and homeland defense topics.

Lieutenant Colonel (Retired) Clarence J. Bouchat flew fighters as an Air Force officer before teaching theater strategy at the U.S. Army War College. He has taught at the U.S. Air Force Academy and published articles on regional and political geography. He currently teaches World Regional Geography at Harrisburg Area Community College in Pennsylvania.

Major Jon A. Bushman is an assistant professor of geography at the United States Military Academy. He is preparing to be a strategic intelligence officer and has taught and researched in the areas of physical, human, and regional geography. He holds a masters degree in geography from the University of Wisconsin.

Dr. Kent Hughes Butts is Professor and Director of the National Security Issues Group at the Center of Strategic Leadership, U.S. Army War College. A former U.S. Defense Attaché in Africa, his books include *Geopolitics of Southern Africa: South Africa as Regional Superpower* and *Economics and National Security: the Case of China.*

Dr. Richard P. Cincotta is the demographic consultant to the Long Range Analysis Unit of the National Intelligence Council in Washington, DC. His research has focused on the demographic transition and its relationships to natural resource dynamics and to the political dynamics of states. He has participated in field research in China, India, and

Morocco, and served in an intelligence field in the U.S. Navy.

Major James Farrell Chastain is an assistant professor of geography at the United States Military Academy. He has taught courses in military geography, urban geography, American history, world history, physical geography, cultural geography, Latin American geography, and the geography of the Middle East and Africa. His research focuses on North African immigration into France and African urbanization. MAJ Chastain holds a graduate degree in geography.

Major Matthew P. Cuviello is an instructor in the geography program at the United States Military Academy. An Army armor officer, he has taught courses in physical geography, military geography and climatology. He holds undergraduate and graduate degrees in geography.

Colonel (Retired) Thomas A. Dempsey is the Professor of Security Sector Reform at the U.S. Army Peacekeeping and Stability Operations Institute in Carlisle, Pennsylvania. Formerly an Army foreign area officer specializing in sub-Saharan Africa, he has served as the U.S. Defense attaché in Liberia and Sierra Leone and was the Director of African Studies at the U.S. Army War College from 1999 to 2006. He holds graduate degrees in African area studies from UCLA and in military arts and sciences from the School of Advanced Military Science at Fort Leavenworth, Kansas.

Major Brian J. Doyle is currently an armor officer serving as a team chief to a border transition team in Iraq. Previously he served as an assistant professor of geography at the United States Military Academy. He has taught and researched in the areas of economic and political geography focusing on the Middle East and Africa. He holds graduate degrees in geography and military arts and sciences.

Major Brian R. Dunmire is an instructor in the geography program at the United States Military Academy. He is a strategic intelligence officer and has taught and researched in the areas of physical and cultural geography, as well as the geography of the Middle East and Africa. He is a doctoral candidate at Old Dominion University, and holds masters degrees from the National Defense Intelligence College, the Army Command and General Staff College, St. Mary's University of San Antonio; and a bachelor's degree from Penn State.

Colonel (Dr.) Laurel J. Hummel is an Academy Professor and director of the geography program at the United States Military Academy. A former Army intelligence officer, she has taught a variety of physical and human geography courses and has researched in the areas of military geography, geodemographics, and geography education. She holds graduate degrees in geography, educational leadership, and strategic studies.

Dr. Amy Richmond Krakowka is an assistant professor of geography at the United States Military Academy. Her research focuses on valuing ecosystem goods and services, energy security, and environmental security. She has published articles in journals such as *Ecological Economics* and *The Energy Journal*.

Dr. Jon C. Malinowski is Professor of Geography at the United States Military Academy, West Point, New York. He has taught a variety of world regional geography courses, including geography of the Middle East and Africa. In addition to academic articles in the field of behavioral geography, Dr. Malinowski is a co-author of or contributor to several textbooks.

Lieutenant Colonel (Dr.) Steven Oluic is Associate Professor of Geography, and has taught courses in urban geography, physical geography, world regional geography and European and Russian regional geography. His research focuses on radical Islam in southeastern Europe and radicalism among the Balkan Muslim Diasporas in the US and Europe. He is the author of one book, numerous book chapters and articles, and is the recipient of several research grants. LTC Oluic holds graduate degrees in environmental science and geography.

Dr. Diana B. Putman is a career Foreign Service Office with the United States Agency for International Development, currently on detail to the United States Africa Command. She has served in Asia and the Middle East, and has spent over twenty years doing research and development work in Africa. Dr. Putman holds graduate degrees in Anthropology and Strategic Studies.

Lieutenant Colonel Luis A. Rios is an assistant professor of geography at the United States Military Academy. An Air Force weather officer, his research interests include environmental security, military geography, climate and climate change impacts on national policy, and natural disaster response and mitigation. He teaches physical geography, meteorology, climatology and environmental security courses and holds undergraduate and graduate degrees in meteorology and tropical meteorology.

Major Megan B. Stallings is a personnel officer in the United States Army. Previously, she served as an assistant professor of geography at the United States Military Academy where she taught and researched in the areas of physical geography and land use planning. She holds graduate degrees in geography, national security & strategic studies, and human resources development.

Major Benefsheh D. Verell is an assistant professor of geography at the United States Military Academy. She has taught and researched in the areas of physical geography and sustainable land use planning, and holds master's degrees in geography and organizational and security management. She has published in *The Geographical Bulletin*.

Dr. Richard Wolfel is an associate professor and Chair of Intercultural Competence at the United States Military Academy. His research focuses on nationalism, identity and the urban built environment in Germany and central Asia. He has published in journals such as *Nationalities Papers, The Pennsylvania Geographer,* and *The Western Humanities Review.*

Data Source: ESRI 2008

Introduction: The Imperative of Understanding Africa

Laurel J. Hummel

Immediately following the 2008 U.S. presidential election, which occurred around the time this book was being compiled, a fracas occurred within the media surrounding some post-election campaign gossip that the Republican party's vice-presidential candidate had revealed during debate and briefing preparations that she did not understand that Africa was a continent, and instead believed it to be a single state. Whether that rumor was true or false is quite beside the point: the larger issue, arguably, is that many people found it even at least somewhat plausible that a person with a high school diploma—let alone a college degree—granted in the U.S. might not know that Africa *is* a continent. Indeed it is a very large one, with 53 independent states fraught with a troubled and complex historical geography. Although most Americans have a general sense that modern Africa is beset with difficulty and some could name a few places and issues related to the limited coverage given African events in the mainstream media, there is little understanding of Africa. Indeed for virtually all Americans, Africa remains "the dark continent."

Americans' knowledge in world events and global systems is infamously poor for a number of reasons. Not least among them is the abandonment of geography from the U.S. secondary public school curriculum, or at least its bifurcation in most U.S. states into earth science and social science courses, with an accompanying loss of the integrative and holistic nature of geography. Indeed, geography is uniquely able to deliver a synergistic and comprehensive view of a place, and the movement away from the discipline has contributed to what Daniel Welch has depicted as Americans' "fog of distortion, ignorance, smugness, [and] disinterest" (2005) about the world outside our borders. If that characterization makes us wince, it is largely because it fits us too well.

American attitudes toward the value of knowing about Africa have changed, but not really progressed, over the last few generations. Before the middle of the twentieth century, there were only a few independent states (Egypt, Ethiopia, Liberia, and South Africa, if one counts being a sovereign state *within* the British empire as true independence), with the rest of the continent carved into colonial possessions tied to their European masters. So what Americans learned about Africa was decidedly within the context of the administrators and resource exploiters, not with respect to the stability or security of Africans themselves. During the Cold War, Americans' predilection toward dividing African states into pro-U.S. and pro-U.S.S.R. camps was reflective of the superpowers' efforts to curry allies, secure continued access to resources, and establish potential forward bases. Along with that alignment came a tendency to apply a double standard to African events; ideology was used to either unfairly attack or uncritically support actions by African governments and regimes, often with a simplistic "they're either with us or against us" stance. For example, a regional drought in the 1980s was seen as the catalyst to agricultural failure in Botswana, a U.S. ally, while the same drought in neighboring Angola was regarded as benign, with the failure of socialism blamed for Angola's similar agricultural breakdown (Bender 1988). The classification process often used toward the end of the Cold War to ascribe "goodness" or "badness" according to West or East leanings left out of the equation how well or poorly a state treated its own people.

In a new world order of multiparty actors—first a multiplicity of unaligned state actors, more recently complicated by the rise of activity by supranationals and nongovernmentals—global relationships are more complicated than ever. The reasons Americans do not frequently think about Africa include that frankly, what little we know tends to make us uncomfortable and confused. The overwhelming theme of Africa as a continual victim of exploitation, be it of human or environmental resources, comes perhaps a little too close to our shores for comfort. As well for most Americans, the incomplete story they know of Africa is bleak and unrelenting. It is all very complicated, and who has the time to devote to understanding it, let alone assisting? Compounded by the heightened pace of life enabled by technologies, increased concern over trans-boundary problems like apparent climate change, and the recent worrisome downturn of global markets and economies, American attention is anywhere but on Africa. My co-editor and I think this is a problem, and we undertook this book in an attempt to help turn attention toward a continent with an enormous amount of environmental value and human potential, and many serious problems which, if not solved, will continue to seriously degrade both.

Toward that end, we offer this book as the fruit of the geographer's art. Geographers are interested in many things at once: indeed we look at the physical environment—climates and landforms, vegetation patterns and stream channels—as well as the processes, patterns, and functions of human settlement on that environment. Geographers study all aspects of the world: the word "geography," after all, derives from the Greek words for "Earth writing." We seek to know both the physical and human characteristics of places, and how those characteristics intertwine and interact to make a place the way it is, and different from other places.

This "place basis" is the theme of Part One. In order to somewhat ease the complexity of Earth, geographers devise regions. This regional concept is a tool to help us simplify and therefore more easily understand a place. The five chapters within Part One are regionalized in a fashion roughly analogous to five of the so-called "pillar" Regional Economic Communities (RECs) of the African Economic Community. The RECs consist of trade blocs, sometimes reinforced by military and political cooperation. These "regional geographies" are a good way to learn about the continent in bite-size geographic pieces. The chapters—one each focused on North, East, Central, Southern, and West Africa—are structured alike. Five geography faculty from West Point: Brian Dunmire, Jon Bushman, Matthew Cuviello, Benefsheh Verell, and Brian Doyle have endeavored to show what characteristics give commonality to each spatial delineation. Each begins with an introduction and basic locational information, moving on to explore the characteristics of the physical environment: physiography and geomorphology, climate and meteorology, and biogeography. The region's human-based characteristics are examined next: first the cogent historical and cultural geographies, followed by an explanation of the region's population geography (also called geo-demographics), its urban geography, aspects of medical geography (that is, the environment of health and disease), economic geography, and finally the current political geography. As one starts to mentally lay each characteristic atop the others, the power of regional geography becomes clear. By making connections between seemingly disparate kinds of information, we can create a means to better understand the totality of a place.

The thirteen chapters comprising Part Two take a decidedly different tack. Each focuses on a different process, system, or characteristic of Africa; and all but one takes a broad brush approach across the continent with case studies as appropriate to highlight extremities and differences. So if Part One attempts to convey a lot of different things about one place (a region), Part Two focuses on particular topics that help us understand how Africa does, and doesn't work. This approach is known as systematic geography, as the object of study is to understand how a system works across space, as opposed to a focus on knowing all the systems and their linkages within a defined space. We hope you enjoy *all* the chapters, and we suspect that you will enjoy them *differently*.

Part Two begins, appropriately, with a look back by political geographer Richard L. Wolfel at one of the unfortunate legacies of Africa's historical geography: that its modern political boundaries are incongruent to its contemporary human landscape because they are vestiges of lines drawn by, and for the enrichment of, the European colonial powers who had exploited Africa's natural and human resources. These illogically positioned boundaries create large amounts of interstate movement of people, goods, and ideas, and also negatively influence intrastate conflict. They also have provided fodder for disputes which have been used as a justification for aggressive expansionist policies.

Chapter 7, "The Importance of Defining Appropriate African Subregions," conveys geographer Megan Stallings' suggestions of ways for the U.S. Department of Defense's (DoD's) newest regional unified command, Africa Command (AFRICOM), to think about organizing their efforts with respect to African space. She explains that most major African issues transcend regional boundaries, which makes the concept of regionalizing quite difficult, and posits that AFRICOM would be well advised to follow a regionalizing scheme already laid out by Africans.

Diana B. Putman, a cultural anthropologist, follows up in Chapter 8 with her own advice for DoD leaders by asking them to thoughtfully address Africans' questions about the legitimacy of establishing and operating AFRICOM. Putman points out that initial response from African leaders, scholars, and media was negative because AFRICOM was not seen by them as legitimate. To gain support from Africans, the U.S. command must demonstrate congruence between American and African strategic interests, support African-led institutions, and understand the complex nature of most African conflict to have a reasonable chance of improving prevention and mitigation activities.

Economic geographer Clarence J. Bouchet gamely tackles two difficult issues. In Chapter 9, he provides a very comprehensive discussion of ways to measure Africa's economic and human development, and a focused review of some of Africa's fundamental development problems. Though it is easy enough to make a blanket statement that Africa is the world's poorest region in terms of economic and social development, Bouchet introduces us to some of the measures commonly used to quantify these indicators of progress and human security. He also shows the results of their application, and reviews their strengths and limitations. Bouchet reminds us throughout that development encompasses not just economic improvement, but also social and demographic advances, political freedoms, economic opportunity, and an overall sense of security. Each development indicator gives only a partial view of the very complex phenomenon of development; the strength of this chapter is the use of many perspectives, which together provide compelling evidence — both direct and circumstantial — that Africa's development is critically lacking.

Bouchet tenaciously follows up his discussion of development measures in Chapter 10 with an engaging primer describing Africa's economic activities and how a host of problems keep the majority of African states from advancing economically. These obstacles are loosely grouped into categories of physical geography, economics, politics, diplomacy, demographics, and culture, and succinctly explained. Finally, Bouchet uses the path of economic development taken by successful states outside Africa as a platform for policy suggestions to help lift African states out of poverty and boost their economic growth. In sum, both chapters dealing with economics and development make very difficult material accessible and also cast light onto some seemingly intractable problems.

The next chapter (11) is the only one of our topical discussions to focus exclusively on one state. In it, Diana B. Putman returns to provide a counterpoint to Bouchet's discussion of the pitfalls of primary economic activities, by looking at how Tanzania's successive governments have adroitly managed its mineral resources — specifically gold — and how this history has lead Tanzania toward the adoption of a broad human security approach which expands traditional notions of state-based security to the individual. Some government policies, however, only reinforced poverty, while others have brought too few benefits to the state. The chapter offers an intriguing look at the nexus between good governance practices and human security, and the possibilities this offers to the many states in Africa currently dependent on primary extractive industries.

In Chapter 12, Megan Stallings offers a succinct introduction of African traditional religions, a survey of how they vary across the continent, some examples of conflict and syncretism at their boundaries, and a forecast for their future. This chapter is invigorating as it introduces us to spiritual belief systems decidedly different than the five major world religions (Buddhism, Christianity, Hinduism, Islam, and Judaism) with which we are most familiar.

As Bouchet points out, people are an important component of development. In Chapter 13, political demographer Richard L. Cincotta and I describe that the preponderance of state population structures are overwhelmingly youthful, with no immediate reduction in fertility on the horizon. Indeed most sub-Saharan African states are expected to experience high levels of population growth through 2025, with concomitant instability and political violence, while the haunting specter of HIV/AIDS in southern Africa will persist. We discuss the ramifications of youthful population structures to include the age structural theory of state performance, and how youthful populations can exacerbate the issue of changes in proportion of competing ethnicities. Finally, we discuss the youth bulge policy dilemma: young men draw the bulk of policy attention because of their role in political violence, but the ultimate key to changing age structure lies in policies that elevate women's status.

More than half of the world's people live in urban areas. This is not the case in Africa as of yet, but sub-Saharan Africa is the most rapidly urbanizing region in the world. In fact, nearly all of its future population growth will take place in its urban areas. This has caused and will cause in the future some distinctive associated patterns and problems, which urban geographers James Farrell Chastain and Steven Oluic explore in Chapter 14. Of note, African urban places are largely overurbanized; that is, they have more residents than their economies and infrastructure can support—and this situation is worsening. Thus, urban places in Africa—especially in sub-Saharan Africa—provide challenges for establishing human security; but if rapidly improved, they will present opportunities for economic and cultural growth.

More so than anywhere else in the world, African diseases hamper human and economic development. Human geographer Jon C. Malinowski introduces the sub-discipline of medical geography in Chapter 15 and uses it to explain the spatial distribution of prevalent diseases and conditions which seriously degrade the health of Africans. Healthcare is poor to practically non-existent for millions of Africans, and providing care for the public is problematic as there is far more need than available resources. This presents a basic geographical problem: how and where to intervene to in order to most effectively elevate Africans' level of health.

The next chapter (16) aims to understand Africa from the perspective of environmental security. This new field of applied geography attempts to determine how the interrelationships between human and natural processes destabilize the environment and potentially undermine human security. Here, climatologist Luis A. Rios and energy geographer (and co-editor) Amy Richmond Krakowka combine their expertise toward analyzing some of the many complex and non-linear interactions that contribute to environmental security issues in Africa. The combination of increasing populations, degraded soils, inconsistent access to fresh water, and changes in climate build the foundation for environmental security concerns. Specifically, the authors use the potential for climate change and variability to impact physical and cultural settings in the Sahel region as a case study. The idea of climate change and variability is especially troublesome here because it threatens to unravel a precariously balanced and volatile region of the continent, likely affecting each of the factors that comprise human security.

Energy geographer Kent Hughes Butts and Brent Bankus call our attention in Chapter 17 to China's developing interest in African stability and long-term access to African resources. As China's population and economy burgeon, it has tapped into a variety of markets to meet increased demand for resources. The expense and extent of Chinese efforts to garner those resources is striking, as their intent is not to compete on the open market for natural resources, but to own them and their associated infrastructure outright to create a secure source of supply. The Chinese Politburo has set down a global directive to *zou chuqu* ("go out"), which has been operationalized in various African locales. Bankus and Butts examine China's efforts in Africa through the lens of the three variables that have characterized recent U.S. national security strategy: diplomacy, development, and defense.

Our last chapter (18) features Africanist Thomas A. Dempsey's analysis of the transformation of African militaries. The good news according to Dempsey is that African militaries are undergoing a transformation that is professionalizing and internationalizing them. Despite this, most African militaries remain limited in capacity by several factors, to include their combat-heavy force structures and lack of a necessary support "tail." Dempsey also discusses some countervailing trends, in that internationalization and the collective security paradigm that supports it are countered by a return to state-versus-state warfare in some more recent African conflict zones. Finally, he makes a forecast for the future of transformation in African militaries—hampered, like so many other systems and processes in Africa—by endemic corruption and a dependence on foreign assistance.

Our overarching goal for those who read this book is that it acts as a catalyst for further reading, consideration, and ultimately, toward an understanding of Africa. If, as geographer George Kimble said in 1951, "the darkest thing about Africa has always been our ignorance of it," we are long overdue to exorcise that ignorance as a necessary first step to help improve conditions for all Africans. Former South Africa President Nelson Mandela once "dream[ed] of an Africa which is in peace with itself" (Godwin 2001). Your editors share the sentiment, and hope this book may in some small way assist its achievement.

References

Bender, Gerald J. 1988. Ideology and Ignorance: American Attitudes Toward Africa. *African Studies Review* 31, no.1: 1-7.

Godwin, Peter. 2001. A conversation with Nelson Mandela. *National Geographic*, September. http://www.nationalgeographic. com (accessed January 2, 2009).

Kimble, George. 1951. Africa Today: The Lifting Darkness. *Reporter*, May 15.

Welch, Daniel Patrick. 2005. What our (US) Kids Don't Know Can Hurt Us: Why it Matters to Know About Africa and the Rest of the World. http://www.redress.btinternet.co.uk/ dpwelch25.htm (accessed December 20, 2008).

North Africa

Brian R. Dunmire

Key Points

- North Africa is separated both physically and culturally from sub-Saharan Africa by the Sahara Desert.

- The region has strong cultural linkages to the Middle East and Southern Europe.

- Mediterranean climate is primarily found along the
  coast, with desert farther inland.

- The largest challenge will remain North Africa's
  economic stagnation.

North Africa is a region that is simple to classify, but
difficult to conceptually connect to the rest of the continent.
North Africa does not quickly fit into easily classifiable molds.
North Africa is often related in academic literature with the
Middle East due to cultural and linguistic similarities, but
does not share geologic underpinnings with the Arabian
Peninsula or the Turkish and Persian regions (Buzan and
Waever 2003). North Africa is physically part of the African
continent; however it fails to have deep cultural or linguistic
connections with sub-Saharan Africa (Bohannan and Curtin
1995, 18-32). It joins the Mediterranean Sea, forming the
southern shore of the greater Mediterranean region. Despite
this relationship, North Africa has distinctly different
natural and cultural landscapes than regions north of the
Mediterranean. The classification problem creates challenges
in integrating North Africa into a holistic treatment of
Africa. However, it can be done. Three ways of looking at
North Africa can be used to evaluate the region: integration
into an African whole, a lack of connectivity between
North Africa and sub-Saharan Africa, and the connectivity

between North Africa and the other Mediterranean states. In order to give a deeper understanding of this region this chapter will examine North Africa's location in relation to the rest of the African continent by focusing on its natural and cultural geographical features.

Location

North Africa's absolute location is 34° north (Tunis) and from 18° West (Canary Islands) to 36° East (Red Sea). Its relative location is south of Europe and north of sub-Saharan Africa. It is bounded by the Mediterranean Sea to the north, the Red Sea to the east, the Sahara Desert to the south, and the Atlantic Ocean to the west. Some of the major geographic features in the region include the Atlas Mountains to the northwest, the Nile River valley to the east, and the Sahara desert to the south. North Africa, if compared to the United States, would stretch from Maine to Washington State and roughly from the United States' northern border south to St. Louis, Missouri. The largest state in North Africa, Algeria (Figure 1) is slightly less than 3.5 times the size of Texas (Nationmaster.com 2008). North Africa extends 7,400 kilometers from east to west from Western Sahara to the eastern boundary of Egypt, and approximately 2000 kilometers from the Mediterranean Sea shore of Algeria to the southernmost portion of Algeria.

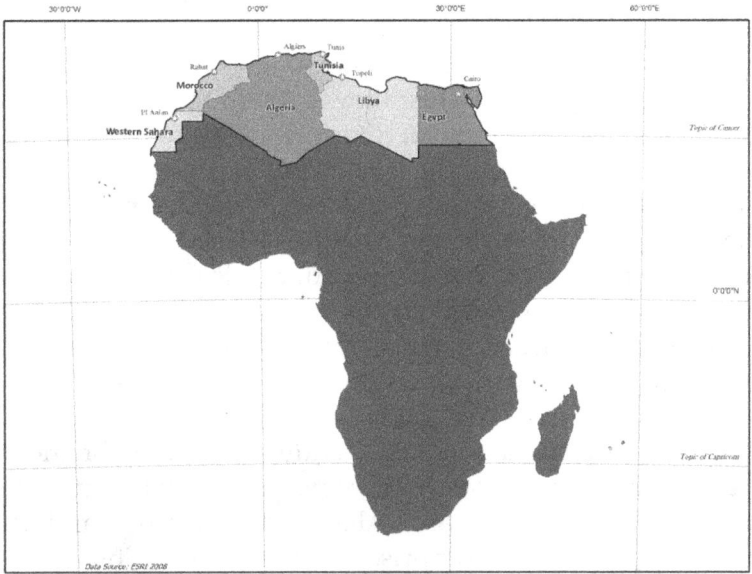

Figure 1. North Africa

Physiography and Geomorphology

North Africa is located on the African lithospheric plate. The two tectonically active regions in North Africa are the convergence zone between the African and Eurasian plates, which passes east-west through the Atlas Mountains, and the northwest-southeasterly oriented divergent tectonic boundary between the African and Arabian Plates. The convergent boundary to the northwest helps form the Atlas Mountains, and the eastern divergent boundary has formed the Red Sea.

The dominant feature of North Africa is the desert. There are virtually no major surface waterways within the region with the exception of the Nile in Egypt. The vast majority of stream channels are ephemeral, meaning they only sporadically contain water. The Nile River watershed is located in sub-Saharan Africa, and does not gain water from the lands found in North Africa. The only location where rainfall occurs in any significant amount is along the Mediterranean, specifically the Atlas Mountains. Maritime topical air (warm and moist) traveling from the northwest to southeast is orographically lifted over the Atlas Mountains and deposits precipitation on the north (windward) side of the mountain range. This allows a thin strip of the land along the coastline of the Mediterranean Sea to be hydrated. However, once inland, the desert landscape predominates. The Sahara Desert is approximately 8.6 million km², roughly the size of the United States (World Bank 2007). Rainfall is extremely scarce due to the subtropical high pressure region, which is formed to the north of the intertropical convergence zone. When precipitation does occur, it often comes in short, intense sessions that can create localized flash flooding.

North Africa is usually divided into two subregions, the Maghreb (the western subregion that usually includes Morocco, Western Sahara, Algeria and Tunisia and the Mashriq (the region comprised of Egypt and Libya). The term Maghreb in Arabic means "where the sun sets" and the Mashriq means "where the sun rises."

The Atlas Mountains in the northwestern portion of the continent are of great importance to the geography of North Africa. The mountains are responsible for many of the fertile valley areas by creating the conditions for lifting of humid air masses from the north and west. The humid Atlantic air masses deposit the majority of their moisture on the northern side of the Atlas Mountains along the Mediterranean coast.

The Nile River is the largest river system in North Africa. The Nile drainage basin extends over an area of 3,038,100 kilometers squared. The source of the Nile River is Lake Victoria in east central Africa; it flows north through Uganda into Sudan and Ethiopia to Egypt. It has a well-defined alluvial valley approximately 1,760 kilometers long and 50 kilometers wide. The river follows a mostly meandering channel path. The average discharge is 2,778 cubic meters per second, with maximum discharge rates in September and minimum discharge rates in April. The alluvial valley is heavily populated, with 95 percent of the

4

Egyptian population living within 20 kilometers of the Nile (World Delta Database Louisiana State University 2008).

Climate

The North African climate is dominated by the annual high pressure systems that form over the Sahara Desert. Based on the Koeppen climate system, the coastal regions are classified as humid temperature climate regions with hot, dry summers (*Csa*) and the interior lands are classified as hot, arid climate regions (*BWh*). That is, the North African climate can be characterized by hot summers and mild winters, with winter precipitation along the Mediterranean coastline less than 30 centimeters and during the summer under 15 centimeters. Inland of the coastal region, North Africa rarely receives more than 20cm of rain for the totality of the year.

Biogeography

The Mediterranean region has unique soils that are often clay-like and rich in organic matter. They are dominated by carbonates. They have good structure, are well-drained, and have adequate water capacity. Given the limited precipitation, leached soils are rare. The main impediments of the Mediterranean soils are excessive limestone and soluble salts. Agriculturally, these soils are fertile (Bationo et al. 2006). The soils are a result of a dry summer season and the prevalence of humus material. The North African interior is characterized by aridisols, which have low organic-matter content and light colored surface areas, and by salts accumulating at or near the surface. Land degradation is a significant concern, threatening food production and natural resource conservation. Water and wind erosion comprise the majority of the land degradation, with overgrazing, agricultural activities, and deforestation being the primary human contributions to land degradation. Desertification is also a significant problem in North Africa, with the excessive exploitation of land by growing populations creating conditions that place at risk fragile desert ecosystems. The areas most affected by desertification are mountain slopes and valleys due to overgrazing the land and poor irrigation practices. These activities clear away ground cover and increase salinity of the soil.

Vegetation in the region is primarily Mediterranean forest, woodland, and scrub in the areas of Morocco, Algeria, and Tunisia that are dominated by the Atlas Mountain range. The Nile River valley primarily consists of tropical and subtropical dry broadleaf forests, and the remainder of North Africa is desert and xeric shrublands.

Growing seasons in North Africa are varied, but tend to be in the summer. The Mediterranean coast and irrigated lowlands can support up to two crops a year, planted with the fall rains and harvested in early spring and again planted with the spring rains and harvested in late summer. In the mountainous regions, most crops are planted after the spring rains, with harvest occurring before the temperatures drop and the snow falls. Tree crops can grow year round.

Land use patterns are varied in North Africa, but can be categorized into three major activities. The first area is the Nile River valley, which is densely populated and intensely used for agriculture. The second major land use area is the northern side of the Atlas Mountains, specifically Morocco, northern Algeria and Tunisia, focused on the cities of Rabat and Tunis. This is primarily an agricultural area (See Table 1), with most major urban areas established along the coast. The third major land use area is the Sahara Desert, comprising all of Western Sahara, and most of Algeria, Libya and Egypt outside of the Nile River valley. This area is used for nomadic herding. There are no major populated areas permanently stationed in the desert.

Table 1. Agricultural Land Use

State	Agricultural Land (% of land area)
Egypt, Arab Republic	4
Algeria	17
Morocco	68
Libya	9
Tunisia	63

Note: figures based on 2005 data. (World Bank Group)

Historical Geography

North Africa has been inhabited by humans for approximately the last 30,000 years. During the last glacial maximum, roughly 20,000 years ago, the climate of northern Africa was much as it is today. North Africa was a combination of inland deserts, with lush mountains and fertile valleys. These viable regions expanded slightly around the Atlas Mountains, and became suitable for animals and crops that grow in Mediterranean climates. The viable areas concentrated on the northern coast expanded into what is now considered the Sahara Desert. People learned to domesticate animals, develop sedentary agriculture, and grow grains. Many people in this region raised animals and would have lived semi nomadic lives. Egypt was a crossroads for the movement of people and practices from the Middle East and southern Europe to what is now considered North Africa.

The most important animal used in North Africa did not arrive until 850 B.C, when the Assyrians presented a camel to Pharaoh Takelot II (Lendering 2006). Camels were initially introduced into North Africa via trade with the region's peoples for the first time. The Berbers now had an animal that was suitable for burden bearing as well as one that produced meat and milk and adapted to their climate. This highly mobile animal created the ability for North Africans to travel across the Sahara Desert by land.

The impact of the introduction of the camel resurrected trans-Sahara trading specifically from Egypt, across the Libyan desert to North Africa, and then penetrating into what is now considered west Africa. This ability to connect North Africa via land routes allowed both ideas and trade to expand. The religions of Christianity and Islam both expanded via these trade routes.

North Africa has been ruled by a series of empires: the Egyptians from 5000 B.C. until 2000 B.C., later the Roman Empire, and then a series of Islamic empires, to include the Umayyads, Abbasids, and the Fatamids. By the 16th century North Africa was part of the Ottoman Empire, and remained so until the beginning of the 19th century (Yapp 1987). European powers from the north moved across the Mediterranean and began to dismember the Ottoman Empire. European colonization efforts divided the Ottoman Empire into multiple colonies. Egypt was first wrested from the Ottoman Empire at the Battle of the Pyramids in 1798 by the French, and then taken by the British. France was more successful in taking Algeria, Morocco, and Tunisia, which remained under French rule until the mid-1950s. Libya fell under the rule of Italy until U.K. forces ejected the Italians in 1943. All the North African nations became independent by the late 1950s.

Cultural Geography

Islam is the dominant religion in North Africa. Brought by the Arab conquests in the seventh century, it has dominated religious discourse ever since. There are small communities of other faiths, with examples being the Christian Coptic communities in Egypt, Tunisia, and Morocco, and a small Jewish population in Tunisia and Morocco. Arabic is the primary language of North Africa. However, there are linguistic regions, especially with Egyptian Arabic in the east and Arab Berber in Algeria and Morocco in the west. These are distinct regional dialects. Written Arabic is primarily modern standard Arabic, which is taught in schools across North Africa. Additionally, former colonial languages are spoken in some areas, such as

English in Egypt, Italian in Libya, and French and Spanish in some areas of Tunisia, Algeria, and Morocco.

Population Geography

The population in North Africa is 166 million people. Given the land area, the resulting arithmetic population density is quite low at fewer than 29 people per square kilometer. However, the population is quite unevenly distributed, with the vast majority concentrated along the Mediterranean coast and on the windward northwestern slopes of the Atlas Mountains in Algeria and Morocco. The desert areas are virtually unpopulated. Egypt is the most populous state, with over 81 million people living primarily within the Nile River valley. Egypt's large population makes it the second most populated state in Africa and largest in North Africa (Table 2); in terms of usage of arable land, it is one of the most densely populated in the world. Libya is the most sparsely populated state, with most of its population living close to the Mediterranean Sea. North Africa had an average growth rate of 2.1 per year from 1990-2003. As such, the region's population expansion is high compared to most of the rest of the world, but low relative to Africa. Current population growth ranges between 1.0 percent per year in Tunisia to 2.2 percent in Libya. (Table 3) The doubling time for populations in the region is between 70 years for Tunisia and 31.8 years for Libya. Population growth rates across the region have been dropping. Still, a youth bulge, illustrated by the Egyptian population profile below (Figure 2), is likely to cause future challenges for all the North African states in creating requirement for job growth and increased social services, such as education, for their increasing populations. Educational rates in the region (Table 4) indicate high rates of primary school completion, which help create the basis for an educated workforce that can be effectively productive in the manufacturing or services sectors of the economy.

Table 2. Total Population (U.S. Census Bureau)

State	Total Population
Algeria	33,770,000
Egypt, Arab Republic	81,714,000
Libya	6,174,000
Morocco	34,343,000
Tunisia	10,384,000

Table 3. Total Population Growth (U.S. Census Bureau)

State	Population Growth (annual)
Algeria	1.2
Egypt, Arab Republic	1.7
Libya	2.2
Morocco	1.5
Tunisia	1.0

Table 4. Primary Completion Rate

State	Primary completion rate, total (% of relevant age group)
Algeria	96
Egypt, Arab Republic	98
Libya	n/a
Morocco	80
Tunisia	99

Note: figures based on 2005 data. (World Bank Group World Development Indicators)

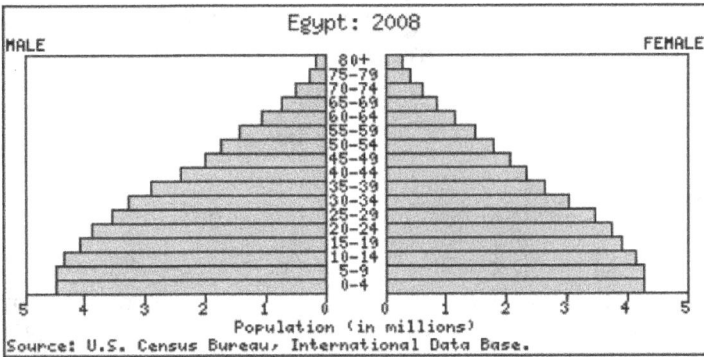

Figure 2. Egypt Population Profile
(U.S. Census Bureau)

Urban Geography

North Africa is a surprisingly urbanized region due to the difficulties of rural agrarian life in an inhospitable environment. In Egypt, 99 percent of the population is concentrated in 5.5 percent of the state area, with only 2.9 percent of the land being arable (Hamza 2003). Urban areas have been recipients of population growth. Indeed, the city's share of total population grew from 48 percent in 1982 to close to 60 percent in 2000, and is expected to exceed 70 percent by 2015. The North African regional average urban growth rate of 4 percent in the past two decades has been exceeded only by sub-Saharan Africa, which is far less urbanized. Cities in the North African region face significant challenges to improve living conditions and contribute to overall economic development. This growth will continue to generate pressures for housing and infrastructure improvements. Slow implementation of economic policy and governance reforms throughout the region has led to growing urban poverty, lack of secure property rights, and the proliferation of slums and informal squatter settlements. The largest cities in North Africa include Cairo, Egypt, population 7.7 million in 2007; Alexandria in Egypt with a 2007 population of 3.8 million; Casablanca, Morocco, with 3.3 million; and Tripoli, Libya with 1.9 million people. Urban structures in North Africa usually include a port

11

and a central business district. Religious structures such as mosques dominate the city centers, with large slums or lower-class areas in the periphery of the city's central district.

Medical Geography

According to the Center for Disease Control and Prevention, North Africa is not a region stricken with some of the epidemics more common to the rest of Africa. HIV/AIDS was at a reported rate of less than 1 percent in 2007 (United Nations 2008). Malaria is not a major issue in the region, nor are many waterborne or water-based diseases due to the region's aridity. Diseases that are most communicable such as typhoid and hepatitis occur in urban areas with exposure through food or communal water sources. Life expectancy is rising, with most North Africans now living beyond 71 years old (Table 5). However, this compares unfavorably with developed states such as the United States, with an average life expectancy of 82 years. North Africa, however, compares favorably to sub-Saharan African life expectancy of 46 years (United Nations 2006).

Table 5. Life Expectancy at Birth, Total Years
(as of 2006)

State	Life expectancy at birth, total (years)
Algeria	72
Egypt, Arab Republic	71
Libya	74
Morocco	71
Tunisia	74

Note: figures based on 2006 data. (World Bank Group World Development Indicators)

Economic Geography

North Africa has experienced a significant improvement in its economic position since the end of the Cold War. The North African economy has become increasingly intertwined with Europe as trade connections have strengthened. The primary export for the region is petrochemicals. Petrochemicals and other goods are usually shipped via sea, with increasing quantities of natural gas shipped to Europe via pipeline (Figure 3).

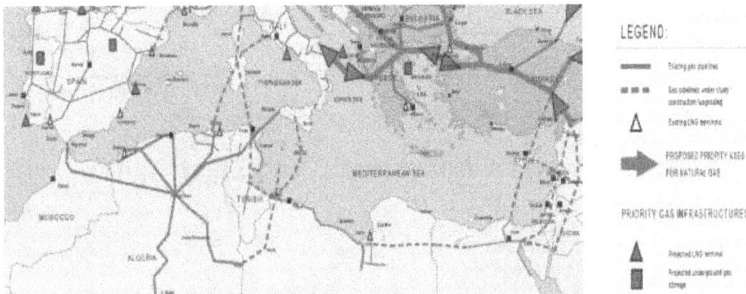

Figure 3. Interstate Oil and Gas Transport to Europe (Interstate Oil and Gas Transport to Europe: Projects of Pan-European Interest 2003)

The economies of the region have been improving, but the overall gross domestic product (GDP) of the five states combined (Table 6) is roughly equivalent to the total GDP of Poland. The dependency on hydrocarbon exports has been both a boon and a challenge to the states in this region. High oil prices result in large amounts of foreign capital. However, corruption is significant and the majority of oil revenues remain in the hands of the elite. This has also led to significant numbers of the local populations not participating in the largesse of the hydrocarbon sales, which has caused social instability in the major urban areas. Libya has the highest gross national income per capita, however, the states with the largest populations continue to struggle to bring the per capita income over the $10,000 (in

13

purchasing power parity) barrier. Agriculture contributes decreasing amounts to national income from a relative perspective. The service sector is increasing in size, but the lack of transparency and high rates of corruption makes growth in this sector problematic.

Table 6. Gross Domestic Product

State	GDP (current $US)
Algeria	114,727,059,456
Egypt, Arab Republic	107,484,037,120
Libya	50,319,732,736
Morocco	65,401,434,112
Tunisia	30,298,490,880

Note: figures based on 2006 data. (World Bank Group World Development Indicators)

Political Geography

The five states in the region have varied governmental structures. All make claims that they are democracies, however, only Morocco, Tunisia, and Algeria can credibly make the argument. Libya has been under the rule of Colonel Muammar Gaddafi since 1969 after he took power in a coup, and President Muhammad Hosni Mubarak has been president of Egypt since 1981. Neither of the easternmost states has allowed credible opposition parties or challengers to publicly surface. The states are generally divided along ethnic lines, with clear distinctions drawn between Egyptian Arabs, the Maghribi Arabs, and the Berbers farther to the west in Algeria and Morocco. All the states in the region have been relatively strong and stable, but all have also faced internal upheaval, generally due to lack of economic growth and lack of access to the political process. Jihadist terrorist groups, often tied to the Muslim Brotherhood in Egypt, have been operating in the region since 1993. Algeria suffered the most from the Islamic terrorist violence, with over 100,000 dead (mostly killed by the terrorists). The primary Algerian Islamic terrorist group

14

is called the al-Qaeda Organization in the Islamic Maghreb, previously known as the Salafist Group for Preaching and Combat. Egypt also suffered from multiple attacks, but in both Algeria and Egypt, the jihadists have alienated majorities of the local population with their attacks.

Conclusion

North Africa is bound together by culture and shared physiogeography. The lack of connection between North Africa and the remainder of the African continent is due primarily to the magnitude of the Sahara Desert. The southern boundary of North Africa is ill-defined. The future of North Africa is tied to its ability to increase its trade and cultural ties with the broader Mediterranean region. The challenges to the region include burgeoning urban populations and desertification. However, the largest challenge will remain its economic stagnation, much of it directly linked to some of the authoritarian tendencies of regional leaders.

Major Brian R. Dunmire is an instructor in the geography program at the United States Military Academy. He is a strategic intelligence officer and has taught and researched in the areas of physical and cultural geography, as well as the geography of the Middle East and Africa. He is a doctoral candidate at Old Dominion University, and holds masters degrees from the National Defense Intelligence College, the Army Command and General Staff College, St. Mary's University of San Antonio; and a bachelor's degree from Penn State University.

References

African Studies Center, Michigan State University. Exploring Africa. http://exploringafrica.matrix.msu.edu/images/ subsaharan.jpg (accessed August 29, 2008).

Bationo, A., A. Hartemink, O. Lungu, M. Naimi, P. Okoth, E. Smaling, and L. Thiombiano. 2006. *African Soils: Their Productivity and Profitability of Fertilizer Use.* http://www. africafertilizersummit.org/Background_Papers/05%20 Bationo--African%20Soils%20-%20Their%20Productivity.pdf (accessed: August 29, 2008).

Bohannan, Paul, and Philip Curtin. 1995. *Africa and Africans.* 4th ed. Prospect Heights, IL: Waveland Press.

Buzan, Barry, and Ole Waever. 2003. *Regions and Powers.* Cambridge: Cambridge University Press.

Centers for Disease Control and Prevention. Egypt. http://www. cdc.gov/ieip/egypt.html. (accessed August 29, 2008).

Hamza, Waleed. 2003. Land use and Coastal Management in the third States; Egypt as a case. http://iodeweb1.vliz.be/odin/ bitstream/1834/383/1/Hamza.pdf (accessed August 29, 2008).

Interstate Oil and Gas Transport to Europe, Projects of Pan-European Interest. http://www.eia.doe.gov/emeu/cabs/ Algeria/images/GAS_updated_111203.pdf (accessed August 29, 2008).

Lendering, Jona. 2006. Camels and dromedaries. http://www. livius.org/caa-can/camel/camel.html (accessed August 29, 2008).

Nationmaster.com. Comparative to US places (most recent) by state. http://www.nationmaster.com/graph/geo_are_com_ to_us_pla-geography-area-comparative-us-places (accessed August 27, 2008).

Louisiana State University. World Delta Database. http://www. geol.lsu.edu/WDD/AFRICAN/Nile/nile.htm (accessed August 29, 2008).

The World Bank. World Development Indicators Online (WDI) and Global Development Finance Online (GDF) 2007. http:// go.worldbank.org/6HAYAHG8H0 (accessed August 29, 2008).

United Nations. 2006.   Life expectancy in sub-Saharan Africa is lower now than 30 years ago: UN. http://www.un.org/ apps/news/story.asp?NewsID=20548&Cr=human&Cr1=de velop (accessed August 29, 2008).

United Nations. 2008 Report on the global AIDS epidemic. http:// data.unaids.org/pub/GlobalReport/2008/jc1510_2008_ global_report_pp29_62_en.pdf (accessed August 29, 2008).

United States Census Bureau, International Data Base (IDB). http://www.census.gov/ipc/www/idb/state/egportal. html (accessed August 29, 2008).

Yapp, Malcolm E. 1987. *The Making of the Modern Near East 1792-1923*. London: Longman.

East Africa

Jon A. Bushman

Key Points

- Cultural pressures from the clash of Islam and Christianity worsen tensions in East Africa.

- Increasing human pressure on the land continues to expand desert areas.

- The persistent legacy of colonialism hinders economic development here.

- Political instability and weak states threaten to balkanize and destabilize the region.

Location

The region of East Africa is located on the east and northeastern part of the African continent. Just to the north of the region is the Tropic of Cancer; toward the south, the equator. The Horn of Africa, which is part of this region, is bounded to the east by the waters of the Red Sea, Gulf of Aden, and Indian Ocean. To the west the region cuts across the Sahel and the edges of the lush forests of the interior. Lakes that are part of the Great Lakes system anchor the southwest corner.

The East Africa regional framework used here is derived from the Intergovernmental Authority on Development (IGAD) economic community. Starting in the north of IGAD and moving east and then south, we include Sudan, Eritrea, Ethiopia, Djibouti, Somalia, Kenya, and Uganda in the regional construct (Figure 1).

It is often difficult for the uninitiated to grasp the size of Africa and regions within Africa. The most common misunderstanding is the underestimation of the size of states and regions. This region is about the size of the continental U.S. west of the Mississippi. Relatively tiny Djibouti is actually larger than the U.S. state of Massachusetts. Eritrea along the Red Sea, is roughly the shape of Idaho, and about 60 percent its size. Ethiopia is slightly larger than the four corners states of Utah, Colorado, New Mexico, and Arizona. Kenya is almost as large as Texas. The Somali east coast, not including the Gulf of Aden, runs approximately the same length as the U.S. eastern seaboard from Maine to northern Florida. Sudan, by far the largest state in the region, is larger than the area between the Rocky Mountains and the West Coast. Uganda is roughly the same size as the states of New York and Pennsylvania.

It is important to explain the rationale for selecting the states comprising the East Africa region. The Intergovernmental Authority on Development (IGAD) in eastern Africa was created in 1996 to supersede the Intergovernmental Authority on Drought and Development (IGADD) which had been founded in 1986 in response to the recurring and severe droughts and other natural disasters between 1974 and 1984 that caused widespread famine, ecological degradation, and economic hardship in East Africa. Although individual states made substantial efforts to cope with the situation and received generous support from the international community throughout this extremely difficult period, the magnitude and extent of the problem argued strongly for a regional approach to supplement state-based efforts. Therefore in 1983 and 1984, six states in East Africa−Djibouti, Ethiopia, Kenya, Somalia, Sudan and Uganda− took action through the United Nations to establish an intergovernmental body for development and drought control in their region. The Assembly of Heads of State and Government met in January 1986 to sign the agreement which officially launched IGADD with its headquarters in Djibouti. The state of Eritrea became the seventh member soon after attaining independence from Ethiopia in 1993.

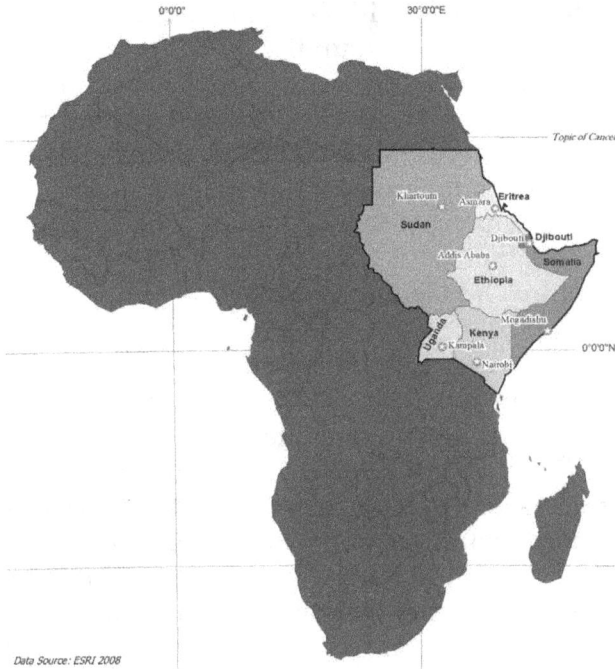

Figure 1. East Africa

In April 1995 in Addis Ababa, the Assembly of Heads of State and Government made a declaration to revitalize IGADD and expand cooperation among member states. On March 21, 1996 in Nairobi the assembly signed the "Letter of Instrument to Amend the IGADD Charter / Agreement" establishing the revitalized groups with a new name, "The Intergovernmental Authority on Development." The new IGAD, with expanded areas of regional cooperation and a new organizational structure, was launched on November 25, 1996 in Djibouti (Africa Union 2008a).

Arguments could be made for the inclusion of Tanzania as part of this regional construct as it holds membership in the East African Community, a smaller regional economic community which also includes Kenya and Uganda (Africa Union 2008b). However, Tanzania is also part of the Southern African Development Community (SADC), a much larger regional economic community, so we include it in the chapter on southern Africa.

21

Other states within IGAD are members of multiple regional economic communities. For example Sudan, Eritrea, Djibouti, Ethiopia, Kenya, and Uganda are member states of the Common Market for Eastern and Southern Africa (COMESA) (COMESA 2008), and Eritrea and Sudan belong to the Community of Sahel-Saharan States (CEN-SAD) (Africa Union 2008c).

Physiography and Geomorphology

The African Rift Valley runs through this region, extending from Lake Nyasa in southern Africa through Kenya, where it is known as the Great Rift Valley, to the Red Sea (Rowntree et al. 2009). The African tectonic plate is slowly tearing apart in this region, causing land subsidence along a north-south trending linear series of extensional faults, and creating a series of structural valleys known as grabens. Since the land is extending and subsiding, magma is able to force its way up through the crust, causing volcanic activity in and around the rift valley. Mountains such as Mount Kenya (5,182 meters), the second tallest on the continent, and the tallest, Mount Kilimanjaro (5,791 meters) in Tanzania, are results of this activity.

The Sahara Desert dominates the northern half of Sudan to the Red Sea, then wraps around the Horn of Africa in a narrow belt, through the states of Eritrea and Djibouti. As the desert turns south, it encompasses Somalia, the Ogaden region of eastern Ethiopia, as well as eastern and northern Kenya. This southern part of the Sahara is also known as the eastern Sahel, or the African Transition Zone between the true desert and tropical Africa.

East Africa, except for Sudan, is part of High Africa, in contrast to Low Africa, farther to the west (Rowntree et al. 2009). As its name implies, this part of the continent is generally higher in elevation, dominated by plateaus and plains 1,000-2,000 meters above sea level, as well as highlands. The Ethiopian Plateau, also referred to as the highlands part of the Sahel, has a dry climate that is cooler than other parts of Africa at this latitude due to the higher elevation. The Sahel is under constant environmental pressure by drought and desertification, contributing to a greater risk of degrading the harvest to the farmers and pastoralists who live there (Rowntree et al. 2009). From 2002-2003 the rainfall was especially sparse in Ethiopia, and millions faced the threat of death by starvation. The same threat loomed for Ethiopia in 2008, as the rains failed once again, especially in the southwest of the state (Hewitt 2008).

Lake Victoria is Africa's largest body of water, lying as a bowl shaped depression where the Rift Valley splits into an eastern and western rift and is surrounded by volcanic uplands. Soils here are well irrigated and very fertile, able to support some of the densest population settlements on the continent. The origins of the Nile, the world's longest river, are found here in the highlands of the Rift Valley zone, in Lakes Victoria and Edward (Rowntree et al. 2009), as well as in the Ethiopian Highlands, with Lake Tana the source of the Blue Nile. Another tributary, the White Nile, runs north through Uganda, descending in southern Sudan into a vast wetland known as the Sudd. Agricultural development projects here in the 1970s greatly increased the potential for growing crops such as peanuts, but several decades of civil war have displaced the farmers, turning them into refugees and harming the agricultural productivity of the region. The White Nile and the Blue Nile come together in Sudan's capital, Khartoum, from which the Nile flows north, eventually through Egypt and into the Mediterranean Sea.

Most major rivers are found in the southwestern areas of this region, especially in Uganda, which is a fertile, well-watered state with many lakes and rivers. Here the climate is more humid and the Intertropical Convergence Zone (ITCZ), which brings constant rainfall, is more persistent. These rivers start out in tropical regions where the vegetation is lush, but many flow north and feed into the Nile, which is classified as an exotic river—one that maintains a continuous discharge despite flowing through desert areas.

Many other rivers in the region, especially in the east and northeast are classified as wadis, where flow is intermittent. Wadis fill with water only when rains come, and quickly empty out after a precipitation event, leaving behind a dry, flat-bottomed, gravel and sand stream bed with steep sides. These wadis usually fill very quickly after the start of a rain event, and flash flooding is common. This happens since the soil forming process here is through calcification. The calcium normally found in soils is not pushed down through the soil horizons by water and gravity, but rather is moved down only a matter of inches by the sparse precipitation. It then collects and forms a hardpan layer similar to concrete, keeping water from deep penetration. Rain water therefore quickly washes over the surface, collecting and filling the numerous wadis dissecting these areas, and causing localized flooding after rainfall events.

Two other major drainage systems in this region have origins in the Ethiopian Highlands. The Shabeelle flows out of the Highlands to the east through the Ogaden region of eastern Ethiopia, bending southward through Somalia to the capital, Mogadishu, where it turns southwest, denied entry into the Indian Ocean by coastal high ground. Eventually the Shabeelle joins the Jubba north of the southern Somali port Kismaayo, where it finally reaches the ocean. The Jubba also begins its journey in the Ethiopian highlands, but takes a more direct path southward into southwestern Somalia on its way to the Indian Ocean. Overall, the region has a few alluvial lowlands that periodically deposit fertile silts suitable for farming.

On the coast several ports are suitable for major shipping operations. On the Red Sea is the Port of Sudan, Sudan's only major port. Farther south are the port cities of Massawa and Assab in Eritrea. On the Gulf of Aden is the economically vibrant port of Djibouti, located near the strategic choke point of the Bab el Mandeb, which is situated on a major world shipping lane. Also on the Gulf of Aden is the port of Berberra in the breakaway Somaliland region of

Somalia. Rounding the Horn of Africa, there are no major port cities until Mogadishu and then farther south the port of Kismaayo, both on the Indian Ocean. Also on the Indian Ocean is the port of Mombasa, serving as the major port for goods in and out of Kenya as well as landlocked Uganda. One inland major port of note is the Kenyan port of Kisumu located on Lake Victoria.

The central highlands of Ethiopia, the lowlands of the Lake Victoria basin, and the Rift Valley zone of Kenya are areas that contain relatively fertile soils able to support and feed larger populations, with the Ethiopian Highlands able to support 70 million people, one of the largest population clusters in sub-Saharan Africa.

A major environmental issue is this region is desertification—the expansion of desert like conditions in the Sahel. Desertification occurs for natural reasons such as fluctuations in climate, but also as a result of human-induced degradation such as expanded agriculture and poor agricultural practices, overgrazing, and deforestation.

This area contains relatively fertile soils, but is subject to periodic drought conditions. Along with drought conditions, the soils are depleted and eroded by farming crops such as peanuts in southern Sudan. Peanut farming is a cause of both soil nutrient depletion and topsoil loss. Since peanuts deplete several key nutrients, farmlands are often abandoned after only a few years. Additionally, since peanuts grow underground, the soil must be overturned at the end of the season to harvest them, which typically coincides with the onset of the dry season. The loose soil is then exposed to the dry Sahara winds that pick up and carry away precious topsoil, leaving the remaining land in a more desert-like condition each year (Rowntree et al. 2009).

The number of livestock has increased greatly since World War II, and with the increase came competition for grazing lands, resulting in overgrazing which has stressed natural pastures. The increased number of livestock, along with the practice of transhumance—the movement of animals between wet-season and dry-season pasture—has degraded the land, and ruins it if not given the proper time to recover (Rowntree et al. 2009).

Deforestation is also a key contributor to topsoil loss (and thus desertification), and is a major problem in the Ethiopian Highlands and Kenya. Highland Ethiopia was once covered with lush forests, but these areas have been significantly diminished as a result of the use of wood and charcoal as fuel for household energy needs. In Kenya, the biofuel scarcity has prompted women to organize into community-based groups, such as the very successful Maathai Green Belt Movement, which has a membership of more than 50,000, mostly women, who have planted millions of trees since 1977 in an effort to meet future energy needs and reduce the amount of time women spend each day gathering fuel wood (Rowntree et al. 2009). Their efforts also help to lessen the human-induced contributions to desertification.

Climate and Meteorology

Most of this region is between the Tropic of Cancer and the equator, with only roughly the southern third of Uganda and Kenya south of the equator. The region therefore is well within the tropics of the northern hemisphere, thus it generally receives approximately 12 hours of daylight year-round. Seasonal rainfall distributions are mainly caused by the convective uplifting associated with the low atmospheric pressure of the shifting ITCZ. Based on temperature and rainfall, there are four different climatic zones in this region. The tropical savanna climate (*Aw* in the Köppen Classification System) (Veregin 2007) exists in the south, including most of Uganda and the southern half of Kenya. In this climate there are generally one or two wet seasons that alternate with dry seasons. Moving north, the climate becomes much drier and is classified as *BSh*, or tropical and subtropical steppe, reflecting a transitional location between the tropical savanna to the south and the desert to the north and east. To the north and east, the climate is very dry and is classified as *BWh*, or tropical and subtropical desert. In the middle of the desert area are the Ethiopian Highlands, a highland climate (classified as *H*) which is too complex to generalize due to the complicated nature of the variable terrain (Rowntree et al. 2009). Local areas within the highland areas will even provide places with humid mesothermal climates (classified as *C*) with relatively mild temperatures and either year-round or seasonal precipitation. Figure 2 provides examples of local climates within the major climate zones.

This region of Africa is too close to the equator to experience weather fronts like those experienced in the United States, or tropical storms such as hurricanes. Precipitation comes from convective thunderstorms or from moisture wrested from the atmosphere through orographic lifting when air is forced aloft by the highlands of the Ethiopian Plateau or the mountain slopes along the Rift Valley.

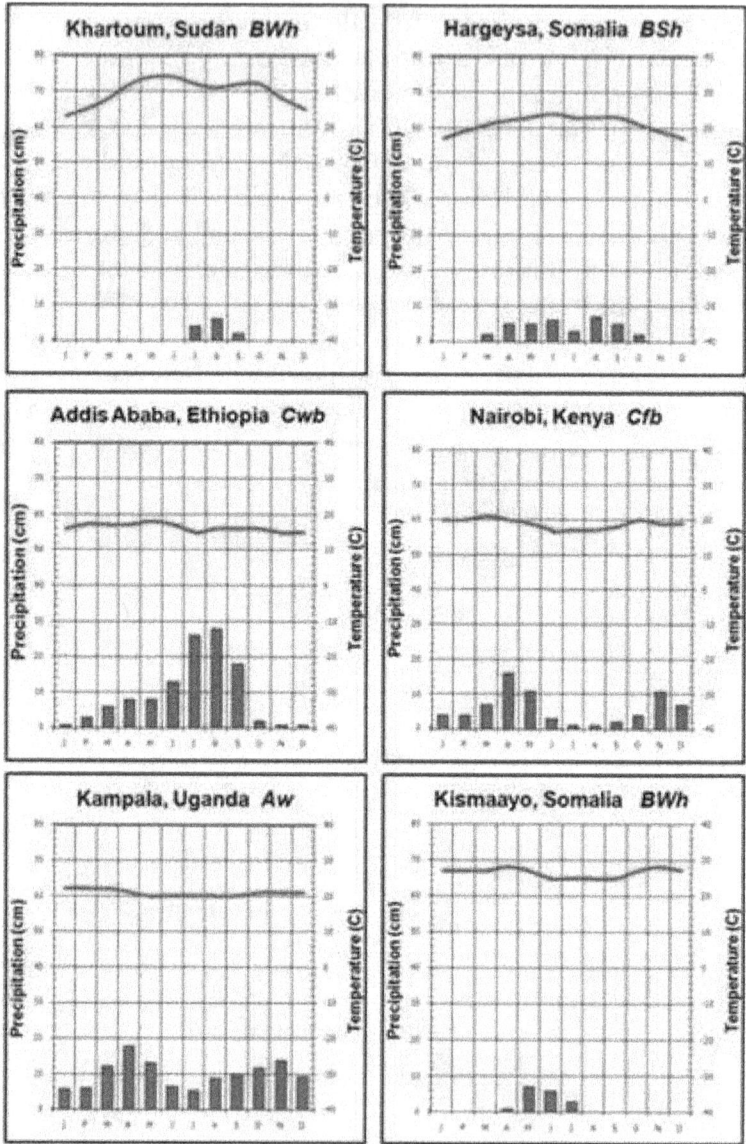

Figure 2. Climographs of Selected Cities
(Weatherbase 2008)

Biogeography

The physical core of the Horn of Africa is the Ethiopian Plateau, rising to over 3,900 meters in many places, but cut deeply by many downward slopes. For the most part this region is higher, cooler, drier, and less forested than areas of central and west Africa. Vegetation is sparse or non-existent in the north and east, and increases along a gradient moving south and west. Trees and other vegetative cover increase and are more closely spaced in areas with increasing amount of rainfall. Lush forests are found in Uganda where rain is plentiful, but become thinner to the north and east as rainfall amounts decrease and the land is unable to support large amounts of vegetation. The forests eventually become savannas, then grasslands, and finally desert.

Historical Geography

Among the more prominent states of pre-colonial east and northeast Africa were the ancient Christian kingdoms of Ethiopia and Buganda, the Arab sultanate of Zanzibar (Martin and O'Meara 1995), and many other minor chiefdoms like Darfur at smaller scales throughout the region. Christianity was long established in Ethiopia; it was adopted, in the fourth century in Aksum, the ancient Ethiopian Kingdom located in northern Ethiopia, Eritrea, and parts of Sudan and Djibouti (Reader 1997). The Ethiopian kingdom resisted the influences of Islam as it penetrated west African states through movement along trade routes from the north and then moved east along the Sahel, which served as a pilgrimage route for adherents making the long journey to Mecca. The nature of the high rugged terrain of the Ethiopian Highlands hindered the penetration of Islam into this ancient Christian kingdom.

Soon after the decisions to divide African space into spheres for colonial rule were made by European powers at the Berlin Conference of 1884, Africans in this region lost any sense of autonomy they once had, whether it was political, economic, or cultural–except for those in Ethiopia. Ethiopians led by Menelik II did not allow European imperialism, manifested mostly by military conquest by Europeans, to defeat their lands. Menelik II even repelled Italian armies that invaded in response to his renouncing a treaty with Italy upon discovery that the Italian version of the treaty made Ethiopia their protectorate (*Columbia Encyclopedia*, 6th ed., s.v. "Menelik II"). Ethiopia was the exception in Africa, as all other areas fell to the mighty European military powers anxious to take as much land as possible before their competitors. Indeed, one of the terms of the Berlin Conference was to "effectively occupy" an area prior to claiming it; this was usually accomplished quite violently (Martin and O'Meara 1995). The rest of the Horn was colonized as the British took control of Sudan, Uganda, Kenya (then British East Africa), and British Somaliland (now the northwestern province of Somalia). Italy conquered Eritrea and Italian Somaliland (the rest of Somalia). Lastly, the French controlled strategically important Djibouti as French Somaliland (Stock 2004).

During the colonial period this region saw varying styles of rule imposed upon different colonies. The British tended to put handpicked locals in control of the government elsewhere in Africa and around the world, but in Kenya where the British had a large white settler presence, the settlers used their considerable power to consolidate and legitimize special privileges (Stock 2004). Here they would grab the most desirable land, displacing Africans who had lived there for generations, and plant the most potentially profitable crops. But even where there were restrictive colonial land policies in place, locals would find ways to resist. For example, the women in Kenya resisted after they were told they had to work on soil conservation projects for the British in addition to their numerous traditional responsibilities. Eventually larger movements such as the Mau Mau Rebellion–an uprising against British rule begun in 1952 after a long buildup of resentment caused primarily by appropriation of land (*Encarta Encyclopedia*, s.v. "Mau Mau Rebellion")-spelled the end for colonial British rule, which was realized with Kenyan independence in 1963.

As mentioned earlier, Ethiopia was never colonized, and during the period of independence from colonial rule in Africa, it continued to be ruled by Haile Selassie. The other states in the region soon gained independence, but problems stemming from the governments left in place by the former colonial powers soon led to instability. In Sudan, military regimes favoring Islamic-oriented governments have dominated national politics since independence from the U.K. in 1956. Britain withdrew from British Somaliland in 1960 to allow its protectorate to join with Italian Somaliland and form the new state of Somalia. According to Somaliland, the former British protectorate should not have been joined with the Italian protectorate. In May 1991, the northern clans, led by the Isaaq clan, declared an independent Republic of Somaliland, and begun the rebuilding that was necessary after the civil war of the late 1980s. Despite the lack of international recognition and help, Somaliland remains autonomous and relatively peaceful (Kaplan 2008).

Uganda became independent from the British in 1962, but the colonial boundaries created by Britain to delimit Uganda grouped together a wide range of ethnic groups with different political systems and cultures. These disparities prevented the establishment of a working political community after independence was achieved. The dictatorial regime of Idi Amin (1971-79) in Uganda was a distinct low point as Amin was responsible for the deaths of some 300,000 political opponents. Guerrilla war and human rights abuses continued to a lesser extent under Milton Obote (1980-85), claiming at least another 100,000 lives. The rule of Yoweri Museveni since 1986 has brought relative stability and economic growth to Uganda.

The French Territory of the Afars and the Issas became Djibouti in 1977. Djibouti occupies a strategic geographic location at the mouth of the Red Sea, one of the global strategic chokepoints for ocean navigation and an important transshipment location for goods entering and leaving the east African highlands. The present leadership favors close ties to France, which maintains a significant military presence in the state, but also has strong ties with the United States. Djibouti hosts the only U.S. military base in sub-Saharan Africa and is a front-line state in the U.S.-led global war on terrorism. In 1993 Eritrea gained a hard-fought independence after three decades of fighting with Soviet-supported Ethiopia. Border tensions continue to this day, with armed conflict between 1998 and 2000. The UN continues to monitor the border, but has recently been forced to pull back due to lack of logistical support from the hosting Eritreans (CIA 2008).

Cultural Geography

Religions of this region can be classified into three main categories; Islam is found in the north and east, Christianity in the center and south, and indigenous/animistic religions are more prevalent in the southwest and west. Animistic religions have for millennia played a role in the life of the people of this region. This began to change when Christianity first came to the people of Axum, in the Ethiopian Highlands, around the 4th century. This orthodox form of the religion has held on in Ethiopia, even with the encroachment of Islam, another universalizing religion. Though Islam was well entrenched in this part of Africa as early as the 14th century (Aryeetey-Attoh 2003), proselytizing Muslim traders were still confined to enclaves in the Nubian lands of Darfur and Sinnar in the 17th and 18th centuries. This was done in West Africa centuries earlier as a tactic to limit the exposure of Islam, and thus limit conversions. Eventually these areas were converted by Arab traders, as were the coastal areas of Kenya and Somalia, but after a jihad promoted by the Ottomans had failed, the Ethiopians in the highlands were able to retain Christianity as their faith (Martin and O'Meara 1995). Due to the close proximity to Arabia, the diffusion process here was different than other parts of Africa since the spread of the religion was also accompanied by the spread of Arab culture. The processes of Islamization and Arabization partly explain the political unrest that continues in both northern and southern Sudan as Islamic religious beliefs, Sharia law, and Arab cultural traits in the north compete with Christian beliefs and African traditional religious practices in the south (Aryeetey-Attoh 2003). A large majority of Kenyans to the south are Christian, but estimates for the percentage of the population that adheres to Islam or indigenous beliefs vary widely (CIA 2008).

Not surprisingly, due to the former colonial connections, western languages are found throughout this region. English is an official language in Kenya as well as in Uganda, where it is taught in grade schools, used in courts of law and by most newspapers and some radio broadcasts. English is also widely spoken in Somaliland, especially in the capital city of Hargeysa. Although English is taught in schools in Ethiopia, the state is dominated by mostly indigenous languages. French is the official language in Djibouti, along with Arabic which is also prominent in the north and eastern parts of this region. Italian can be found to some extent in Puntland (the other autonomous Somali region) and Somalia proper, as both were formerly part of Italian Somaliland. Ganda or Luganda, the most widely used of the Niger-Congo languages, is preferred for native language publications in Kampala, the capital of Uganda, and may be taught in school (CIA 2008).

Ethnic and tribal ties are still quite important in this region, often superseding loyalty to the state. In Uganda, the incompatibility between traditional power and the British style of governing pitted the powerful and relatively wealthy, educated, and politically strong Buganda tribe against the tribes of the north. This set the stage for the downward spiral and the eventual rule of Idi Amin and the instability and atrocities that followed (Aryeetey-Attoh 2003). Political power in Kenya is very much influenced by tribal association and size. The recent bloody aftermath to

Kenya's elections pitted the dominant Kikuyu tribe, the tribe of President Mwai Kibaki, against members of the Luo tribe to which the defeated politician Raila Odinga belongs. Kenya had not seen high levels of violence since its independence, but the early 2008 violence, mostly conducted by organized machete-wielding mobs, was thought to be comparable to the early stages of the Rwanda genocide. The fighting resulted in over 1,500 dead and 500,000 displaced, with many small villages lying in ruins and displaced citizens afraid to return to their homes. Ethnic tensions are also present in the Horn of Africa. The Somali ethnic tribe covers a vast part of the Horn, and frequently crosses the Somali/Ethiopian border as they follow traditional seasonal herding and migration patterns (known as "transhumance"), creating border tensions in the area as the tribe simply ignores the superimposed boundary separating the two states.

Population Geography

In general, fertility rates are high in this region, with women averaging at least five children over the course of their lifetime (U.S. Census 2008), regardless of religious affiliation; Muslim, Christian, and animistic communities all have similarly high birthrates (Rowntree et al. 2009). Fertility rates have remained high because large families are seen as an asset, especially in rural areas. Children can tend to crops, livestock, and gather fuel wood, contributing more to the household than they take. Children also provide a family with a measure of security as grown children are expected to take care of parents when the parents' health begins to falter (Rowntree et al. 2009). For centuries large families were also encouraged in places with tribal divisions (for example, Kenya), wherein tribal size affects political influence (Rowntree et al. 2009).

Currently there are no extreme policies driving family size, such as the one child policy of China, but governments have haltingly begun to address family planning. Following the 1994 United Nations International Conference on

Population and Development in Cairo, governments began pursuing smaller family sizes by encouraging the use of contraception (Rowntree et al. 2009). With states averaging between four and seven children per woman, the region will grow very rapidly and soon have larger percentages of its population under the age of 15. Currently, 44 percent of the population of the region is under 15 years old (Table 1) compared to 20 percent in the U.S. (CIA 2008).

The high proportion of youth presents an economic crisis for these states as the young people will soon be seeking employment in a job-poor environment. The resulting masses of unemployed youth are prone to disenfranchisement and criminal activity. Some of these children are kidnapped or fall victim to forced-labor schemes, where parents send them away with the hope they will work and send back remittances. They are also co-opted as child soldiers, especially in northern Uganda. The rebel Lord's Resistance Army has kidnapped thousands of children in recent years, training the boys as fighters and using the girls as servants and sex slaves. In southern Sudan, groups of boys flee into the bush in order to escape potential captors from the north (Stock 2004).

Some factors seem to be mitigating the population growth rates. Urbanization here discourages large families and children are increasingly seen as an economic liability as they are no longer needed for the tasks found in a rural setting. AIDS also is slowing overall growth in the region as it cuts a wide swath across the working age population, with many negative effects. However with birth rates among the highest in the world and death rates high but declining, the region is experiencing a population explosion. As medical technologies and improved sanitation conditions continue to become available and adopted, and especially if the incidence of HIV is suppressed, death rates should further decline. This demographic transition will continue as urbanization changes the predominant view of children as economic producers, to one of children as economic liabilities. Once this happens, population growth will likely slow down. In the meantime, the states of the region will experience rapid population growth and will have to deal with a very young population who face a number of stresses.

Table 1. Population Data for East African States
(Population Reference Bureau 2008a, 2008b)

State	Popu-lation Mid-2008 (millions)	Rate of Natural Increase (%) (2008)	Projected Pop. 2050 (millions)	Infant Mortality Rate (2008)	Total Fertility Rate (2008)	% Pop of Age <15 (2008)
Djibouti	0.8	1.8	1.5	67	4.2	38
Eritrea	5.0	3.0	11.5	59	5.3	43
Ethiopia	79.1	2.5	147.6	77	5.3	45
Kenya	38.0	2.8	65.0	77	4.9	43
Somalia	9.0	2.7	23.8	117	6.7	44
Sudan	39.4	2.1	73.0	81	4.5	41
Uganda	29.2	3.1	106.0	76	6.7	50
US	304.5	0.6	438.2	6.6	2.1	20

Urban Geography

East Africa continues to be characterized by rural societies. While there is a high proportion of people living in urban areas in Djibouti (82 percent), mostly due to its lack of arable land, this situation is the exception in the region. Only 12-19 percent of people in Uganda, Ethiopia, and Eritrea and around 35 percent of Somalis, Kenyans, and Sudanese live in urban areas. Urban growth is high in primate cities such as Nairobi, Kenya where the population has grown from just 119,000 in 1948 to over 3 million in 2008. Every state in the region has a primate city, one that according to Stock (2004, 461) is "a city that is much larger than other cities in the same country, and that typically has a very high proportion of the nation's modern economic development and political power." Usually a primate city is at least twice as large as the next largest city and also a cultural hearth–a crucible of culture for the rest of the state. Unfortunately, much of that urban growth has come in the outskirts of Nairobi, in Africa's largest slum Kibera, where nearly 800,000 people live a very marginal existence (Harding 2002). Shantytowns like Kibera continue to grow since the high rate of urbanization outstrips the ability of cities to keep pace in housing, jobs, industry, and basic social services (Cole et al. 2007). Sudan's capital, Khartoum, and its close neighbor, Umm Durman, function closely together, in effect primate city (Table 2).

Table 2. Largest Cities in Each State, Rates of Growth
(world-gazetteer.com 2008)

City	State	Mid 1980s Pop.	Mid 1990s Pop.	2008 Pop. Calculation	% Annual Growth
Djibouti	Djibouti	No data	No data	596,396	No data
Asmara	Eritrea	275,385	No data	632,315	No data
Addis Abeba	Ethiopia	1,412,575	2,084,588	3,144,918	2.81
Nairobi	Kenya	1,324,570	2,143,254	3,038,533	3.95
Mogadishu	Somalia	No data	No data	1,609,050	No data
Umm Durman	Sudan	526,284	1,271,403	2,395,159	4.31
Khartoum	Sudan	476,218	947,483	2,203,987	5.79
Kampala	Uganda	No data	774,241	1,507,042	3.75

The mostly rural East Africa region has begun to rapidly urbanize in ways seen in South America, where the myth of jobs and better economic prospects, exacerbated by a tradition of oral communication pull the desperate in to already overburdened cities. They then quickly realize that employment prospects are dim, and they are forced to settle in large urban slums on the outskirts of the major cities.

Many migrants to the urban slums work in the informal sector in order to get by on a day-to-day basis. Women in East African slums are much like women in other parts of Africa; responsible for the care of children and the household, they must also seek some way to provide supplemental income to support the family. In the slums this often takes the form of joining the informal sector of the economy, and conscripting the children in their care to jobs for supplemental income. Ninety percent of the women in the Mathare Valley, a squatter settlement community in Nairobi, work in the informal sector of the economy doing jobs such as brewing beer in their houses from maize, at times supplementing their incomes from beer sales with sexual liaisons with the men they meet as customers (Stock 2004).

Medical Geography

Malaria is endemic in the Shebeelle and Jubba River valleys, especially in the upper reaches in Ethiopia. Other areas affected significantly by malaria include the southern half of Uganda and all areas around Lake Victoria. The city of Nairobi also sees high rates of infection, along with areas of northeastern Ethiopia where the Awash River flows into an inland delta, never reaching the Red Sea, creating swampy conditions and attracting the mosquitoes that are the vectors for the disease (de Blij and Downs 2007).

Trypanosomiasis, or sleeping sickness, is generally not a major problem in East Africa, except in the southwest of the region in Uganda, where climatic conditions allow for the presence of the tsetse fly, which transmits the disease to humans and cattle. In 1905, just four years after the disease was first recognized in Uganda, about 200,000 people died of sleeping sickness in the Busoga Province alone. The disease is less common in the more open savanna and higher elevations of East Africa (above 1,220 meters), where it is too cool for the tsetse fly to survive (Cole et al. 2007). It is possible here to raise large numbers of cattle, unlike in west and central Africa where only certain types of cattle are resistant to the disease.

Many Ethiopians are again facing starvation due to chronic food deficits exacerbated by high risks of drought and crop failure (Stock 2004). AIDS is as well a major problem for East Africans, affecting all segments of society as the disease takes its toll on the very demographic that provides the labor to help run the economies, and orphans large numbers of children.

High infant mortality rates (deaths of infants prior to their first birthday, measured per thousand infants) indicate a poor health care system with a low number of doctors and hospitals per capita in the cities and lack of access to health care in rural areas (see Table 1). The persistence of high infant and child mortality also tends to delay the lowering of birth rates, as families have little surety that a baby will survive to adulthood.

Economic Geography

At independence, Kenya went through planned resettlement of European farms in a very successful program wherein middle and lower class Kenyans resettled the farms that were left unoccupied by white settlers who had departed as independence appeared imminent. During the 1960s and 1970s, this project expanded and became known as the Million-Acre Scheme, increasing agricultural productivity by 4 percent (Stock 2004). Ethiopia also saw planned resettlement, but it was not nearly as successful. The program aimed to move families from the densely populated heartland of the state to the sparsely populated western and southwestern peripheries, in order to lessen the state's dependence on foreign aid by opening up fertile, underutilized territory. However, the program was implemented hastily without careful planning and with inadequate resources to ensure an orderly and successful transition. Expansion of the program also coincided with the 1984-1985 drought, when over a half million people moved in just over a year, almost ensuring the program's failure.

Kenya is the European Union (EU)'s largest supplier of fresh horticultural produce, such as fresh-cut flowers, under an economic arrangement known as production under contract. This arrangement allows the buyer to dictate the conditions under which the flowers are grown, the quantities, and even the type and amount of pesticides used. This horticulture industry creates conflicts such as water shortages due to irrigation and health threats from pesticide use to women and children who do most of the labor in this industry. The economic relationship, however, is tenuous since the European supermarkets that dictate the terms from afar can suddenly shift to another producer if Kenya fails to maintain a comparative advantage with respect to price, quality, and assured supply (Stock 2004). Horticultural exports are Kenya's biggest economic producer after tourism; so the economic stability of the state is dependent on the continued success of the industry. Annual growth has averaged over 10 percent for the past five years and is projected to continue this trend.

Of all Kenyan horticulture exports in 2006, the value of floriculture exports was $300 million (46 percent), the value of fresh produce $230 million (36 percent), the value of processed fruits and vegetables $100 million (14 percent), and the value of nuts and fresh fruit $25 million (4 percent). About 96 percent of exports are to the EU, with flowers mainly to U.K. and Holland, vegetables mainly to U.K. and France, and fruits (predominantly avocado) to France (Kenya flowers 2008).

Millet is an important food crop in Sudan, Ethiopia, and Uganda (Cole and de Blij 2007). Sorghum is also economically important or considered a staple for parts of all states except Djibouti, with Sudan and Ethiopia leading as the number two and three producers for all of Africa in 2001 (Cole and de Blij 2007). Ethiopia's economy relies heavily on its coffee exports for which it is regionally well known.

The most important regional cash crop, quat (pronounced "chat"), is found in great quantities in the eastern Ethiopian Highlands. Quat leaves have an intoxicating effect when chewed. Large quantities are exported to neighboring states, especially Somalia, Djibouti, and Yemen (Stock 2004). Quat is legal in Great Britain where

90 percent of male Somali migrants there use it, but its use is banned in the rest of Europe, Canada, and the U.S. Quat has narcotic properties that have been known for centuries (Ross 2004).

Ownership of livestock in East Africa is important both socially and economically as they are a visible sign of amassed wealth, and they reproduce, adding value to the farmer's herd (Cole and de Blij 2007). Pastoralism, a social and economic system based on the raising and herding of livestock, is practiced throughout East Africa. Pastoralists utilize large areas of savanna, semi-desert, and desert to raise livestock in marginal conditions that are too rocky, dry, or steep for successful farming. Cattle are the most important and valued animals, rarely eaten by the pastoralists except for ceremonies and in times of emergency (Stock 2004). Herds in this region include large numbers of cattle (99 million), sheep (92 million), and goats (86 million), mostly in the Ethiopian Highlands and southern Sudan. Thirty-three percent of Africa's sheep and 31 percent of goats are found in Sudan, Ethiopia, and Somalia (Cole and de Blij 2007). Ethiopia has the largest number of livestock in all of Africa (Stock 2004), which demonstrates the ability of the highlands climate to support larger populations of people, livestock, and vegetation than all of its neighbors except for Uganda, which has much greater amounts of vegetation. The rural economies and way of life for pastoralists such as the Kereyu of the arid Awash region in the Ethiopian Rift Valley are under increasing pressure due to a declining resource base as they are deprived access to traditional rangelands by the creation of national parks and the expansion of irrigated agriculture, in this case sugar farms. Because of these competing demands for use of the land, there is often conflict and sometimes violence between neighboring pastoralist groups as well as nearby farmers (Stock 2004).

Other livestock of note include camels (11 million) which are mostly found in Somalia and Sudan, in the desert areas that do not support cattle; asses (6 million) of which 86 percent are in Ethiopia and a notable number in Sudan; pigs (almost 2 million) found mostly in Uganda, with a small number in Kenya; and horses (2.8 million) mostly in Ethiopia. Pigs, along with chickens, are important as they do not cost much to maintain because they are raised almost entirely on family-produced garbage. Raising these animals with low operating costs and high returns is a very prudent measure for rural families with scarce land resources (Aryeetey-Attoh 2003). In the region, pigs are found almost exclusively in Uganda, one of Africa's leading pig producing states (Cole and de Blij 2007). Only small numbers of pigs are found in Kenya and Ethiopia, where the environment is ill-suited. Pigs are entirely or mostly absent from the region's predominantly Muslim states of Eritrea, Djibouti, Somalia, and Sudan due to the religious prohibition against eating pork.

Political Geography

The post-colonial period in East Africa has been marked by political turbulence. The superimposed boundaries established by the Europeans have split cultural groups, and artificially bound rival tribes, kingdoms and ethnicities together. States of East Africa have experienced civil wars (Sudan, Uganda, Ethiopia, Somalia) and frequent border wars (Ethiopia and Eritrea; Ethiopia and Somalia). Without a working government since 1981, Somalia has simply failed as a state. Perhaps new states will emerge as the region experiences a degree of balkanization – political fragmentation, often accompanied by hostility.

In 1991 Somaliland declared independence from Somalia, and had everything in place for viable independence except international recognition. Therefore it remains part of Somalia from the perspective of the international community, but in reality it is far different than the war-torn state of Somalia. Autonomous Somaliland has a functioning government, its own currency, a military force for internal and border security, and a functioning economy. It even maintains an open border with Djibouti, not through permission from Mogadishu, but rather through its own negotiations with its neighboring state. Somaliland continues to advocate for international recognition, and encourages tourism. The neighboring Somali region of Puntland has also achieved autonomy from the war-torn southern part of the state, but does not seek independence.

Sudan may also split into an Arab-Islamic north and a Christian-animistic south. The fighting in the western province of Darfur continues to create countless refugees and hundreds of thousands of deaths.

Kenya has not experienced civil war since independence (Cole and de Blij 2007), but democracy was recently tested when tribal and ethnic violence followed the December 2007 presidential elections, resulting in over 1,500 dead. The president and parliament, with UN mediation, resolved the crisis by creating a power sharing agreement by appointing the losing candidate to the newly created post of prime minister. Djibouti benefitted from Ethiopia's loss of Eritrean territory and its resulting landlocked status; Eritrean and Ethiopian border tensions and wars have forced Ethiopia to route its cargo through Djibouti as well as Somaliland.

Piracy off the coast of Somalia has gained the attention of the world in 2008. The shift of attacks from the southern part of the coast of Somalia to deep water attacks far off shore in the Indian Ocean, into the Gulf of Aden, has begun to threaten shipping and trade passing through this extremely important trade route between Asia and Europe. The International Maritime Bureau (IMB) Live World Piracy Map (www.icc-ccs.org) well illustrates this geographical shift in piracy activity. Of the 63 reported incidents in the Somalia area in the first nine months of 2008, 51 were reported in the Gulf of Aden, with the remainder off the east coast of Somalia. Attacks in the Gulf of Aden involved automatic weapons, as well as the use of Rocket Propelled Grenades (RPG) (International Maritime Bureau 2008a).

Most of the pirate attacks in the Gulf of Aden) took place east of Aden, Yemen and near the Yemeni coast (Figure 3). The attacks increased to the east, north of the semi-autonomous Puntland, where piracy is an economic means to survival. Pirates hijack passing vessels and sail them to Somali waters where they demand ransom. The long-range attacks are made possible by "mother vessels" that carry smaller boats close that are then launched as assault craft. Piracy has become an important part of the economy of Puntland, where all levels of government from the police to president are charged to be involved (Al-Mutairi 2008). With a weak economy inside a failed state, Puntland will continue to be a safe haven for pirates, and the pirates will continue to operate in the Gulf of Aden as long as they avoid an increasing and active UN mandated naval presence.

Perhaps international recognition of smaller, stable states as seen in the Balkans with the relatively recent independence of Montenegro and Kosovo will bring greater stability to the region. An independent Somaliland could act as a model of stability that is needed in this tumultuous part of Africa.

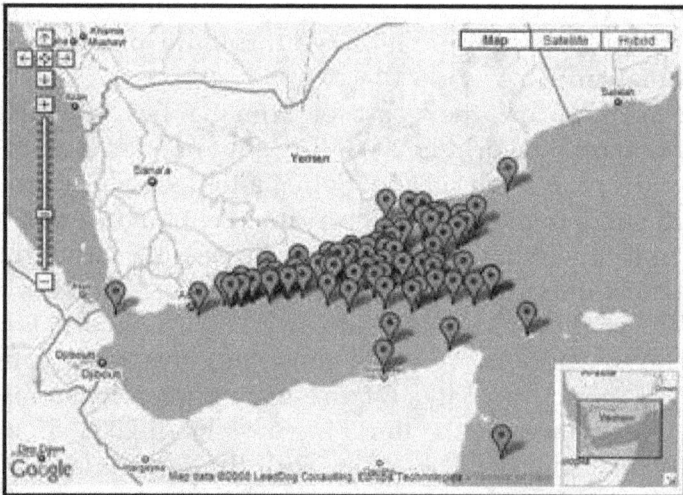

Figure 3. Reported Pirate Incidents in the Gulf of Aden, Jan-Sep 2008 (International Maritime Bureau 2008b)

Major Jon A. Bushman is an Assistant Professor of Geography at the United States Military Academy. He is preparing to be a strategic intelligence officer and has taught and researched in the areas of Physical, Human, and Regional Geography. He holds a masters degree in Geography from the University of Wisconsin.

References

Africa Union. 2008a. http://www.africa-union.org/root/au/RECs/igad.htm (accessed June 10, 2008).

Africa Union. 2008b. http://www.africa-union.org/root/au/RECs/EAC.htm (accessed June 10, 2008).

Africa Union. 2008c. http://www.africa-union.org/root/au/recs/cen_sad.htm#memberstates (accessed June 10, 2008).

Al-Mutairi, Abdulaziz. 2008. Puntland's Lucrative Piracy Business. http://www.arabnews.com/?page=7&section=0&article=113 717 (accessed November 29, 2008).

Aryeetey-Attoh, Samuel. 2003. *Geography of Sub-Saharan Africa.* 2nd ed. Upper Saddle River, NJ: Pearson Education Inc.

CIA World Factbook. 2008. https://www.cia.gov/library/publications/the-world-factbook/index.html (accessed October 22, 2008).

Cole, Roy and H.J. de Blij. 2007. *Survey of Subsaharan Africa: A Regional Geography.* Oxford: Oxford University Press.

COMESA. 2008. Common Market for Eastern and Southern Africa. http://www.comesa.int/countries (accessed June 13, 2008).

de Blij, H.J., and Roger M. Downs, eds. 2007. *National Geographic College Atlas of the World.* Washington, DC: John Wiley & Sons, Inc.

de Blij, H.J., and Peter O. Muller. 2006. *Geography; Realms, Regions, and Concepts.* 12th ed. New York: John Wiley & Sons, Inc.

Harding, Andrew. 2002. Nairobi slum life: Kibera's children. BBC News online. http://news.bbc.co.uk/2/hi/africa/2297265.stm (accessed October 2, 2008).

Hewitt, Gavin. 2008. Ethiopian children face starvation. BBC News online. http://news.bbc.co.uk/2/hi/africa/7449523.stm (accessed June 13, 2008).

Kaplan, Seth. 2008. The Remarkable Story of Somaliland. *Journal of Democracy* 19, no. 3: 143-157.

Kenya Flowers. 2008. http://www.kenyaflowers.co.ke/FAQ's.htm (accessed July 31, 2008).

International Maritime Bureau. 2008a. Unprecedented Rise in Piratical Attacks. http://www.icc-ccs.org/index.php?option=com_content&view=article&id=306:unprecedented-rise-in-piratical-attacks&catid=60:news&Itemid=51 (accessed November 29, 2008).

International Maritime Bureau. 2008b. World Piracy Map. http://www.icc-ccs.org/index.php?option=com_fabrik&view=visualization&controller=visualization.googlemap&Itemid=89&phpMyAdmin=F5XY3CeBeymbElbQ8jr4qlxK1J3 (accessed November 29, 2008).

Martin, Phyllis M., and Patrick O'Meara, eds. 2005. *Africa*. 3rd ed. Bloomington, IN: Indiana University Press.

Population Reference Bureau. 2008a. 2008 Africa Population Data Sheet. Washington: Population Reference Bureau.

Population Reference Bureau. 2008b. 2008 World Population Data Sheet. Washington: Population Reference Bureau.

Reader, John. 1997. *Africa: A Biography of the Continent*. New York: Alfred A. Knopf, Inc.

Ross, Paul. 2004. Smuggling – Khat. BBC News online. http://www.bbc.co.uk/insideout/extra/series-1/smuggling_drugs_khat.shtml (accessed November 14, 2008).

Rowntree, Les, Martin Lewis, Marie Price, and William Wyckoff. 2009. *Diversity Amid Globalization: World Regions, Environment, Development*. 4th ed. Upper Saddle River, NJ: Pearson Prentice Hall.

Stock, Robert. 2004. *Africa South of the Sahara*. 2nd ed. New York: Guilford.

U.S. Census Bureau, International Data Base (IDB). 2008. http://www.census.gov/ipc/www/idb/ (accessed October 2, 2008).

Veregin, Howard, ed. 2007. *Goode's World Atlas*. 21st ed. Hoboken, NJ: John Wiley & Sons, Inc.

Weatherbase. 2008. http://www.weatherbase.com (accessed July 15, 2008).

World-gazetteer. 2008. http://world-gazetteer.com (accessed October 16, 2008).

Central Africa

Matthew P. Cuviello

Key Points

- The history of colonization has shaped the states in the region.

- Central Africa is rich in resources but poor management, destabilized governments and civil war have limited development of industries.

- Central Africa possesses distinct climate zones that affect the economy, habitation and culture.

This book will define Central Africa as Burundi, Cameroon, Central Africa Republic, Chad, Congo, Democratic Republic of Congo (DRC), Equatorial Guinea, Gabon, Rwanda and Sao Tome and Principe. These states were born from a colonial past, thrust into a post-colonial world, and are still reliant on the connections to the European powers.

Location

Relative to the other regional divisions of Africa as delineated in this book, Central Africa is a small region, about one-third the size of the United States. The region extends from about 13°S to 20°21' N latitude. From the west, the region starts at the Atlantic Ocean and extends to almost three-quarters of the continent to the east. The equator splits the region, with approximately 40 percent of the land area falling south of 0° latitude. Central Africa is bordered to the north by Nigeria, Niger, and Libya; to the east by Sudan, Uganda and Tanzania; to the south by Malawi, Zambia and Angola; and to the west by the Atlantic Ocean. The largest state in the region is the DRC, and the smallest is Sao Tome and Principe (Table 1).

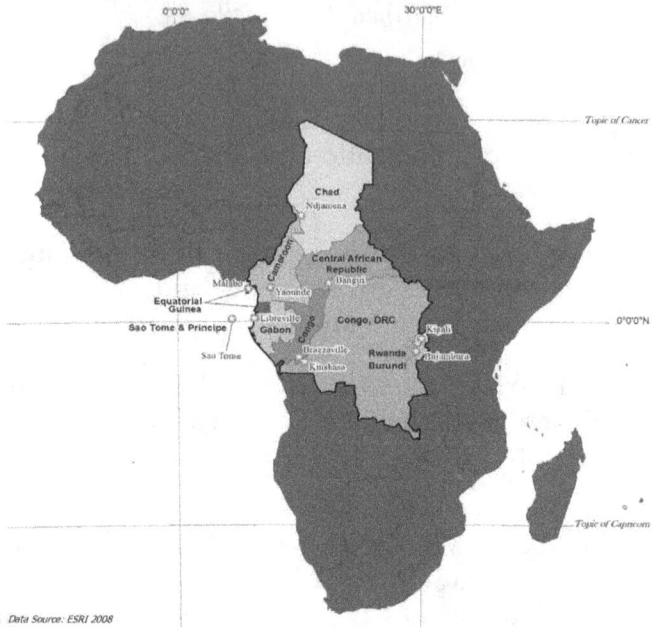

Figure 1. Central Africa

Table 1. Surface Area (World Bank 2006)

Country	Surface area (sq. km)
Burundi	27,800
Cameroon	475,400
Central African Republic	623,000
Chad	1,284,000
Congo	342,000
Democratic Republic of Congo	2,344,900
Equatorial Guinea	28,100
Gabon	267,700
Rwanda	26,300
Sao Tome and Principe	1,000

Note: surface area is defined as a state's total area, including areas under inland bodies of water and some coastal waterways.

Physiography and Geomorphology

Central Africa is one of the most physically diverse regions in the world. The region contains a vast array of landform types (desert, mountains, basins, plateaus, coastal plains) and is a perfect case study for the effects of the global circulation model (GCM) on rainfall patterns and corresponding landscapes. Central Africa is located in the middle of the African tectonic plate and therefore has little seismic activity.

From west to east there are distinct topographic regions. The narrow coastal plain along the Atlantic Ocean ranges from 64 kilometers to about 200 kilometers inland. To the east there is a series of hills, mountains and plateaus running parallel to the coast. Located here are the Mayombe Massif (400-600 meters) and the Chaillu (up to 1500 meters) mountain ranges that help form a topographic barrier that influences local precipitation patterns. To the east of these mountains is the great Congo Basin which is a large plateau (2 million square kilometers) with an average elevation of about 400 meters. This area was once covered by an ancient inland sea. The region is bounded in the west by the mountains of the Great Rift Valley that rise to heights of 1500 meters to 5000 meters (Hance 1975).

Rivers are abundant throughout the southern two thirds of Central Africa. They are the lifeline of the region and are sustained by high amounts of precipitation. The Congo River (Figure 2) is the largest in the region and the second largest in Africa, after the Nile. Eleven thousand kilometers of navigable waters flow in the Congo basin. It has ten main tributaries, the largest being the Lualaba and the Luaoula (Du Bois 2007). The main sources of water for the river are runoff from the Rift Valley Mountains, Lake Tanganyika and Lake Mweru to the east, and the Chambeshi River from the south. Other important rivers in the region include the Oubangi, Chari and the Ogooue. All serve as important transport systems, carrying goods and services to the interior areas of the region. Also the rivers provide a tremendous source for hydroelectric power.

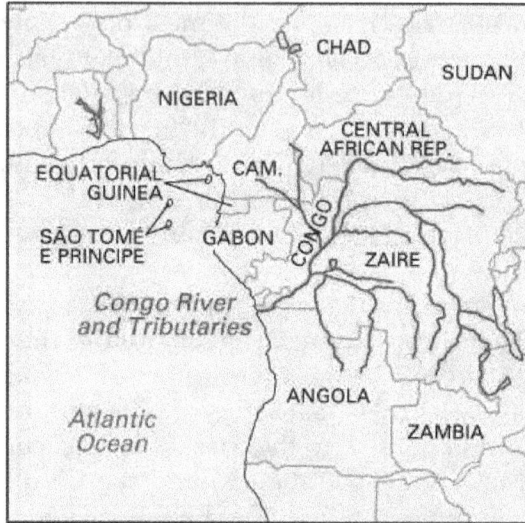

Figure 2. The Congo River (Encarta)

The northern position of Central Africa, specifically Chad, is part of the Sahara desert. There is very limited surface water except for Lake Chad in the west. This lake is recharged only by limited rainfall and is depleted by evaporation and human use. Drought often plagues this part of the region, affecting Chad, the northern provinces of Cameroon, and Central African Republic the hardest. The lack of water puts a heavy strain on agriculture and limits sources of drinking water for people and livestock.

Climate

Central Africa's climate is dominated by its proximity to the equator and the position of the subsolar point-the location on the earth where the sun's rays hit at a 90° angle and thus receives the most intense insolation. This heating from the sun causes air to rise, expand and cool, and eventually condense to form clouds. The area of greatest atmospheric lift is referred to as the intertropical convergence zone (ITCZ). As the earth revolves around the sun, this belt of precipitation shifts seasonally north and south of the equator.

The majority of central Africa is dominated by the ITCZ all year long. Just south of the equator, the area in the DRC receives a great amount of average annual precipitation (150 centimeters) (CIA Fact Book 2008). North of the equator, there is a steady decrease in annual precipitation values as the influence of the ITCZ diminishes. In the northern part of the region Chad receives little precipitation. Some stations record as little as one centimeter annual rainfall (weatherbase.com 2008).

Chad's northern half is under the influence of the sub-tropical high pressure belt where there is consistent subsidence of air. Sinking air does not allow for the development of clouds and is typically devoid of rainfall. Water is a constant concern for the people of the Sahara.

Biogeography

The Central African rainforest is the second largest in the world and dominates the region. All states in the region encompass some equatorial rainforest except Chad. The rainforest biome (classification of vegetation) consists of dense vegetation. Consistent precipitation can be attributed to many of the problems in the region as well as possibilities for the future. People in the rainforest tend to cluster around rivers and transportation networks. There is little infrastructure and communication is hindered or relatively non-existent in many other areas throughout the region (Ramsey and Edge 2004).

The biome progression in Central Africa closely follows the global circulation model. As the amount of annual precipitation decreases from south to north, a clear pattern of different biomes follows. Near the equator is the tropical rainforest biome. Here thick vegetation and countless species of plants and animals exist. The soil in the rainforest is typically poor due to a great amount of leaching (loss of nutrients from the continual downward movement of water through the soil). Therefore, commercial farming is not profitable. However the forest is rich in other natural resources, such as rainforest timber, palm oil, and rubber (Hance 1975). These resources have been the focus of European states for over a century.

North of the rainforest is the savanna, a transitional region between the rainforest and grasslands. The savanna provides movement corridors for people and agricultural as well as pastoral opportunities. There are two distinct growing seasons that correspond to the movement of the ITCZ in and out of the region: precipitation in the summer, and little to no precipitation in the winter.

North of the savanna are grasslands and desert. The amount of precipitation in the grasslands limits vegetation growth and is insufficient for large trees. In Central Africa, the grassland region is relatively small and transitions rapidly to desert. The desert biome receives the least amount of precipitation. One third of Chad is located in the Sahara. Despite this, more than 80 percent of Chad's laborers utilize over 39 percent of the land for agriculture.

The land used for agriculture varies for different reasons (Table 2). Rwanda and Burundi are both poor landlocked states where ninety percent of the population relies on subsistence farming. Economic growth in both states depends on tea and coffee exports, which account for ninety percent of exports (CIA 2008). Although Central African Republic can only use 8.4 percent of its land for farming, the state is a self sustained provider and potential exporter of food (CIA 2008).

Table 2. Agricultural Land Use (World Bank 2005)

State	Agricultural land (% of land area)
Burundi	90.6
Cameroon	19.7
Central African Republic	8.4
Chad	39.1
Congo	30.9
Democratic Republic of Congo	10.1
Equatorial Guinea	11.6
Gabon	20.0
Rwanda	78.6
Sao Tome and Principe	59.4

Historical Geography

The modern history of Central Africa is dominated by European powers. At the Berlin Conference (1884-1885), the colonizing powers of Europe divided Africa into ruling jurisdictions. Colonization of Africa did not take into account the traditional tribal area boundaries. Large ethnic groups including the Fangs, Batekes, Kongos, the Hutus and the Tutsis cross many modern day state boundaries (Ramsey and Edge 2004). Conflict between the Hutus and the Tutsis is a major theme in the region, specifically in Rwanda and Burundi.

In Rwanda, the majority ethnic group, the Hutus, overthrew the ruling Tutsi king in 1959. They proceeded to kill thousands of Tutsis, forcing over 150,000 into exile in neighboring states. In 1990, the children of the exiled Tutsis, the Rwandan Patriotic Front (RPF), began a civil war. The four year war culminated in the genocide of roughly 800,000 Tutsis and moderate Hutus. The Tutsi rebels defeated the Hutu regime and ended the killing in July 1994, but approximately 2 million Hutu refugees fled to neighboring Burundi, Tanzania, Uganda, and Zaire (now the DRC).

Many Hutus have returned to Rwanda, although a faction of extremists exists in the DRC, determined to regain control by force. In Burundi, ethnic tensions between the Hutus and the Tutsis led to a twelve year civil war displacing many to neighboring states (CIA 2008).

The French sphere of influence was the largest in the region. Other than Burundi and Rwanda (Germany then Belgium), Equatorial Guinea (Spain), the Democratic Republic of Congo (Belgium) and Sao Tome and Principe (Portugal), all other states were colonized by France. The Central African Republic, Chad, the Congo, and Gabon were all once a part of French Equatorial Africa. France allowed private companies to exploit resources and labor with no long term sustainability plan. The Belgians were the only ruling power with a plan for long term development in the Belgian Congo (present day DRC). Even so, conflict during the 1990s in the DRC was a destabilizing force in the region.

As of 2008, former colonial powers still project influence in the region. Expatriots hold key positions in local governments and businesses. France has the most influence in the region (Ramsey and Edge 2004). France has troops stationed in Chad, Central African Republic and Gabon. The main purpose of the French military is to promote regional stability. Gabon serves as a main base of operations with headquarters units. In Chad, over 1200 French troops are stationed to protect French nationals, to support the pro-French government and to provide intelligence assistance to the Chadian military. France has also spearheaded a European peacekeeping force in 2007 and 2008 (Hanson 2008) which quelled an attack by Sudanese-backed rebels desiring to overthrow the government. In Central African Republic, France stations about 300 troops as advisors to local armed forces (Hanson 2008).

Political Geography

Political instability throughout the region is a common theme since most states gained independence in the early 1960s. Post-colonial governments have ranged from conservative democracies to military dictatorships to Marxist-Leninist regimes. Multi party democracies have been established by many states in the region, although second or third parties find it hard to get representation (Ramsey and Edge 2004). Many of these new governments have grown out of much unrest and internal strife between ruling parties and rebel organizations.

Since independence, there have been attempts to unite the Central African states into economic and political alliances aimed at promoting regional cooperation. In 1983 the Economic Community of Central African States was established to stimulate industrial activity, increase markets, and reduce the dependence on France and other colonial ties. This, like other organizations, failed due to lack of participation and financial support.

Civil unrest and political instability have compromised more recent efforts to reengage on common endeavors, specifically in the Democratic Republic of Congo. The civil war that raged from 1996 to 2002 caused tensions when rebel forces were backed by Rwanda, Uganda and Zimbabwe. Interventions from across borders are not uncommon. Most often, rebel forces seek refuge in a neighboring state and when strong enough, return with force.

Cultural Geography

The dominant religion in Central Africa is Christianity. Islam has had little influence in the region except for Chad and northern Cameroon. Christianity and Islam coexist with many indigenous tribal religions; many professed followers still secretly follow traditional African religions or have incorporated tribal customs into Christian or Islamic practices in order to fulfill their spiritual needs (Ramsey and Edge 2004).

Portugal was the first state to bring Christianity to Central Africa around 1490 by establishing Roman Catholic missionary communities. By the eighteenth century, these missions had all but dissolved, in part due to the slave trade (Ramsey and Edge 2004). The missionaries returned in the late nineteenth century, following repatriated freed slaves to the area who had previously converted to Christianity. The missionaries built schools and infrastructure, providing a different outlook for many of the followers. Many of the elite class of the Central African states were educated in Christian schools. This influence has lead to strengthened links to the West.

Population Geography

The population distribution in Central Africa is varied depending on the physical landscape, largely following the vast network of rivers and lakes. The Democratic Republic of Congo is by far the most populous state in the region (Table 3). Population densities are among the highest in the Great Lakes region; Burundi and Rwanda, for example, have arithmetic population densities of 387 and 312 people per square kilometer respectively (Cole and de Blij 2007).

Increasing populations are recognized as a contributing factor of underdevelopment. Most states in the region have instituted policies in order to slow population growth. The Democratic Republic of Congo, Central African Republic, and Rwanda are among the African states that have no government-supported fertility control measures. Even in states with a governmental policy, family planning, contraceptives and education have met with varied results due to societal and religious norms (Cole and de Blij 2007).

Table 3. Total Population (US Census 2008)

State	Total Population
Burundi	8,691,000
Cameroon	18,468,000
Central African Republic	4,444,000
Chad	10,111,000
Congo	3,903,000
Democratic Republic of Congo	66,515,000
Equatorial Guinea	616,459
Gabon	1,486,000
Rwanda	10,186,000
Sao Tome and Principe	206,178

Urban Geography

According to the United Nations, Central Africa's shift from rural areas to an urban environment has slowed slightly since the late 1990s (UNEP 2008). The decreasing state of health in some rural areas, due especially to HIV/ AIDS, increasing cost of living, and high unemployment are contributing factors of this decrease in urbanization. Most states are still highly rural based. For example, only 10 percent of the population of Rwanda and Burundi live in cities (Stock 2004). Most of the large cities in Central Africa such as Libreville, Kinshasa, Brazzaville, Bangui and Pointe-Noire are located on the coast or on rivers, and are tied to the region's colonial past. During the colonial period coastal towns were created in order to ship goods and resources back to Europe and provide command and control centers for European powers. As demand for material and natural resources increased, these urban centers grew quickly to meet demand.

After independence, these cities continued to grow and remained the economic and governmental centers. Many of the urban centers are primate cities-those with populations more than double the next most populous city, and dominant in terms of economy and culture. For instance, the capital city of Libreville comprises 50 percent of the population and provides 50 percent of the employment of Gabon. The rapid growth of these few cities in the region has led to environmental, medical, and poverty concerns. Lack of clean water, land degradation, flooding, and poor sanitation are but a few of the increasing problems that primate cities in Central Africa face (UNEP 2008).

Medical Geography

Due to its climate, population densities and lack of sanitation, Central Africa is plagued by many infectious diseases. Most notably, there is a prevalence of malaria and trypanosomiasis. The tropical jungles near the equator provide an optimum breeding ground for mosquitoes, the vector for malaria. The disease is endemic in the population which helps explain the low life expectancies in most states (Table 4). Malaria often kills youth and the elderly due to weaker resistance to fight the disease. Deaths in these demographic groups greatly affect the economy by reducing the potential workforce and disrupting the family structure. The tsetse fly, the vector for trypanosomiasis, thrives in the tropical and savanna biomes found in Central Africa. Instability in the region has compromised efforts to control the disease. HIV/AIDS also affects every state in Central Africa.

Table 4. Life Expectancy at Birth, Total Years
(as of 2006) (World Bank 2006)

State	Life expectancy at birth, total (years)
Burundi	49
Cameroon	50
Central African Republic	44
Chad	51
Congo	55
Democratic Republic of Congo	46
Equatorial Guinea	51
Gabon	57
Rwanda	46
Sao Tome and Principe	65

Economic Geography

Central Africa is an economically depressed region of Africa. The total GDP of the region is just below 74 billion US dollars (Table 5). In contrast the estimated 2008 GDP of the State of Utah is 76 billion US dollars. Cameroon has the highest GDP due to its oil as well as its cacao exports. The island state of Sao Tome and Principle has the lowest GDP. It lacks natural resources and its one cash export, cacao, has suffered because of mismanagement and drought.

Central Africa's economy is primarily based on its rivers. All of the rivers flow to the Atlantic Ocean due to the topography of the region. This fact has lead most of Central Africa to focus economic development strategies toward Europe and the Americas (De Bois 2007). These trends toward trading with Europe mirror the colonial past marked by exploitation of resources by foreign powers. The relative location of the United States makes it an easier trading partner than Asian states.

Natural resources are abundant in the tropical regions and there is potential for a positive economic future. Resources in the region include timber, cotton, and agricultural products. Diamonds and precious metals are found in Central African Republic and the DRC. Oil is present and refined in Chad, Cameroon, Congo and Gabon, but until population and governments stabilize, the riches of many of these resources will not be realized.

Table 5. Gross Domestic Product (Data as of 2008, Current USD) (World Bank 2006)

State	GDP (current US$)
Burundi	1,000,000,000
Cameroon	20,650,000,000
Central African Republic	1,714,000,000
Chad	7,095,000,000
Congo	7,675,000,000
Democratic Republic of Congo	10,140,000,000
Equatorial Guinea	10,490,000,000
Gabon	11,300,000,000
Rwanda	3,320,000,000
Sao Tome and Principe	144,000,000

Conclusion

Natural resources are the key to a sustained economic and stable political future in the Central Africa region. The development of the oil, timber, precious metals, and agricultural distribution industries could help create the conditions for a stable future. However, state governments must also establish safe environments free from civil unrest and war. Neocolonial ties continue to influence the region negatively. The states of Central Africa must emerge from the shadow of these former ruling powers to establish a region with a global footprint.

Major Matthew P. Cuviello is an instructor in the geography program at the United States Military Academy. An Army Armor officer, he has taught courses in Physical Geography, Military Geography and Climatology. He holds undergraduate and graduate degrees in Geography.

References

Cole, Roy, and H.J. de Blij. 2007. *Survey of Subsaharan Africa: A Regional Geography*. Oxford: Oxford University Press.

Du Bois, W.E.B. 2007. *Africa: Its Geography, People, and Products and Africa–Its Place in Modern History*. New York: Oxford University Press.

Encarta. 2008. http://encarta.msn.com/media_461520491/congo_river.html (accessed January 6, 2009).

Hance, William Adam. 1975. *The Geography of Modern Africa*. New York: Columbia University Press.

Hanson, Andrew. 2008. The French Military in Africa, Council on Foreign Relations. http://www.cfr.org/publication/12578/ (accessed on November 23, 2008).

MetroRoommates. http://www.metroroommates.com/images/states/CentralAfrica.gif (accessed September 13, 2008).

Ramsay, Jeffress, and Wayne Edge. 2004. *Global Studies: Africa*. 10th ed. Guilford, CT: Mc-Graw Hill/Dushkin Company.

Stock, Robert. 2004. *Africa South of the Sahara*. 2nd ed. New York: Guilford.

United Nations Environment Program Online. http://www.unep.org/dewa/Africa/publications/aeo-1/216.htm (accessed September 27, 2008).

United States Census Bureau, International Data Base (IDB). http://www.census.gov/ipc/www/idb/country/egportal.html (accessed August 29, 2008).

World Development Indicators Online (WDI) and Global Development Finance Online (GDF). The World Bank, Washington, DC. http://go.worldbank.org/6HAYAHG8H0 (accessed August, 29 2008).

West Africa

Brian J. Doyle

Key Points

- West Africa possesses the greatest energy reserves of any region in Africa.

- The population of West Africa is the most diverse of any in Africa.

- West Africa straddles the transition zone between Christianity and Islam, increasing the volatility of the region.

West Africa is the most dynamic region in sub-Saharan Africa. Anchored by Nigeria, the most populous African state, West Africa forms a region of contrasts that blends many cultures and cradles potential for wealth in its abundant natural resources and human capital.

Location

West Africa is bordered on the north by the Sahara Desert, to the south and west by the Atlantic Ocean, and to the east by the Congo River basin. In absolute terms, West Africa is located between 5° N latitude and 20° N latitude and 17° W and 20° E latitude. This region is only slightly smaller in size than the continental United States.

There are many different mappings of the states that compose West Africa. For the purpose of this book, West Africa will include, starting in the northwest and working counter-clockwise: Mauritania, Senegal, The Gambia, Guinea-Bissau, Guinea, Sierra Leone, Liberia, Mali, Burkina Faso, Ivory Coast, Ghana, Togo, Benin, Niger, and Nigeria. Although there is much discussion and debate regarding this grouping, this delineation is also shared by the noted

geographers de Blij and Muller (2006) and Stock (2004).
This is also the grouping that forms the supranational
organization known as the Economic Community of West
African States or ECOWAS.

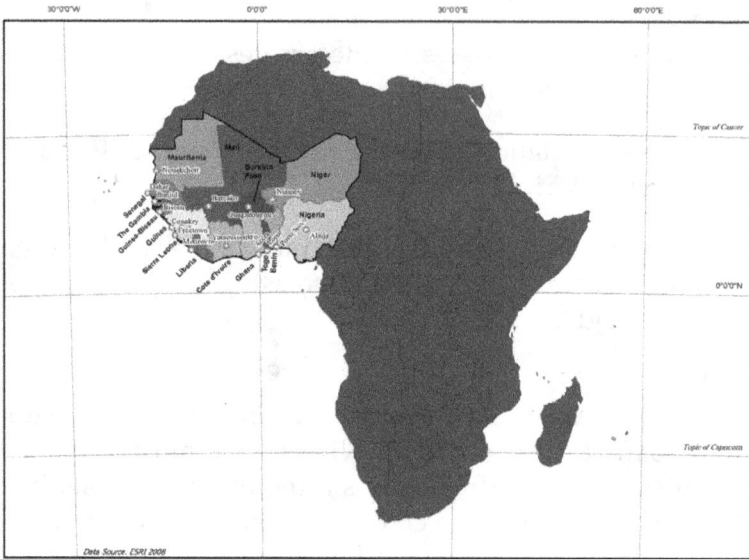

Figure 1. West Africa

Physiography and Geomorphology

From the standpoint of physical geography certain
features of West Africa are particularly notable. Situated
in "Low Africa," West Africa is bordered on the east by the
Adamawa Highlands, anchored at the Gulf of Guinea by the
soaring volcanic peaks of Mount Cameroon (Stock 2004).
To the west is the Guinea Highlands and to the north the
Sahara Desert (Stock 2004). The only geologic fault line in
the area runs north-northeast from Mount Cameroon along
the Nigeria - Cameroon border (Stock 2004).

West Africa also sits astride a transition zone known
as the Sahel. The Sahel is a semi desert region between
the Sahara Desert and the coastal plain (Stock 2004). This
region is embroiled in an environmental crisis in which
more and more land is being claimed annually by the

desert–a process known as desertification. Some recent literature has expressed some hope that with better farming techniques, places like Niger may be reclaiming some of the agricultural land lost to desertification (Polgreen 2007).

An interesting geologic formation that occurs throughout the region are the rock domes known as "inselbergs" (see Figure 2) (Army n.d.). These are large formations of Precambrian rock that dominate the surrounding plains (Stock 2004). It is believed that these rocks are the result of weathering that has eroded the surrounding material and left the exposed domes of more resistant material behind (Stock 2004).

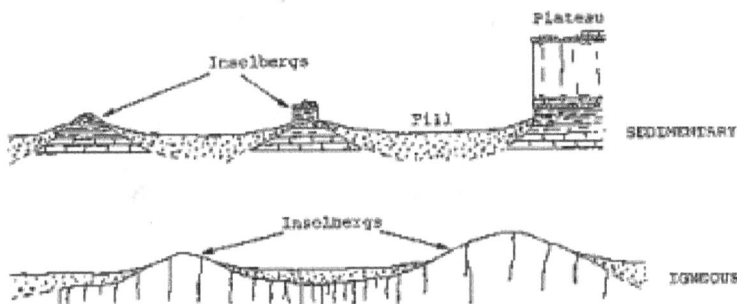

There are several significant river systems in the region; the most dominant is the Niger River. This river forms in the Guinea highlands and flows through Guinea, Mali, and Niger before reaching the sea through its delta found on the coast of Nigeria (Veregin 2007). In addition to providing much needed irrigation to this region, the river also serves as a traditional boundary between many of the cultural groupings found in the area. On the far west coast, the Gambia River's watershed forms the state of The Gambia, which in most locations extends only about twenty miles to either side of this body of water.

The coastline of West Africa provides some of the only harbors in Africa south of the Sahara. These port cities are connected to the colonial past and notably the slave trade and exploitation of natural resources.

Climate

Located just north of the equator, West Africa is most heavily influenced by the effects of the intertropical convergence zone or ITCZ. This belt of convective atmospheric lifting shifts north and south across this region in a seasonal variation resulting from the angle of the sun's rays relative to the surface of the earth and the heat that phenomenon produces. Within the ITCZ rainfall is frequent and winds are light and variable (Strahler and Strahler 2005). Variability in rainfall is closely associated with the migration of the ITCZ especially in West Africa (Stock 2004). In the summer months the region experiences almost all of its precipitation as the ITCZ predominates. During the dry winter season, winds carrying great amounts of dust sweep southwesterly from Chad into Nigeria (Stock 2004). These winds are known as *harmattan* and can cause episodes of low visibility for several days (Stock 2004). This impacts the lives of those who make this region home by restricting travel and commerce.

Biogeography

Vegetation in West Africa is extremely diversified. Tropical rain forests mark the southern fringe in Nigeria and along the Gulf of Guinea, while the arid Sahara Desert marks the northern border. Between these two contrasts is a broad savanna that transitions between moist and arid (Cole and de Blij 2007). These contrasts greatly affect the people and their corresponding patterns of population and agriculture.

Human alteration of the environment has also led to changes in the patterns. Of particular note is the devastation to the tropical rainforests in the south due to increased urbanization, and the process of desertification in the north.

Livelihoods and food supplies are greatly affected by the patterns of vegetation. Much of the cultural and economic diversity of West Africa is due to the biogeographic patterns observed (Stock 2004).

Historical Geography

West Africa in pre-colonial times was a very rich and prosperous region. This prosperity was due to trade routes which connected the Sahara to Europe, and also with east and South Africa. Centers of learning and culture, such as those found in the legendary Timbuktu, eclipsed European institutions of the same era (Cole and de Blij 2007). This period of prosperity was ended by slavery, the saddest chapter of African history. Slavery has deep and enduring roots in West Africa. The coastline, which has some of the only natural harbors on the continent, served to support the shipping and trading of humans (Rowntree et al. 2006). European powers established trading centers along the coast which facilitated this trade and stripped Africa of its greatest natural resource–people.

Around 1870, this devastating period of slave trade ended and colonialism began in earnest in the region (Stock 2004). Much of this region fell under the control of French West Africa. A notable exception to this is the British control of the economic and demographic powerhouse that is now Nigeria. The British also controlled the Gold Coast (Ghana), Sierra Leone, and The Gambia. The Portuguese controlled Guinea, and the Germans colonized Togo (Rowntree et al. 2006). The state of Liberia was an independent state throughout this period of colonialism. The United States used this territory as a place to relocate freed slaves who wished to return to Africa. This, however, created other problems similar to those resulting from colonialism, specifically that foreign populations, in this case repatriated slaves, were put in positions of control and began the process of subjugating indigenous populations.

In the period of independence beginning around 1960, the states of West Africa generally followed the trajectory of the rest of the continent. Periods of boom and bust were accompanied by the transfer of power between duly elected governments and military coups.

Cultural Geography

The most obvious cultural divide in West Africa is that created by the diffusion of Islam. The northern portion of this region is strongly influenced by Islam. The southern portion is populated by practitioners of Christianity and traditional tribal religions. This creates a tenuous rift between the peoples of the region (Stock 2004). Interestingly, the tribal religions are seeing resurgence within this region as Africans view these faith systems as an alternative to foreign religious thought (Stock 2004). Many indigenous people see Islam as a foreign system of domination as much as Christianity. Tribal beliefs are presenting a uniquely African identification to religion.

West Africa is composed of multiple ethnic and linguistic groupings. The Berlin Conference (1884–1885), which laid the groundwork for the period of colonialization, imposed lines on maps that had little to no relation to existing cultural groupings (Stock 2004). This has caused disastrous repercussions to this day for the peoples that occupy the land and attempt to create effective civil government in these European devised states.

Nigeria serves as an excellent example of how states attempt to create a functioning federal government despite disparate ethnic identities. Stock (2004) has identified three manners in which this state has attempted to create unity and functionality. The first was the creation of additional administrative sub-units based on ethnic groups. At independence Nigeria had three divisions roughly corresponding with the largest of the ethnic groups. Today the federal system is composed of thirty-six states and continues to grow as groups assert their differences and desire representation. Secondly, Nigeria moved its capital from the colonial primate city of Lagos to a new city, the forward capital Abuja. Abuja was located so as to remove it from any association with a major ethnic grouping. Finally, Nigeria has attempted to build unity through ensuring that resources and projects were equally distributed across the population (Stock 2004). These policies have created numerous long-term problems relating to sustainability while only creating passable short-term relief.

Population Geography

West Africa is sub-Saharan Africa's most populous region (de Blij and Muller 2006). Within the region Nigeria is the single most populous state. The spatial pattern of population is directly related to the proximity to water, either the Atlantic coast or along the major river systems. The states located within the Sahel have considerably lower populations.

Overall the population of West Africa is increasing at what many consider to be an unsustainable rate with regard to the environment; that is the population growth is rapidly outstripping the natural resource base. The birth rate for all of the states in West Africa is staggering with the lowest fertility rate (roughly the average number of children per woman) in Ghana at 3.8 to the highest in Guineau–Bissau and Niger at 7.1 and 7.2. Only the equally staggering mortality rate of the region, affected by the devastating toll of AIDS, has kept overall population growth from being even greater (Cole and de Blij 2007). On the whole there has not yet been the cultural shift to lower birth rates that the model of demographic transition would predict, which would result in the overall population leveling off.

Urban Geography

Beginning in the ninth century Islamic cities were established at the end of trans-Saharan trade routes in West Africa (Stock 2004). These cities flourished for a period, but then were largely abandoned as external entities wielded increasing power with the onset of the slave trade and the beginnings of colonization. Only within the last century did urban centers again become established in this region. Colonial powers established cities as administrative centers and to house European officials. Often the indigenous population was not a part of these cities except in positions of service (Stock 2004).

At present West Africa remains predominantly rural (Cole and de Blij 2007). This fact exists despite the challenges presented by the densely-packed urban centers in Nigeria and other coastal locations. Much of this is caused by the necessity of agriculture to feed and sustain the people.

Medical Geography

Cole and de Blij (2007) explain that the predominance of infectious diseases in Africa is due to the patterns observed in populations, environments, behavior, socioeconomic development and climate (Cole and de Blij 2007, 150). The diversity in West Africa of all the factors listed above explains the equally diverse pattern of disease in this region. This pattern of disease has always affected the mortality rates in this region, and in turn has stifled the economic development of the area by limiting the labor pool and imposing burdensome health care issues on individuals and families.

In discussing landscape epidemiology, Meade and Earickson (2000) explain that economic growth is altering the environment in ways that increase the risk of disease. This is certainly true in West Africa. For example, in Nigeria the drive to produce greater amounts of oil has taken a devastating toll on the people of the Niger Delta. The alteration of the landscape, most often in the form of pollution, has contaminated drinking water, reduced irrigation and destroyed productive fields. This not only increases susceptibility to infectious disease, but leads to malnutrition and hunger related ailments (Stock 2004).

As discussed in the medical geography chapter, AIDS has taken a toll on West Africa. The disease has many effects. Obviously the toll on the individual is devastating. The second and third order effects on family and on communities are often overlooked, but one effect is on the national economy. This is what Stock refers to as the "ripple effect" (2004, 318). The loss of laborers, through death or through caring for those who are sick is likely hampering the full economic potential of these states. Further, the cost of paying for health care and for associated concerns has diverted capital flows that could be put to use building the economies of these states (Meade and Earickson 2000).

Economic Geography

The economic geography of West Africa is marked primarily by the impact of oil. Currently, "Nigeria is Africa's largest supplier of oil, and is the fifth largest global supplier of oil to the United States" (Ploch 2008). This is fueling a boom that is providing great wealth for the elite, while inflicting ecological and social devastation on the majority of the people due to poor planning and corruption. This pattern is likely to continue due to the current global economy's thirst for oil. Ploch (2008) has posited that with Nigeria on course to supply 25 percent of U.S. oil imports by 2015, the security of Nigerian oil fields may well become a U.S. military mission.

Aside from oil and its associated industries, there is very little in the formal economies of West Africa. As with most of the states in Africa, informal economies sustain the daily life of the people in this region. The unfortunate side effect of the reliance on informal economic institutions is the lack of a tax base or accountability for labor practices. This further impacts the development of these regions (Stock 2004).

Political Geography

As with most of Africa, West Africa is still dealing with the effects of colonialization. The political divisions of the region were created without any consideration for ethnic, cultural, linguistic or cultural groupings. This has created a host of problems affecting stability and prosperity. The states of this region have attempted to deal with these issues in a variety of ways. Unfortunately these strains are often resolved only through force of arms.

The conflicts that have plagued this region have and will continue to sap resources and capital. Too often debt has been accumulated that cannot be overcome by struggling economies. Much of this debt is incurred by one administration which is subsequently overthrown, but the debt is held over. This results in situations where reformist governments cannot even begin the process of rebuilding their states because of debt burden. The governments of these states have been unable to move forward as a result of these debt constraints.

Given debt relief, and reining in endemic corruption, it is possible that many of these states could provide a level of prosperity for their populations which could in turn allow for security and stability. The states of West Africa have an enormous amount of resources, both natural and human, which could provide for their populations. Age-old rivalries and disputes will continue to hamper development, and the resolution of these issues can lead to peace and stability.

Major Brian J. Doyle is currently an Armor officer serving as a Team Chief to a Border Transition Team in Iraq. Previously he served as an Assistant Professor of Geography at the United States Military Academy. He has taught and researched in the areas of Economic and Political Geography focusing on the Middle East and Africa. He holds graduate degrees in Geography and Military Arts and Sciences.

References

Cole, Roy, and H.J. de Blij. 2007. *Survey of Subsaharan Africa: A Regional Geography.* Oxford: Oxford University Press.

de Blij, H.J., and Peter O. Muller. 2006. *Geography; Realms, Regions, and Concepts.* 12th ed. New York: John Wiley & Sons, Inc.

Meade, Melinda, and Robert Earickson. 2000. *Medical Geography.* 2nd ed. New York: Guilford.

Ploch, Lauren. 2008. *Africa Command: U.S. Strategic Interests.* CRS Report for Congress, Washington, DC: Congressional Research Services.

Polgreen, Lydia. 2007. In Niger, Trees and Crops Turn Back the Desert. *New York Times,* February 11.

Rowntree, Les, Martin Lewis, Marie Price, and William Wyckoff. 2006. *Diversity Amid Globalization; World Regions, Environment, Development.* Upper Saddle River, NJ: Pearson Prentice Hall.

Stock, Robert. 2004. *Africa South of the Sahara.* 2nd ed. New York: Guilford.

Strahler, Alan, and Arthur Strahler. 2005. *Physical Geography; Science and Systems of the Human Environment.* 3rd ed. Hoboken, NJ: John Wiley & Sons, Inc.

United States Army. http://www.tec.army.mil/research/products/desert_guide/lsmsheet/lsinsel.htm (accessed October 4, 2008).

Veregin, Howard, ed. 2007. *Goode's World Atlas.* 21st ed. Hoboken, NJ: John Wiley & Sons, Inc.

Southern Africa

Benefsheh D. Verell

Key Points

- Southern Africa has the highest HIV rates in the world.

- South Africa dominates the region politically and economically.

- Vast mineral resources support a rich mining industry for many southern African states.

- Pressure from increasing population is worsening land degradation.

Southern Africa is extremely diverse both geographically and culturally. Economic troubles, political instability, and ethnic tensions hinder the region. South Africa is the economic and political powerhouse of the region and has the most potential for development. AIDS, however, has darkened the future for many southern Africans and could lead to regional instability (Cole and de Blij 2007).

Location

The southern region of Africa includes the following states: Angola, Botswana, Lesotho, Madagascar, Malawi, Mauritius, Mozambique, Namibia, Seychelles, South Africa, Swaziland, Tanzania, Zambia and Zimbabwe (Figure 1). The region is bounded by the Indian Ocean on the east at 40°E; the Atlantic Ocean on the west at 11°W; and the Indian Ocean on the south at 34°S. Angola, Zambia, and Tanzania bound the northern area of the region. Madagascar is an island approximately 258 miles east of Mozambique. The island of Mauritius is 546 miles east of Madagascar and the islands of Seychelles are 661 miles northeast of Madagascar.

The entire region minus the islands is roughly the same in area as the continental United States.

Tanzania is considered part of East Africa in most regional divisions; however it is included in this text as part of the southern region because it is a member, along with the other aforementioned states, of the Southern African Development Community (SADC). The goal of the SADC is to improve the overall quality of life for Africans in the region as well as promote peace and economic growth (Aryeetey-Attoh 2003). This is much easier said than done.

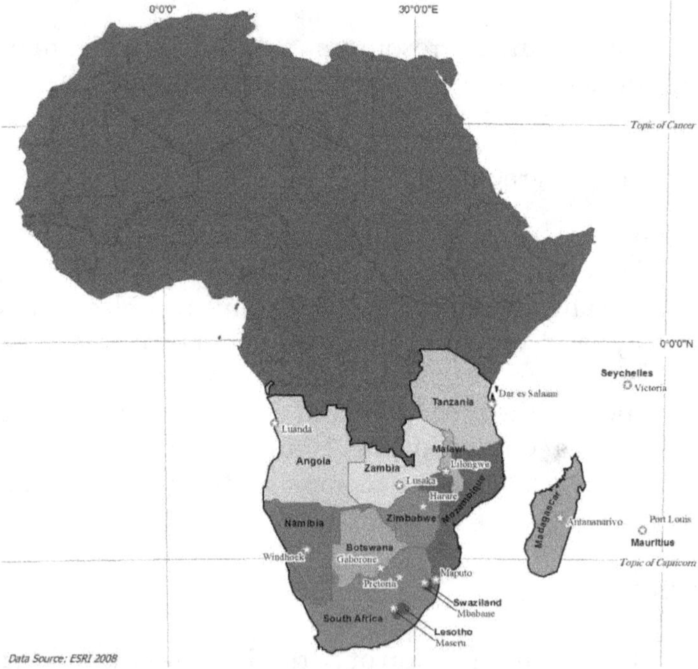

Figure 1. Southern Africa

Physiography and Geomorphology

Southern Africa's landscape varies widely. The principle land feature in this region is the Great Escarpment which rises sharply like a mountain wall a few dozen miles inland all along the coast. As a result, the region has very little coastal plain and low-lying territory (Cole and De

Blij 2007). The Cape Ranges Mountains, which are 1,800 to 2,100 meters high (6,000 to 7,500 feet), are located in the southwestern area. Beyond them is a semi-arid area which transitions to the deserts of Botswana and Namibia. Other key land features are the Drakensberg Mountains in South Africa which reach 3,350 meters (11,000 feet) and the Okavango Swamp in Botswana, which during the wet season is a valuable resource and habitat for numerous species. Southern Africa has several rivers, but the many falls and rapids limit navigability. The Orange River in South Africa provides water for irrigation, urban centers, and industrial needs. Coastlines are dominated by narrow lowlands of marshes, deserts, and sandy beaches with very few natural harbors (Areetey-Altoh 2003; Cole and de Blij 2007).

Climate

The climate in the region varies from savanna in the northern areas to desert in the southern regions. The Mediterranean climate of the South African coast, mild winters with temperatures above freezing and moderate dry summers, made this area desirable for early settlements. Regional variations in climate are caused by various climate controls such as seasonal wind patterns, ocean currents, and the influence of a marine or continental location. For example, Mocamedes, Angola; Mongo, Zambia; and Tamatave, Madagascar all have similar average yearly temperatures but vastly different precipitation (Figures 2a, 2b, and 2c). Mocamedes is dry all year round, in part because the winds blow from east over land, but also because the city's location on the coast near a cold ocean current exacerbates the dry conditions. Mongo receives its precipitation from October through March as a result of the proximity of the intertropical convergence zone with its predominance of convective lifting and cloud formation. From April through September, the subtropical high pressure zone dominates the region, inhibiting atmospheric lifting and producing dry conditions. Tamatave is on the windward side of a mountain range and thus receives ample precipitation all year round. These three cities demonstrate the southern region's climatic diversity and the impact of local topography.

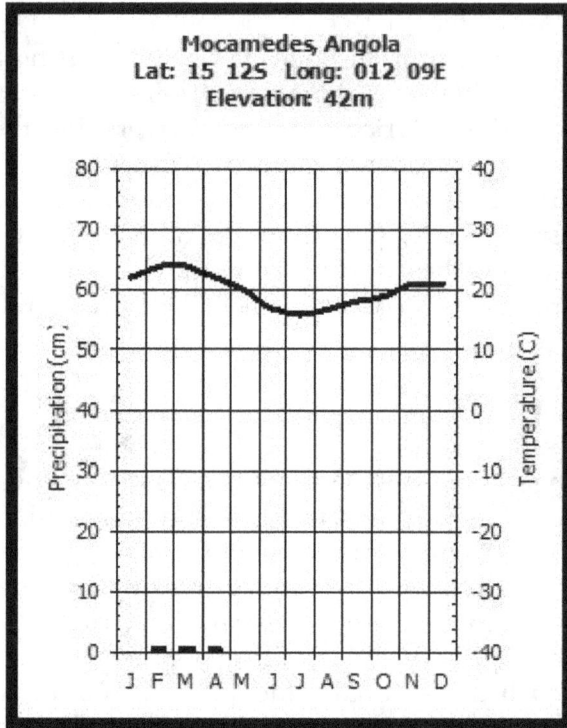

Figure 2a. Mocamedes' Desert Climate
(New York Times 2008)

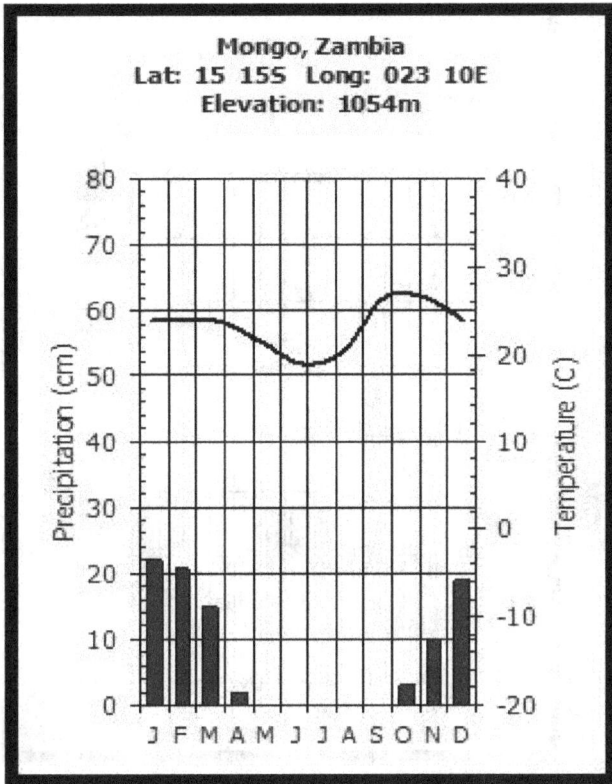

Figure 2b. Mongo's Savanna Climate
(New York Times 2008)

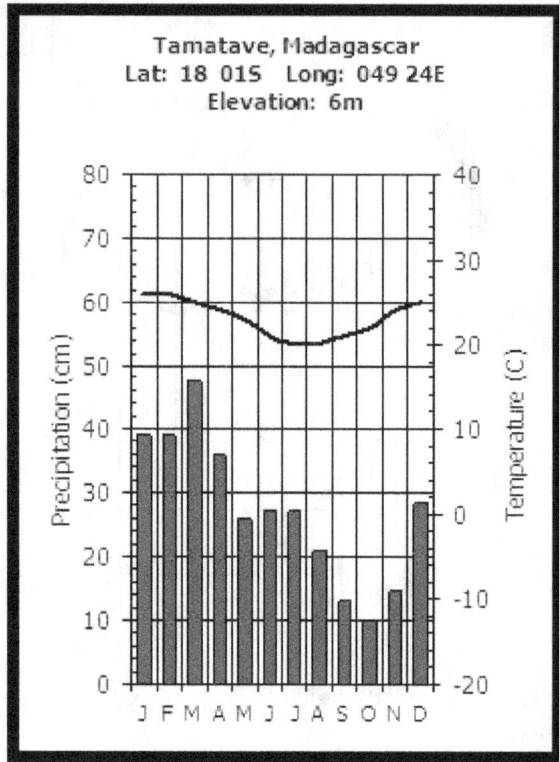

Figure 2c. Tamatave's Tropical Rainforest Climate
(New York Times 2008)

Biogeography

The landscape in the southern African region is mostly grassland or shrubs though in the southwest the Namib and Kalahari Deserts join to form an arid region. Mean annual precipitation on the coast is 16 millimeters (0.6 inches) in the Namib Desert. Further inland where the Namib and Kalahari deserts join, the area is moister with 127 millimeters (5 inches) of annual precipitation (Cole and de Blij 2007). Parts of Zimbabwe, Mozambique, Zambia, and Angola have forests, but these are dry open woodlands, not tropical forests. The southern tip of South Africa has Mediterranean vegetation such as broadleaf evergreen shrubs. Eastern Madagascar has tropical forests, but with increased deforestation and encroachment by humans, the forests and the habitats they provide are becoming seriously degraded (Aryeetey-Attoh 2003).

Southern Africa has little arable land in the aggregate as a result of population increases and poor farming, mining, and grazing practices, which have left the region in distress. Wildlife habitats suffer not only from human land use practices, but also from excessive poaching. Limited fresh water resources are a problem for Botswana, Swaziland, Zimbabwe, Angola, Malawi, Mozambique, Madagascar, and South Africa. South Africa's growth in water usage is outpacing the supply, and runoff from urban areas adds to the degradation of the water quality (CIA 2008).

The entire southern region suffers from varying degrees of desertification, which is land degradation attributable to poor land use practices, deforestation, and overgrazing. Population pressures have worsened the problems. This is noticeable in Lesotho, where forced migration and settlement into marginal lands has resulted in overgrazing and severe soil erosion and desertification (CIA 2008). Soil erosion has contributed to both decreases in agricultural yields and water pollution, leading to inadequate supplies of potable water. Deforestation of the tropical rain forest, both for international timber demand and domestic fuel, has led to a loss of biodiversity as well. Zimbabwe and Zambia rely heavily on their mining industry, but lack of technology has led to toxic waste and heavy metal pollution of both soil and water.

Historical Geography

Southern Africa was greatly affected by colonial European powers. Britain, Portugal, France, and the Netherlands all had a stake in the region. The colonization period spanned from the late 1880s to the early 1960s with an emphasis on settlement due to moderate and healthful climates. As European power and populations grew, their level of power in southern Africa increased as well. Native peoples were pushed to homelands or reserves on environmentally marginal lands (Cole and de Blij 2007). This process is most notable in South Africa with apartheid. Apartheid is an Afrikaans word meaning "apartness" or "separateness." Based on the concept that integration would result in a loss of cultural identity, the white government imposed strict racial laws on blacks, Asians, and Coloreds (mixed racial heritage) and developed a brutal police state to enforce them (Cole and de Blij 2007).

Implementation of apartheid began officially in 1948 after the electoral victory of the Afrikaner National Party though South Africa had been subject to white domination for three hundred years (Stock 2004). European settlers established Cape Town in 1652. Dutch (Boers) migration into the interior followed for the next two centuries, but the pace increased after the British settled on the coast in 1820, eventually leading to a clash with native black Africans like the Zulu. Diamond and gold discoveries in 1874 and 1886 respectively encouraged more British migration into the area, bringing in more capital and technology. Blacks lost their lands and livelihood as laws were passed to restrict their movement and employment opportunities. The British continued to acquire lands and seized control of South Africa from the Dutch in 1902 (Stock 2004). The Union of South Africa was formed in 1910 and discrimination laws continued. These segregation laws, which included separate residential areas and skilled jobs reserved only for whites, were not sufficient enough to satisfy extreme nationalist groups among the Boers. They formed the "Purified" Nationalist Party in 1934, won the 1948 election, and implemented racist laws under the premise that different groups should live and develop separately with their own culture and resources. The actuality was extreme inequality as whites controlled the government, economy, and the best lands (Stock 2004). Apartheid was in force in South Africa until 1990.

Cultural Geography

Southern Africa contains numerous ethnic groups and tribes. For example, Tanzania has more than 130 tribes from the Bantu family; Malawi has eleven ethnic groups, and Namibia has eight. Many states have at least three ethnic groups. One of the few common themes is that Europeans and whites are a minority in all states. The eastern islands of Madagascar and Mauritius have substantial Indonesian mixed ethnicities; Malayo-Indonesian and Indo-Mauritian respectively. The islands of Seychelles have mixed French, African, Indian, Chinese and Arab ethnicities (CIA 2008).

Indigenous religions vary just as widely, but Christianity is prominent throughout the region. States like Swaziland and Zimbabwe have adopted a blend of both Christianity and indigenous traditional faith such as Zionist and Syncretic respectively. Another commonality is that Islam is a minority religion found in the eastern portion of the region in Zambia, Tanzania, Malawi, Madagascar, Mozambique, Swaziland, and Mauritius (CIA 2008).

Many states use English as one of the official languages mainly for government and business, but by no means is English dominant. The range of indigenous languages throughout the region is great. For example, Zambia has 77 indigenous languages. Many states have more than one official language while several other indigenous languages are commonly spoken. For example, six languages are spoken in Mozambique, seven in Malawi, and eight in South Africa. This diversity of ethnic groups, religions, and languages makes southern Africa a complex region to study (CIA 2008).

Population Geography

The majority of Southern Africa's states are reflective of stage two of the demographic transition model (DTM), with more than 43 percent of their populations under the age of 15, and birth rates are high (Aryeetey-Attoh 2003).

Population and population densities (Table 1) vary widely throughout the region: from the island of Mauritius at 618 people per square kilometer to Botswana and Namibia, the least dense, each having three people per square kilometer. When considering only arable land (physiologic density), population densities for all states rise dramatically. Many southern African states like Angola, Malawi, Mozambique, and Tanzania rely heavily on subsistence agriculture, thus the high physiologic densities for these states stress the carrying capacity of the land's limited resources.

Crude birth rates (CBR) have decreased significantly from 1975 to 2005 for Botswana, Lesotho, Mauritius, Seychelles, and South Africa, suggesting that population growth has now begun to slow. (Cole and de Blij 2007). The declining birth rates represent a shift to a more industrialized and urbanized society. However, population increases have put stress on the carrying capacity of the land leading to land degradation, and this trend will continue. Additionally, the youthful population impacts the social infrastructure of southern Africa's states as the need for programs in health care, education, and job training is acute. Couple this requirement with government corruption in states like Zimbabwe and Swaziland, and the social situation becomes dire (Cole and de Blij 2007).

Crude death rates (CDR) have actually increased from 1975 to 2005 in Botswana, Lesotho, Zambia, and Zimbabwe, which suggests that political instability, famine, and most likely AIDS have taken a toll on the population. CDR projections for 2025 are the same or even greater for these states, with South Africa having a significant increase as well (Cole and de Blij 2007).

Migration patterns center on refugees emigrating from unstable states such as Zimbabwe to Botswana or South Africa. Tanzania has in excess of 500,000 refugees — more than any other African state — from Burundi and the Democratic Republic of the Congo. South Africa also has refugees from Burundi, DRC, Somalia, and other African states. Most often people emigrate to escape political persecution, economic dysfunction, famine, and war.

Table 1. Current Population Data for States in Southern Africa

State	Arithmetic Density (pop/sq km)	Physiologic Density (pop/ sq km arable land)	Population (July 2008 est.)	Population Growth Rate (2008 est. %)
Angola	13	379	12,531,357	2.1
Botswana	3	484	1,842,323	1.4
Lesotho	59	645	2,128,180	0.1
Madagascar	31	685	20,042,552	3.0
Malawi	110	716	13,931,831	2.3
Mauritius	618	1280	1,274,189	0.8
Mozambique	25	499	21,284,700	1.7
Namibia	3	255	2,088,669	0.9
Seychelles	190	9138	82,247	0.4
South Africa	39	330	48,782,756	0.8
Swaziland	65	640	1,128,814	-0.4
Tanzania	41	1072	40,213,160	2.0
Zambia	15	225	11,669,534	1.6
Zimbabwe	34	356	11,350,111	-0.7

Note: the low and sometimes negative growth rates are in part a result of the AIDS/HIV crisis. (CIA 2008)

Urban Geography

South Africa and Botswana are the most urbanized states of the region at around 50 percent (Aryeetey-Attoh 2003). South Africa's apartheid policies divided the cities into racial zones which led to a housing crisis for blacks, as they were forced into desolate areas with little or no infrastructure. As a result, squatter settlements sprang up on the peripheries of South African cities. Many cities still struggle with disparities in housing availability and quality (Stock 2004).

For the rest of the region, about 34 percent of the population lives in urban areas. The fastest urbanizing cities are in the states of Malawi (8.5 percent) and Tanzania (6.3 percent). Rapid urbanization here has led to acute housing and job shortages and inadequate infrastructure (Aryeetey-Attoh 2003).

Many of the capital cities are former colonial capitals and are primate cities, meaning that the city is at least twice the size of the next largest. The primate cities, primarily created for European settlement, contain imprints of both indigenous and colonial culture (Aryeetey-Attoh 2003).

Medical Geography

HIV and AIDS have been devastating for the southern region of Africa. The disease will shorten or seriously degrade the lives of at least one-third of the young men and women in the region, and two-thirds in states like Botswana and Zimbabwe (Cole and de Blij 2007). The economic impacts of HIV are immense. Less money is spent on food and schools because more resources must go to healthcare, and public health services have become overwhelmed caring for the sick and the orphaned. The population structure of southern African states has changed as well. The workforce (ages 15 – 30) is depleted, and women are especially affected. Life expectancy has dropped and negative growth rates are projected for Botswana, South Africa, and Zimbabwe (Cole and de Blij 2007). The social influences of multiple partners, intergenerational sex, and labor migration has made the disease very difficult to control. Southern Africa is the crux of the epidemic and will face this problem for decades into the future (Aryeetey-Attoh 2003).

Economic Geography

Subsistence agriculture plays an important role in the region, specifically for: Angola, Malawi, Tanzania, Namibia, Mozambique, Lesotho, and Swaziland. The majority of

Angola's population relies on subsistence agriculture for its livelihood, yet the state does not produce enough to feed itself and must import half of its food (CIA 2008). Prior to independence in 1975, the state led the continent in coffee production. When the Portuguese left, production decreased dramatically due to lack of capital and a weak political system that did not enhance economic investment. Angola is still recovering from a 27 year civil war which badly damaged its economy and infrastructure. The state needs to improve the development of its domestic markets and transport systems before the economy can fully recover (Cole and de Blij 2007). Malawi, one of the world's most densely populated states, is also one of the least developed. Agriculture accounts for 90 percent of the export revenues with tobacco making up more than half of the exports (CIA 2008). Tanzania is one of the poorest states in the world. Agriculture employs more than 50 percent of the workforce yet the topography and climate of the state limit the amount of arable land. By 2005, the state had received $1.5 billion in aid from the International Monetary Fund, the World Bank, and other donors to help restructure the economy (CIA 2008). An in-depth analysis of the primary extractive industries in Tanzania and their relationship to human development is available in the chapter: "Minerals and Human Security in Tanzania." Although 50 percent of Namibia's population depends on subsistence farming, mining provides more than 50 percent of foreign exchange earnings and the state is a primary source for gem quality diamonds (CIA 2008).

Diamond mining is also an extremely important industry for Botswana, South Africa, Angola, and Tanzania which all have highly productive diamond fields (Aryeetey-Attoh 2003 and Stock 2004). Diamond mining in Botswana makes up 70 to 80 percent of the state's export earnings. Botswana has one of the world's highest economic growth rates and through fiscal discipline has transformed itself from a poor state to a middle income state with a GDP per capita of $16,400 (2007 estimate). For comparison,

Zimbabwe has a GDP per capita of $200 while the United States is at $45,800 (CIA 2008). However, Botswana still has high rates of unemployment and the second highest HIV rates in the world (Swaziland has the highest) which threaten all the previous economic gains (CIA 2008). Though mining brings in revenue for the region, many southern African states lack the access to technology and finances necessary for geological surveys for the mining industry, resulting in degraded habitats and scarring from primitive extraction methods, or reliance on externally owned mining companies. (Aryeetey-Attoh 2003; Stock 2004).

South Africa is the economic power of the region. It has the largest endowment of natural resources, which include gold, diamonds, iron ore, coal, alloys, and copper. Also, it has the most developed agriculture and manufacturing, including a highly productive iron and steel industry, and more than 50 percent of the industrial plants in Africa. South Africa is the continent's leader in the production of gold, platinum, coal, chrome, sugar cane, and corn. With the best infrastructure in the region and a robust road and rail transportation network, it is well-linked to neighbors. Seasonal migration to the state is high, as employment in the mining or manufacturing industries depends heavily on surrounding states for the work force. South Africa is considered rich compared to the rest of the states in the region and has the most opportunities for economic development (Cole and de Blij 2007). Despite this relative economic power, poverty and lack of further economic empowerment among the disadvantaged groups lingers from the apartheid era (CIA 2008).

Lesotho and Swaziland's economies are closely tied to South Africa and its currency, the South African Rand, as Lesotho relies heavily on remittances from miners working in South Africa. Lesotho's economy is primarily based on subsistence agriculture as is Swaziland's, with 70 percent of the population depending on it. Swaziland receives more than 90 percent of its imports (motor vehicles, machinery, petroleum products, and food stuffs) from South Africa and in return, sends 60 percent of its exports which include sugar, wood pulp, cotton yarn, citrus, and canned fruit (CIA 2008).

Government corruption is also an issue in the region, most notably in Zimbabwe (CIA 2008). President Robert Mugabe and his party have led Zimbabwe into an economic and political abyss. The state has an unsustainable fiscal deficit and hyperinflation. Its involvement in a war with the Democratic Republic of the Congo from 1998 to 2002 cost the economy hundreds of millions of dollars. Mugabe's long neglect of the unequal land distribution between European settlers and black Zimbabweans led to his implementing a hasty and disastrous plan in the late 1990s and 2000: the seizure of land from white farmers, without compensation, to give to landless black families (Cole and de Blij 2007). The land reform program badly damaged the commercial farming sector, leaving the state – formerly an exporter of agricultural products–now a net importer of food products. The IMF has suspended their support as the government is in arrears on previous loans and refuses to enact reforms that would stabilize the economy. Inflation reached the staggering number of 26,000 percent in November 2007 and continues to climb because the Reserve Bank of Zimbabwe routinely prints money to fund the budget deficit. Zimbabwe's financial turmoil has put stress on neighboring states as refugees emigrate (CIA 2008).

Despite the financial turmoil of Zimbabwe, the island states of Mauritius and Seychelles serve as positive economic examples. Since its independence in 1968, Mauritius has risen to a middle income economy with a GDP per capita of $11,200 and diversification into industrial, financial, and tourist sectors. Life expectancy has increased from 68 years for both sexes in 1985 to 73 years in 2005 and a projected 77 years in 2025 (U.S. Census 2008). Seychelles has followed suit and the islands rank in the upper middle income group of states in the world with a GDP per capita of $16,600 (CIA 2008).

Political Geography

The states in southern Africa have undergone much turmoil in recent decades. Angola is still recovering after the aforementioned disastrous 27 year civil war that ended in 2002. Zimbabwe has one of the most corrupt governments in Africa with Mugabe as president. His failed land redistribution campaign led to wide shortages of basic necessities and crippled the economy. He rigged the election to ensure a win in 2002 and his party did the same in 2005 to secure a majority in parliament. Elections in 2008 were hampered by violence against the opposition and vote tampering. In order to find work and escape political persecution, refugees have fled by the thousands into Botswana and South Africa causing the former to build an electric fence and the latter to place military forces along the border. Violence against Zimbabweans is common in South Africa as the native South Africans compete with the influx of refugees for jobs.

South Africa, post apartheid, has undergone several changes in political space. The 1993 constitutional agreement replaced the old provinces and homelands with nine new ones in an attempt to deconstruct tribal identities associated with former territories. The provinces vary greatly in size and population. For example, the Northern Cape Province has the most land area, but only two percent of the population and two percent of South Africa's economic productivity. The province of Gauteng, which includes Johannesburg, is considerably smaller but has 20 percent of South Africa's population and 40 percent of its economic production (Stock 2004). The inequality of space and resources contributes to the weakness of the local governments. However, the non-white South Africans, with new political freedoms, have formed numerous organizations dedicated to human rights, gender equality, HIV/AIDS education, reduction of violence, and environmental education (Stock 2004).

Conclusion

The southern African region faces many challenges in the decades to come. Many of these challenges directly impact the region's potential for economic development. The impact of AIDS/HIV on the working population has negatively affected the economy and stressed the region's human security. Corruption in governments like Zimbabwe must end for any real economic gains or unity in the region. Though the area is rich in natural resources, the mining techniques used by many states are fairly primitive and lead to environmental degradation. The states must evolve beyond subsistence agriculture for their livelihood as the amount of arable land is limited and population growth is stressing the carrying capacity of the land.

Positive economic growth is possible with sound fiscal discipline and honest leadership. These burdens will most likely fall on South Africa as the state has adopted the role of regional leader in the past and it possesses the economic resources, technology, and infrastructure to do so. States like Botswana, Mauritius, and Seychelles have made great strides to improve their economic stability and others in the region could benefit from their example.

Southern Africa is an extremely diverse region in ethnicity, language, and religion. The region must find a common thread around which to unite, while still preserving unique cultural heritage. The Southern African Development Community is a positive step to reach regional unity.

Major Benefsheh D. Verell is an Assistant Professor of Geography at the United States Military Academy. She has taught and researched in the areas of Physical Geography and Sustainable Land Use Planning, and holds master's degrees in Geography and Organizational and Security Management. She has published in 'The Geographical Bulletin.'

References

Aryeetey-Attoh, Samuel. 2003. *Geography of Sub-Saharan Africa*. 2nd ed. Upper Saddle River, NJ: Pearson Education Inc.

Canty and Associates LLC. 2008. http://www.weatherbase.com (accessed September 29, 2008).

Central Intelligence Agency. 2008. *The 2008 World Factbook*. Washington, DC: Central Intelligence Agency.

Cole, Roy and H.J. de Blij. 2007. *Survey of Sub-Saharan Africa: A Regional Geography*. Oxford: Oxford University Press.

New York Times. 2008. http://geography.about.com/library/blank/blxafrica.htm (accessed September 29, 2008).

Population Reference Bureau. 2008. http://prb.org (accessed October 24, 2008).

Stock, Robert. 2004. *Africa South of the Sahara: A Geographical Interpretation*. 2nd ed. New York: Guilford.

United States Census Bureau, Population Division. 2008. http://www.census.gov/ipc/www/idb (accessed October 24, 2008).

The Tyranny of the Map and Modern Instability: The Ramifications of Incongruent Political and Ethnic Boundaries on Modern Africa

Richard L. Wolfel

Key Points

- National identity is a social construction: a process that is highly politicized.

- The Berlin Conference created boundaries that had no historical logic and limited national development in the era of independence.

- The haphazard boundaries of Africa create large amounts of interstate movement of people, goods and ideas and also influence intrastate conflict.

- Boundary disputes have been used as a justification for aggressive expansionist policies.

The last half of the twentieth century was an era of dramatic change in Africa. With independence for Ghana in 1957, the age of independence in Africa began. The 1960s were a time of great excitement as state after state separated from their former colonizers and charted a path of independence. By the start of the decade of the 1970s, disillusionment set in as Western and Soviet models of development had failed to achieve a level of economic success. This was coupled with increased ethnic, regional, and national conflicts which tempered the excitement of independence seen a decade earlier. This disillusionment manifested itself in continued geopolitical maneuverings and ethnic and regional conflicts, for example the Amin regime of Uganda and increased conflicts in Sudan.

By the 1980s, the hope of political and economic development had faded away amongst the rise of humanitarian crises, civil wars and Cold War alliances. The 1990s ended the Cold War maneuvering, but saw the continuation of humanitarian crises and ethnic and regional conflicts. This trend continues in the early 21st century as ethnic conflicts in Rwanda and Darfur provide a sad continuation to the trend of recent African history.

Many issues have contributed to the failure of political and economic development in sub-Saharan Africa. A critical underlying cause is the incongruence of political and ethnic boundaries. Starting with the scramble for Africa at the Berlin Conference (1884-85) the boundaries of Africa were drawn out of convenience for the European powers with little regard to the ethnic landscape of Africa. The result of this decision has been an extended era of tribal and ethnic conflict. Most of the modern ethnic conflicts can be tied to the creation of multinational states, incorporating ethnic and tribal groups with a long history of animosity.

This chapter will explore the evolution of political and ethnic boundaries in Africa as an important influence on modern conflict in Africa. The grouping of ethnic and tribal groups with long histories of conflict has created not only humanitarian crises as seen in Rwanda, Nigeria and Sudan, but has also facilitated authoritarian rule in various regions of the continent. In order to successfully understand the nature of ethnic conflict in Africa, one must begin with a discussion of colonization and the division of Africa as initiated in Berlin over 120 years ago.

Nationalism and Territoriality as a Social Construction

An important debate within the geographic community concerns the definition of space and how it is produced. According to Lefebvre (1991, 1), until recently, space had a "strictly geometrical meaning." In other words, space was not something that was influenced by cultural or political actions; it was innocent, and isolated from the political process. Lefebvre (1991, 31) challenges the innocence of space in the political development of a region by prominently stating "that every society...produces a space, its own space." Space is now widely viewed as an active player in the political development of a region. It influences change and is also changed during the process of political development.

Landscape and the Archeology of Knowledge

Philosopher and sociologist Michel Foucault has emphasized throughout his work that knowledge is based on layers of existence or an archeology of sorts. An understanding of society is based on an evaluation of the power structures that exist at each layer. Furthermore, modern society is based on several levels (Rabinow 1984). This leads to a conclusion that modern governments utilize several layers of historical evolution in an effort to provide justification and legitimacy for their conception of national development.

One of the key issues raised in Foucault's analysis is his discussion of discourses — communication that involves specialized knowledge. It is important to ask whom the discourse serves. In this analysis, Foucault emphasizes that discourses are not naturally evolving processes, but are actively manipulated by power elites in a society to promote their goals (Rabinow 1884).

The conclusion of discourse as a mechanism to gain power is also consistent with discussion of truth. According to Foucault (1980, 118), "truth is produced." Truth should be understood as a regulated process. Societies produce truth that is consistent with the beliefs of the identity they are creating. This is key in studies of nationalism. Truth is presented as part of the national discourse. Societies utilize symbols to provide a set of instruction for the members of the nation.

Geography plays an important role in the discussion of the use of power in the construction of a nation. A nation, according to Smith (1988) is a group of people who share a common identity that is created through a political process. Nations differ from ethnic or tribal identities in that a nation is a modern phenomenon, created "out of modern conditions and ideally suited to those conditions" (Smith 1988, 3). Foucault emphasizes that geography has an important influence on the power structures within a society. According to Foucault (1980, 77), "tactics and strategies deployed through implantations, distributions, demarcations, control of territories and organisation of domains" are important tools in an evaluation of the power relationships within societies. Especially important in landscape studies is a discussion of the organization of domains. A state constructs landscapes in an effort to promote its idea. This is done through a conscious selection of sites to promote or preserve ideologies. Architecture is used by a society in an effort to show people what they should believe for the purpose of developing a group identity. This is shown to them constantly as they move throughout a city. Also, states can either destroy or disavow sites in an effort to hide themes that are not consistent in the national identity being constructed, and they can use boundaries to separate people.

Foucault's discussion of power and the construction of societies provide important insights into discussions of the development of the borders of Africa. Boundaries are often created in an effort to promote power. This can be done through either the concentration of an ethnic group within a boundary, or the dispersal of an ethnic group across boundaries. During colonization, the borders of regions were developed for the convenience and benefit of the European powers. When the African states became independent, they were left with borders that benefited the European colonizer. This created a major hindrance to development for the newly independent African state.

Colonization and the Need for "Order"

The Berlin Conference underlies one of the most common problems for colonization: how to divide territory in an effort to maximize control over space. Generally, there have been two major methods of imposing boundaries on a region. First, a colonizing power divides territory in an effort to divide the local population and reduce its influence. An excellent example of this process is in central Africa where the Hutus and Tutsis were divided by the Belgians based on cattle ownership, physical measurements and church records in an effort to keep the local population from uniting against colonial rule (Mamdani 2001).

The second method of dividing territory is to eliminate conflict between colonizing powers. This was the rationale for the Berlin Conference, organized by Otto von Bismarck in 1884-85. The early 1880s was the start of the scramble for Africa as most European powers began claiming territory. Quickly the competition escalated, especially in the Congo River basin. Belgium, under King Leopold II, claimed the economically wealthy region of Congo, but the French, Portuguese and English all managed to landlock the Belgian colony. This created a crisis and at the request of Portugal, Germany, a rising colonial power, seized the opportunity to host a conference to resolve the conflict in the Congo basin.

The result of the conference was the division of Africa, creating spheres of influence for the colonial powers in Africa. The key result of this conference was the establishment of rules governing how Africa was to be divided. The interesting, and often mentioned, observation of this conference is the lack of representation from the African people. Bridges (1998, 63) emphasizes "the situation in Africa itself seemed to cry out for the imposition of a European civil order." This statement shows the arrogant mindset of the Europeans as they prepared for the Berlin conference. As many have pointed out, the Europeans treated Africa as if it was a child in need of European guidance. The result of this mindset was the creation of boundaries that did not follow the traditional demarcation of Africa, since these boundaries were seen as contrary to the goal of the Europeans. The boundaries delimited by the Berlin Conference became the foundation on which independent states in Africa would later be built. The lack of concern for the national and tribal boundaries in Africa would lead to conflict as Africa decolonized.

The Ramifications of the *"Tyranny of the Map"*

The Berlin conference streamlined colonization in Africa and eventually the decolonization of the continent. However, as the former colonies began to develop into independent states, four problems became apparent. First, pan-Africanism became a force that challenged the identity of the newly independent states. Three synergistic forces worked to create a pan-African movement in the region: establishment of a European-style education system, the systematic racial discrimination that catalyzed a call to action, and cultural bonding after emigration outside the continent. First, schooling in Europe was established to create a class of leaders for the African colonies. These elite Africans from many different regions were educated together in an effort to govern based on the plans of England (Adi 2000). This common education created an environment in which the new elite started viewing Africa in its entirety, as opposed to understanding Africa in smaller ethnic divisions.

As part of this schooling, a second major force developed that united Africans. The education system also introduced them to discrimination while in Europe. Lake (1995, 22) noted that Africans "were made to internalize notions of their inferiority." Adi (2000) also notes that racial discrimination was one of the major influences leading Africans to form their own organizations. These organizations cut across ethnic lines and focused on common issues facing Africans. The result was a movement toward a common African solution to these problems, leading to greater calls for unity at a larger level than the current state structure.

The third issue that promoted pan-African identity was the creation of a diaspora community outside the continent. As Africans from all regions lived, worked and were educated in Europe and parts of the Americas, they faced common issues, especially discrimination. This led to increased interconnections across ethnic/colonial boundaries. The result was a set of common issues that led to a call for greater unity.

Pan-Africanism is a major barrier to the development of modern African states. As the elite and the diaspora community began to think of Africa in a unified identity as opposed to individual states, this created a challenge for the leadership as the intellectual elite tend to place allegiance to a larger entity than the state. As a result, national development in Africa has been slowed as loyalty has been split between the local identity of the state and the larger African identity.

The second major issue that hindered the development of states in Africa was the cross-border cultural and economic relationships that worked to undermine loyalty to the state. Cross-border relationships work to weaken loyalty and identity to an individual state as people maintain loyalty on both sides of the border. The migrant communities in southern Africa are outstanding examples of the creation of multiple identities that dilute the national identities in the modern states of the region. For instance, the Mozambican males who sojourn in South Africa to find employment often marry South African women to ensure their political and economic stability, despite having a family in Mozambique (Lubkemann 2000). This form of polygyny has created a class of transnational males with an interest in two communities, making them neither completely Mozambican nor South African. With a wife in each community, a somewhat jumbled sense of identity is felt by men as they are not necessarily just using South Africa as a labor market, but they have established ties there.

At the same time, keeping a wife in Mozambique limits their ability to sever ties to that state. Thus, their identity becomes transnational, diluting their Mozambican identity, but not completely accepting a South African identity, and resulting in neither state earning their full allegiance.

The third major hindrance is the intrastate violence that has been the major source of conflict within Africa. Several examples of intrastate violence exist, including in Rwanda, Sudan and Nigeria. The interesting issue here is that very few interstate conflicts have taken place in modern Africa and most of the conflict has been within states. Newbury (2002, 5) notes that of the sixteen wars fought in Africa between 1990 and 1997, only two were interstate, the rest within a single state. This propensity toward intrastate violence shows both the problematic boundaries the newly independent states of Africa inherited and also the inability of the leadership of these states to create an environment in which multiple national groups could flourish and share in the identity of one state.

Finally, Africa has developed a complex set of rules governing colonial boundaries. The boundaries that were created by the Europeans in Berlin were artificial and built out of convenience. One example of this, identified by Herbst (1989), is that 44 percent of Africa's state borders are straight lines. This is an outstanding example of the lack of regional knowledge and a lack of concern for the existing cultural or natural landscape that went into the construction of borders which were superimposed on established cultural landscapes. This may well have led to massive conflict and redrawing of borders in the early years of decolonization. Fortunately, there have been minimal interstate conflicts stemming from border disputes, largely due to a policy laid down by the Organization of African Unity (OAU) in 1963 in which it declared "any change in the inherited colonial boundaries to be illegitimate" (Herbst 1990, 124). This principle was also promoted by the United Nations (UN) with the statement that "the territorial integrity of the states thus created must be safeguarded against attack from within or without" (Emerson 1969, 298). This leads to the conclusion that both the global leadership and the African leadership would not allow major wars over border conflicts to occur. With this in mind, it became necessary to create nations within the former colonies.

Miles and Rochefort (1991) study two groups from the same ethnic community who were on different sides of the Nigeria/Niger border. Their work showed that state identification was more important than ethnic identity to the local citizens within Nigeria. This is significant as it shows that states are starting to separate a single ethnic group, now living in different states, through the process of nationalism. The nation building process is highly complex and problematic. Uchendu (1977) emphasizes that "African nations face the problem of how to select national, inspirational symbols that do not alienate their traditions." In other words, African states must construct a national identity that does not ignore their history. Mazuri (1972, xv) employs the term "cultural engineering" to refer to the process of building national cohesion. This term is very illustrative as the process of nation building is not a natural process in an artificially divided Africa. As in other regions of the world, those in leadership undertake conscious decisions on which elements are included as part of the national discourse. In Africa this is very complex as elements must be selected that do not alienate minority groups within a state.

Examples of Boundary Conflicts and Political Actions

Two major types of conflicts can be observed in Africa as a result of the boundaries that were created in Berlin. Regional conflict within a state is the most common type. This can result from longstanding ethnic confrontations or from conflict over resource allocation. Several examples of internal conflicts exist in Africa including Nigeria, where several ethnic groups have historically engaged in open conflict in a struggle that also includes religious

103

confrontation between Christianity and Islam. In Rwanda, internal conflict was well documented between Hutus and Tutsis engaged in genocide during the 1990s. As well, Sudan is a state rocked by civil war and genocide over the last 30 years. The Darfur region of Sudan is a classic example of an ethnic conflict that has escalated to a major humanitarian crisis.

Since 1955, Sudan has seen several major conflicts within its borders. These conflicts have focused on regionalism and ethnic-based dispute. The civil wars of Sudan (1955-1972; 1983-2005) focused on religious and linguistic variations; the problems in Darfur differ in that the conflict is primarily regionally and resource based (UN 2005), as both sides speak the same language (Arabic) and share the same religion (Islam). Historically, the Darfur region was an independent sultanate until incorporation into the British Empire. The region was then included as part of Sudan. While many accounts of the conflict exist, the emphasis here is upon its regional nature. The lack of understanding at Berlin led to the incorporation of this region into Sudan, and the OAU and UN confirmed this incorporation through their admonition against boundary changes. The result has been a dramatic humanitarian crisis.

The second major boundary conflict type is international conflict over a border. While the OAU and UN have expressly condemned conflicts over boundaries, there have been some boundary conflicts in Africa. Also, some leaders have used the history of colonization or the inappropriateness of boundaries as a source for increasing their power within the state. One example of a leader using decolonization to further his power base is Idi Amin and his regime in Uganda. Amin's emphasis on blaming the British for the problems of the state and using the boundary issues as justification to promote his aspirations to become the geopolitical power in Central and East Africa ultimately led to his downfall.

Idi Amin became leader of Uganda through a military coup in 1971. Amin used colonization and border conflicts as justification to promote his power within the state. Tactically, Amin came to power by dividing the state along ethnic lines. Most of his support came from the West Nile region, while his opponents, primarily members of the Acholi and Lango ethnic groups, were purged from the military, with some being executed. Amin extended his list of victims to other African ethnic groups. However, Amin garnered international reproach when he expropriated property from the Asians and Europeans in Uganda and eventually expelled the Asians from the state. This was all done in an effort to gain control of the economy of Uganda as he attempted to justify the expropriation under the umbrella of decolonization by blaming British ownership of businesses for the poverty of the state. To that end, when the United Kingdom broke diplomatic relations, he claimed that he had defeated the British in Africa and added the title "Conqueror of the British Empire" to his name.

Amin's war with Tanzania proved to be his downfall. The large group of exiled Ugandans living in Tanzania, opposed to Amin, seemed to be the major reason for his declaration of war, but Amin publically declared that the war was to annex the Kagera region of Tanzania, which he claimed was historically part of Uganda. These irrendentist notions proved to be Amin's downfall as his forces were routed and Amin was forced to flee Uganda and abdicate the presidency.

Amin's rule in Uganda demonstrates how those in power in Africa can use the Berlin Conference borders to justify their efforts to seize greater power. Amin tied the economic problems in Uganda to British colonial subjects, mainly Indians, and this led to their expulsion. Finally, in his international conflicts, Amin always justified military aggression as an effort to regain territory lost by Uganda. Though he ultimately failed, both the internal and international policies of Amin show the potential for serious conflict in Africa as a result of colonial boundaries and the ability of corrupt leaders to manipulate these boundaries for their own gain.

Conclusion

Boundaries are a powerful entity in the contemporary geopolitical system. One of the major issues the global community will face in Africa is how to deal with multiethnic states and multistate nations. Also, the continent will face shifting and multiple forms of identity as a result of the construction of new identities based on pan-African concepts. As Lefebvre and Foucault have emphasized, we must be careful of the motives of leaders espousing new boundaries as they are often trying to create space for their own gain in power.

Based on the strength of the UN and OAU's statements, international boundary conflict seems to be an unlikely event in the foreseeable future. Also, as states mature and develop their own national identities, it is possible that the previously dominant ethnic identification will be superseded by the civic nationality created by the states. However, as seen in Sudan, internal conflict is likely to continue as economic and environmental resources become scarcer and a more likely source of conflict.

Boundary conflicts are not seen only in Africa. They are common across most of the decolonizing world. The lines on the map gain power as they are internationally recognized and it becomes extremely difficult to change the lines as states begin to vie to protect their own interests. The future of newly independent states is strongly tied to their boundaries, especially when state and national boundaries are not congruent. One of the major projects facing the global community is to move beyond the incongruity of the state and nation and create viable states in the post-colonial world.

Dr. Richard Wolfel is an Associate Professor and Chair of Intercultural Competence at the United States Military Academy. His research focuses on nationalism, identity and the urban built environment in Germany and Central Asia. He has published in journals such as 'Nationalities Papers,' 'The Pennsylvania Geographer,' and 'The Western Humanities Review.'

References

Adi, Hakim. 2000. Pan-Africanism and West African Nationalism in Britain. *African Studies Review* 43, no.1: 69-82.

Bridges, R.C. 1998. The Source of the Nile Debate. In *Cultural Atlas of Africa*, ed. Jocelyn Murray. New York: Checkmark Books.

Emerson, Rupert. 1969. The Problem of Identity, Selfhood, and Image in the New Nations: The Situation in Africa. *Comparative Politics* 1, no. 3: 297-312.

Foucault, Michel. 1980. *Power/Knowledge: Selected Interviews and Other Writings, 1972-1977*. Ed. Colin Gordon. New York: Pantheon.

Herbst, Jeffery. 1989. The Creation and Maintenance of National Boundaries in Africa. *International Organization* 43, no. 4: 673-692.

Herbst, Jeffery. 1990. War and State in Africa. *International Security* 14, no. 4: 117-139.

Lake, Obiagele. 1995. Toward a Pan-African Identity: Diaspora African Repatriates in Ghana. *Anthropological Quarterly* 68, no.1: 21-36.

Lefebvre, Henri. 1991. *The Production of Space*. Trans. Donald Nicholson-Smith. Oxford: Blackwell.

Lubkemann, Stephen. 2000. The Transformation of Transnationality among Mozambican Migrants in South Africa. *Canadian Journal of African Studies* 34, no.1: 41-63.

Mamdani, Mahmood. 2001. *When Victims Become Killers: Colonialism, Nativism, and the Genocide in Rwanda*. Princeton, NJ: Princeton University Press.

Mazuri, Ali. 1972. *Cultural Engineering and Nation Building in East Africa*. Evanston, IL: Northwestern University Press.

Miles, William and David Rochefort. 1991. Nationalism versus Ethnic Identity in Sub-Saharan Africa. *The American Political Science Review* 85, no.2: 393-403.

Newbury, Catharine. 2002. States at War: Confronting Conflict in Africa. *African Studies Review* 45, no.1: 1-20.

Rabinow, Paul, ed. 1984. *The Foucault Reader*. New York: Pantheon.

Smith, Anthony. 1988. The Myth of the Modern Nation and the Myths of Nations. *Journal of Ethnic and Racial Studies* 11: 1-26.

Uchendu, Victor. 1977. The Challenge of Cultural Transition in Sub-Saharan Africa. *Annals of the American Academy of Political and Social Science* 432: 70-79.

United Nations. 2005. *Report of the International Commission of Inquiry on Darfur to the United Nations Secretary General*. http://www.un.org/News/dh/sudan/com_inq_darfur.pdf#search=%22un%20report%20darfur%20genocide%22 (accessed July 9, 2008).

The Importance of defining Appropriate African Regions

Megan Stallings

Key Points

- AFRICOM must be divided into logical subregions to effectively build partnerships, assist African needs and interests, and achieve U.S. objectives at the same time.

- It is nearly impossible to differentiate distinct regions that have any sort of common basis. Furthermore, most major African issues transpose boundaries; they cannot be confined and delineated within official lines.

- The U.S. needs to demonstrate support for African initiatives and strengthen their existing alliances so Africans can solve problems on their own. Therefore, rather than make new boundaries that do not completely fulfill the role, AFRICOM would be best suited to follow the initiatives already laid out by Africans.

Introduction

President George W. Bush officially established the regional unified combatant command for Africa (AFRICOM) on October 1, 2007, with operations to commence one year hence. The success of AFRICOM is not only in the national interest of the United States, but is important to the stability of the international community. As stated in the National Defense Strategy, "International partnerships continue to be a principal source of our strength" (Rumsfeld 2005, 4). Africa, replete with abundant resources but fraught with conflict, becomes more significant every day with the rise of globalization. Therefore, the U.S. must be proactive and deal with challenges in a clear and definitive manner to secure its interests. Similar to how Central Command (CENTCOM) divided the Persian Gulf region into smaller operational regions, AFRICOM needs a regionalizing scheme to allow better focus on specific areas. In addition to the bilateral engagement that already exists, this means that multilateral engagement is necessary. AFRICOM must be divided into logical regions to effectively build partnerships, assist African needs and interests, and achieve U.S. objectives at the same time.

Africa is an extremely large and diverse continent; all states cannot be considered together for effective strategic engagement and accomplishment of AFRICOM's objectives. Numerous factors could be used to delineate regions within Africa, with some factors more prevalent in one state than another. Some possible defining characteristics include, but are not limited to: climate, crime, culture, disease, economics, environmental degradation, failed/ failing states, famine, internal and cross-border conflict, physical geography, piracy, politics, population growth, refugees, regional alliances, religion, terrorism, trade, and the presence of ungoverned spaces. Regions may be more effective if established along commonalities such as these factors. Consequently, AFRICOM may be more successful if divided logically to tackle the most pressing issue(s) in each region.

The structure and organization of AFRICOM will by necessity be different than other combatant commands (COCOMs), primarily by the augmented role of the State Department and the subjugation of the military warfighting objective to more immediately constructive interests. For success, the combatant commander needs to ensure AFRICOM is perceived as a different organization than the other COCOMs. There are many audiences across the globe who must believe the difference: but primarily the African audience. The creation of regions should reinforce that difference and encourage support from within Africa. In order to accomplish this, AFRICOM must present itself transparently.

Background

AFRICOM tentatively plans to establish regional integration teams (RITs) in several locations across the continent (Defense Senior Leadership Council 2007). The combatant commander needs to decide where to place the RITs throughout the area of responsibility (AOR) for effective engagement; appropriately designed regions can help. There are many approaches to regionalizing Africa, all along different criteria. Textbooks and academia divide Africa in many ways, while non-governmental organizations use other approaches, the African Union (AU) uses still another, and the U.S. military proposes to further complicate the picture. Careful consideration and analysis is needed to determine the most beneficial division of the AOR to support Africa's and AFRICOM's objectives. Regions could be demarcated based on one main criterion, or a merger of the most prominent and strategically important criteria, where each state is wholly contained within one region. Another alternative is to assign regions based on major issues and assign states within regions that focus on their most pressing needs. In this scenario, one state could belong to several. In any of these options, geographically contiguous regions are not necessarily essential. In this case African space can be (notionally) divided in new ways, according to the task(s) at hand. The ability to shape the landscape into regions according to AFRICOM's objectives is a blank canvas; no convention or preset pattern needs be followed. But always-to increase security and stability on the continent, AFRICOM's objectives must be aligned with Africa's own.

Discussion

The sheer diversity of the 52 states within AFRICOM provides innumerable factors to consider. Therefore it is essential to narrow the focus to the most important interests. Four main published objectives for AFRICOM focus on 1) democratic governance and political freedom, 2) economic growth and opportunity, 3) the battle against disease (primarily HIV and malaria), and 4) combating internal state conflicts (Carson 2004; Craddock 2007; Frazer 2006). Each of these objectives could reasonably be used to establish a regional construct.

U.S. European Command (EUCOM) analyzed the African states when under its watch to determine levels of democratic governance, the first objective. As can been seen in Figure 1, EUCOM named Libya, Central African Republic, Democratic Republic of Congo, Equatorial Guinea, Swaziland, and Burundi as dictatorships, and The Gambia, Guinea Bissau, Guinea, Liberia, Burkina Faso, Angola, and Zimbabwe as superficial, repressive, and corrupt democracies. Other states were either deemed democracies or developing democracies (Jones 2004). The span of non-democratic governance is quite wide and involves a large number of states, infeasible for grouping within one contiguous region. Thus, EUCOM had already mapped African space into discontinuous regions.

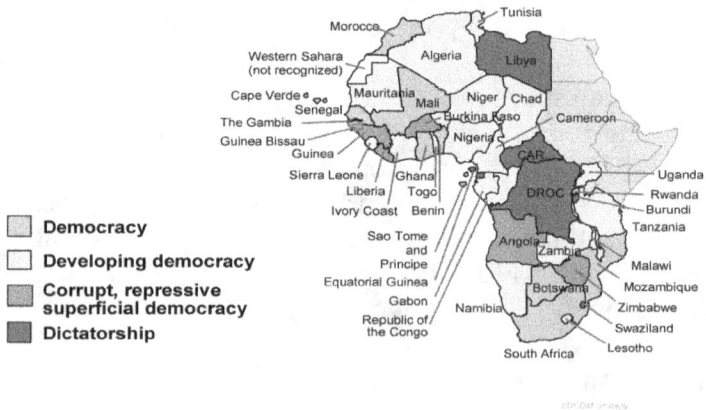

Figure 1. 2004 EUCOM Political Map of Africa, Showing an Assessment of Levels of Democratic Governance (Jones 2004)

The second objective, economic development, is extremely important to the region. As 71 percent of the population is under the age of 25, a potential economic work force of over 900 million people could have a positive impact on the rest of the world under the right economic, environmental, and security conditions (Cobb 2005). Africa already has many regional economic alliances, some more focused and successful than others. According to the AU, the recognized regional economic alliances (RECs) established within Africa are: AMU (Arab Maghreb Union), COMESA (Common Market for East and Southern Africa), CEN-SAD (Community of Sahelo-Saharan States), ECCAS (Economic Community of Central African States), ECOWAS (Economic Community of West African States), IGAD (Inter-Governmental Authority for Development), EAC (East African Community), and SADC (Southern Africa Development Community) (African Union 2007). These alliances are geographically contiguous and there are several states belonging to more than one alliance. In addition, both COMESA and CEN-SAD cover such broad areas that they would be inefficient for use as regions. Similarly, the EAC is so geographically small that it would be equally inefficient. However, the existence of economic alliances supports strong regional foundations potentially capable of spurring development; combined focused effort can achieve more than individual states. In particular, ECOWAS demonstrates achievement in many economic areas and has been a regional stability partner for EUCOM (Jones 2005). The AU is attempting to capitalize on the stronger RECs as they create their regional brigades along similar boundaries (African Union 2007).

The third objective focuses on the two primary diseases drastically affecting African lives, HIV/AIDS and malaria. Both diseases are epidemics within the continent and severely affect large portions of the population. There are many governmental and non-governmental groups concerned with the state of health and the preponderance of

113

disease in Africa. The ability for a region to focus on a specific aspect of health and disease could be helpful. According to the World Health Organization (Figure 3) the highest levels of malaria (more than 25,000 cases per 100,000 people) are in Liberia and Ghana, closely followed by Togo, Uganda, Guinea, Malawi, and Mozambique. Figure 4 shows the HIV infection rates are the highest (more than 30 percent of the population) in Botswana and Zimbabwe, closely followed by South Africa, Lesotho, and Namibia (UNAIDS 2006). Indeed, nine African states (Uganda, Democratic Republic of Congo, Kenya, Tanzania, Zambia, Zimbabwe, Mozambique, Nigeria, and South Africa) have more than one million people affected by HIV (UNAIDS 2006). Clearly, the health problems in Africa are scattered throughout the continent, with HIV maintaining a stronghold in the southern portion. Therefore, a southern region could be established based on HIV prevalence, to be able to concentrate efforts on this critical issue. However, there are no other easily delineated regions that could follow suit for other diseases or health issues.

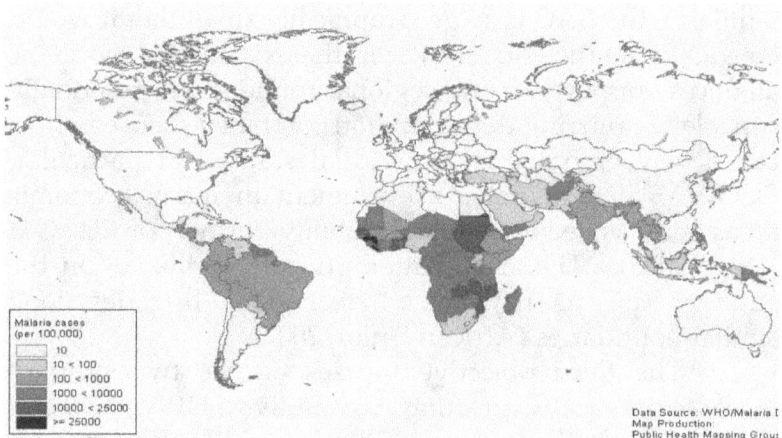

Figure 3. Malaria Cases (per 100,000), 2004
(World Health Organization)

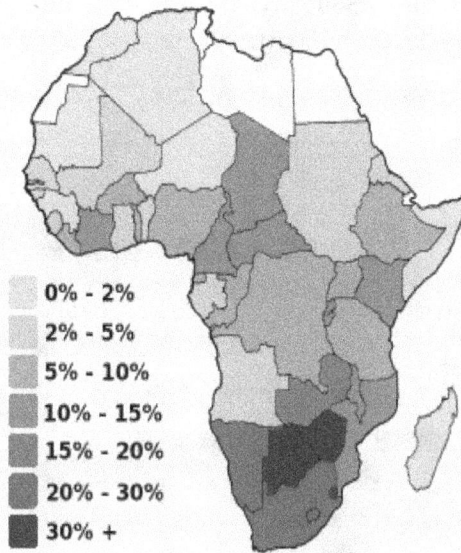

Figure 4. African HIV Infective Rates (UNAIDS 2006)

The fourth objective is combating internal state conflict. There are numerous ways to look at the level of internal conflict within Africa. One option, the Human Security Report, analyzes conflict from a viewpoint of insecure states, as measured by a combination of political instability, violence, and human rights abuses. The analysis, as depicted by Table 1, lists the worst performing states in each category (Human Security Centre 2005). The most dysfunctional states appear in all three categories. Considering just the combination of the top 16 states in each separate category (shown in Table 1), 28 of the total 48 states are African. Four−Liberia, Burundi, Democratic Republic of Congo, and Algeria appear in all three categories of dysfunction. An additional five African states are listed in two categories (Human Security Centre 2005).

Table 1. Severity of Internal Conflict
(Human Security Centre 2005)

Fatalities from political violence	rate per 100000	Core human rights abuses	Amnesty International (2003)	U.S. State Depart ment (2005)	Average ranking (2003)	Political instability/violence	World Bank (2002)
Liberia	69.4	Colombia	5	5	5	DRC	0
Iraq	35.1	DRC	5	5	5	Liberia	0.5
Burundi	18.2	Iraq	5	5	5	Afghanistan	1.1
Sudan	8.5	Algeria	5	4	4.5	Burundi	1.6
Uganda	6.5	Indonesia	5	4	4.5	Cote d'Ivoire	2.2
Israel/Palestine	5.8	Israel	5	4	4.5	Sudan	2.7
Nepal	4.4	Liberia	5	4	4.5	Somalia	3.2
DRC	4.2	Afghanistan	4	4	4	Colombia	3.8
Somalia	3.9	Angola	4	4	4	Palestinian Territories	4.3
Colombia	1.6	Brazil	4	4	4	Iraq	4.9
Philippines	1.4	Burma (Myanmar)	4	4	4	CAR	5.4
Eritrea	1.3	Burundi	4	4	4	Georgia	5.9
Afghanistan	1.1	Cameroon	4	4	4	Nepal	6.5
Cote d'Ivoire	0.7	CAR	4	4	4	Congo-Brazzaville	7
Algeria	0.7	China	4	4	4	Algeria	7.6
Senegal	0.4	Congo-Brazzaville	4	4	4	Zimbabwe	7.6

A second way to look at internal conflict within Africa is to study the diversity of failed states. Failed or failing states are a dramatic indicator of the amount of internal violence likely in an area. Without an effective government, and with an increase in ungoverned spaces, individual groups clamor for power with no mechanisms available to restrain them. Merging numerous criteria to delineate regions results in too much overlap and complexity. These four factors are only a starting point; considering the need to engage with these states, different languages and dialects as well as disparate cultures are additional complicating factors. It is nearly impossible to differentiate distinct regions with any sort of common basis. Furthermore, focusing a regionalization scheme on multiple criteria based on four different objectives will not provide a strong approach. There are too many states that require assistance in all four areas; each of the resulting regions would be very large and cumbersome. In addition, most major African issues transcend boundaries; they cannot be confined and delineated by law. However, creating new boundaries based on transcendent issues is not feasible as 1) those boundaries would change as the issue morphed; and 2) AFRICOM needs its regional operational boundaries to coincide with state political boundaries in order to support current political structures (however fragile) and coordinate more easily among states when issues overlap. For AFRICOM to coordinate with sub-state level governments in impractical and does not support African state legitimacy. In these cases multiple parties can be the beneficiaries. Therefore, a simple focus on one of the four factors discussed above without attempting to incorporate other characteristics provides the clearest solution to creating a coherent regional schema.

Of the four stated AFRICOM objectives, fostering economic trade and development seems most promising as economic development and the creation of jobs bring the capability to solve other issues. If Africans have jobs, they are better able to feed, clothe and shelter themselves. Without constraints on these resources, there is less impetus for conflict and violence. In addition, uncorrupted economically viable states are better able to sustain schools, healthcare, and critical infrastructure and thus provide for human security (Gration 2007). Using the economic factor as a basis for regionalization also better supports the existing African structure of regional organizations. This enhances AFRICOM's ability to build partnership capacity with established, recognized multinational organizations (AFRICOM 2007). As Deputy Assistant Secretary of Defense for African Affairs Theresa Whelan stated, this approach allows the U.S. not to "reinvent the wheel," but reinforce and capitalize on the work Africans have already done (Smith 2007). Likewise, the Director of the Africa Program, Center for Strategic and International Studies (J. Stephen Morrison) emphasized the need for AFRICOM to enlarge the foundation of existing regional and economic alliances and ensure their development in the future (Morrison 2007). In addition, National Security Presidential Directive (NSPD) 50, dated September 28, 2006, states the U.S. must work to strengthen regional organizations in Africa (Whelan 2008). Clearly, there is already traction for this idea among U.S. policymakers. As well, U.S. initiatives must have approval and support of Africans if they are to succeed (Smith 2007), and focusing on fostering economic trade and development issues wil garner that cooperation. Africa has vested more importance in the REC structure than just economic concerns; the AU's use of the REC structure when proposing their regional brigade concept shows the esteem vested in RECs.

Conclusion and Recommendation

Attainment of Africa's and AFRICOM's objectives is heavily dependent on successfully dividing the 'workspace' of the Area of Responsibility. Regions must be effectively aligned in order to accomplish preliminary goals, and consequently overall objectives. AFRICOM's decision on regions will have a great effect on how the command is viewed, particularly from the public and political perspectives of Africans.

If "the purpose of AFRICOM is to encourage and support...African leadership, not discourage and suppress it...it would be counter-productive for AFRICOM to take actions that undermine that goal. AFRICOM is intended to complement, not compete with the African Union" (Whelan 2007, 7). U.S. officials provide a lot of "talk" when it comes to AFRICOM and what it will do for Africans. The U.S. must support the talk with appropriate and respectful action to encourage Africans' perception of AFRICOM as a credible and trustworthy agent. AFRICOM should take a first step to demonstrate its support for Africans by aligning regions along already established African initiatives, such as the RECs.

The Department of Defense is considering many innovative approaches to the organizational construct of AFRICOMandits locations (Whelan 2007). Researching ways to divide and organizing the staff in an innovative manner is a good idea; but the most creative and new approach the U.S. could use to regionalize the continent now is to follow Africa's lead. Instead of developing a new structure and forcing western thoughts of proper boundaries on Africa, which would be unfortunately reminiscent of colonialism, AFRICOM should try to build upon the already established regions of the RECs.

Furthermore, AFRICOM should create regions that follow the AU's proposal for its regional brigades, as seen in Figure 5 (EUCOM Strategy 2004). The proposed North Region corresponds with the AMU, with the addition of Western Sahara (that did not belong to any regional alliance), and the subtraction of Egypt (which is not part of AFRICOM's AOR). The proposed West Region, Central Region, and South Region correspond with the ECOWAS, ECCAS, and SADC, respectively. Each of these regions are almost duplicates of the respective RECs. The East Region follows the makeup of the SADC, with the addition of Rwanda, Tanzania, Seychelles, and Comoros. In addition, the established Combined Joint Task Force – Horn of Africa (CJTF-HOA) AOR, a current subset of CENTCOM, will become part of the East Region of AFRICOM, providing detailed knowledge of the area from its past endeavors.

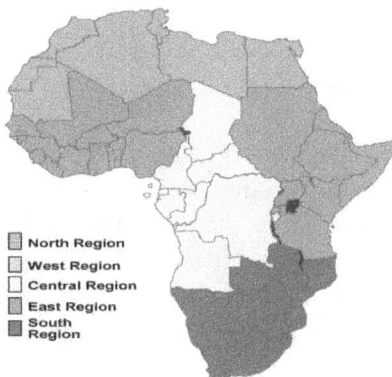

Figure 5. Proposed African Union Brigades & AFRICOM
Regions (EUCOM Strategy 2004)

While this may not seem like a new or an out-of-the-box idea, that is the point. The U.S. needs to demonstrate support for African initiatives and strengthen their existing alliances so Africans can solve problems on their own. Based on this and previous analyses, there is no concise way to divide the regions of Africa, and no clear boundaries that can separate complex issues which move freely across space. Therefore, rather than make new boundaries that do justice to the human landscape and instead just add another layer of bureaucracy, AFRICOM would be well advised to follow initiatives already in place. As a result, the Africans will justly receive the credit and the world will gain strategic benefit.

In addition, AFRICOM should base the Regional Integration Teams in an "anchor state" within each region. The RITs will have a different makeup than the current embassy and bilateral teams and will vary according to needs of a specific region. The RITs can leverage the credibility and strength of the anchor state within the region to pursue AFRICOM's objectives. And beyond a regional and multilateral approach, AFRICOM should continue to deal with individual states on a bilateral basis. The strategic regional work is important, but there are some issues better handled on a state-to-state basis. If developed properly, the individual agencies within the AFRICOM organization and RITs will be well suited to accomplish bilateral missions as well as the regional charges.

Major Megan B. Stallings is a personnel officer in the United States Army. Previously, she served as an Assistant Professor of Geography at the United States Military Academy where she taught and researched in the areas of physical geography and land use planning. She holds graduate degrees in Geography, National Security and Strategic Studies, and Human Resources Development.

References

African Union. 2007. Regional Economic Communities. http://www.africa-union.org (accessed September 24, 2007).

Carson, Johnnie. 2004. Shaping U.S. Policy on Africa: Pillars of a New Strategy. *Strategic Forum* 210:1-7.

Craddock, Bantz J. 2007. A Statement before the House Armed Services Committee. March 15.

Cobb, Charles E. 2005. Africa in Fact. *National Geographic Magazine*, September.

Defense Senior Leadership Council. 2007. USAFRICOM Discussion, October 1. Accessed through Naval War College class PowerPoint brief, pp. 5.

European Command. 2007. EUCOM Strategy. http://www.eucom.mil/english/index.asp (accessed September 23, 2007).

Frazer, Jendayi E. 2006. Current Themes in U.S. – Africa Policy. U.S. Department of State. Washington DC, May 16.

Fund for Peace. 2007. Failed States Graph. http://www.fundforpeace.org/programs/fsi/fsindex.php (accessed October 2, 2007).

Gration, Jonathan S. 2007. Testimony on Africa before the Senate Foreign Relations Committee, August 1.

Human Security Centre. 2005. The Human Security Report, 2005. http://www.humansecurityreport.info (accessed September 25, 2007).

Jones, James L. 2005. A Statement before the Senate Armed Services Committee. March 1.

Jones, James L. 2004. European Command Strategy. Germany.

Morrison, J. Stephen. 2007. Exploring the U.S. Africa Command and a New Strategic Relationship with Africa. Testimony before the Senate Foreign Relations Subcommittee on Africa, August 1.

Rumsfeld, Donald H. 2005. The National Defense Strategy of the United States of America. Washington, DC.

Smith, Steven D. 2007. Africa Command Poised to Help Continent's Security, Stability. American Forces Press Service. http://www.defenselink.mil/news/newsarticle.aspx?id=47529 (accessed September 23, 2007).

UNAIDS. 2006. 2006 Report on the Global Aids Epidemic. http://www.unaids.org/en/HIV_data2006GlobalReport/default.asp (accessed September 26, 2007).

United States Africa Command. 2007. AFRICOM 101 Briefing. http://www.cpms.osd.mil/africom/docs/AFRICOM101.pdf (accessed September 15, 2007).

Whelan, Theresa. 2008. Personal communication in classroom discussion, April 2.

Whelan, Theresa. 2007. Why AFRICOM? Statement to the Press, May.

World Health Organization. 2004. Malaria, 2004. http://www.who.int/topics/malaria/en (accessed September 28, 2007).

Addressing African Questions About the Legitimacy of the U.S. Africa Command (AFRICOM)

Diana B. Putman

Key Points

- The creation of AFRICOM symbolizes the strategic importance of Africa to the U.S.

- Initial response from African leaders, scholars, and media was negative because AFRICOM was not seen by them as legitimate.

- To gain buy-in from Africans, it is important for AFRICOM to demonstrate congruence between American and African strategic interests, and support African-led institutions.

- Understanding the complex nature of conflict on the continent is essential for AFRICOM to improve prevention and mitigation activities.

On February 6, 2007, the Bush Administration (Bush 2007) announced the creation of a new combatant command, U.S. African Command (AFRICOM), to focus on Africa. For over a decade Africans and others had proposed that the continent's strategic importance warranted greater attention and planning than was possible when U.S. responsibility for Africa was distributed among three separate commands (American Enterprise Institute 2007). Nonetheless, the African press, academics, and leaders expressed fears about AFRICOM (Reed 2007; Mills et al. 2007).[1] The United States

---

[1] In addition, using a daily Google search for AFRICOM, the author reviewed 368 media articles between August 3, 2007 and February 25, 2008. About three quarters came from African media; the rest came from all over the world.

needs to appreciate why Africans voice such concerns. The success of AFRICOM depends on its legitimacy in the eyes of Africans. This requires interacting differently with African leaders and institutions than has been customary.

This chapter is based on a snapshot in time from February 2007 through February 2008 to reflect the types of concerns raised by some African leaders, academics, and the media about the creation of AFRICOM. A review was conducted of information available in the public domain, contacts in Africa were interviewed. Because this methodology focused on perceptions and messages as opposed to determining "truth," there may be inaccuracies in the depiction of certain events and the opinions described here may differ from the facts.

AFRICOM has made a major effort to be responsive to the concerns expressed not only by Africans but also by other U.S. government (USG) agencies, and by American and international non-governmental organizations. That Brigadier General Jean de Martha Jaotody, Head of the Operations and Support Unit, Peace Support Operations Division of the African Union (AU) was designated to represent the AU at the October 17, 2008 Unified Command Status ceremony demonstrates that African leadership has determined that the Command can play a positive role on the continent. Similar positive sentiments toward the command were expressed by other African leaders around that time.

This was definitely not the case in late 2007, when prominent African journalist Abba Mahmoud expressed a common view, "For a majority of African patriots, the question being asked is: if America cannot protect itself from being attacked by terrorists on September 11, 2001, how can it protect us in Africa, thousands of kilometers away?" He continued with the motto of the Nigerian Army, "*Victory is from God alone...* For us in Africa, protection is from God alone and not any superpower" (Mahmood 2007). Therefore, how the AFRICOM issue was resolved, Mahmood asserted, would determine the continued sovereignty, territorial integrity, and dignity of Africa — or otherwise.

This view was not confined to journalists; an important American ally was equally dismissive. Nigeria's Foreign Minister, Chief Ojo Maduekwe, emphatically stated that foreign troops were unwelcome in Africa, and he demanded to be better informed and more closely consulted in the matter of AFRICOM's establishment (Maduekwe 2007). More troubling was the public statement of General Tsadkan Gebretensae of Ethiopia, former Chief of Staff of the Ethiopian Defense Forces, who served as an advisor on the transformation of liberation forces into legitimate armies. Gebretensae indicated "widespread skepticism even in countries where the security policy of those countries is very much in line with the security thinking in Washington" (AEI 2007).

To keep AFRICOM attuned to local issues, planners hoped to locate the headquarters (or several small offices) on the continent, which did not gladden Africans. Additionally, the South African and Southern African Development Community (SADC) rejected any idea of locating AFRICOM forces in the region (Webb 2007). This discord over AFRICOM's location further confirmed the need to understand African sensibilities.[2] Many states (e.g. Nigeria, Algeria, Zambia) and regional institutions (including SADC and the Arab Maghreb Union) opposed a physical AFRICOM presence. Only President Johnson-Sirleaf of Liberia invited AFRICOM to establish a headquarters and said the command was good for the continent (Butty 2007). However, other Economic Community of West African States (ECOWAS) leaders expressed reservations. Recognizing

---

[2] The vast majority of the articles reviewed raised questions or concerns about AFRICOM's intentions on the continent. Almost all of the positive articles involved interviews with American officials or scholars. In an email message to the author on March 7, 2008, Brian Chigawa, on staff at COMESA's Headquarters, noted "the location of AFRICOM on the continent needs legitimacy and that legitimacy can only come about through reaching 'common ground' by the US government through the African Union."

that the mission was more important than the location, in mid-February 2008 General William "Kip" Ward, AFRI-COM's Commander, stated that the headquarters would remain in Stuttgart, Germany for the foreseeable future (Ward 2008). While visiting Ghana, President Bush also confirmed that the U.S. had no intention of establishing bases in Africa (Accra Daily Mail 2008).

This chapter analyzes why legitimacy matters, and discusses how AFRICOM can attain legitimacy. Americans must understand the colonial and neocolonial legacy and current African sensitivities about outsiders or they will always be baffled by African interpretations of what Americans consider benign behaviors. The chapter will not dwell on cross-cultural understanding and linguistic skills needed for successful interactions overseas since these are already recognized by the USG, but rather articulate additional factors required for AFRICOM to find legitimacy and influence.

Based on over fifty years of program experience in Africa, legitimacy-enhancing principles adopted by the United States Agency for International Development (USAID) merit AFRICOM's careful consideration. AFRICOM needs to emphasize the commonality of U.S. and African strategic interests and demonstrate an appreciation of the complexity of conflict in Africa. Unless the multi-faceted nature of African conflict is recognized, there is a high risk that AFRICOM would design simplistic, inappropriate interventions. AFRICOM needs to clearly define how it will support the Department of State and USAID's diplomatic and development mandates. Finally, AFRICOM must utilize the new institutional arrangements that have evolved on the continent since the mid-1990s. Asserting leadership, Africans have defined agendas at the state, sub-regional and continental level. AFRICOM would gain partner trust and effectiveness by listening to these leaders and articulating the commonalities between African agendas and American security interests.

The Common Market for Eastern and Southern Africa's (COMESA's) strategic plan illustrated the necessity of implementing multilateral programs and operating at a pace consistent with African priorities and agendas (COMESA 2006). COMESA recommended that indirect assistance may be as important as direct training of African forces. In order to gain legitimacy, AFRICOM has to function in multiple arenas, each meaningful to Africans.

Africa's potential problems were significant enough to warrant specialized attention and engagement and justify the creation of a unified geographic command. Structured to support ongoing security, diplomatic, and development objectives on the continent, AFRICOM has learned in its early days from the experience of American military interventions after the Cold War. AFRICOM will have an expanded focus on conflict prevention and capacity building (AFRICOM 2007). Improved security in Africa is essential to reduce poverty, raise standards of living, stem environmental problems, enhance trade and investment and promote economic growth. These are all goals of common interest to Africans and Americans.

Why Legitimacy Matters

There is a lack of consensus in the political science literature on a definition of the concept of "legitimacy" although it is frequently invoked in international political disputes. Edward Luck (2002, 47) states that "in the disparate literature on the meaning and sources of legitimacy, two characteristics stand out: first, that legitimacy is a subjective condition, a product of one's perceptions; second, that legitimacy matters." The definition used in this chapter is that an action is perceived as legitimate internationally when it is in compliance with the law, is authentic or genuine, or is seen as reasonable.

When the United States decided to use its power to overthrow the Taliban in Afghanistan after the 9/11 attack on the United States, the action was fully endorsed and had legitimacy in the eyes of the global community. There appeared to be a direct connection between Taliban support of Al Qaeda and the terrorist attacks in the U.S. This contrasted with the views of much of the world over the U.S. decision to invade Iraq. The U.S. claimed that Iraq had weapons of mass destruction in defiance of United Nations (UN) sanctions and inspections, and asserted that Saddam Hussein supported international terrorism. Many states were concerned about the U.S.'s decision to invade in the absence of fuller endorsement from the UN, without which the U.S. action lacked legitimacy as being inconsistent with international law.

From a review of over 368 media articles and a paper from the Center for Defense Information (Reed 2007), it is evident that Africans expressed grave reservations about the purported mandate of AFRICOM and doubted its legitimacy. Sensing that the main purpose for AFRICOM was to increase control over — or even seize — critical resources, including oil and minerals, Africans also feared that more overt attention by American troops would bring more terrorist attacks to their states. They worried that the U.S. would intervene unilaterally, preventing African institutions from leading.[3] Some Africans expressed concern that the U.S. and China intended to battle out their rivalries on African soil. Finally, there was anxiety that the U.S. planned to establish sizeable bases and deploy large numbers of troops that would infringe on African sovereignty.

Writing in *Military Review*, Sean McFate succinctly summarized the many U.S. strategic interests in Africa. These included "the needs to counter terrorism, secure natural resources, contain armed conflict and humanitarian crisis, retard the spread of HIV/AIDS, reduce international crime, and respond to growing Chinese influence" (McFate

---

[3] In email communication with the author on March 7, 2008, Brian Chigawa of COMESA explained, "Given the recent experience of the world with regards to the actions of the US government in defying the United Nations Security Council to go to war in Iraq and experiences of their pre-emptive actions on the African continent like Sudan, Africa has genuine concerns for the location of AFRICOM on the continent."

2008, 12). Africans correctly identified these main U.S. strategic interests. Their overwhelmingly negative perceptions of American intent were rooted in the past and reinforced by current events. To build legitimacy for AFRICOM, the United States should have studied and addressed this history.

The first large AFRICOM activity, the Africa Partnership Station (APS), was based off-shore from the *USS Fort McHenry* on a seven-month training mission to West Africa. Media reports suggested its purpose was to suppress drug smuggling and maritime threats in the Gulf of Guinea, bordering the southern Nigerian oil fields (Flynn 2007), where impoverished residents have attacked Western oil interests as a symbol of exploitation and greed. The area of operation also included the Bakassi oil region, until recently under dispute by Nigeria and Cameroon. The objectives of APS were well intentioned, and supported by many West African states (Barnett 2007). Yet with increased U.S. dependence on African oil which is approaching 25 percent of U.S. imports, (DOS/USAID 2007), this first activity frightened many Africans who interpreted the creation of AFRICOM as driven more by securing U.S. access to natural resources than enhancing security in the region (Flynn 2007). Whatever the true motivations, in reality the improved security was a boon for Africans.

The Colonial Legacy of Extraction and Cold-War Engagement

Based on the legacy of colonial resource extraction and post-colonial superpower involvement in internal affairs, coupled with poor African leadership over the decades, Africans are deeply suspicious about U.S. intentions. AFRICOM needs to first absorb this history, and then demonstrate that while the U.S. wants to guarantee access to key resources, it must foremost not harm African stability and prosperity. Otherwise AFRICOM would not be viewed as a legitimate player on the continent.

From an African perspective, the continent was for centuries a place where outsiders stole valuable natural resources—humans as slaves, ivory, gold, timber, copper, tin, diamonds, rubber, cotton, and more recently oil, and coltan—a metallic ore used in making consumer electronic products. Outside powers brought new legal and political systems, imported new religions, established arbitrary boundaries, and governed either benevolently or tyrannically. Colonial rule supplanted traditional political systems without developing new effective institutions. Tribal belief systems were not necessarily abolished, but were displaced. Relationships and power balances between tribal groups were disrupted. New types of education and cultural systems were imposed over traditional values that were not eliminated, but were subjugated.

Following World War II, many colonies demanded their freedom. By the late 1950s, the "winds of change" had swept over Africa (Macmillan 1960). Most states had been granted independence by 1965, although white rule continued in parts of southern Africa. While many states remained peaceful, conflicts began almost immediately in others, including the former Belgian Congo (Klinger 2005). European colonists had done little to develop African governance and civil society. It was not uncommon for fewer than a dozen university-trained individuals to manage vast places. With scarcely any educated citizens, limited or no experience of democracy, poor manufacturing capacity, underdeveloped agriculture, and an absence of government services, newly-liberated states hobbled. Infrastructure was minimal and usually confined to regions near extractable resources, having been developed for exploitation during the colonial era.

As African states gained independence and experimented with socialist and capitalist models of development in the 1960s, a proxy Cold War started on African soil. Both the United States and the Union of Soviet Socialist Republics (USSR) exercised disproportionate influence over all African policies. Aptly described by Linda Thomas-Green-field (AEI 2007), "...there were no advantages to Africa in the Cold War; it was the blade of grass caught in the battle between the elephants." African leaders were in no position to resist. The creation of the Organization of African Unity (OAU) in 1963 was an early attempt by idealistic leaders to control their destiny, but the political immaturity of many heads of state bent on protecting state sovereignty made it impossible for unified actions. Even prior to the OAU, President Kwame Nkrumah of Ghana suggested the creation of an African High Command because of his concern over how the two rivals — the U.S. and the USSR — were manipulating United Nations peacekeepers in the Congo (Imobighe 2007).

Poor leadership, misguided development policies, and Cold War activities had negative and destabilizing consequences on Africa (USAID 1997). A notable trend of the Cold War was superpower support for highly militarized, centralized, and authoritarian regimes, which fueled the burgeoning arms trade. Military expenditures frequently outpaced social spending, and production sustained bloated government bureaucracies and defense capacities instead of basic needs. Fierce economic decline characterized this period of misplaced priorities. Donors experimented with development theories, but rarely stayed the course long enough to achieve success. Decades of aid to corrupt, purportedly anti-Communist dictatorial regimes, support for South Africa's racial segregationist policy known as apartheid, and inconsistent levels of foreign assistance undermined U.S. credibility, especially in southern Africa. Frustrated Africans determined to liberate southern African states from their difficulties themselves. Perhaps this dissatisfaction explains why SADC members expressed such hostility toward AFRICOM, and accounts partially for South Africa's desire to exert a regional leadership role today.

Post-Cold War Africa

The end of the Cold War coincided with important changes in Africa. Unchecked foreign involvement began encouraging African leaders to explore indigenous solutions to political and economic problems. Ineffective U.S. and UN interventions in Somalia and Rwanda, a peaceful transition to majority rule in South Africa, and the end of conflict in Mozambique acted as wake-up calls for African leaders.

African leaders have begun to recognize the need to take responsibility for the continent's future. To capitalize on their engagement, it is imperative that external actors play supporting roles and not impose solutions. In the governmental and non-governmental arenas, the rise of new African actors determined to solve their own problems is highly significant. They merit applause and require enthusiastic direct and indirect support.

The deepening political maturity of many leaders, coupled with a parallel desire to reduce the continent's dependence on foreign aid led to this change. Benefiting from a transition in many states to democratic or quasi-democratic systems, the markedly more open atmosphere encourages public debate about the continent's problems and possible solutions. While individual state sovereignty remains an obstacle to further integration, most leaders acknowledge multilateral institutional norms and oversight mechanisms. Long-standing traditional, local, and regional knowledge and perspectives are beginning to emerge.

African leaders called for new institutional frameworks and arrangements over a decade ago. Today these structures (some more advanced than others) form the core of a new "African renaissance" (COMESA 2006). Improvements in African multilateral institutions began in the early 1990s. A radical step was the 1993 creation of the OAU Conflict Resolution Mechanism. This marked the first time that conflict—previously of concern only to individual states—might be subjected to a regional or continental forum (Imbobighe 1980).[4] When African leaders grasped that the OAU

---

[4] According to Imobighe, the original attempt to create an Africa High Command had failed, and in its place a much weaker Defense Commission was created by the OAU. Over the years

was collapsing they created a new institution, the African Union (AU) in 1999. The African Union's charter promotes African solidarity, defends state sovereignty, protects people's rights, advances peace in the region, and furthers good governance and democracy. A number of AU institutions exist including a Peace and Security Council; a Pan African Parliament; an Economic, Social and Cultural Council; and a Court of Justice. The AU Commission is responsible for the day-to-day management of the AU.[5] An outside scholar, Mauro De Lorenzo, suggests "that the United States articulate AFRICOM's purpose in terms of African security priorities," including support for the AU's Zone Security and Defense Policy (AEI 2007).

Initiated and adopted by African leaders of the Organization of African Unity in 2001 and now promoted by the African Union, the New Partnership for Africa's Development (NEPAD) is a vision and strategic framework for Africa's renewal. Key principles include:

> good governance as a basic requirement for peace, security and sustainable political and socio-economic development; African ownership and leadership, acceleration of regional and continental integration; and forging a new international partnership that changes the unequal relationship between Africa and the developed world (NEPAD 2007).

---

various alternatives had been proposed, such as the African Taskforce and the Collective Intervention Force, but they were unable to gain much traction due to continuing disagreement over appropriate roles and logistics.

[5] The African Union Summit (in February 2008) selected a new chairman, President Jakaya Kikwete of Tanzania and a new chair, Jean Ping and Deputy Chair, Erastus Mwencha of the Commission. Mr. Ping is the ex-Foreign Minister of Gabon and Mr. Mwencha is the outgoing Secretary General of COMESA. http://www.africa-union.org/root/au/index/index.htm (accessed December 16, 2008).

In NEPAD, individual states assess their progress toward common objectives using an innovative peer review mechanism, and a "Panel of the Wise" allows highly respected Africans to advise heads of state in times of crisis.

While the AU operates across the continent, most daily implementation of decisions by the AU is decentralized to eight Regional Economic Communities (REC) of varying capacity, which also implement their own regional agendas (AU 2007).[6] Francis Crupi (2005-2006) persuasively argues that it is in the U.S. national interest to support sub-regional organizations because of their vested interest in establishing peace and security. Mansfield et al. (2000, 116) demonstrate empirically that participants in the same preferential trade agreement are less likely to become involved in military disputes. This chapter proposes that it is important to support all eight RECs' peace and security priorities and programs. For some RECs, AFRICOM could train the AU's new military stand-by brigades, a role endorsed by Nigeria's President Yar'Adua and other ECOWAS members (Eze 2007). The five multinational stand-by brigades will assume peace-keeping roles on the continent and relieve the burden on the United Nations and other external partners. Composed of inter-disciplinary units of civilians, police and military, the brigades remain in their home stations until called upon, but will enable faster response to crises than has been the case in the past.

---

[6] The eight Regional Economic Communities are: 1) Economic Community of West African States (ECOWAS), 2) Community of Sahel-Saharan States (CENSAD), 3) Southern African Development Community (SADC), 4) Common Market for Eastern and Southern Africa (COMESA), 5) East African Community (EAC), 6) Arab Maghreb Union (UMA), 7) Economic Community of Central African States (ECCAS), and 8)Inter-governmental Authority on Development (IGAD). See "Other Pages/RECS" on the African Union website. (http://www.africa-union.org/root/au/index/index.htm (accessed December 16, 2008).

Successful Principles of Engagement

Africans perceive Americans as unwilling to listen and learn. According to journalist Lindsay Barret, "the major stumbling block to such cooperation in the past has been the display of imperial arrogance and unilateral prejudice of the U.S. in its attempts to implement or execute military strategies on the ground in Africa" (Barret 2007). In the early 1990s, intensifying food insecurity and conflict in the Horn of Africa, joined with the failure of American interventions in Somalia, prompted President Clinton to request USAID (1997) to develop a new approach in consultation with Africans. In this endeavor, over one thousand African stakeholders identified strategic linkages between food security and conflict. They also proposed that development agencies learn to interact differently with the continent.

Pursuant to this input, USAID designed the Greater Horn of Africa Initiative (GHAI) around innovative solutions proposed by Africans. The GHAI implemented new business practices designed to break the cycle of poverty, conflict, and despair in the Horn of Africa. Five principles or rules of engagement were adopted by USAID in designing and implementing regional development programs. They are:

- African Ownership: seeks widespread consultation by building and responding to the growing evidence of African leadership with the added element of capacity strengthening

- Regional Perspective: involves analysis and response to events within the context of a regional perspective

- Promoting Stability: places a priority on preventive measures, flexibility,

and promoting positive change in the
midst of crisis

- Strategic Coordination: streamlines
  United States Government (USG),
  multilateral and regional coordination to decrease duplication of effort
  and contradictory action

- Linking Relief and Development:
  improves linkages between humanitarian and development assistance
  through deeper understanding of
  transitions out of crises and focusing
  on long-term impact from the beginning (USAID 1997, 13).

African leaders (Ketema 2005; Mwencha January 23,
2008) cite the use of these principles as the basis for greatly increasing the acceptance of USAID's programs. These
principles involve Africans in identifying challenges and
solutions. Placing Africans in a leadership role requires the
U.S. or other donors to support indigenous efforts to bring
about economic growth, peace, and stability. Recognizing
that change does not take place linearly requires patience.
A multidisciplinary approach includes diplomatic, development, and military assistance. These principles continue to
influence how USAID designs both its bilateral and regional
programs in Africa today (Anderson 2008). That AFRICOM
espouses the need to adopt similar principles should serve
to reassure Africans.

AFRICOM's Commander, General William "Kip"
Ward, has stated repeatedly he intends to listen. In December 2007, he established a Dialogue Forum on AFRICOM's
website. His welcome stated:

As we build U.S. Africa Command, we want
to talk to people about what the U.S. mili-

tary is doing in Africa. Just as importantly, I want everyone on the staff to also listen and learn. AFRICOM will add value and do no harm to the collective and substantial on-going efforts on the Continent. AFRICOM seeks to build partnerships to enable the work of Africans in providing for their own security. Our intent is to build mutual trust, respect, and confidence with our partners on the Continent and our international friends (Ward 2007).

General Ward is correct to emphasize partnerships, on doing no harm and on listening to African voices. If AF-RICOM leadership and staff respect these principles, they will reduce negative perceptions and temper African skepticism.

Common U.S. and African Interests

The U.S. National Security Strategy (NSS) states: "Our goal is an African continent that knows liberty, peace, stability, and increasing prosperity" (2006, 37).[7] The African Union (AU) voices similar objectives: "To promote peace, security and stability on the continent...to promote demo-

---

[7] According to the *National Security Strategy of the United States of America* (2006, 37), "Africa holds growing geo-strategic importance and is a high priority for this Administration. It is a place of promise and opportunity, linked to the United States by history, culture, commerce, and strategic significance. Our goal is an African continent that knows liberty, peace, stability, and increasing prosperity...The United States recognizes that our security depends upon partnering with Africans to strengthen fragile and failing states and bring ungoverned areas under the control of effective democracies. We are committed to working with African nations to strengthen their domestic capabilities and the regional capacity of the African Union to support post-conflict transformations, consolidate democratic transitions, and improve peacekeeping and disaster response."

cratic principles and institutions, popular participation and good governance…and to promote sustainable development" (AU 2007).[8] Thus, at the most fundamental level, the U.S. and the community of African states are aligned, yet they harbor different ideas on how to achieve their goals.

At a conference in South Africa at the Brenthurst Institute in April 2007, Mills et al. (2007) noted two key points about AFRICOM:

> The first is that AFRICOM is still an enigma. No one is sure what it will do or how, and

---

[8] The African Union home page states that the objectives of the African Union are: "To achieve greater unity and solidarity between the African countries and the peoples of Africa; To defend the sovereignty, territorial integrity and independence of its Member States; To accelerate the political and socio-economic integration of the continent; To promote and defend African common positions on issues of interest to the continent and its peoples; To encourage international cooperation, taking due account of the Charter of the United Nations and the Universal Declaration of Human Rights; To promote peace, security, and stability on the continent; To promote democratic principles and institutions, popular participation and good governance; To promote and protect human and peoples' rights in accordance with the African Charter on Human and Peoples' Rights and other relevant human rights instruments; To establish the necessary conditions which enable the continent to play its rightful role in the global economy and in international negotiations; To promote sustainable development at the economic, social and cultural levels as well as the integration of African economies; To promote co-operation in all fields of human activity to raise the living standards of African peoples; To coordinate and harmonize the policies between the existing and future Regional Economic Communities for the gradual attainment of the objectives of the Union; To advance the development of the continent by promoting research in all fields, in particular in science and technology; and, To work with relevant international partners in the eradication of preventable diseases and the promotion of good health on the continent." (http://www.africa-union.org/root/au/index/index.htm (accessed December 16, 2008).

what it means for Africa. The second is that AFRICOM's success will ultimately depend on how well the U.S. understands and responds to the security priorities of Africans (2007).

Five months later, African military leaders confirmed that the command's intentions were still not clear. The Defense Minister of Liberia, Brownie Samukai, suggested the need for a better communications strategy with Africans to reassure skeptics and to explain AFRICOM. According to Sumukai, success in this will involve travel and engaging with various stakeholders:

> Policy makers who are helping to bring this concept together will need to get out of Washington and go maybe to Ethiopia and the like...it has to go to Africa to be sold at a continental level; that is, with the AU...and you will need to make sure that those sub-regional bodies are themselves well-informed (AEI 2007).

Greater effort at a working level is also required to convince stakeholders that AFRICOM will adopt solutions proposed by the Africans. In January 2008, the Secretary General of COMESA reiterated a theme when stated that he was not sure what AFRICOM would do and how it would interact with prominent African organizations (Mwencha 2008). African leaders have repeatedly said that improved communication is an imperative for future success.

General Ward has already stated that AFRICOM intends to listen and respond to African needs (Ward 2007). This is an important first step. Starting now, AFRICOM needs to put major effort into understanding how Africans define Africa's security concerns, and then as Mills et al. (2007) suggest, they must "align AFRICOM's rhetoric, focus, and resources robustly and publicly to African concerns."

Minister Samukai identified several possible areas for such cooperation including disaster prevention and response, technical support in areas such as mapping and satellite imagery, capacity building for crisis prevention, and assistance in addressing transborder issues such as terrorism, maritime security and the like. Said Samukai:

> You have to provide the kind of confidence that this is not a wishy-washy kind of relationship and partnership you are trying to establish, but a partnership that has mutuality of interest, as well as continental-wide interest, so that it reduces the apprehension and it improves the environment for cooperation (AEI 2007).

In September 2007, former Assistant Secretary of Defense Paul Wolfowitz stated that the Department of Defense (DoD) is not eager to send troops into Africa—in fact there is an expressed preference on DoD's part to support other nations' peacekeeping roles (AEI 2007). This is consistent with the conflict prevention role that AFRICOM has described. AFRICOM should work closely with the African Union and African states with strong security forces willing to shoulder the burden, and with states aspiring to play leading roles on the continent such as Nigeria, South Africa and Ethiopia. By focusing on common interests, AFRICOM is more likely to overcome negative perceptions and achieve legitimacy. AFRICOM must highlight that U.S. security interests can benefit both Americans and Africans and must not undermine legitimate African interests. AFRICOM must work hard to allay African suspicions.

Military and civilian leaders addressing the US Army War College Class of 2008 reiterated that the nature of warfare has changed. While conventional war is not obsolete, the U.S. can expect to engage extensively in conflicts that involve irregular, asymmetric and terrorist tactics (U.S. Army/U.S. Marine Corps 2006). African history is replete with unconventional conflicts. Close study of successful and unsuccessful efforts to impose order on the continent can inform US doctrine. Being open to learning from African experiences of conflict will also improve AFRICOM's legitimacy.

Conflict in Africa

A key objective of AFRICOM is to enhance security and prevent conflict. Lacking a deep understanding of the multi-faceted nature of conflict in Africa, outsiders continue to espouse simplistic, one-dimensional causes of conflict. African leaders now appreciate that the multi-dimensional nature of conflict has the capacity to destabilize entire regions. Without a sophisticated comprehension of the nature of African conflict, AFRICOM risks failing to "do no harm," a key principle espoused by General Ward (2007).

Traditional analyses of conflict frequently focus on class, race, ethnicity, religion, poor governance and other variables. However, based on case studies in Rwanda (land), Burundi (coffee), the Democratic Republic of the Congo (minerals), Sudan (oil), Ethiopia (Nile waters) and Somalia (pastures), the environmental basis of conflict in Africa is evident (Lind and Sturman 2002). Joao Porto's overview of contemporary conflict analysis emphasizes that there is no single cause of a conflict. Once begun, conflict evolves over time based on internal and external variables that come into play (2002). He stresses that sophisticated analysis is needed to understand the complex relationship between ecological factors and conflict in Sub-Saharan Africa, which involves multiple internal and external actors and diverging and conflicting interests. Both grievance and greed are usually motivators, although the latter is often masked by other rationales that play better to international audiences. Porto asserts "access to and control of valuable natural resources including minerals, oil, timber, productive pastures and farming land, have been crucial factors in the occurrence of violent conflicts across the continent"(2002, 2).

141

This sentiment is also recognized by USAID:

> Competition is an inevitable part of life for virtually every citizen, whether it is competition over natural resources — a plot of land, a scrap of pasture, or access to a watering hole — economic position and access, or political power... combined with a proliferation of small arms, despots who refuse to relinquish power and entrenched corrupt elites, creates a high level of volatility in the region...The costs of these conflicts, ranging from ethnic cleansing to intergroup cattle rustling to genocide and war, can retard or reverse a state's development efforts by years (1999, 9).

Porto concludes that conflict prevention and management practitioners must learn three important lessons:

> One, conflict in sub-Saharan Africa is structurally and functionally open. Conflicts in sub-Saharan Africa operate within broader regional and international systems. Apparently isolated conflicts are in reality intimately linked to broader political and economic contexts involving multiple, and often times, competing individuals and group actors, and interests. The institutions, policies and legal regimes governing these, moreover, are overlapping and mixed. Policy makers, therefore, must explicitly recognize the role of external engagers, and incorporate their involvement in policy formulation and interventions. Two, conflict systems in sub-Saharan Africa are operationally complex. The levels of engagement and the number of variables underlying conflict are many; and

more often than not the operation of conflict is uncertain. Tracing the role of different conflict variables, including ecological, demands scrupulous policy attention to such operational vagaries. Three, the ecological variable is clearly an important factor in conflict. Moreover, it is also important that policy research and analysis trace the relationship of ecology to conflict through different pathways. Policies will vary depending on how the ecological variable is linked to conflict. Identifying and assessing linkages is critical to targeting effective policy interventions that have lasting impact (2002, 32).

To sum, conflict in Africa is always geographically and functionally complex, and often tied to or an agent of environmental issues. Understanding conflict's root causes is critical to any eventual attempts to prevent or solve it. By the early 1990s, African leaders appreciated the complexity of conflict and created new multilateral institutions and approaches to thwart it. Acknowledging that multiple state and non-state actors contribute to solutions for poverty, food insecurity and conflicts led to the decision to expand, strengthen, and revitalize sub-regional African organizations.

Outsiders, including AFRICOM, need to perform detailed analyses before conflict prevention or mitigation campaigns are begun. Joint doctrine's standard political, military, economic, social, institutional, and infrastructure (PMESII) analytical construct during theater campaign planning has merit for this (Standing Joint Forces Headquarters 2006). However, it is unlikely to identify the complexity of any particular conflict without an in-depth and sophisticated sense of history, geography, and modern geopolitical dynamics.

The Common Market for Eastern and Central Africa (COMESA)

To achieve legitimacy, AFRICOM must learn the agendas, strengths and weaknesses of the new African institutions, and engage them appropriately. Never in the post-colonial era has there been a stronger effort on the part of African leaders to address their fundamental challenges. If AFRICOM chooses to ignore or bypass these new institutional arrangements, Africans will interpret this policy as a lack of genuine interest in promoting a mutual U.S.-African security agenda.

Uniquely, COMESA has successfully promoted regional economic integration and an indirect approach to security. Americans tend to favor direct action to solve problems, but, according to a famous Maasai proverb: "Progress never follows a straight line. It occurs through zigzags" (Strauss 1995). AFRICOM support for COMESA's indirect efforts will enhance conflict prevention and mitigation, achieving greater legitimacy than engaging only with RECs possessing stand-by brigades.

Created in 1994, the establishment of COMESA replaced a Preferential Trade Area established in 1981. With nineteen member states (COMESA 2006) and a population of 389 million, COMESA covers a land area of 19.2 million square kilometers (7.4 million square miles), larger than the United States. The total GDP is $275 billion (less than Belgium's), with some of the world's most resource rich states and some of the poorest, where millions live on less than $2 per day. Total trade is at $159 billion with $82 billion of exports (mainly oil and minerals), demonstrating the region's tremendous economic potential. The COMESA region also contains some of the most volatile conflict zones in Africa.

COMESA envisions achieving economic integration in eastern and southern Africa through regional cooperation in core areas of trade, investment, infrastructure, and science and technology development. The Free Trade Area

(FTA), established by COMESA in 1999, has thirteen members. COMESA's goal is to establish a fully operational customs union by December 2008, and a common market by 2014. According to COMESA's *Strategic Plan 2007-2010* (2006):

> Poverty eradication and development are the ultimate goals of our organization. It is therefore crucial to promote the adoption of the appropriate mix of economic and social policies, a process for which we cannot wait for the world. It is our responsibility, in the context of the 'African Renaissance.'

The COMESA heads of state recognized that that their ad hoc approaches to peace and security neither reduced conflict nor promoted economic growth. To focus on preventive diplomacy they created the Peace and Security Programme in 1999. Within the framework of the African Union's Mechanism for Conflict Prevention, Management and Resolution, COMESA's Ministers of Foreign Affairs meet at least annually to consider modalities for promoting peace, security and stability.

Within the COMESA structure, ministers and the Secretary General engage in quiet diplomacy. Meeting regularly with heads of state, the Secretary General can encourage peacemaking prior to or during an outbreak of conflict. For example, when violence erupted after the Kenyan elections in December 2007, the Secretary General invited several current and former heads of state to mediate between President Kibaki and opposition leader Raila Odinga before the United Nations and the AU became involved (Mwencha 2008).

The evolution of COMESA's Peace and Security Programme shows the growing African awareness of the complexity of internal and regional conflict and recognition of the intersection of conflict prevention, peace building, and economic activities. If AFRICOM bolsters these efforts,

Africans will recognize that Americans are willing to play a supporting role, and AFRICOM's reputation will be enhanced.

COMESA acknowledges the importance of training and equipping the AU's regional stand-by brigades, a key area where AFRICOM can assist. However, it has chosen a more indirect approach to its involvement in peace and security matters (Mwencha 2007). For instance, in 2001, the ministers recommended involving private sector and civil society organizations in discussions on peace, security and economic integration because of the important role of non-state actors. In 2002, they noted the need for leadership by elected government officials. COMESA has now trained over seventy parliamentarians on conflict prevention and management. Another way to ensure peace is through COMESA's Court of Justice, established in 1994 to adjudicate trade disputes that could turn into larger, violent conflicts.

In September 2004, COMESA sponsored the workshop entitled "Linking Peace, Security and Regional Integration in Africa" in order to "present current research, identify gaps, and propose additional studies to help design prevention and mitigation steps and capacity building measures for stakeholders" (McDermott 2007). With much conflict in Africa commencing internally and later migrating to neighbors, a central question was how regional integration can nurture peace and security.

In 2005, the Ministers of Foreign Affairs requested detailed research on the Democratic Republic of Congo (DRC) as a guide to devise practical mitigation strategies. Neighboring states interested in profiting from natural resources had abetted internal conflict, and with Congolese instability punishing the entire region, COMESA wanted to learn whether changes in economic institutions, infrastructure, and behavior could offer relief. Supported by the United Kingdom's Department for International Development (DFID) and USAID, the research investigated trade flows from the DRC through the Great Lakes region and into East Africa in a project called Trading for Peace (DFID/ USAID/COMESA 2007). COMESA wanted to improve the governance and functioning of local and regional markets through understanding the regional dimension of natural resource exploitation in the DRC. The study described systemic institutional problems that have inhibited trade and allowed it to be dominated by political elites in a 'militarized' economy. The project concluded, "presently in the DRC it is actually easier to do business illegally than legally" (DFID/USAID/COMESA 2007, 8). A critical finding was that governments and donors risk inflaming conflict if they rush in without comprehending the nature of the socio-political and economic dynamics involved.

The data from this project were presented to government and civil society representatives in late 2007 and early 2008. Subsequently, COMESA was asked to design economic, trade and governance activities to diminish variables that exacerbate conflict and promote legal exploitation of resources. Many of the activities proposed can be added to ongoing economic development and good governance projects, thus reinforcing the link between regional integration and conflict mitigation. COMESA is also investigating the cost and effects of conflict on regional integration through a "War Economies" program (Karangizi 2007) and it participates in the AU's Conflict Early Warning system (CEWS).

AFRICOM will naturally concentrate on the RECs which host the AU's stand-by brigades, and strengthen the peacekeeping capacity of these forces. But this emphasis will detract from the additional preventive role AFRICOM has assumed. AFRICOM must also engage with COMESA and other RECs that are actively trying to understand the nexus between economic activity and conflict, and design innovative interventions.[9]

---

[9] Reacting to a draft of this chapter, Chigawa reinforced the importance of political as well as military action: "Most conflict situations cannot be addressed by military solutions only as we have

Concluding Thoughts

Many reasons have contributed to AFRICOM's perceived lack of legitimacy in the eyes of Africans. New principles for interacting with Africans were proposed in this chapter, assigning Africans the leadership role in defining problems and solutions. A summary of colonial and neo-colonial legacies demystified some of the sensitivities surrounding the role of outsiders in Africa. The complex and dynamic nature of conflict and its links to natural resource exploitation and economic variables have been elaborated. Preventive activities need to encompass broader variables than those usually assumed as the root causes of conflict. This chapter argued that AFRICOM needed to engage with many different African institutions to surmount the challenges facing the continent. The example of COMESA suggested that detailed consultations with RECs will provide AFRICOM with useful activities to support beyond training of defense forces.[10]

Strategic coordination with other USG agencies is critical. By far, the largest and most constant USG engagement in Africa includes development assistance administered by USAID, the Millennium Challenge Account, the President's Plan for Emergency AIDS Relief (PEPFAR) and other similar mechanisms. Although the continent has the lowest lev-

---

seen with the case of Iraq and Somalia. All the eight RECs have specific roles for addressing issues of peace and security within the continental architecture for peace and security, whose main component is political aid, and not the military." E-mail message to author. March 7, 2008.

[10] Brian Chigawa: "The role of the African stand-by brigades should have synergies with all political initiatives of their member states which are handled by RECS such as COMESA, EAC and IGAD which are not hosting any brigade but can provide the much needed political oversight." E-mail message to author. March 7, 2008.

els of foreign direct investment abroad, American commercial interests are on the increase. Joint doctrine discusses the importance of "supported" and "supporting" roles in any campaign (Joint Publication 2006). To win, AFRICOM must cooperate closely with other agencies in the USG, especially the Department of State and USAID, and it must articulate clearly when and where it will support their efforts, and when and where it will need support by other "softer" elements of national power. AFRICOM needs to explain now how it intends to support and enhance, not supplant, other USG efforts. Explicit definition of its role will also enhance AFRICOM's legitimacy with African leaders and the public.

USAID experience over the last several decades shows that insufficient attention to the continuum between humanitarian relief, post-conflict reconstruction, and development assistance leads to failure. Recent experience in Afghanistan and Iraq confirms this. Working with stakeholders, AFRICOM must confirm what direct humanitarian activities it will undertake, how it will support the lead USG agency (USAID) for humanitarian interventions, and how it intends to play only a supporting role in the development arena.

Lieutenant General Daniel Opande, ex-Vice Chief of the Kenyan Army and an experienced peacekeeping commander, confirmed the consonance of African and U.S. security interests: "international terrorism; cross-border trafficking of arms, persons, and drugs; environmental degradation; natural and man-made disasters; and conflicts" (AEI 2007). But, he also noted that to effectively address these interests, "there is a need for in-depth discussions...to develop trust and closer cooperation" (AEI 2007). The current Chief of Staff of the Ghana Armed Forces, Brigadier General Robert Winful's measured conclusions about AFRICOM best summarize the situation:

> The establishment of AFRICOM presents both opportunities and pitfalls. However,

we can overcome these by crafting policies
that will lead to a form of cooperation between Africa and the U.S. that is mutual and
cordial. Only through such forms of cooperation will AFRICOM become a useful tool
in achieving its objectives (AEI 2007).

In his speeches, General Ward has repeatedly asserted that AFRICOM intends to be a learning organization. Changes haves already been made to the mission, to
forms of engagement with African organizations and leaders, and in strategic communications since establishment of
the Command was first announced. The next few years will
provide an opportunity for AFRICOM and its staff to prove
its ability to assist the continent to meet its security challenges.

*Dr. Diana B. Putman is a career Foreign Service Office with the
United States Agency for International Development, currently
on detail to the United States Africa Command. She has served in
Asia and the Middle East, and has spent over twenty years doing
research and development work in Africa. Dr. Putman holds
graduate degrees in Anthropology and Strategic Studies.*

References

African Union. http://www.africa-union.org/root/au/index/
index.htm (accessed December 16, 2008).

African Union. The African Union in a Nutshell. http://www.
africa-union.org/r6/au/AboutAu/au_in_a_nutshell_en.htm
(accessed December 27, 2007).

American Enterprise Institute for Public Policy Research. 2007.
Transcript of Event: AFRICOM: Implications for African Security and U.S.-African Relations. Washington, DC: American Enterprise Institute. (http://www.aei.org/events/filter.
all,eventID.1571/transcript.asp).

Anderson, Cheryl. 2008. Mission Director, USAID East Africa Mission. E-mail message to author. February 26.

Barnett, Thomas. Continental Ambitions. http://commentisfree. guardian.co.uk/thomas_barnett/2007/12/continental_ ambitions.html (accessed December 20, 2007).

Barret, Lindsay. Nigeria and AFRICOM: No Time for Knee Jerk Diplomacy. http://www.sunnewsonline.com/webpages/ opinion/2007/dec/27/opinion-27-12-2007-001.htm (accessed December 20, 2007).

Bush, George W. 2006. *The National Security Strategy of the United States of America.* Washington, DC: The White House.

Bush, George W. 2007. *President Bush Creates a Department of Defense Unified Combatant Command for Africa.* Washington, DC: The White House. http://www.whitehouse.gov/news/ releases/2007/02/ 20070206-3.html (accessed February 26, 2008).

Bush, George W. 2008. On AFRICOM and U.S. military base in Ghana: Baloney! Accra Daily Mail. http://www.accra-mail. com/mailnews.asp?id= 3949 (accessed February 26, 2008).

Butty, James. Liberia Assured of Help with Debt Relief during U.S. Visit. http://128.11.143.121/english/archive/2007-10/2007-10-25-voa4.cfm?CFID=213011222&CFTOKEN=6865 8320 (accessed October 25, 2007).

Chigawa, Brian. 2008. E-mail message to author. March 7.

Common Market for Eastern and Southern Africa. COMESA Strategic Plan. http://www.comesa.int/copy_of_about/ (accessed March 14, 2008).

Congressional Research Service. 2007. *CRS Report for Congress, Africa Command: U.S. Strategic Interests and the Role of the U.S. Military in Africa.* Washington, DC: CRS.

Crupi, Francis. 2005-2006. Why the United States Should Robustly Support Pan-African Organizations. *Parameters* 35, no. 4: 106-123.

Eze, Ikechukwu. 2007. AFRICOM: Furor over America's African Trail. http://www.businessdayonline.com/analysis/features/1718.html (accessed December 24, 2007).

Flynn, Daniel. 2007. U.S. Seeks to Woo Africans with Naval Diplomacy. http://in.reuters.com/articlePrint?articleid=INIndia-30459020071112 (accessed November 12, 2007).

Imobighe, T.A. 1980. An African High Command: The Search for a Feasible Strategy of Continental Defense. *African Affairs* 79, no. 315: 241-254.

Joint Publication 5-0. 2006. *Joint Operation Planning.* Washington, DC.

Karangizi, Stephen. 2007. Director Peace and Security Programme, COMESA. E-mail message to author. October 26.

Ketema, Seyfu. 2005. Personal communication with the author. May 25.

Klinger, Janeen. 2005. Stabilization Operations and Nation-Building: Lessons from United Nations Peacekeeping in the Congo, 1960-1964. *The Fletcher Forum of World Affairs* 29, no. 2.

Lind, Jeremy, and Kathryn Sturman, eds. 2002. *Scarcity and Surfeit: The Ecology of Africa's Conflicts.* Pretoria: The Institute for Security Studies.

Luck, Edward. 2002. The United States, International Organizations, and the Quest for Legitimacy. In *Multilateralism and US Foreign Policy*, ed. Steward Patrick and Shepard Forman. Boulder, CO: Lynne Rienner Publishers, Inc.

Macmillan, Harold. 1960. *Winds of Change* Speech by Harold Macmillan, Accra, Gold Coast (now Ghana). http://en.wikipedia.org/wiki/Wind_of_Change_percent28speechpercent29 (accessed March 14, 2008).

Maduekwe, Chief Ojo. 2007. U.S. AFRICOM and African Development. http://allAfrica.com/stories/printable/200710110233.html (accessed February 26, 2008).

Mahmood, Abba. 2007. Nigeria: Looking into the Year 2008. http://allafrica.com/stories/200712280417.html (accessed December 28, 2007).

Mansfield, Edward D. et al. 2000. Preferential Trading Arrangements and Military Disputes. In *Power and the Purse: Economic Statecraft, Interdependence and National Security*, ed. Jean-Marc F. Blanchard, Edward D. Mansfield and Norrin M. Ripsman. London: Frank Cass.

McDermott, Paul. 2007. USAID East Africa Director, Regional Conflict Management and Governance Team Leader. E-mail message to the author. October 23.

McFate, Sean. 2008. U.S. Africa Command: A New Strategic Paradigm? *Military Review* 88, no.1 (January-February): 10-21.

Mills, Greg et al. 2007. AFRICOM and African Security, The Globalization of Security or the Militarization of Globalization? http://www.thebrenthurstfoundation.org/Files/Brenthurst_Commisioned_ Reports/BD0704_What_Africom_means_for_Africa.pdf (accessed February 27, 2008).

Mwencha, Erastus. 2008. Secretary General of COMESA. Telephone interview by author. January 26.

Mwencha, Erastus. 2008. Secretary General of COMESA. Personal communication with author. January 23.

Mwencha, Erastus. 2007. Secretary General of COMESA. Telephone interview by author. October 24.

New Partnership for Africa's Development. http://www.nepad.org/2005/files/home.php (accessed December 29, 2007).

PACT. 2007. Researching Natural Resources and Trade Flows in the Great Lakes Region. Washington, DC: DFID/USAID/COMESA Study.

Porto, Joao. 2002. Contemporary Conflict Analysis in Perspective. In *Scarcity and Surfeit: The Ecology of Africa's Conflicts,* ed. Jeremy Lind and Kathryn Sturman. Pretoria, South Africa: The Institute for Security Studies.

Reed, Valerie. 2007. Straus Military Reform Project: Prospects for an African Headquarters for AFRICOM. Washington, D.C.: Center for Defense Information. http://www.cdi.org/friendlyversion/printversion.cfm?documentID=4160&from_page=../program/document.cfm (accessed December 18, 2007).

Regional Economic Development Services Office for Eastern and Southern Africa. 1999. *Strategic Plan 2001-2005: Strengthening Partnerships and Capacity.* Nairobi: U.S. Agency for International Development.

Standing Joint Force Headquarters. 2006. *Commander's Handbook for an Effects-Based Approach to Joint Operations.* Washington, DC: Standing Joint Force Headquarters.

United States Africa Command (AFRICOM) official website. 2007. About AFRICOM from the U.S. Africa Command. http://www.africom.mil/AboutAFRICOM.asp (accessed August 5, 2007).

United States Agency for International Development. 1997. *Greater Horn of Africa Initiative (GHAI) Strategic Plan FY 1998-2002.* Washington, DC: USAID.

United States Army/United States Marine Corps. 2006. *FM 3-24, Counterinsurgency.* Washington, DC: U.S. Government Printing Office.

United States Department of State/United States Agency for International Development. 2007. *Strategic Plan, Fiscal Years 2007-2012.* Washington, DC: DOS/USAID.

Ward, William. 2007. General Ward Discusses Goal for AFRICOM. http://www.africom.mil/ getArticle.asp?art=1539 (accessed December 24, 2007).

Ward, William. 2007. AFRICOM Dialogue. http://www.africom.
mil/getArticle.asp?art=1539 (accessed December 21, 2007).

Ward, William. 2008. US shifts on AFRICOM base plans. http://
newsvote.bbc.co.uk/mpapps/pagetools/print/news.bbc.
co.uk/1/hi/world/africa/7251648.stm (accessed February
26, 2008).

Webb, Boyd. 2007. SADC snubs US force on African Soil.
http://www.iol.co.za/index.php?from=rss_Africa&set_
id=1&click_id=68&art_id=vn20070830041224745C804400
(accessed September 2, 2007).

Measuring Africa's Economic and Human Development

Clarence J. Bouchat

Key Points

- Africa is the world's poorest region in economic, demographic, and social development.

- No single measure can fully explain the poverty and challenges faced by African states, but analyzing several factors shows that African people and economies lag behind the rest of the world.

Introduction

In 1957, after 136 years under colonial occupation, Ghana's independence was the beginning of the shift from colonial to majority rule in Africa. Ghana was chosen as one of the first states because it was best prepared for sovereignty with a relatively efficient civil service and education structure, abundant natural resources, and a viable economy. That same year, by contrast, the Republic of Korea was rebuilding a state devastated by 45 years of brutal Japanese imperialism and the opening bloody conflict of a long cold war. South Korea then labored under a dictatorial regime, was bereft of natural resources, and entirely dependent upon international aid (Gyekum 2005). In 1957 Malaysia also gained its independence after 446 years under Portuguese, Dutch, and British colonialism, as well as Japanese occupation. Independence was given while the then Malayan Federation was still in the midst of an ethnic and ideological insurgency, although, like Ghana, Malaysia also inherited a stable British civil structure and a larder of natural resources (Saraswathi 2007). The per capita income of these new states was about the same that eventful year (Gyekum 2005; Saraswathi 2007; Mbaku 2004), but Ghana with an economic growth rate of five percent seemed to promise the brightest prospects of the three (Clawson et al. 2008). Yet fifty years later Ghana's gross national income (GNI) stood at just $520 per person and is ranked 177th globally by the World Bank. Malaysia's GNI was 10 times greater at $5490 and 80th in the world, and South Korea's GNI 34 times larger at $17,690 and 49th (World Bank GNI 2006). Why has one of the better regarded states of Africa with such early promise fared so poorly economically compared to less favorably positioned states? The explanation for these differences in economic standing between the states of Africa and the rest of the world helps to explain some of the causes for the problems endured by Africans today.

Economic activities are the most central of all human endeavors. They are what satisfy the basic human physical needs of food, shelter, protection, and health. Economic activities also enable other higher order human endeavors including cultural and political activities. Although rich in human and geographic diversity, Africa has lagged behind the rest of the world in its economic development, adversely impacting its human development. To better understand economic problems in Africa and offer potential solutions, this chapter explains African development by comparing the few more-developed and many lesser-developed states and areas of this continent in terms of economic, demographic, and social measurements. This complements the next chapter which explores, on a macro scale, some of Africa's primary economic activities (subsistence and commercial agriculture, and mineral and energy resource extraction), manufacturing, and service activities to describe the nature of local African economies and their impact on development. Throughout these discussions the causes and potential obstacles that slow Africa's economic development are then evaluated in order to recommend ways in which the United States and other interested parties can better support and develop states and regions. Economic development is the foundation upon which future African security, stability, population growth, environmental protection, and improvement in standards of living depend. Africa's natural and human resources are among the last great underused assets left on earth, and their proper development should be of concern to all.

Measuring Africa's Economic Development

To understand the economic development of Africa, it is necessary to resort to statistics describing economic, demographic, and social conditions. Such statistics are often used (and misused) freely in the media and academia to prove points and explain enigmas, but too often the numbers themselves are a mystery. How useful is such data and what underlying conditions does it relate? The opening example of this chapter, comparing the economic standing of Ghana, Malaysia, and South Korea is a case in point. Is GNI a fair way to make such economic comparisons across continents and half a century? If so, what does it mean and can it explain the causes of poverty and underdevelopment?

Economic size and growth is not the same as economic development, although each suffers in Africa. Development in this chapter is used in a broad sense as the "progressive improvement of the human condition in both material and nonmaterial ways" (Clawson et al. 2008). As this chapter will show, economic growth may occur without improving human or physical well-being. Economic development is closely associated with human development and together they lay a foundation for an economy to sustainably boost itself through more sophisticated value-added activities by building social capital in education, equality, freedoms, culture, stability, and good governance; demographic well-being through improved health and population distribution; and economic capital in terms of better infrastructure, investment, diversification, and management. Economic development seeks to lessen environmental degradation, social and political inequality, and other distresses that sometimes accompany unregulated economic growth. These concepts put Africa's regional and representative states' economic, demographic, and social development into

159

perspective. The measures examined here will include GNI, gross domestic product (GDP), purchasing power parity (PPP) adjustments, the human development index (HDI) and its health and education components, social measures such as freedom and equality, and other material economic and demographic indicators that may prove useful to planners and implementers of policy to better understand the conditions encountered on the African continent, and help improve those conditions.

By any measure of national income, the economies of Africa fare poorly when compared to the rest of the world. An economy is defined as "production, development, and management of [the] material wealth...system of a state or region" (Morris 1976, 413). Based upon this definition it is easy to conclude that the best way to measure an economy is to aggregate its production, development, and management of wealth over a specific time period and for a defined area. If such a summation is done for the total value of goods and services produced over the period of a year for a designated state or region, that measure is known as the gross national product (GNP) or GNI (there is a slight difference between GNP and GNI, but for the purposes of this chapter that difference is insignificant) (Getis et al. 2006). This measure attempts to quantify all the value-added human activities in the private (reported currency exchange), public (government spending), and informal (barter and gray market) sectors of an economy in goods, services, and net return on investments originating from one state (Getis et al. 2006). Typically such measures are based on a common currency like the U.S. dollar, requiring conversion rates and estimates, and thereby inducing some degree of error. Since large states with large populations are expected to produce more goods and services, GNP compares economic size and relative contribution of states to the global economy. However, total GNI or GNP by itself is not a ready indicator of the wealth or development status of a state. To meaningfully compare the development status between states using GNP, GNP per capita must be used. The numbers used in the Ghana comparison at the beginning of this chapter were adjusted in this way to enable fair comparisons among the three states. GNP per capita compensates for increase in population along with growth in the economy at any given time, so that comparisons can be made chronologically as well as laterally among states. GNP fails to incorporate non-marketed production, however, so such activities as parenting and maintaining one's own dwelling are not included in the measure as economic pursuits (Holloway 1992). By measuring national income per capita, sub-Saharan Africa has fared poorly, showing virtually no growth between 1960 and 2000–compared to the significant growth registered in other low income areas of the world. Rather, sub-Saharan Africa's economy grows only as fast as its population. With only 10 percent of the world's population, Africa has 30 percent of its poor. The number of poor people doubled in the twenty years since 1980 (300 million people), making Africa the only region in the world where the number of poor is rising (Feleke et al. 2007). In summary, GNP is a relatively straightforward means to gauge the aggregate value-added economic activities of a state over time in order to measure economic progress and offer meaningful comparisons. In Africa this reveals relative and absolute poverty.

The use of GNP to measure development, however, has flaws which are corrected through other related measurements. GNP, for instance, includes the net returns of investments made overseas and infers increased wealth for the originating state, even if there was no real value added. This skews the perception of wealth to the investing rather than producing state. To make the distinction between value-added production *within* a state rather than *by* a state, gross domestic product (GDP) is more often used than GNP for comparisons (Rubenstein 2008). In all other ways GDP measures total market value as does GNP, and both use per capita measurements as an indicator of economic development for a state. Among African states, use of GDP should bolster economic development measures since

Africans are more likely recipients of overseas investment and aid than originators (kleptocrats excluded), so return for investments made from abroad are credited to the local African economies. Even with that edge it is depressing to learn the per capita GDP of sub-Saharan Africa from 1960 to 2000 grew at a very low annual rate of 0.1 percent, while the rest of the world averaged growth of 5 percent annually from 1980 to 2000 (Collier 2006). Such a meager growth rate means that the African economies could barely outgrow the rate of their populations' expansion, and helps to explain why Africa remains the world's least developed region.

Another method used to correct flaws in national income measurements is to weight GNP or GDP to reduce the fluctuations induced by currency exchange or price distortions. This process is known as purchasing power parity (PPP). The PPP attempts to measure the domestic purchasing power capability in local currencies giving a more genuine evaluation to the measure of economic development and a society's standard of living (UNDP HDR 2007). "It is based on the idea that identical baskets of traded goods should cost the same" (Getis 2006), and if they are not the same the difference should be used to adjust the national income measures. PPP measurements reduce the error that transitory U.S. dollar exchange rate spikes have in skewing the perception of economic development and standard of living, and account for the difficulty in obtaining common basic requirements for living in a society. Using the GDP PPP usually reduces the perception of poverty suffered when compared to unadjusted figures. The differences in measuring economic development in terms of per capita value of GNI, GDP, and GDP PPP are apparent in Table 1. The GNI and GDP at the official rate vary somewhat between them, as expected. However, the GDP at the official exchange rate diverges significantly from the GDP PPP, in this example by factors of 1.7 to 3.2. For the more developed U.S. and U. K., the differences between the three measures are less. As is usually the cases when using GDP PPP, the citizens of some developing states have more purchasing power than GNI or GDP may indicate–often making the PPP measure an equalizing indicator. Not surprisingly, as a region sub-Saharan Africa still ranks below the rest of the world in average GDP PPP at $1,998. This value is significantly below the low-income-state world average of $2,531. By any standard of economic measure, many states in Africa seriously lag behind the rest of the world's development standard and rates.

Table 1. Comparison of Development
Measures of Economic Indicators

State	Gross National Income	Gross Domestic Product, Official Exchange	Gross Domestic Product, PPP
Algeria	3,030	3,800	8,100
Botswana	5,900	6,900	14,700
Chad	480	700	1,600
Congo, Rep	950 (2005)	1,800	3,700
Ethiopia	180	200	700
Ghana	520	600	1,400
Kenya	580	800	1,600
Mauritius	5,450	5,600	11,900
Nigeria	640	900	2,200
Sierra Leone	240	250	800
South Africa	5,390	6,200	10,600
UK	40,180	45,500	35,300
USA	44,970	45,800	46,000

Note: all figures in U.S. dollars and are per capita data. GNI uses 2006 data and GDP uses 2007 data.
(GNI: World Bank, "Key Development Data and Statistics." GDP PPI and GDP Official Rate: Central Intelligence Agency, *The 2008 World Fact Book*. 2008)

Measuring Africa's Human Development

Using economic measurements like GNI and GDP PPP to gauge human development may still not adequately describe a development situation. Not all societies favor material wealth equally, and those that desire it less may seem less developed than they actually are (Clawson et al. 2008). For that reason social and demographic measures are also used to give a more nuanced understanding of development, which should generate better solutions to weigh and counter poverty. If material goods are not universally held in the same high regard, there are other things that most modern societies cherish and are willing to expend scarce resources to attain. Education and health care are two such social metrics, and are crucial to the development of a vibrant economy. Both are human indicators of economic development, since the amount of resources allocated to these indicates the wealth of an economy, and dedicating such resources is an investment in future economic and human well-being. The health of a people can be measured by markers such as expenditures on medical care as a percentage of national wealth, proportion of patients to doctors or nurses, or even by calories and protein received in an average daily diet. Such social indicators of development, however, are often indicated through related demographic statistics. For example, a long average life expectancy is an agglomerate gauge of the strength of a state's health care, food supply, sanitation, and public assistance support. The difference in life expectancy between developed states and underdeveloped states shows men and women living significantly longer in wealthier societies, which is a reflection of their social resources and organization.

Regionally, sub-Saharan Africa's life expectancy is only 49.6 years, while that of high income states averages is 79.2 on average and low income states 60.0 (UNDP HDR 2007). United Nations Development Programme data in Table 2 indicates that even otherwise promising states, such as Botswana and South Africa, show their less developed nature in life expectancy, while reflecting the grave toll that AIDS and other diseases have taken.

Infant mortality rate (IMR), the number of babies that survive to their first year per 1000 live births, and child mortality rates (CMR), the number of children who live to their fifth year, are other common measures of health and welfare systems. Childhood survival, however, is based more upon basic medical care like immunizations, parental knowledge, and ability to combat common forms of death from illness, malnutrition and diarrhea, so this measure is somewhat less dependent on wealth and more on community organization. Sub-Saharan Africa's regional CMR is 172 deaths per thousand while that of high income states is only 7 (UNDP HDR 2007). An IMR of 60 deaths per 1000 births is a mark of lesser developed states (Rubenstein 2008), and many sub-Saharan African states exceed that. Table 2 shows most African states in excess of the U.S. and U.K. IMR rate by ten to twenty times. Thabo Mbeki, former President of South Africa, stated that "the world's biggest killer and the greatest cause of ill health and suffering across the globe ... is extreme poverty," a sentiment shared by many researchers and medical professionals (Jacobs 2007). In most basic demographic indicators, the people of Africa fare worst in the world.

Table 2. Comparison of Development Using
Demographic and Social Indicators

State	Life Expectancy (years)	Infant Mortality (rate)	Adult Literacy Total Pop (%)	Gross Enrollment Ratio (%)
Algeria	71.7	34	69.9	73.7
Botswana	48.1	87	81.2	69.5
Chad	50.4	124	25.7	37.5
Congo, Rep	54	81	84.7	51.4
Ethiopia	51.8	109	35.9	42.1
Ghana	59.1	68	57.9	50.7
Kenya	52.1	79	73.6	60.6
Mauritius	72.4	13	84.3	75.3
Nigeria	46.5	100	69.1	56.2
Sierra Leone	41.8	165	34.8	44.6
South Africa	50.8	55	82.4	77
UK	79	5	99	93
USA	77.9	6	99	93.3

Note: all figures based on 2005 data. (United Nations Development Programme, Human Development Reports, 2007/8, 2005 data. U.S. and U.K. literacy rates from CIA *The 2008 World Factbook*, 2008)

A healthy work force is not sufficient, however, to develop an economy. The work force must also be skilled and literate to be productive. Two important measures of the level of social development are the quantity and quality of education. Quantity may be measured by how long a student attends school, because even in mediocre schools the longer a student attends the more likely he or she is to learn. To measure quantity of education the United Nations uses the gross enrollment ratio (GER), which is the ratio of all students in primary, secondary, and tertiary (college) levels of schooling compared to the official population of school age students for those three levels as established by the state and expressed as a percentage (UN Gender Statistics 2008). This statistic helps to show how many eligible students may actually be attending school and can be an indicator of future literacy. Table 2 shows that the highest African rates of GER are found in northern Africa, South Africa, and Mauritius at around 75 percent enrollment—below the average developed state's rate of 93-98 percent. These states are not representative of most of Africa, however, which falls far short with only 58 percent of African children enrolled in primary education and far fewer at higher levels (UNDP HDR 2007).

Quality of education can be measured by the student-teacher ratio or by the literacy rate, which is the percentage of a state's adults who can read and write in their own language (Rubenstein 2008, 297-8). High income societies usually give 12 years of school to their students, and offer relatively easy access to higher education. This results in a typical literacy rate of above 98 percent for adult men and women. Sub-Saharan Africa's literacy is only 59.3 percent (UNDP HDR 2007) which helps explain why its economic development is low. The lower GER rates in the youngest generation also forecast illiteracy and a shortage of needed skills for future higher order economic activities, trapping Africans in another cycle of poverty. Together, literacy rates and GER constitute what the UN refers to as the Education Index, and are important indicators of a population's current ability to participate in advanced economic activities and its potential to improve future human and economic conditions. So important are health and education to an underdeveloped population that the UN Millennium Development Goals, which aim to reduce absolute poverty by half worldwide by 2015, specifically target universal primary education, greater gender balance in schools, and reduction in the CMR as key development goals (Independent Task Force 2005, 112).

Measurements of development that combine both social and demographic characteristics are urbanization and the total fertility rate. Both reflect population growth or distribution, but are highly influenced by cultural norms and organization. Urbanization is the total population of a state or region living within a city or its immediate surroundings (the definition of which varies by state). Economically cities represent a dense pool of laborers needed by industry, and allow economic specialization of services like banking, insurance, and a stock exchange that are the hallmark of advanced economies. In a rich state, urbanization usually exceeds 75 percent of its total population. Some states in Africa have approached 60 percent urbanization (see Table 3), but none have yet built world class manufacturing regions. Ties to ancestral land, willingness to embrace the changes that come with migrating to a city, and organization within the city are all cultural traits and systems that affect urbanization. At 244 million people or 30 percent of the population, sub-Saharan Africa has the lowest current urban population among the world's regions, but the highest city growth rate (Clawson 2008). A more complete discussion of urbanization in sub-Saharan Africa can be found in Chapter 14.

Another social and demographic characteristic is the total fertility rate, which is (roughly speaking) the number of children the average woman in a state or region will bear during her lifetime. A rate of 2.1 children is considered a long term zero population growth rate, while more than that creates a growing population and is another indicator of a less developed state (see Table 3). Sub-Saharan Africa's TFR average is 5.5, significantly higher than that of middle income states (2.1) and even low income states (3.8) (UNDP HDR 2007). That so many babies are born is an indicator of agriculture as a mainstay of an economy, low standard of health care since many children do not survive, low level of government support so that children act as insurance for the elderly, and cultural preference for large families. The negative aspect of large families is that they disperse the concentration of available funds, delaying a surplus of massed capital needed for development. High urbanization reinforces a low TFR, since city dwellers rarely have the room or economic motivation to have large families. Social and demographic indicators, such as urbanization and

TFR, are just a few among a host of other economic, social, and demographic measures used to better understand a specific area's development through a broader perspective. Social and demographic traits often are the foundation upon which a modern economy is built, and are therefore excellent indicators to supplement economic measures of development. Since health, education, and urbanization require community resources and organization, they are also signs of how much wealth and ability a community has to fulfill these aspirations.

Table 3. Comparison of Development Using Urbanization, TFR, and HDI Indicators

State	Urbanization (% population)	Total Fertility Rate (births per woman)	Human Development Index (World Bank rank)
Algeria	40.3	2.5	0.733 (104)
Botswana	57.4	3.2	0.654 (124)
Chad	25.3	6.5	0.388 (170)
Congo, Rep	60.2	4.8	0.548 (139)
Ethiopia	16	5.8	0.406 (169)
Ghana	47.8	4.4	0.553 (135)
Kenya	20.7	5	0.521 (148)
Mauritius	42.4	1.9	0.804 (65)
Nigeria	48.2	5.8	0.470 (158)
Sierra Leone	40.7	6.5	0.366 (177, bottom)
South Africa	59.3	2.8	0.674 (121)
Sudan	40.8	4.8	0.526 (147)
U.K.	98.7	1.7	0.946 (16)
U.S.	80.8	2	0.949 (12)

Note: HDI and urbanization is 2005 data, TFR is 2000-5 data. Urbanization data is based on state-derived definitions of an urban area, and varies. (United Nations Development Programme, Human Development Reports, 2007/8, 2005 data)

Since 1990 the United Nations has published the human development index (HDI) as a shorthand single aggregate measure of human development to facilitate chronological and lateral comparisons. The HDI includes the economic measure of GDP PPP to determine standard of living; a social measure using the educational index including both GER and literacy rates; and a demographic dimension for health in the form of life expectancy. Combined, these provide a broader index ranging from a value of 1 (best score) to 0 (dismal) to show human and economic development levels (Table 3, last column). Sub-Saharan Africa ranks lowest among the world's regions with an HDI of 0.493 due to having the world's lowest standard of living, and worst health and education levels. The region of North Africa, including Egypt, rates significantly higher with an HDI of 0.740 (UNDP HDR 2007). This is about the same development level as the relatively prosperous region of East Asia (without Japan) (UNDP HDR 2007). In comparison, the regions of Anglo-America, Japan, and Western Europe each place around 0.93-0.94 in HDI (Rubenstein 2008) and average middle and low income states at 0.776 and 0.579 respectively. Although often cited for its broadness, even the HDI has limitations since it includes just a few important measures of the many available, and thus still gives a less than comprehensive picture. The UN Development Programme's 2007 Human Development Report judges its own HDI measure:

> It does not, for example, include important indicators such as gender or income inequality and more difficult to measure indicators like respect for human rights and political freedoms. What it does provide is a broadened prism for viewing human progress and the complex relationship between income and well being.

Because it accounts for at least one significant economic, social, and demographic measure, the HDI is a better balanced, although still limited, single indication of economic and human development. Using this measure, sub-Saharan Africa is again the least developed region in the world.

Measuring Other Development Indicators in Africa

To add a deeper understanding of the economic and human development of a state, additional indexes may be used to compensate for the acknowledged weaknesses in the HDI. The gender development index (GDI, see Table 4), which compares the level of human development between women and men, is one such method which uses the same criteria found in the HDI. The greater the disparity between men and women in these measures, the lower the GDI. In parts of Africa where overall literacy runs at 50 percent of the population or below, for example in Ethiopia, Sierra Leone or Chad, female literacy is only half to a quarter of male literacy. The gross enrollment ratio confirms this current trend and bodes slow future improvement for African women overall with only 25 to 75 percent of age-eligible females enrolled in school, lower than the enrollment rate for males. This means that the female half of the population of these states have less opportunity than males to reach the levels needed to contribute to economic development, which retards overall growth potential, since not all human resources are used. Such differences may result from a fiscal allocation system where limited available resources are expended mainly on males, or there may be a cultural cause where girls are put to work earlier in house-based tasks.

Lower education results directly in lower earned income for females (Table 4) in many African economies, by a difference of two to three times. When women can work outside the home, less education often means women remain in menial or entry level jobs and cannot progress to higher level technical or management positions. Lack of education also reduces women's chances of holding elected or appointed positions in government. Only in life

171

expectancy do African females fare better than their male counterparts among the development measures, but this is also true everywhere in the world where rudimentary modern medical care and public health are practiced; and in sub-Saharan Africa women's relatively longer life expectancies have been mitigated by HIV/AIDS. Not surprisingly, of all of the regions in the world, sub-Saharan Africa ranks lowest in GDI (Rubenstein 2008), and of all the states Niger is the lowest at 0.278 (Clawson et al. 2008). Such a low GDI indicates that African women have less influence in the affairs of their communities and families, which in turn hinders economic and human development.

Table 4. Comparison of Development Measures Using Gender Development Index Measures

State	Earned Income (estimated U.S. $) Male / Female	Life Expectancy (in years) Male / Female	Adult Literacy (% total pop) Male / Female	GER of Total Pop (%) (GER of Females)	Gender Dev Index (rank
Algeria	10,515 / 3,546	70.4 / 73.0	79.6 / 60.1	74 (72)	0.720 (94)
Botswana	19,094 / 5,913	47.6 / 48.4	80.4 / 81.8	69 (62)	0.639 (108)
Chad	1,735 / 1,126	49.0 / 48.4	40.8 / 12.8	37 (23)	0.370 (151)
Congo, Rep	1,691 / 841	52.8 / 55.2	90.5 / 79.0	51 (40)	0.540 (119)
Ethiopia	1,316 / 796	50.5 / 53.1	50.0 / 22.8	42 (37)	0.393 (148)
Ghana	2,893 / 2,056	58.7 / 59.5	66.4 / 49.8	50 (44)	0.549 (116)
Kenya	1,354 / 1,126	51.1 / 53.1	77.0 / 70.2	60 (53)	0.521 (126)
Mauritius	18,098 / 7,407	69.1 / 75.8	88.2 / 80.5	75 (70)	0.804 (65)
Nigeria	1,592 / 652	46.6 / 47.1	78.2 / 60.1	56 (44)	0.456 (138)
Sierra Leone	1,114 / 507	40.2 / 43.4	46.7 / 24.2	44 (65)	0.320 (156)
South Africa	15,446 / 6,927	49.5 / 52.0	84.1 / 80.9	77 (72)	0.667 (106)
UK	40,000/ 26,242	76.7 / 81.2	99/ 99	93 (95)	0.944 (10)
USA	40,000/ 25,005	75.2 / 80.4	99 / 99	93 (97)	0.937 (16)

Note: all figures based on 2005 data. U.S. and UK earned income shows maximum allowed in report.
(United Nations Development Programme, Human Development Reports, 2007/8. U.S. and U.K. literacy rates from CIA *The 2008 World Factbook,* 2008)

Other inequalities found in the HDI are balanced by also examining factors addressing income distribution and human freedom—each a factor influencing economic and human development. With income inequality a state may have a relatively high GDP per capita, but rich elites may be the primary beneficiaries while the rest of the population is significantly below the national average and suffers inadequate education and health care. The poverty line is an absolute way of measuring such disparity, based on the definition of being poor in each state. A relative way to measure the degree of income inequality allowing comparisons across borders is a Gini Index used by the United Nations Development Programme (UNDP) as a ratio of values of 0 to 100, with 100 representing perfect inequality (one person earns everything, and the rest nothing).

The World Bank ranked Namibia as having the world's most unequal distribution of wealth in 2006 with a Gini index of 74.3, a result of its white minority owning most of the state's land and commercial farms (Cutter 2007). Botswana and South Africa also have unequal income distribution for similar reasons (UNDP HDR 2007). Gordon and Gordon note that "Africa now rivals Latin America as the region of the world with the greatest inequality between the rich few and the many poor" (2007, 399). Anecdotal evidence from oil rich Nigeria shows that despite suffering a net decline in GNI per capita over past decades, six of the world's one hundred richest people are Nigerian, and each one is politically powerful (Gordon and Gordon 2007). Economic inequality often is associated with political inequality in Africa, leaving the poor not only destitute but powerless to change their situation.

Attempts to better balance the HDI using more subjective factors, such as political freedom, have created measures like the UNDP's human freedom index (HFI). First tabulated in 1991 to address the lack of human rights when measuring development through the HDI, the UNDP concluded there was a high correlation between human development and human freedom (Lewis 1991). Some political freedoms may directly contribute to economic development including property rights (Cowin 1992), such that political freedom bolsters human development, and human development reinforces political freedom. However, the UNDP HFI is no longer tabulated, probably because it proved to be too politically contentious. For the past 35 years the non-government organization (NGO) Freedom House has offered a similar index on a 1 (best) to 7 (worst) scale to measure political rights and civil liberties (Table 5). In its 2006 analysis, 46 states were rated in the 6 or 7 category for political rights and 19 of those were found on the African continent. That means Africa hosts nearly half of the world's repressive regimes but represents only a little over a quarter of the world's states. Some blame the cause for such abuses on a lack of economic resources resulting in a "human rights rationing" (McGreal 1999).

Indeed among Africa's three wealthiest states in terms of GDP PPP and HDI, Mauritius, Botswana, and South Africa, are also found the freest societies in Africa—but there are also exceptions to ponder. In the states tracked in this chapter, Algeria is second in HDI and fourth in per capita wealth (indicators of economic development) yet still is categorized by Freedom House as not free. In part this may be due to African aspirations that value democracy more for its potential to deliver necessities like water, shelter, and education than for its freedoms (*Afrobarometer* 2002). Although not entirely correlated to economic development, some factors such as income distribution and human freedom offer a fuller understanding of a state's development situation.

Table 5: Comparison of Development Using Income
Inequality and Freedom Measurements

State	Income Inequality (0 =equality)	Political Rights / Civil Liberties / Freedom Index
Algeria	35.3	6 / 5 / Not Free
Botswana	60.5	2 / 2 / Free
Chad	n/a	6 / 5 / Not Free
Congo, Rep	n/a	6 / 6 / Not Free
Ethiopia	30	5 / 5 / Part Free
Ghana	40.8	1 / 2 / Free
Kenya	42.5	3 / 3 / Part Free
Mauritius	n/a	1 / 1 / Free
Nigeria	43.7	4 / 4 / Part Free
Sudan	n/a	7 / 7 / Not Free
Sierra Leone	62.9	4 / 3 / Part Free
South Africa	57.8	1 / 2 / Free
U.K.	36	1 / 1 / Free
U.S.	40.8	1 / 1 / Free

Note: income equality data is from 2005, and political rights
data from 2006.
(Income data from United Nations Development Programme,
Human Development Reports, 2007/8; political rights and
civil liberties from Freedom House, Freedom in the World
State Ratings, 2006)

The economic, social and demographic characteristics
introduced so far in this chapter are just a few of many
possible ways of measuring development in order to gain
a more holistic view of economic conditions. The more
characteristics that are evaluated, the more comprehensive
the analysis of a state's economic situation, including some
of the material gains examined in this section. One such
economic factor to consider is productivity, defined as the
value of a particular product or service compared to the

amount of labor needed to produce it. Developed states' workers have access to tools and capabilities through capital that make their work more productive and able to generate more wealth than that of underdeveloped states' workers, who rely on less efficient human and animal power (Rubenstein 2008). One characteristic of productivity tracked by the UN Development report is electricity consumption per capita, which tells how much power is used to operate tools and equipment at work and home. Africa's most industrialized and wealthiest societies, here represented by Mauritius, South Africa, and Algeria, are also the states that consume the most electricity. Electricity consumption, along with internet and cell phone usage (see Table 6), also portend a large investment in physical infrastructure, suggesting national wealth to invest and confidence in future stability by doing so.

Consumer goods such as appliances, transportation, computers, and phones are also essential to a modern economy since they allow access to jobs, services, and information. Consumption of such goods is a result of high economic development, but they in turn promote even higher levels of development through their ability to create increased efficiency and availability of more workers. Such gadgets also indicate a societal proclivity for embracing change which is another prerequisite for advancing economically along Western norms. States with more than 500 telephones, 400 motor vehicles, and 300 Internet users per 1000 people are more developed, while those with less than 100 of each per 1000 are considered underdeveloped (Rubenstein 2008). Such consumer goods tracked in Table 6 reinforce earlier conclusions that categorize all of Africa as underdeveloped, but they differentiate Mauritius, South Africa, and Algeria as the more developed states within Africa.

One bright spot for sub-Saharan Africa is that its regional cellular phone use average of 130 per 1000 people is almost twice that of other low income states, which may suggest a willingness to embrace technology, although internet users at 26 per thousand are half that of the other low income states which average 45 (UNDP HDR 2007). Such differences in communication may be explained by the fact that a cellular network is cheaper to join and requires less infrastructure than internet usage. Indicators such as productivity through energy and goods consumption are just a few among a host of other economic, social, and demographic measures used to better understand Africa's low economic development status.

Table 6: Comparison of Development Using Consumption Indicators

State	Electricity Consumption Per Capita (kilowatt-hrs)	Internet Users (per 1000)	Cell Phone Subscribers (per 1000)
Algeria	899	58	416
Botswana	n/a	34	466
Chad	11	4	22
Congo, Rep	229	13	123
Ethiopia	36	2	6
Ghana	289	18	129
Kenya	169	32	135
Mauritius	1,775	146	574
Nigeria	157	38	141
Sierra Leone	24	2	22
South Africa	4,818	109	724
Sudan	116	77	50
U.K.	6,756	473	1,088
U.S.	14,240	630	680

Note: figures based on 2005 data, except electricity consumption which is 2004 data.
(United Nations Development Programme, Human Development Reports, 2007/8)

Conclusion

Development encompasses more than just economic improvement; it is also composed of social and demographic advances, political freedoms, economic opportunity, and even perhaps a sense of collective contentment. Development therefore requires both material wealth and non-material enhancement because they reinforce one another in bettering society. When gauging improvement, development measures have their limitations in that each only partly describes this complex phenomenon. For the best understanding of development, different perspectives are needed including economic measures such as a state's GNP per capita, GDP PPP, income equality, and consumption of goods; social measures including GER, literacy, urbanization, gender equality, and political rights; and the demographic characteristics of life expectancy, CMR, IMR, and TFR among others. For ease of use, these measures can be grouped into a single indicator, such as the HDI or GDI, but even those do not fully explain the situation unless considered with other trends.

Africa's development may also not completely follow Western norms which emphasized production of goods and services using the twentieth century's model that burdened future generations and the environment (Clawson et al. 2008). Despite reliance on quantifiable measurements and a Western-centric view of what development is, Africa still presents a picture of low economic and human development in both absolute terms and relative to other regions of the world. Sub-Saharan Africa's HDI of 0.491 lags behind the HDI average of the world's low income states at 0.570 (UNDP HDR 2007), making it the poorest of the poor. Even worse, the trend is moving towards more economic poverty. The number of people living in extreme poverty (earning less than $1 a day) has increased in most of sub-Saharan Africa since 2000 when 189 states pledged to promote development, freedom, and peace through the UN's Millennium Development Goals. In fact, none of the eight major human development goals are on track to be reached in Africa by the target date of 2015 (Gordon and Gordon 2007).

In Africa, economic growth is not necessarily about gaining more or better material possessions, desirable as this may be in reducing poverty. Economic growth is just as concerned with the intelligent sustainable growth that also ensures demographic and societal development with it. A World Bank report emphasizes:

> Development is about improving the quality of people's lives, expanding their ability to shape their own futures. This generally calls for higher per capita income, but it involves much more. It involves more equitable education and job opportunities. Greater gender equality. Better health and nutrition. A cleaner, more sustainable natural environment. A more impartial judicial and legal system. Broader civil and political freedoms. A richer cultured life (2000, xxiii).

The Republic of Korea as late as the 1960s was also afflicted with many of the same problems faced by most African states today. However, by 2007 South Korea's GNI of $410 million was larger than all of the economies of sub-Saharan Africa combined at $310 million (Clawson et al. 2008). Such growth supports April and Donald Gordon's remark that South Korea "is now a model of development as one of the world's most prosperous Newly Industrialized States..." (2007, 399). The African states are the last to start this rapid climb, but the models and assistance needed for economic, social, and demographic development are available if the states of Africa can set their own fundamentals in order. To further explain why such poverty persists, despite native advantages including substantial natural resources and a relatively low population density, and how to help Africa develop, the next chapter analyzes some of the causes responsible for hobbling the African people in their human progress and possible solutions to improve the situation.

Lieutenant Colonel (Retired) Clarence J. Bouchat flew fighters as an Air Force officer before teaching Theater Strategy at the U.S. Army War College. He has taught at the U.S. Air Force Academy and published articles on regional and political geography. He currently teaches World Regional Geography at Harrisburg Area Community College in Pennsylvania.

References

Afrobarometer. 2002. Key Findings About Public Opinion in Africa. Institute for Democracy in South Africa, no.1 (April).

Central Intelligence Agency. *The 2008 World Factbook.* 2008. https://www.cia.gov/library/publications/the-world-factbook/index.html (accessed on March 28, 2008).

Clawson, David L., Douglas L Johnson, Viola Haarman, Merrill L. Johnson. 2007. *World Regional Geography.* Upper Saddle River, NJ: Peason-Prentice Hall.

Collier, Paul. 2006. Africa: Geography and Growth. Oxford: Centre for the Study of African Economics.

Cowin, Andrew J. 1992. UN Report Backtracks on Link Between Freedom and Development. http://www.heritage.org/Research/InternationalOrganizations/bu180.cfm (accessed December 11, 2008).

Cutter, Charles H. 2007. *Africa 2007.* Harpers Ferry, WV: Stryker-Post Publications.

Feleke, Elisabeth, and Louis A. Picard. 2007. *African Security Policy in the Twenty-First Century, an Overview of Issues.* Washington, DC: National Defense University.

Freedom House. Freedom in the World State Ratings 1972-2006.
http://www.freedomhouse.org/template.cfm?page=15
(accessed May 19, 2008).

Getis, Arthur, Judith Getis and Jerome D. Fellmann.   2006.
Introduction to Geography. New York: McGraw Hill.

Gordon, April A. and Donald L. Gordon.   2007. Trends and
Prospects. In *Understanding Contemporary Africa*, ed. Gordon
and Gordon. Boulder, CO: Lynne Reinner Publishers.

Gyekum, Frank A. 2005. South Korea: A Success Story Worth
Emulating.

http://www.ghanaweb.com/GhanaHomePage/features/
artikel.php?ID=92213 (accessed March 19, 2008).

Holloway, Steven and Kavita Pandit. 1992. The Disparity between
the Level of Economic Development and Human Welfare.
Professional Geographer 44, no. 1: 57-71.

Independent Task Force Report No. 56.   2005. More Than
Humanitarianism: A Strategic U.S. Approach Toward Africa.
New York: Council of Foreign Relations, Ind.

Jacobs, Sean and Krista Johnson. 2007. Media, Social Movements
and the State: Correcting Images of HIV/AIDS in South
Africa. *Africa Studies Quarterly* 9, no. 4 (Fall).

Lewis, Paul. 1991. UN Index on Freedom Enrages Third World.
New York Times, June 23. http://query.nytimes.com/
gst/fullpage.html?res=9D0CE2DA103FF930A15755C0
A967958260 (accessed March 31, 2008).

Mbaku, John.Mukum 2004. *Institutions and Development in Africa*.
Lewiston, NY: Edwin Mellen Press.

McGreal, Chris. 1999. Another Horrific Year Ends Century of
Blood. *UK Observer*, October 24.   http://www.guardian.
co.uk/rightsindex/0,2759,201749,00.html (accessed March
31, 2008).

Morris, William, ed. 1976. *The American Heritage Dictionary of the English Language.* Boston: Houghton Mifflin Company.

Rubenstein, James M. 2008. *An Introduction to Human Geography.* Upper Saddle River, NJ: Peason Prentice Hall.

Saraswathi, M. 2007. Malaysia Has Made the Best of What It has, Says Kofi Annan. http://www.bernama.com.my/bernama/v3/printable.php?id=272943 (accessed March 19, 2008).

United Nations Development Programme (UNDP). Human Development Reports. http://hdr.undp.org/en/statistics/ (accessed May 15, 2008).

United Nations Gender Statistics Programmes. Glossary G. http://www.escwa.un.org/gsp/glossary/g.html (accessed March 29, 2008).

World Bank. 2007. GNI per Capita 2006: World Development Indicators Database. September 14. http://siteresources.worldbank.org/DATASTATISTICS/Resources/GNIPC.pdf (accessed March 19, 2008).

World Bank. 2006. Key Development Data and Statistics. http://web.worldbank.org/WBSITE/EXTERNAL/DATASTATISTICS/0,,contentMDK:20535285~menuPK:1192694~pagePK:64133150~piPK:64133175~theSitePK:239419,00.html (accessed March 29, 2008).

Africa's Economic Activities

Clarence J. Bouchat

Key Points

- Most Africans are engaged in subsistence agriculture, which slows development.

- Most of Africa's internally generated foreign revenue for development comes from commercial agriculture and energy and mineral resources, but its economies should be more diverse.

- Most of Africa's earnings and aid revenue are mismanaged or misappropriated; African states must improve how they govern and manage their governments and economies.

- Foreign aid should continue in more development-centered ways to promote Africa's prospects.

Economic Activities and Development

Although a society's welfare and development are more than an agglomeration of its economic activities, the economy is the foundation for social, demographic, and material gains. A state's economy provides the funding for new wells, clinics, schools, ballots, and the income to buy life- enhancing goods and services. Africa lags behind the rest of the world in development in large part because its economies are the smallest and least productive in the world. This comparative global disadvantage has grown rapidly since the great age of European discovery began in the 1450s. At that time the difference between Europe and Africa was small, with Europeans impressed by the African empires' wealth, organization, and strength. Europeans traded with Africans as equals and the Portuguese entered into alliances with African states (Garraty and Gay 1972).

Today, despite the often negative indicators of Africa's situation, there are some success stories on the continent and a general, although not universal, trend toward economic growth averaging over 5 percent annually between 2000 and 2007 (Economic and Trade Overview 2007). In order to continue this progress, the factors contributing to economic success must be determined. Since its inclusion into the world economy by Arab traders in the eleventh century and European merchants in the fifteenth century (and earlier for North Africa through the classical-age Mediterranean empires), Africa's economy has been grounded primarily on agriculture and has been a source of raw materials for the world (Garraty and Gay 1972).

Early European names for parts of the continent—the Grain Coast, Gold Coast, and Ivory Coast—attest to these enduring relationships. These resources were a main cause for European imperialism, and why some leaders today accuse outside powers of continuing their control in Africa through a form of neo-colonialism. Unlike Europe, however, Africa's main economic activities over the centuries remained primarily the same. It is the continued reliance on such economic pursuits that may explain why Africa is economically underdeveloped. In Africa, farming remains the most important economic activity, and mineral and energy resources its biggest exports. Such activities are the most basic form of human production to meet fundamental needs, but tend to advance economic development very slowly. Elsewhere in the world, economic, social, and demographic improvement has been fueled by engaging in higher order economic activities such as manufacturing, building, and production (secondary economic activities), or services to and from individuals, businesses, and government (tertiary economic activities) to include communications, transportation, education, research, and personal services.

This chapter examines Africa's primary, secondary, and tertiary activities, to show how the reliance on the primary economic activities has put it at a disadvantage. It also explores how better administration and governance, diversification into higher order economic activities, and foreign assistance can leverage human and natural resources into furthering development in Africa.

There are several components that contribute to development, especially economic development: the natural environment, people, and culture. The natural environment is particularly important to the success of the primary economic activities (Clawson et al. 2008) which include agriculture, forestry, fishing, hunting and gathering, grazing, mining, and drilling. These primary activities share the same limitations that hobble them from contributing to a state's development. The most basic hindrance is that the vagaries of natural supply, due to its basis in physical geography, expose such activities to risk and shortages. Primary economic activities also earn less from human input and capital than higher order activities do for the overall cost of the commodity. Less added-value derives less profit from primary commodities than from manufactured goods or services. The economic value of these commodities depends on the rise and fall of international demand, since domestic and regional demand in Africa for its own commercial primary products is small.

Economic policies of industrialized states are made in their favor, which makes participation in the global economy by less developed states less advantageous. Even occasional high global primary commodity prices, as occurred in the 1970s and in the 2000s, may not contribute to economic and human development enough over time since inevitable drops make investment in such activities risky, and their roller-coaster economic returns are too unreliable for modern development schemes that depend upon stability. Thus, around the world and throughout history, there has been a strong correlation between a predominant engagement in primary economic activities and relatively low economic and human development of a region or state. Although the most basic of human activities, the inconsistent returns, less predictable supply, lower added value, and dependence on outside demand for primary commodities like food, fibers, timber, hydrocarbons, and mineral resources make them a weaker and less reliable means by which to further development.

Agriculture

Workers who engage in agriculture for the principle purpose of feeding their families are considered subsistence farmers and are at the lowest level of development. They typically employ small or desolate plots of land using little machinery, capital, or fertilizer. Subsistence agriculture may include intensive farming such as rice growing, slash and burn methods in the jungle, and pastoralist farming. Subsistence farmers engage sporadically in the national economy and do not contribute in an appreciable way to a state's tax base or economic development.

A state is considered developed if it employs less than ten percent of its labor in agriculture, and is underdeveloped if more than half are farmers (Rubenstein 2008). A high percentage of the work force engaged in agriculture is an indicator of an economically underdeveloped state because "a high percentage of agricultural workers in a state indicates that most of its people must spend their days producing food for their own survival ... not in more wealth creating enterprises like manufacturing and services" (Rubenstein 2008, 259). On average, African agriculture employs about two-thirds of all workers, but accounted for less than a quarter of GDP in 1999 according to the World Bank (Bread for the World 1999). Table 1 shows 80 percent of the work force in Ethiopia, Chad, and Sudan is engaged in agriculture, with 75 percent for Kenya and 70 percent for Nigeria.

The relatively low contribution of agriculture to the GDP for so much human involvement demonstrates the relative inefficiency of subsistence farming in the state economy. Drought, disease, and pests make all types of farming risky, but especially subsistence farming which has fewer resources and depth with which to mitigate such disasters. The poverty of subsistence farming is compounded by a growing population that often accompanies traditional farming, so less food is available per capita. Subsistence farmers must therefore adopt more intense or more modern farming methods, or face possible dire consequences such as famine, which has plagued sub-Saharan Africa for several decades (Rubenstein 2008).

The need to adapt "is all the greater because the AIDS pandemic is cutting down the number of agricultural workers in Africa, reducing Africa's ability not only to feed itself but also to cope with periodic natural calamities" (ITFR 2005, 121). An extreme consequence of subsistence agriculture over-burdened by population growth is evident in Rwanda, Africa's very agriculture-dependent and most densely populated state (CIA 2008, Rwanda). Paul Magnarella, former President of the Association of Third World Studies, concludes that the cause of the

> Rwandan genocide was the increasing imbalance in land, food, and people that led to malnutrition, hunger, periodic famine, and fierce competition for land to farm. Rwanda's leaders chose to respond to these conditions by eliminating the Tutsi portion of the population as well as their Hutu political rivals (2002, 34).

It is difficult for primary economic activities to significantly advance economic development because of the risk and low economic return from such commodities. Subsistence agriculture remains the predominant form of economic activity in Africa, but contributes the least to an economy and tax base. This condition plays a dominant role in the underdevelopment in sub-Saharan Africa, and in its famines and conflicts.

For this mainstay of Africa's economy to overcome hunger and contribute to society's development, a surplus in food production is a requirement. A surplus will not only feed sub-Saharan Africa's population, but generate revenue through the sale of excess goods, and allow unneeded labor to engage in higher order economic activities (Clawson et al. 2008). Elsewhere in the world similar situations were converted from subsistence farming into the modest base upon which more developed economies were built. Since the 1940s, the engine for such transformation has been the Green Revolution, originally a U.S.-Mexican project to attain food security by developing high-yield, disease-resistant grain varieties (Clawson et al. 2008). Through scientific research and the technological application of "mechanized equipment, chemical fertilizers, insecticides, herbicides, and hybrid seeds...yield[s of] two to four times more than traditional crops" were realized (Clawson et al. 2008, 609).

Despite its success in Asia and Latin America, the Green Revolution has not delivered a dramatic increase in food in Africa (ITRF 2005). One reason is that African tuber staples (cassava, yams, and cocoyams) are not part of the diet of other underdeveloped parts of the world and were not addressed. Green Revolution crops (such as rice) grown in parts of Africa require heavy investment in capital for machinery, chemical enhancements, specialized seeds, and access to larger plots of land (Clawson et al. 2008). Basic literacy to read manuals and understand more complicated new methods is also helpful, as is a willingness to embrace change. However, the pre-requisites for capital, land, and education are often out of reach of most Africans, creating a dilemma that prevents them from advancing. To gain the resources needed to participate in the Green Revolution, farmers may depend on government or international assistance, or incrementally transform into commercial agriculture by growing food for international trade (Rubenstein 2008). Either way, "increasing agricultural productivity is the engine of economic development in agricultural economies. Agricultural productivity improvement and rural development are also the most effective ways to improve conditions for poor people" (Bread for the World 1999). The Green Revolution is a proven method which yields higher development, but initiating that change requires assistance in Africa.

Unlike subsistence agriculture, commercial crops are grown primarily for sale, and depend on capital-driven inputs like machinery, chemical enhancements, and large plots of land — all of which increase crop production while reducing the percentage of laborers involved (Rubenstein 2008). Such produce may include grains, fruits and vegetables, nuts, fibers, meat and dairy, timber, fish or more of nature's bounty that grows on land or sea and whose harvest exceeds local needs. Malawi offers a classic example of commercial agriculture through tobacco, which accounts for 70 percent of all of its export revenues. However, Malawi's case also cautions against using mono-agriculture to fuel economic development, since so much needed revenue is dependent on the survival of a single crop and the vagaries of global competition (Cutter 2008). Perhaps for this reason Malawi places low in the Human Development Index (HDI) (at 0.437 ranking 164 of 177 states), and last world-wide in Gross Domestic Product Purchasing Power Parity (GDP PPP), earning only U.S. $667 per capita annually (UNHD 2008).

Ethiopia's coffee crop is also a major part of its foreign revenue, which has stunted Ethiopia's economic growth because of recent droughts, exacerbated by a simmering war with Eritrea and depressed international demand (CIA 2008, Ethiopia). Uganda's exports are dependent upon primary commodities too, accounting for 83 percent, but Uganda "diversified its agricultural sector to include nontraditional exports, such as fruits, vegetables, tobacco, and flowers..." (Clawson et al. 2008, 612). In Table 1, the primary exports category is an indicator of the amount of commercial agriculture (but also mineral and energy resources, and logging depending on which state is examined) sold abroad. For Ethiopia 60 percent of its exports are from commercial crops like coffee; but that excludes the vast number of subsistence farmers who grow few cash crops (CIA 2008). Another typical example is Ghana's 35 percent of export revenue from agriculture, mainly cocoa, in which few of Ghana's 55 percent of agricultural workers participate (CIA

2008). Currently, commercial agriculture is only a boon to a small elite portion of Africa's population.

Commercial and subsistence agriculture often exist side by side in a dual economic system, which explains why some states have both a high percentage of workers engaged in agriculture and yet are very dependent on exports from agricultural goods. As noted earlier, such commercial enterprises may be the engine for gaining resources needed to transform subsistence agriculture through a new Green Revolution, whereby "foreign innovations are first adapted on large scale farms…before descending to the level of small holder" (Clawson et al. 2008, 609). The dark side to a dual structure is that the wealthy elite who gain the resources to be commercial farmers or ranchers also have the power to control poor subsistence farmers or drive them to marginal land which is quickly overworked before a transition occurs (Clawson et al. 2008). On the other hand, during the 2000s Zimbabwe demonstrated the negative impact on food security and exports of unwisely breaking up large commercial farms.

Within families such dualism also exists, which is a legacy of colonial policies that today reinforces gender inequality (DeLancey 2007). For example, women are often relegated to traditional subsistence farming to feed the family, growing up to 80 percent of Africa's total food supply, while men work for wages or grow commercial crops as part of the transition from subsistence farming (Rubenstein 2008; Bread for the World 1999). Creating surplus food in agriculture dependent Africa is the key to economic development. Participating in a new Green Revolution is one way to transition to more lucrative commercial agriculture and assure better access to food, but to achieve success, a balanced transition from subsistence to commercial agriculture must occur.

Table 1: Comparison of Primary Economic Employment and Production Indicators

State	Employment In Agriculture (% total employ)	Primary Exports (% exports)	GDP from Agriculture (% of total)	Primary Economic Activity Exports
Algeria	14	98	8	Petroleum, natural gas
Botswana	n/a	13	2	Diamonds, copper, nickel, soda ash
Chad	80	n/a	22	Oil, cattle, cotton, gum arabic
Congo, Rep	n/a	n/a	6	Petroleum, lumber, sugar, cocoa
Ethiopia	80	89	49	Coffee, qat, gold, livestock, oilseed
Ghana	56	88	37	Gold, cocoa, timber, tuna, manganese
Kenya	75	79	24	Tea, horticultural products, coffee, fish
Mauritius	9	29	5	Sugar, cut flowers, fish
Nigeria	70	98	18	Petroleum, cocoa, rubber
Sierra Leone	n/a	93	49	Diamonds, rutile, cocoa, fish
South Africa	9	43	2	Gold, diamonds, platinum, other metals
Sudan	80	99	31	Petroleum, cotton, sesame, livestock
U.K.	1	18	1	
U.S.	1	15	1	

Note: data based on most recent years from 2000-7. Botswana, Congo, and Sierra Leone's agriculture employment data are not available, but each at least exceeds half of the work force. (Primary Exports: UN Development Programme; Human Development Reports; 2007/8 Employment, GDP from Agriculture, and Exports: Central Intelligence Agency 2008)

Since agriculture is crucial to the well-being of Africans, its proper management is the key place from which to develop the continent's economies and societies. Africa's under-performance in agriculture is a function of the region's corruption of the dual economic system, unsuitable climate and bad weather, and institutional factors such as low levels of investment, instability, inefficient resource use, and poor administration (Clawson et al. 2008). The antidote to these problems is better state governance, and international assistance to prod Africa's stagnant development trend. Maintaining basic internal stability, external peace, transparency, and representative government are necessary first steps in gaining local and foreign investment in agriculture, but one that many African governments seem unable to achieve. To encourage change towards these goals the United States started the Millennium Challenge Account (MCA) which offers "a fifty percent increase in development assistance for those states meeting its qualifications... [which] stress good governance, peace, security, the rule of law, human rights..." (Crupi 2005-2006, 118). Benin, Ghana, Mali, and Senegal have gained eligibility in MCA for their improvement efforts.

With basic good governance in place, external assistance could help to ensure that commercial agriculture becomes a boost to development and not just another form of supporting the elite. For instance, professional agricultural planning that respects or restores the environment is crucial to increase production and ensure that any gains made can be sustained for future generations. State governments should be proactive through reforestation, revegetation, soil conservation, and through their organizational responses to problems, rather than reactive as has usually been the case (Clawson et al. 2008). Such steps will mitigate the effects of adverse weather, and somewhat prepare for changes in the environment.

Since farmers and state governments often lack the resources and capital to spur a Green Revolution and more efficient commercial agriculture, foreign aid may prove very useful at the start. One example of such assistance is the U.S. government's Africa Seeds of Hope Act which aims to increase agricultural productivity and rural development through food security for subsistence agriculture and higher income for commercial endeavors. Through this act, the U.S. Agency for International Development (USAID) consults with the rural poor to establish micro credit with private entities and nongovernment organizations (NGOs), extends the benefits of the Green Revolution to African crops, enables increased flexibility in food aid, and ensures accountability towards progress (Bread for the World 1999). Other international, foreign government and NGOs are also active in similar initiatives and all efforts should be cooperatively optimized. A partnership of African governments willing to improve governance and international assistance is one way to advance Africa's development.

A second way to promote development, establish food security for Africans, and create a surplus of commercial crops for international trade is to enhance the supply side of agriculture. International supply side demands for African agricultural products may better ensure development is sustainable in the long run and does not just continue ineffective aid and grants. The United States and European Union could play a much larger, if more controversial, role by opening up their domestic markets to African agricultural goods, similar to the access that African manufactured products now have. This would eliminate a World Bank estimated $270 billion of trade-distorting price supports, and spur African economies (IFTR 2005). However, every change made to the precarious balance of Africa's economies needs to be carefully considered. In such a case, African farmers

> would require substantial financial, human and physical investment in developing land for growing agricultural products, and agro-industrial development for

processing, packaging, meeting health and sanitary standards, and marketing to the supermarkets of the world. It would require human capital and expertise in farming, food processing, and food product marketing of precisely the kind that Africa has been carelessly exporting... (Mistry 2005, 674).

Uganda's past policy and Zimbabwe's present policy of land reapportionment have driven away much of the human capital needed to achieve such a goal, whereas Kenya and Namibia's policies have better retained the expertise needed, although perpetuating other problems. Developing agriculture is the key to advancing Africa's economic and human development. To achieve these goals, African governments must govern better and ensure an efficient and equitable transition to food security and commercial agriculture. International assistance can spur the transformation by offering aid in starting the process and opening markets to African products. This may be the key piece in a complex puzzle of helping Africa develop.

Extractive Resources

Vast mineral and energy wealth are just as important as agriculture in underpinning Africa's economies. These are all primary commodities that may be the foundation upon which to develop a society or economy if properly managed, but often they are not. Because Africa is relatively land and resource abundant but underachieving in human efforts, natural resources play a larger role in its fortunes than in any other region except the Middle East (Collier 2006)

Between 1965 and 2000 "most of the growth that has taken place in export trade has come primarily from extractive processes and agriculture," with primary commodities accounting for more than 90 percent of foreign revenues in many African states (Elu 2000, 3). Natural resources are "naturally occurring, exploitable material that society perceives as useful to its economic and material well being" (Gettis 2006, 135). Some resources are renewable, like solar, wind, and geothermal energy. Africa has much potential to harness these for its benefit using its mighty rivers like the Congo or Niger to generate electricity, but also through numerous small rivers such as Liberia's St Paul River which once supplied half of that state's electricity. Although Africans desperately need cheap clean energy from these renewable sources, their establishment has been slow and under-funded compared to non-renewable resources which are exportable and of greater interest to overseas companies and governments that invest in Africa's infrastructure.

Nonrenewable, or fund, resources include metallic and nonmetallic minerals and fossil fuels. To be useful natural resources must be accessible, exploitable, and economically needed. Accessible refers to the distribution and occurrence of a resource. Many African states have few or less-than-adequate natural resources and cannot depend on this avenue for revenue to develop. Exploitability requires technology to recover and fashion it in an economically viable way. Although some resources are relatively easy to obtain, such as the alluvial diamonds of Sierra Leone and Liberia (a characteristic that fueled the civil wars in both states), most need capital, technology and expertise, usually requiring the intervention of foreign interests. Economic need is based on the recognition that a resource has value and fills a niche within an economy, generating trade or industry. Natural resources can be more influential in speeding development than agriculture because the payoff is greater, but with increased risks.

The finite geographical distribution of natural resources gives them a value that rises and falls with international demand and therefore they may be unreliable sources of funding for development plans. The requirement for foreign demand and assistance to recover and use these resources also means that a state government often has less control over its fate than is true of more-localized agriculture. Because of the advanced level of technology and expertise involved in extraction activities, their potential return to spur development is higher because of the capital cost and value added, but they usually reward only an elite fraction of the population unless government intervenes to spread the wealth. Raw materials and agriculture alone can be used to spur development, as coal and iron ore were used in the United Kingdom to start the Industrial Revolution in the eighteenth century. Other European states, the United States, and Japan followed suit with an increasing need for raw materials to continue their development. This appetite, however, resulted in the colonization of Africa and other parts of the world, thereby inhibiting further development in the newly colonized regions (Rubenstein 2008). Natural resources offer more potential to enhance development than agriculture, if properly governed, but to a less extent than industry or services. Below are examples of how natural resources are contributing to African states' development and the pitfalls that finite resources pose to the development process.

Natural resources in some states have remained the primary source for funding economic and human development, resulting in both notable successes and negative effects (Elu 2000). Since 2000, oil exporting states have led Africa's economies with an impressive 7 percent growth rate (Economic and Trade Overview 2007). Gabon is a typical state benefiting from this trend. An exporter of timber, gold, iron ore, and manganese into the 1970s, Gabon saw significant economic growth with the discovery of oil. This single commodity, which now accounts for 50 percent of GDP and 80 percent of export revenues, grew the GDP PPP to an impressive $13,800 in 2007. Gabon's national income per capita based on oil is near the highest in sub-Saharan Africa and is four times that of most other African states (CIA 2008; Clawson et al. 2008). On the negative side, Gabon's rapid growth has also produced a high income inequality level, which keeps power in a small group and most of its population poor and uneducated. Oil also dominates Nigeria's economy at 25 percent of GDP and 95 percent of exports. Although oil revenues produced respectable growth from 1965 to 1982, the Gross National Income (GNI) per capita since then has dropped from $1110 to $300 in 2000. This demonstrates the inherent transitory nature of riches from natural commodities. The drop in GNI was further exacerbated by the government's mismanagement of its economy, high population growth (with a Total Fertility Rate of 5.41 in 2007), and internal ethnic divisions—each an example of problems that other African states face in developing (Elu 2000).

Not only has Nigeria's oil production not increased the general welfare of its people, but in some cases it has had a direct negative impact by harming agriculture through polluting the land and diverting funds from agricultural development (Elu 2000). In the oil producing Niger River delta, the deprivations from inequality and environmental degradation have ignited an insurgency, which in turn disrupts oil production and limits overall economic growth (U.S. State Department 2007). Natural resource wealth has stoked instability and violence in other places too. Impoverished Chad is currently hoping for oil reserves to be an economic boost through foreign investment. However, internal ethnic unrest and cross border incursions produced a negative 1.3 percent growth rate in 2007 (CIA 2008) due in part to violent disruption of oil production and poor governance (Economic and Trade Overview 2007). Even where a government genuinely tries to develop its population through its fund resources, it may not succeed.

Algeria earns 60 percent of its budget revenue and 95 percent of its export earnings from hydrocarbons as the world's 4th largest natural gas exporter and 14th in oil. Yet the government's attempt to diversify the economy in order to reduce high unemployment and raise living standards has been unsuccessful, with reforms slowed by corruption

197

and bureaucratic inertia (CIA 2008). The perceived blessings of oil may backfire in other ways too.

In the Republic of Congo, rising oil revenues since the 1980s have been the main source to finance large-scale development resulting in a substantial GDP growth averaging 5 percent annually. To do so, however, the government has mortgaged a substantial portion of its oil earnings through oil-backed loans that have contributed to a growing debt burden and chronic revenue shortfalls. Congo's success is also threatened by the cyclical nature of oil prices, an uneasy internal peace, and incomplete government and economic reform (CIA 2008).

Natural resources in Africa have only partially realized their potential in helping the world's least developed region advance. Throughout Africa the benefits of fund resources are diminished for many of the same recurring problems found in agriculture: the cyclical nature of the demand for natural resources, poor government management in using the earnings from raw materials, internal instability which may actually be caused by the presence of such wealth, and population growth that simply outstrips the economic growth rate. Despite these hindrances, resource rich states are envied since many in Africa are bereft of natural resources and their potential to assist development.

Natural resources can obviously be both a help and hindrance to development, so analyzing Africa's sources of natural wealth beyond hydrocarbons is instructive. Oil and natural gas-poor African states can sometimes rely on other fund resources to generate foreign revenue. Guinea, for example, is a major producer of bauxite and gemstones which along with other primary products make up 75 percent of its exports, but they do not advance a low Human Development Index (HDI) of 0.456, ranking 160th in the world (USGS 2006; UNDP 2008).

Zambia is an important world supplier of cobalt and copper, a major portion of its 91 percent of primary exports. Zambia has an even lower HDI of 0.434 and is 165th in the world (USGS 2006; UNDP 2008). The Democratic Republic of Congo has 80 percent of the world's cobalt reserves, 10 percent of its copper, 30 percent of its diamonds, and other diverse mining resources that contribute to 25 percent of GDP output and 75 percent of total exports, along with rich renewable energy and agricultural sources. Yet the Democratic Republic of Congo has not realized its development potential for many of the same factors cited for other African states: "government corruption, mismanagement, and profligacy... War only furthered the collapse" (Cutter 2008, 125; Clawson et al. 2008, 638).

South Africa is its continent's largest and most diverse source for important metallic and nonmetallic minerals, placing in the world's top five in production and reserves in anthracite coal, antimony, chromium, industrial diamonds, gemstones, titanium, and vanadium along with other lesser mineral reserves, and leads the world in platinum and gold (USGS 2006). These raw materials account for nearly all of South Africa's primary exports, which at only 48 percent of all exports indicates a diversification of the economy that few other natural resource exporting states in Africa share. South Africa is a rare case that breaks the trend of resources seemingly holding back economic and human development because of its relatively better governance and economic management, greater stability, and diversification into higher order economic activities. Morocco, on the other hand, is not as well endowed with physical resources, although it is the world's leading exporter of phosphates (used in fertilizer) which make up 92 percent of its mining earnings (Cutter 2008).

Together with some food products, primary commodities only make up 35 percent of Morocco's exports, but this contributes to a higher HDI of 0.646, ranking 126th — very close to South Africa's level (UNDP 2008). Why is it that despite the abundant natural resources found in Africa, only 3 of Africa's 53 states rank in the top 100 of the HDI (Seychelles, Mauritius, and Tunisia), and none maintains this ranking through just its agriculture or raw natural resources (UNDP 2008)?

Despite its potential benefits, a case can be made that reliance on Africa's huge endowment of natural resources is actually a detriment to development because Africa's wealth is so mismanaged as to retard real growth elsewhere. Thomas Friedman calls this the "curse of oil," but the curse could be extended to reliance on any fund resources sold as a state's primary means of revenue. Friedman explains:

> As long as the monarchs and dictators who run these oil states can get rich by drilling their natural resources—as opposed to drilling the natural talents and energy of their people--they can stay in office forever. They can use oil money to monopolize all the instruments of power—army, police, and intelligence—and never have to introduce real transparency or power sharing... States focused on tapping their people have to focus on developing real institutions, property rights, rule of law, independent courts, modern education, foreign trade, foreign investments, freedom of thought, and scientific enquiry to get the most out of their men and women (2005, 460-1).

This describes a plutocracy common in Africa. Self-serving elites maintain a grip on power and wealth that is simplified by the concentrated, in-place, self-contained nature of mineral extraction between a single foreign or local entity with capital and expertise and a willing government that advances the elites' financial interests, and keeps the state in a dependent relationship with international institutions (Delancey 2007). An example is tolerating "piracy and bunkering, or the theft of oil out of pipelines, [which] are estimated to drain $1 billion to $4 billion annually from West African oil production. An estimated 25 percent of Cameroon's is stolen." (ICG 2005, 26) Worse is the kleptocracy, where elite outright steal national wealth. For example, the books of Angola's state oil company, Sonangol, are treated as virtual state secrets.

In 1998 more than a billion dollars was secured for exploration permits but "much of it disappeared off of the books" (Cutter 2008, 108). Natural resource wealth has also fueled violent conflict that so readily plagues the continent. The most notorious were blood diamonds smuggled out by warring factions and sold on the world market to finance war and insurgency. Africa's bloodiest civil war in the Democratic Republic of Congo, killing an estimated 3.8 million people, was funded through diamonds and its other resources (Gordon and Gordon 2007). The source of the natural wealth doesn't matter as much as how it is applied to achieve development, or misapplied to prevent it. Unfortunately most resources are squandered through lack of judicious governance and administration, meaning such natural wealth may be a detriment under the wrong circumstances.

For all of their promise, natural resources have many multi-faceted limitations in advancing development. Some limits are due to the inherent traits of natural resources which concentrate their wealth in only a few fortunate economies, and whose price, and therefore aid to development, fluctuates with an international market. The outside assistance needed to generate supply and demand has opened fund resource extraction to past colonial and alleged neocolonial relationships. Internal and external conflict may be exacerbated by fighting over control of natural resources, and ethnic divisions have also been factors in diminishing the returns. However, the most significant factor, and one over which Africans themselves hold the most control, is that of mal-governance and poor administration which divert the benefit of natural resource revenue from developing economic and human resources to ineffective schemes or outright corruption.

The proper administration of natural resources for the betterment of society is often an unrealized dream in Africa, but can assist with economic and human prosperity as states from Norway to Australia have accomplished, and of which Botswana is the best example in Africa. The key to such success is the same as in successful resource-poor states such as Japan, Switzerland, South Korea, Finland, and Taiwan—good governance that invests in its people. That is why measuring the social and economic measures are so important in understanding development. Good economic planning and developing people are also some of the best ways to invest in the future, by harnessing natural resources and people skills through diversifying the economy into higher order activities.

Industry

If Africans wish to attain the same levels of economic, social, and demographic development as did Europe, North America, and Japan, they could follow a similar path to advancement from primary to secondary economic activities. These regions showed that the economic development process' most important component is its people, in terms of numbers, literacy, health, and productivity. The people and demographic characteristics of a state are a second major component of the economic development process, and one that is particularly suitable for aiding development and building secondary economic activities by some African states. Secondary economic activities are manufacturing, construction, power production and other activities "that process, transform, and assemble raw materials into useful products [or] take manufactured goods and fabricate them into finished consumer products" (Rubenstein 2008, 294). Industry depends on the productivity of people, which is the labor value-added to a product beyond the cost of raw material and energy inputs (Rubenstein 2008).

The productivity of people depends on their literacy, skills, and health as enhanced by processes and capital inputs like tools, transportation, and communications. The dividends from value-added human intellect and fabrication using capital and technology have been earlier demonstrated in the higher returns from commercial agriculture over subsistence. People are key to both farming and industry, but in farming the population is relatively dispersed while in industry workers are concentrated—usually in cities or their surroundings—which results in economy of scale in production, concentration of support facilities like transportation and communication nodes, and allowance for more efficient consumption of products produced. Although mining and drilling of fund resources are considered primary economic activities, extraction does share many characteristics with industry such that they are sometimes analyzed together similar to the data used in Table 2.

The similarities between extraction and manufacturing are that both operate from point locations, involve higher level worker skills and technology, require expensive capital infrastructure investments and access to power, and offer higher economic returns. Because of the economic advantages that secondary activities provide, "one of the markers of underdevelopment today is the relative absence of modern manufacturing capability" (Clawson 2008, 24). In sub-Saharan Africa, industry has fared poorly, declining in relative world share since 1975 from 4.8 percent to 2.4 percent in 1990 (Clawson 2008). In 2006, according to United Nations Industrial Development Organization Director, General Kandeh Yumkella, sub-Saharan Africa's share of world industrial output stood at 1 percent, and half of that came from South Africa. In contrast, South Korea alone produces 3.4 percent of the world's industrial output (Deen 2006). Clearly, industry has played a much smaller role in Africa's economies than agriculture or resource extraction. Industry has remained stagnant in absolute terms and declined in relative terms over the past decades. If African societies wish to develop further, then industrialization is one path to follow, similar to developed states.

All African states have some light manufacturing tailored to domestic markets, which may range from a village blacksmith to a small local bottling plant. It is at the regional and international levels that African manufacturing remains paltry and uncompetitive. However, Africans possess some comparative advantages in order to develop themselves through industries in which native components are significant. Most major industrial areas in Africa are centered in urban areas near natural resources such as West Africa's petroleum fields, Southwest Africa's "ring of diamonds," South Africa's mineral rich Witwatersrand, copper in Zambia and the Democratic Republic of Congo, and the agricultural regions of Lake Victoria and central Ethiopia (Clawson 2008).

Dependence on primary goods is common in the early stages of industrialization because it builds upon existing economic specialization. For example, Ethiopia's small industrial sector is dependent upon agriculture to produce textiles from its cotton crop, and leather goods from its cattle herds (Cutter 2008; CIA 2008). Such agriculturally-based manufacturing accounts for 66 percent of Ethiopia's manufacturing base, 73 percent in Uganda, and 90 percent in Burundi (Clawson 2008). These efforts are only a small first step, however. Botswana, on the other hand, has been remarkably successful in using its main natural resource, diamonds, to attain one of the world's highest sustained economic growth rates. Stability and good governance are major contributors to this success, but they have also benefited from performing higher level activities, going beyond being the world's largest producer of crude diamonds (CIA 2008).

In order to gain the economic benefits of value-added human fabrication, the government insisted that its partner, the giant diamond company DeBeers, move its sorting operations from London and cutting, polishing, and marketing operations from India to Botswana (Cutter 2008). This lucrative arrangement has continued one of Africa's highest GDPs per capita–shared by a small population composed mostly of subsistence farmers.

South Africa, the continent's economic powerhouse, has an industrial base founded on natural resources and local requirements. However, a well developed infrastructure in communications, transportation and energy, a strong business services sector, and relative stability have developed within South Africa diverse industries producing automobiles, metalwork, machinery, textiles, iron and steel, and chemicals (CIA 2008). Yet despite these advantages, South Africa's manufacturing remains as stagnant as the rest in Africa (ADB 2001).

Mauritius's industry also started with a basic commodity, sugar, but the government aggressively diversified it to achieve a middle income economy. In the 1960s raw sugar accounted for 86 percent of export earnings because it is the island's only viable commercial crop. Since then Mauritius has expanded to processing molasses, and more recently to producing biofuel from sugar waste to generate 60 percent of the state's electricity. Mauritius has purposely grown beyond its natural resources to enter into the labor-intensive textile industry as a means to continue to advance its economy further. At its peak in 2004 such light manufacturing accounted for 21.4 percent of GDP, almost all for export (Cutter 2008). To become competitive internationally the government of Mauritius invested heavily in its human potential and physical infrastructure and is showing the benefits in its favorable development measurements including an equitable income distribution (CIA 2008). Industry based on using native natural resources is a basic stepping stone towards development, but because Mauritius is resource poor the state has purposefully enabled and harnessed its human resources.

Nearly all states in Africa have started down the industrialization path, but except for South Africa and Mauritius, few have gone far. The fundamentals of stability, good government planning, and proper investment again show their worth in development. However, even with some successes achieved, Africa's most advanced states face problems in continuing their development and maintaining their relatively high standards of living.

Table 2: Comparison of Industry and Services Employment and Production Indicators

State	Employ-ment In Industry (% total employ)	GDP from Industry (% of total)	Industrial exports	Employment In Services (% total employ)	GDP from Services (% of total)	Inter-national Tourists (000s)
Algeria	23	61	Petroleum products	63	30	866
Botswana	n/a	51	Textiles	n/a	47	843
Chad	8 (approx)	47	None	12 (approx)	31	44
Congo, Rep	n/a	57	Plywood	n/a	37	26
Ethiopia	8	13	Leather products	12	38	125
Ghana	15	25	Aluminum	29	38	373
Kenya	10 (approx)	17	Petroleum products	15 (approx)	59	990
Mauritius	30	25	Clothing, molasses	61	70	n/a
Nigeria	10	53	Petroleum products	20	29	813
Sierra Leone	n/a	2531	None	n/a	20	10
South Africa	26	27	Machinery	65	71	6,026
Sudan	7	36	Petroleum products	13	33	39
U.K.	18	24		81	75	24,900
U.S.	23	21		76	78	52,690

Note: data from 2007. Tourism data from 2000, except Botswana and South Africa which is 1999. Employment in industry, and GDP percent in industry include resource mining and drilling activities. (Central Intelligence Agency 2008; Tourism: Nevin 2003; U.S. and U.K. Tourism: World Tourism Organization 2001)

Despite the previous examples, Africa cannot be construed as an industrialized region. Even with a few bright examples, African economies must surmount daunting intrastate and interstate obstacles to grow their industrial bases to become competitive. Continuing to examine Mauritius' manufacturing illustrates some of the problems that African states face. The gains made by Mauritius in industrialization by harnessing its one natural asset—sugar, and its people's abilities in the textiles industry, were challenged by changes to international trade policy. In 2005, the European Union started to remove preferential trade agreements in sugar given to former colonial states (Mauritius was a British possession until 1968). This has severely strained sugar farming and its attendant industries, the island's most important employer and revenue source. To remain competitive, seven of eleven sugar processing plants closed, farming practices modernized, and alternate derivative products developed—strong government responses to adverse circumstances. A second blow also ended favorable textile import quotas by the United States and Europe, which had successfully stimulated industry in the world's poorest states, and in 2005 the changes closed hundreds of factories in Mauritius, at the time the world's second largest exporter of woolen knits (Cutter 2008).

Lesotho's burgeoning textile industry suffered the same fate in 2005. Under the U.S. African Growth and Opportunity Act (AGOA) passed in 2000, African development was promoted through increased trade and investment (Copson 2001). East Asian manufacturers took advantage of African states' cheap labor and reduced U.S. duties to invest $100 million in Lesotho, employing 50,000 people and producing 10.5 percent of its GDP. The end of preferential imports brought the near overnight collapse of this industry in Lesotho and other African states (Cutter 2008). Another hindrance to developing through international trade exists beyond trade barriers. Africa's young industries lack the fundamentals to gain entry into developed markets- the same quality, safety, marketing, and other problems that African agricultural produce also faces. International standards are higher and more ubiquitous than in decades past, and integrating into multilateral trading systems like the World Trade Organization (WTO) is more difficult (Deen 2006). Thus African industry needs to improve its production capacity, but its efforts are undercut by an inability to attract foreign capital and expertise, and by international trade regulations.

In many cases Africans and their governments have also undermined their own industrial development. Zimbabwe once boasted one of Africa's more diverse economies and modern industrial sectors. It successfully exported textiles, footwear, and agricultural machinery to regional markets. However, inept management, corruption, and a draconian one-party state polarized society and eviscerated an industrial success story (Clawson 208). Violence and social tension are perhaps the biggest causes of underdevelopment in Africa, since industry requires capital investment and investors demand stability to reap a return. Even after investments are made, stability is needed to operate, as the Democratic Republic of Congo shows with its long-running internal conflict that contributes to an industrial capacity producing at just 25 percent and an unemployment rate of 85 percent in 2005 (Cutter 2008).

Lack of investing in infrastructure is another chronic problem for industrialization. A $1.2 billion mega aluminum smelter was located in Mozambique to take advantage of cheap hydroelectric potential from the Zambezi River. However, the finished plant will consume four times Mozambique's average electricity production and requires major investment in additional dams and Mozambique's fledgling natural gas industry for more energy to keep it running. The project is stalled after its first phase until more power can be generated. Needed investment is arriving, however, from foreign investors impressed with the government's open economic regime and capitalist development which have made Mozambique one of the most dynamic economies in Africa (Cutter 2008).

Mozambique is benefiting from its government's policies, but many states do not, and poor governance and administration may be the second biggest cause for lack of development. An example is Ethiopia where private land ownership is illegal, hampering investment in industry such that only a small part of Ethiopia's economic production is by manufacturing (CIA 2008). Governments such as the ones in Nigeria or Cameroon also misallocate public funds undercutting important sectors like agriculture, by investing in the more glamorous extraction industry (Elu 2000). Sometimes these misallocations "stimulated rural-urban migration, yet there were insufficient jobs to absorb those who left the stateside" and were a cause for food shortages on the continent (DeLancey 2007, 115). Government imposed import substitution strategies to strive to build young native industries by protecting them in their local market from competition abroad. Inevitably, though, such policies produce inefficient, low-quality companies whose products are uncompetitive globally, and expensive for local consumers. African government efforts are better spent making their industries competitive through establishing "institutions for industrial standards, testing, expert support, quality assurance, training, technology information, research, and technical extension and assistance for investors, suppliers, subcontractors, and local African entrepreneurs" (Clawson 2008, 612).

Neoliberal trade policies, such as the "Washington Consensus," advocate an export-led development strategy which opens up African economies to world trade starting with African agricultural and extractive products. This might reverse Africa's declining share of world trade which now stands at only 1.5 percent (Gordon and Gordon 2007). In 2001, *Afrobarometer* cited several African states for their positive market reforms and democratization including Botswana, Ghana, Lesotho, Malawi, Mali, Namibia, South Africa, Tanzania, Uganda, and Zambia (*Afrobarometer* 2002). Should their efforts continue, these are the states that have positioned themselves for success through internal measures, adapting to the international market and using international support to lead African economies past old negative tendencies and into real development.

Services

A third part of an economy is its tertiary economic activities: its services. These complement and enhance the primary and secondary activities and add robustness to an economy through diversity and greater depth. As with the other two, tertiary activities rely on the economic development components of people, the natural environment, and culture. Whereas the success of primary activities was particularly sensitive to the natural environment, and secondary activities related to the quality of a population, tertiary activities are especially dependent on culture. Culture is the way that a society "organizes itself in terms of beliefs, values, customs and lifestyles [which] greatly influence both the direction and degree of development" (Clawson et al. 2008, 20).

When service activities are used to generate international revenue, the manner in which a culture embraces change and globalization is a key to success. Services are "any activity that fulfills a human want or need and returns money to those who provide it." There are three types of services with numerous sub-types that include: consumer services such as retail and wholesale, education, health, leisure and hospitality; business services such as financial, professional, transportation and communication; and public services like security and social services (Rubenstein 2008, 398-400). Like industry, the added-value of people's involvement and investment required for many tertiary activities give these higher order economic endeavors greater returns. The human-to-human aspect of services for international revenue puts a premium on the culture component of development in order to interact sufficiently with other societies, and embrace the constant fast-paced changes that globalization requires. Some examples are typical personal-societal obligation traits that could impact the success of international services like concept of time (Western economies are "monochromic," being more schedule driven than "polychronic" societies, as typically found in Africa), attitude towards uncertainty (Western economies are more accepting of uncertainty and risk than "uncertainty avoidance cultures"), and acceptance of authority (participation in Western economies is more flat and distributed than in "high power distance cultures") (Peace Corps n.d., 71-72, 104-107, 112-3, 118-9).

The service sector of most African economies is composed primarily of internal personal services ranging from retail vendors to primary schools to cell phone providers. At some level, services have existed throughout Africa's history alongside agriculture and basic industries. Tertiary activities in Africa can include high technology and support other parts of the economy at the same time. One prime example would be African universities engaging in Green Revolution research to find better adapted crops, and techniques to spur subsistence and commercial agriculture. Other examples of service support to African activities include banking and insurance to cover factories and mines, and public transportation and security to help bring crops to market. Although all African states have some services, the strongest and largest economies have broadened themselves to offer international services. Among several such activities in Africa, tourism and regional business services are two of the more important that will be presented here as examples. Even though only a small part of the overall economy, expanding global tertiary activities should be a goal for Africans, since these activities tend to use higher order human skills, are more lucrative, and are a catalyst to higher economic and human development. They have also been the best method of development for states like Singapore and Switzerland, which are resource-poor but invest heavily in the skills and well-being of their people.

One natural resource for which Africa is renowned, but isn't mined or drilled, is its inspiring landscape and abundant wildlife from the tropical rain forests to the vast grass savannas. In 2001 28.4 million international tourists visited these sights, generating $11.7 billion in much needed foreign income for Africa (Diecke 2003). Many states see tourism as vital in generating revenue for economic development. Tourism can be a boon to job creation, attract foreign expertise to develop local skills, balance intrastate development, and diversify an economy. With Africa being the destination choice for only 4.1 percent of international tourists worldwide, there is much growth potential in this sector (Diecke 2003). One Zambian businessman summed up the promise and challenges of tourism when he said, "Virtually Africa-wide, the tourism industry has been identified as the sector most likely to build national economies. The painful question is how to stimulate the political will, persuade governments and private sectors to fund tourism infrastructure...and, probably most importantly, for governments to inspire the confidence of foreign investors" (Nevin 2003, 56). Some African states have answered these questions and succeeded in attracting tourists, especially Kenya in the east; Mauritius and the Seychelles on the Indian Ocean; Morocco, Tunisia, and Egypt in the north, Cote d'Ivoire and Senegal in the west, and South Africa (Diecke 2003). Some of this success is a result of scenic natural resources and climates: which are advantageous but not equitably distributed elements of tourism. Another geographic advantage is close proximity to Europe which helped North Africa attract over a third of Africa's tourists (10.6 million) and receipts ($4.2 billion) in 2001 (Diecke 2003). A third important factor is stability. Quite simply, tourists are attracted to safe and secure areas for vacation, and investors look for macroeconomic stability to realize a return in infrastructure investments like lodging, transportation, and attractions.

Zimbabwe is a case in point. It slipped from 1.2 million visitors in 1999 to a few thousand in 2002 because of the political and economic problems which threaten violence in that state. The expectation of stability in the rest of southern Africa plays an important part in World Tourism Organization predictions that this region will become Africa's top tourist destination by 2020 with 36 million visitors, nearly quadruple the number it had in 2000 (Nevin 2003).

Tourism also tends to succeed in states where other foreign enterprises already exist with functioning investment ties, open channels of communication, and where foreign cultures are better understood (Britton 1998) — meaning established integration into the international community, or continuing dependence through neocolonialism, depending on one's perspective. Kenya is an example of these conditions where "pioneer facilities development was in place because Kenya had a vigorous expatriate community which sought to advance foreign commercial interests, including tourism." (Diecke 2003, 294)   Not coincidentally, East Africa was the third most visited African region with 5.9 million visitors in 2001, and is expected to grow proportionately through 2020 (Diecke 2003; Nevin 2003).   By establishing good economic fundamentals of a stable environment and global connections, Africa's tourism can greatly boost its development aspirations.

As with other endeavors, good governance and political will is also required to attain the stability and globalization needed to thrive in international tourism, but also to support human development in terms of health and education, legal rights for private enterprise and political freedoms, and to construct and maintain a basic physical infrastructure (Diecke 2003).   Such good governance also enhances other economic endeavors, but is particularly important to activities like tourism which have a strong international component to them. The Seychelles is a model for applying these criteria towards tourism.   It hosted 140,000 elite tourists in 2006 accounting for 70 percent of its foreign earnings and an impressive GDP per capita. Most African states have been unable to establish such criteria, and as a consequence have not built higher end activities like tourism. Establishing tourism in an environmentally sustainable way is another form of good governance and critically important to maintain the assets that tourists seek (Diecke 2003). Sustainability is also attained through building native human resources in order to develop quality services, and to encourage skills which could improve other economic sectors as well (Hodge 1999).

Even if all of these conditions are properly set, unexpected events such as terrorism may undercut any efforts, which is why diversity of activities in an economy is important. For example, Morocco registered decreases in its important tourism businesses after the attacks of September 2001, and even more after the U.S. invasion of Iraq in 2003 (Cutter 2008). In Tanzania tourism has dropped significantly following the Al -Qaeda attack on the US embassy in 1998 and with the subsequent rise in Islamist moralism (Cutter 2008). Although often seen as a main engine for development in Africa, the broad requirements for natural or cultural attractions, human development skills, cultural sensibilities and globalization, stability, and good governance have set a high bar for entry into tourist services. Much like mineral extraction and manufacturing, tourism can also disturb fragile balances in local societies, infrastructure, and the environment. However, those states that succeed in tourism experience a synergistic effect that improves other economic sectors. For these reasons, rather than being the engine of African development, tourism may reinforce the gulf between developing and the poorest states, and for most states, may simply be a mark of development rather than a way to reach it (Nevin 2003).

Often states sophisticated enough to establish a tertiary sector like international tourism also have the skills and resources to diversify into other higher service activities as well. Higher level services include the banking, insurance, brokering, and other activities commonly grouped under the financial sector of business services. A strong financial services sector is particularly prized in an economy because it is not only a lucrative sector in its own right, but one that can financially support and boost other economic activities from agriculture to services. In the weak financial markets often found in Africa, a strong indigenous financial sector can fill a void to become a regional hub, gaining foreign revenue and attracting international expertise for local companies and their workers. This, however, usually requires liberalizing the local economy and removing barriers. Although considered risky to open an economy to global competition, the advantages are a larger potential market, and the effort of compelling native businesses to sharpen their skills, broaden services and products, and lower costs to other businesses. Becoming a competitive regional financial hub also requires sophisticated communications, transportation, research, and managerial skills and infrastructure that bolster those and other sectors as well (Hodge 1999). Mauritius has deliberately expanded its economy beyond sugar, textiles, and tourism to embrace banking, communications, and information technology by creating cyber cities, tapping into the fiber-optic cable that runs from Europe to India's high tech corridor (Cutter 2008). In so doing it has become a regional financial hub, luring over 32,000 off-shore entities worth $1 billion to transact business in India, China, and Africa (CIA 2008). Mauritius also benefits from its predominately Indian culture to serve as liaison for businesses in India and the rest of the world. To bridge the shortage in needed skilled workers, Mauritius has invested heavily in education, extended the school day, and added technological subjects to its curriculum. A lack of qualified people remains its biggest obstacle to growth (Cutter 2008).

South Africa has built a well-regulated and sophisticated financial sector that attracts many foreign financial businesses to the region because its technology, infrastructure, and supervision meet competitive world standards (Hodge 1999). These attributes have grown South Africa's stock exchange to the 17th largest in the world. It now includes many foreign brokerages that control up to 40 percent of the market, but the bourse's overall size grew so much that few of the local traders lost revenue; thus it has been a win-win situation (CIA 2008; Hodge 1999). South Africa is the continent's leader in commercial loans, financial advisory services, foreign exchange, securities trading, and insurance: all of which make South Africa an important launching point into Africa for international business (Hodge 1999). In 2003, South Africa also had 38,000 people working in call centers, taking advantage of its communications infrastructure and human skills. Ghana, Senegal, Kenya, Morocco, and Madagascar have also started international call center operations, but among them have only 16,000 jobs (Gordon and Gordon 2007). Striving to become a financial hub requires liberalizing economic policies, investing in requisite infrastructure and people skills to take advantage of regional financial services.

Not all international financial dealings are by large transnational corporations, as just described. Because of Africa's unequal distribution of resources, wealth, and opportunities, many workers are migrant, sending remittances to their families at home Lesotho for instance has few resources, prompting many of its 50 percent unemployed to South Africa to work. Although declining, in 1996 remittances accounted for a third of the entire GDP of Lesotho (Cutter 2008). Cote d'Ivoir, Ghana, Nigeria, and overseas states like Spain, Great Britain, and France host many African workers who need to send money home. Kenya is the regional hub in East Africa for financial services, dealing in both large commercial and small micro-fund transfers (CIA 2008, Kenya; Sander 2003). Kenya's claim as the regional hub comes from its relative strength in regulation, and better coverage in terms of numbers of banks and population served. Despite its position as a regional economic power, Kenya does not reach global standards (Sander 2003). The small and informal nature of such exchanges makes tracking them difficult, but they remain major sources of income and part of Kenya's strength as a regional financial hub.

As desirable as financial and other services may be as part of an economy, the high cost of capital to develop the infrastructure and human skills needed to participate has severely limited or barred most African states from developing them (Hodge 1999). An ironic twist for African states is that international banking is mature enough to be used in a "reverse transfer of wealth" because African states must repay huge debts they incurred– $15 billion for interest alone in 2003 (Gordon and Gordon 2007, 402). International debt relief as pioneered by the British government at the G8 Gleneagles conference in 2005 started a welcome trend of debt reduction for 38 states, most of them African, based on demonstrated improved governance (McLaughlin 2005). These actions should help right financial systems, lower balance of payments, and divert debt payments into states' physical and human capital. Debt relief and rewarding good governance are welcome steps in reinforcing basic requirements for development: stability, government transparency, liberalized economies, and investment in human and physical capital. In banking, as in most of the other international services, Africans are woefully deficient—both a cause and an indicator of their underdeveloped status.

Summary of Africa's Economy

Although often described and conceived as a single entity, Africa's people and economies are no monolith. Africa presents a complex environment with many factors affecting its diverse parts. Africa boasts success stories, but also some of the most destitute people and conditions. Almost half of sub-Saharan African states averaged an economic growth rate of 5 percent or more in 2003, and over a third achieved this mark in 2006, with 16 states sustaining growth over 4 percent for a decade. Although sub-Saharan economies have grown by over 4.5 percent since 2000, the growth rate did not keep pace with the higher average of other underdeveloped states, but did outperform the world average and, most important for real gains, exceeded the population growth rate (ITF 2005; U.S. Department of State 2007). Despite recent relative success, Africa's 53 states still occupy 26 of the world's bottom 32 rankings in GDP PPP per capita (Malawi is last), 28 of the lowest 36 in literacy rates (Burkina Faso is last), 35 of the lowest 37 states in life expectancy (Zambia is last), and 34 of the worst 40 states in the HDI (Sierra Leone is last, but Liberia and Somalia did not report and may be in worse shape) (UNDP 2008).

What caused these differences? The problems bringing about such poverty are many, as discussed in the preceding sections, and are gathered here in the categories of geography, economics, diplomacy, politics, demographics, and culture. Geographic causes of poverty included selective distribution or lack of natural resources, adverse weather conditions, climate change, and poor proximity. Economic reasons are low human labor value-added in most African activities, low or fluctuating commodity prices, lack of investment in physical infrastructure and human capital, over-reliance on one primary economic product for foreign revenue, difficulty in meeting world standards in products and globalization requirements, dependence on one or a few international markets in which to sell goods, state domination of the economy, poor corporate administration and oversight, and import price shocks. Political problems include lack of stability or violence through frequent coups, civil wars, and cross border fighting, dominance of self-serving elite, inadequate citizen participation and representation, and poor or counter-productive government policies. Diplomatic challenges are little control in the international trading environment, crippling debt burdens, the role of foreign aid, and foreign states' adverse domestic policies. Cultural problems include internal ethnic divisions, gender and economic inequality, and colonial legacies. Demographic problems continue to include low literacy and education skills, low health and life expectancies, high rates of debilitating diseases, and high population growth rates. These lists of representative problems hindering African states' economic and human development are not fatal, and are not unique to Africa. However they seem to be chronic, and must be addressed to better develop the people and resources of this continent.

Other states around the world faced similar problems and were able to advance into the ranks of developed or developing states. They accomplished this by manipulating the three basic components of development: natural resource assets, human skills and abilities, and the cultural strengths and willingness to embrace change to meet the specific conditions faced by each state. To exploit these foundational components to development, successful developing states need to focus on: the tools of proper economic and environmental administration to enhance the fundamentals of macroeconomics; good political governance that enables the energies and resources of an entire population; economic diversification and higher economic activities by investing sufficiently in human abilities and common infrastructure; and revenue to finance these improvements through attaining surpluses to trade on the world market or obtain foreign investment or aid to power the development process. Trade liberalization is also useful in setting the conditions for African development, but a UN economic report in 2004 argued that that would be insufficient to lift Africa out of poverty or boost growth on its own (Gordon and Gordon 2007). To achieve these goals in Africa, the United States and others have assisted African states with a raft of economic programs like the African Seeds for Hope Act, Millennium Challenge Account, the African Growth and Opportunity Act, and debt relief. Africans have developed their own strategy to deal with these problems and employ these solutions through the African Union's New Economic Policy for African Development (NEPAD). This is a bootstrap strategy that stresses peace and security, good governance, regional cooperation, and building of human capacities. Not surprisingly, its priorities are in agriculture, human development, physical infrastructure, diversification, protecting the environment, and cooperation (DeLancey 2007). The combined efforts of Africans and the developed states are the best hope for lifting the world's poorest region into position to better contribute to global — and its own — prosperity.

Lieutenant Colonel (Retired) Clarence J. Bouchat flew fighters as an Air Force officer before teaching Theater Strategy at the U.S. Army War College. He has taught at the U.S. Air Force Academy and published articles on regional and political geography.

*He currently teaches World Regional Geography at Harrisburg
Area Community College in Pennsylvania.*

References

Africa Development Bank. 2001. *Africa Development Report 2001.*
    Oxford: Oxford University Press.

Afrobarometer. 2002. Key Findings About Public Opinion
    in Africa. http://www.afrobarometer.org/papers/
    AfrobriefNo1.pdf, (accessed June 5, 2008).

Bread for the World. 1999. Africa Seeds of Hope—What Will
    It Do? http://www.africa.upenn.edu/Urgent_Action/
    apic_2599.html. (accessed June 5, 2008).

Britton, S. G. 1998. The Political Economy of Tourism in the Third
    World. *Annals of Tourism Research* 9, no. 3: 331-58.

Central Intelligence Agency. 2008. *The 2008 World Factbook.*
    https://www.cia.gov/library/publications/the-world-
    factbook/index.html. (accessed March 28, 2008).

Clawson, David L., Douglas L. Johnson, Viola Haarman, and
    Merrill L. Johnson. 2007. *World Regional Geography.* Upper
    Saddle River, NJ: Peason-Prentice Hall.

Collier, Paul. 2006. Africa: Geography and Growth. http://
    eitransparency.org/UserFiles/File/collier_africa_
    geography_growth.pdf. (accessed June 2008).

Copson, Raymond W. 2001. Africa Backgrounder: History, U.S.
    Policy, Principle Congressional Actions. Washington DC:
    Library of Congress Congressional Research Service. January
    5.

Crupi, Francis V. 2005-2006. Why the United States Should
    Robustly Support Pan-African Organizations. *Parameters* 35,
    no. 4 (Winter): 106-123.

Cutter, Charles H. 2007. *Africa 2007.* Harpers Ferry, WV: Stryker-
    Post Publications.

Deen, Thalif. 2006. Third World Industrial Output Mushrooms. *Asia Times Online*, November 9. http://www.atimes.com/ atimes/Global_Economy/HK09Dj01.html. (accessed June, 11 2008).

DeLancey, Virginia. 2007. The Economies of Africa. In *Understanding Contemporary Africa*, ed. April A. Gordon and Donald L. Gordon. Boulder, CO: Lynne Reinner Publishers.

Dieke, Peter U. C. 2003. Tourism in Africa's Economic Development: Policy Implications. *Management Decision* 41, no. 3: 289-86.

Elu, Juliet. 2000. Human Development in sub-Sahara Africa: Analysis and Prospects for the Future. *Journal of Third World Studies* (Fall). http://findarticles.com/p/articles/ mi_qa3821/is_200010/ai_n8927632/pg_2. (accessed June 5, 2008).

Friedman, Thomas L. 2005. *The World is Flat: A Brief History of the Twenty-first Century*. Basking Ridge, NJ: Farrar, Straus and Giroux.

Garraty, John A., and Peter Gay. 1972. *The Columbia History of the World*. New York: Harper and Row Publishers.

Getis, Arthur, Judith Getis, and Jerome D. Fellmann. 2006. *Introduction to Geography*. New York: McGraw Hill.

Gordon, April A. and Donald L. Gordon. 2007. Trends and Prospects. In *Understanding Contemporary Africa*, ed. April A. Gordon and Donald L. Gordon. Boulder, CO: Lynne Reinner Publishers.

Hodge, James. 1999. Examining the Cost of Services Protection in a Developing State: The Case of South Africa. http://www. tips.org.za/files/280.pdf (accessed June 17, 2008).

International Crisis Group. 2005. Islamist Terrorism in the Sahel: Fact or Fiction? Africa Report No. 92, March 31. http:// merln.ndu.edu/archive/icg/islamistterrorisminthesahel.pdf (accessed June 10, 2008).

Independent Task Force Report. 2005. *More Than Humanitarianism: A Strategic U.S. Approach Toward Africa.* New York: Council of Foreign Relations, Ind.

Magnarella, Paul. 2002. Review of When Victims Become Killers, by Mahmood Mamdani. *Human Rights and Human Welfare* 2, no. 1 (Winter): 25-34.

McLaughlin, Abraham. 2005. What Debt Relief Means for Africa. *Christian Science Monitor.* June 13. http://www.csmonitor. com/2005/0613/p01s02-woaf.html. (accessed June 21, 2008).

Mistry, Percy S. 2005. Commentary: Reasons for sub-Saharan Africa's Development Deficit that the Commission for Africa did not Consider. *African Affairs* 104, no. 417 (October): 665-678.

Nevin, Tom. 2003. African Tourism Review. *African Business,* no. 284 (February):54-60.

Peace Corps Information Collection and Exchange. n.d. *Culture Matters: The Peace Corps Cross-Cultural Workbook.* Washington DC: Peace Corps.

Rubenstein, James M. 2008. *An Introduction to Human Geography.* Upper Saddle River, NJ: Peason Prentice Hall.

Sander, Cerstin. 2003. Passing the Buck in East Africa: The Money Transfer Practice and Potential for Services in Kenya, Tanzania, and Uganda. http://www.microfinancegateway. org/files/22081_ST_Money_Transfer_in_East_Africa_ Sander.pdf. (accessed June 17, 2008).

United Nations Development Programme (UNDP). n.d.. Human Development Reports. http://hdr.undp.org/en/statistics/. (accessed May 15, 2008).

United States Department of State. 2007. *2007 Comprehensive Report on U.S. Trade and Investment Policy Toward Sub-Saharan Africa and Implementation of the African Growth and Opportunity Act.* Office of the United States Trade Representative. May: 21-36.

United States Geologic Survey (USGS). 2006. *Mineral Commodity Summaries 2006.* Washington DC: U.S. Department of the Interior.

World Tourism Organization. 2001. *Millennium Tourism Boom in 2000.* Madrid, Spain: WTO. January 30.

Minerals and Human Security in Tanzania

Diana B. Putman

Key Points

- Human security is a new paradigm that expands the notion of national security beyond the state to the individual.

- Appreciating how Tanzanians may view the mineral sector today requires an understanding of the state's post-colonial history and the important legacy left by its first President, Julius K. Nyerere.

- Conflict over minerals does not have to be the norm on the continent of Africa if solid governance structures are in place.

"Human security" refers to an emerging paradigm for understanding global vulnerabilities. The proponents of the concept of human security challenge the traditional notion of national security by arguing that the proper referent for security should be the individual rather than the state. Human security holds that a people-centered view of security is necessary for national, regional and global stability. Blessed with abundant resources (minerals, fertile agricultural and pasture land, wildlife, forests), yet remarkably stable since independence, Tanzania is an anomaly in a region where conflict rages over either a scarcity or surfeit of these same resources (Lind and Sturman 2002).[1]

---

1 Jeremy Lind and Kathryn Sturman, eds. *Scarcity and Surfeit: The Ecology of Africa's Conflicts* (Pretoria: The Institute for Security Studies, 2002). Based on case studies in Rwanda (land), Burundi (coffee), the Democratic Republic of Congo [DRC] (minerals), Sudan (oil), Ethiopia (Nile waters) and Somalia (pastures), the contributors to *Scarcity and Surfeit: The Ecology of Africa's Conflicts* describe why environmental security is a key issue on the continent. Joao Porto, in turn, stresses that sophisticated analysis is needed to understand the complex relationship between ecology and conflict in sub-Saharan Africa that involves multiple internal and external actors and diverging and conflicting interests. Both grievance and greed are usually motivators, although the latter is usually masked by other rationales that play better to international audiences. Porto asserts "access to and

By reviewing Tanzania's post-colonial political history and the legacy of its first President, Julius K. Nyerere, this chapter explores how successive governments in Tanzania have strategically managed its mineral resources, and how this history has lead Tanzania toward the adoption of a broad human security approach. A brief history of the gold mining sector is provided from colonial days to the present. This is followed by a political and economic overview of Tanzania in which President Nyerere's vision of development has influenced successive decisions about the sector. The concept of human security resonates in Tanzania because of Nyerere's legacy and is central to the current debate about the need to renegotiate gold mining contracts. Looking at gold mining through a human security lens provides insights into the next steps the government may take in interacting with international mining companies.

Gold Mining

From prior to World War II until the mid-1960s, gold mining and export was a major industry and principal earner of foreign exchange. Then as deposits were exhausted, mine closings resulted in a substantial drop in output. Some prospecting was carried out in the early 1970s, but in 1976, the state's reported production was negligible. Artisanal miners continued to operate, however, smuggling gold out of the state, resulting in significant foreign exchange losses. When thousands of miners moved in from neighboring states, the government banned all private prospecting in gold fields in 1977 (Kaplan 1978). Artisanal mining remained the norm for the next twenty years and the government exerted some effort to benefit from it.

The Government of Tanzania (GOT) slowly began liberalizing the economy in the early 1990s. With World Bank

---

control of valuable natural resources including minerals, oil, timber, productive pastures and farming land, have been crucial factors in the occurrence of violent conflicts across the continent."

encouragement, they GOT invited international mining companies to prospect and new lucrative sources of gold were discovered. The first mining contracts were signed in 1994 and fell under the Mining Act of 1979. Later contracts fell under the Mineral Policy of Tanzania of 1977 and the Mining Act of 1998 (Ministry of Energy and Minerals 2006). Each year since 1998, a new gold mine has been opened in Tanzania. The mines are owned by Resolute Ltd.; Ashanti Goldfields in joint venture with AngloGold; Barrick Gold Corp; Placer Dome Inc.; and Pangea Goldfields Inc. in joint venture with Miniere du Nord (Gold Mining in Tanzania 2008). Astonishingly, six large-scale gold mines have come into production in Tanzania within the same number of years.

In 2003, Tanzania became the continent's third-largest gold-producing state after South Africa and Ghana. Annual production of gold has increased from around 43.2 Ton in 2002 to about 52.2 Ton in 2005. Tanzania's estimated gold reserves have been calculated at about 1,400 Ton (United States Geological Survey 2005). In 2003, Tanzania reported a 20 percent increase in gold exports to $504 million from $414 million. This accounted for more than 62 percent of total export revenues, compared with 49 percent in 2002 (Gold Mining in Tanzania 2008). Other sources note that gold represented 90 percent of mineral exports, but mining accounted for only 3.8 percent of Tanzania's GDP in 2006 (Revenue Watch Institute 2008). This limited contribution of mining to the GDP is noteworthy, and will be discussed later.

Social, Political, and Economic Background

On 9 December 1961, Tanganyika, on the mainland, became independent from a U.K.-administered UN Trusteeship. Independence for Zanzibar (composed of two islands: Ugunja and Pemba) followed in 1963. In 1964, after a bloody revolution on Zanzibar, where the majority African population overthrew the minority Arab and Asian political rulers, Zanzibar and Tanganyika joined to form the United Republic of Tanzania. The population of mainland Tanzania consists of over 120 tribes mainly of Bantu origin, only a few having a population of over one million in a state with an overall population of about 37 million (Cotter 2007). The population is fairly evenly divided between Christians and Muslims, with some animists. Prior to independence, until his retirement from the presidency in 1985, the political landscape was dominated by Julius K. Nyerere (1922-1999) or *"Mwalimu"* (Swahili for teacher), as he was commonly called.

Over twenty years have passed since *Mwalimu* stepped down but the influence of his fundamental philosophy of a socially just and equitable society continues. His handpicked successor, President Ali Hassan Mwinyi (1985-1995), began the process of economic and political liberalization. 1995 heralded the first multi-party elections with Benjamin Mkapa winning the presidency then, and again in 2000, with a greater margin. In 2005, Jakaya Mrisho Kikwete, a well liked and charming ex-military man who had been groomed by Nyerere, became President (Associates in Rural Development 1999).

The economy is still dominated by subsistence agriculture, providing more than 44 percent of the GDP and 80 percent of the employment. The majority of export earnings are generated by cash crops including coffee, tea, cotton, cashews, sisal, cloves and pyrethrum, but the quality of the crops and the marketing structures remain seriously problematic. Tanzania's industrial sector is one of the smallest in Africa at less than 10 percent of the GDP. This sector is dominated (90 percent) by small and medium enterprises specializing in food processing, production of textiles and apparel, leather tanning and plastics. A few larger factories manufacture cement, rolled steel, corrugated iron, aluminum sheets, cigarettes, beer and other beverages, raw materials, import substitutes and processed agricultural products (United States Department of State 2008).

The GDP in 2006 was almost $12 billion. Overall real GDP growth has averaged about 6 percent a year for the last seven years, higher than the average of less than 5 percent for most of the 1990s. Most Tanzanians, though, are mired in poverty with a per capita income of $319 in 2006 (U.S. Dept. of State 2008). Despite the lack of economic progress for the majority of the citizens, Tanzanians have not revolted against the ruling party, in part because other political parties have not organized effectively. There also seems to be a general acceptance by Tanzanians that movement away from one party rule should be gradual to avoid the violence that has plagued neighboring states (ARD 2003).

Nyerere's Social, Political, and Economic Vision

Most Western observers have severely criticized President Nyerere's economic policies and downplayed his other accomplishments. Ignoring his economic shortcomings, Africans across the continent refer to Nyerere as one of the "Fathers of Africa" for his role as one of the original nationalists fighting for independence from colonialism, and for his contributions to the liberation of southern African states (Johnson 2000). Some dismiss the importance of Nyerere's moral and material support for liberation fighters (Johnson 2000). Tanzanians and other Africans passionately mourned his death in 1999 (Pratt 2002).[2] In addition to being called *Mwalimu*, Nyerere is called "*Baba wa Taifa*" (Father of the Nation) and many Tanzanians continue to esteem his political vision while deploring how it was operationalized in the early decades.

President Nyerere's fundamental ideas, taken from his 1968 book *Uhuru na Ujamaa: Freedom and Socialism*, remain important in the political and economic culture of modern Tanzania (1968). A review of his policies during

---

2 Cranford Pratt, "The Ethical Foundation of Julius Nyerere's Legacy" in *The Legacies of Julius Nyerere: Influences on Development Discourse and Practice in Africa*, ed. David A. McDonald and Eunice Nyeri Sahle (Trenton: Africa World Press 2002), 39-52. Also personal observations by the author and Adam Messer in October 1999 when President Nyerere died.

the 1960s though 1980s illuminates current discussions of the mining sector in Tanzania. Furthermore, Nyerere's promotion of a national identity and his successful effort to keep the Tanzanian People's Defense Forces completely under civilian control (Lupogo 2008) may be the biggest reason that control of mineral resources in Tanzania has not caused the level of strife seen elsewhere.

Uhuru na Ujamaa, translated as "Freedom and Socialism" in the 1968 book title, actually means something else. While *Uhuru* is translated correctly, *Ujamaa* in Kiswahili refers to "family-hood" or "togetherness." Notice the difference: Nyerere's original conception of socialism was a truly African concept with little in common with Marxism or Leninism. He deplored the deification of these two theories as well as the uncritical adoption of socialist ideas and practices. Nevertheless, the Arusha Declaration in 1967 resulted in the adoption of many mainstream socialist practices.

Despite implementation of misguided economic ideas during his twenty-five year presidency, Nyerere's original vision focused primarily on the equality of all humans.[3] Here he stood apart from most other African "liberationists" by insisting that discrimination was inappropriate. He applauded the sense of communal responsibility that existed in traditional Africa and wanted to find economic and political paths to accommodate this. He wanted to follow a socialist model for he feared that any other route would focus only on financial rewards, "money for money's sake," and exacerbate the differences between the "haves and have-nots." He called for economic self-reliance. He understood that Tanzania was a poor state that needed to leapfrog into the modern world, but he wanted to accomplish this in his own way. Nyerere's frequent exhortations to his statement on this theme led William

---

3 Nyerere, 1-34. The introduction provides a very coherent overview. Mark Curtis and Tundu Lissu, "A Golden Opportunity: How Tanzania is Failing to Benefit from Gold Mining." (Dar es Salaam: Colour Printing, 2008), 4-5. The foreword to this document illustrates this very clearly.

Edgett Smith (1971) to title his biography *We Must Run While They Walk: A Portrait of Africa's Julius Nyerere*.

From the beginning, Nyerere's vision of African or Tanzanian socialism met with a mixed reception. Some in the West decried a socialist approach; others, mainly from the Scandinavian states, applauded his wisdom. The People's Republic of China provided substantial aid for infrastructure, including a railroad and small-scale irrigation works. Robert McNamara, president of the World Bank, willingly provided loans for Nyerere's experiment for an extended time period.[4] Despite American dismay over Nyerere's policies, the United States supported Tanzania during the Cold War to keep the state within its sphere of influence.

Reviewing *Uhuru na Ujamaa* after thirty-five years provides fascinating insights on Nyerere's successes and failures as a leader.[5] It is easy to be seduced by Nyerere's persuasive language and to agree with the deeply ethical and humanist thrust of his vision. One awakens with a jolt to the reality of the application. Scholars, outside observers, and Tanzanians provide contradictory reviews of how this vision played out.

Various assessments of Nyerere's Tanzania reveal the abysmal failure of many of his economic and political policies. The exception is the success of his effort to forge a

---

4 Michael Lofchie, Chair of the Political Science Department at UCLA and long-time scholar of Tanzania, suggested that Nyerere's brilliant, gifted and very magnetic personality might have blinded many people to the flaws in the application of his vision in Tanzania. Interview by author, October 10, 2007.

5 My family first lived in Tanzania from 1972-1975. Even this soon after Independence, Nyerere's economic policies were turning out to be disastrous. There was widespread starvation because the push toward collective villages was already wrecking havoc with agricultural production. Nyerere's thrust toward nationalization of successful private enterprises was beginning to scare people into voluntary exile, and those who did not choose that path soon found themselves in jail. At the same time, the switch from English to Kiswahili as the national language threw the educational system into disarray. I was sent to Switzerland to complete my last two years of secondary school because there were insufficient age appropriate textbooks available in Kiswahili at that time. When I informed my family in late 1993 that I was considering an assignment in Tanzania, I was read the "riot act" for wanting to go to such a "basket-case" state.

national identity. Economically, socialism was a disaster for Tanzania. When farmers refused to adopt Nyerere's ideas of collectivization as the way to improve efficiencies, he forcibly relocated some six to eleven million people (between one-fourth to one-third of the population) within less than a decade through a process known as *ujamaa* or "villagization."[6] Anyone could be accused of economic sabotage by Nyerere's government, including indigenous Tanzanians.

Despite the rhetoric of racial and political tolerance, foreign-owned enterprises—white and Asian owners of productive farms and factories—who declined to move to socialist modes of production, bore the brunt of his policies when Nyerere decided to nationalize their enterprises.[7] A critic would conclude that these policies illustrate a lack of concern for human security, but it was the application of *Uhuru na Ujamaa* that was problematic, not the very humanistic, egalitarian philosophy behind all of Nyerere's undertakings.

Nationalization occurred despite the clear lack of governmental capacity to manage these assets more productively. For instance, the Williamson Diamond Mine (named after its discoverer) in Mwadui was the first significant diamond mine outside of South Africa. It has been operating continuously since 1940. Post World War II, Williamson piloted many technological innovations. In 1958 he sold the mine to a joint partnership of DeBeers and the pre-independence Tanganyika government. By 1971, Nyerere nationalized it. Mine performance deteriorated significantly under government management.

In 1994, the GOT invited DeBeers back and they purchased 75 percent of the mine. Since then it has returned

---

6 This interpretation of *Ujamaa* is quite different than the original "familyhood" discussed earlier and much more like mainstream Chinese communism
7 Interestingly, by the 1990s, if one was an Asian and had been jailed for 1-3 years during this era for "economic sabotage" it was worn as a mark of pride for it proved that one had been successful early on. Those entrepreneurs who had staying power remained and rebuilt their fortunes one, two or three times recognizing their critical role in the economy and benefiting (sometimes unduly) from their longevity and understanding of the system.

to modern standards of production excellence (Williamson Diamond Mine 2008). Additionally, at a time when achieving economic growth required zero tolerance for mistaken policies, Nyerere's government adopted a series of macroeconomic judgments that failed the people and repelled most remaining Western allies (Helleiner 2002). As he was stepping down, Nyerere lamented that despite his early successes in providing universal education and health, per capita income had dropped from $280 to $140 (Johnson 2000). It took another twenty years to recover.

Uhuru na Ujamaa praised the rule of law and the importance of grassroots democracy. But these fared no better under Nyerere. When his grand social project did not seem to be moving fast enough, and when local institutions, which he initially extolled, did not implement the central government's plans, they were abolished. Many trade unions and local cooperatives were shut down and some of their leaders jailed (Johnson 2000). Nyerere's failure was his fear of alternative power structures that did not blindly follow his orders. He knew where he wanted to go with his vision and he brooked no opposition. The jails were full of political and economic sabotage prisoners of all races. Civil society, as understood by Westerners, was effectively eliminated.

In contrast, some other early controversial policies of Nyerere's have led to a sense of national identity unparalleled elsewhere in Africa and still underappreciated by the West.[8] Some scholars suggest these are of no consequence because there were no longstanding conflicts among the more than120 small tribes in Tanzania, but I disagree (Johnson 2000). Tanzanians who experienced these policies, although differing in age, concur on their importance.[9] These key

---

8 The author asserts this based on personal observations and on many fascinating conversations with Tanzanians and other East and Central Africans between 1994-2005. One can claim that this does not hold true for Zanzibaris who continue to feel they are separate and different from Mainlanders. Certainly some of the actions taken by the Zanzibari government such as joining the Organization of Arab States unilaterally without consultation with mainland politicians suggests this.
9 The author frequently heard these types of assertions during her most recent

policies were: 1) adoption of Swahili as a national language; 2) movement of secondary school students to other regions (the equivalent of the American busing during the civil rights era); and 3) mandatory national service. Together, they help to explain the absence of conflict and the emphasis on human security in Tanzania today. Everyone, regardless of tribe, would thereby participate in national development.

Gold Mining and Human Security in the 21st Century

Once Nyerere retired from public office, President Mwinyi slowly began liberalizing the economy. The pace accelerated under President Mkapa. Based on advice from the World Bank in the early 1990s, very generous agreements were negotiated with international mining companies to exploit Tanzania's minerals and metals, including tanzanites, diamonds and gold. At the time, Tanzania's economy was floundering with low yields from agriculture, insufficient revenues from tourism and huge external debts racked up in previous decades. It was thought that the combination of royalties and taxes, and employment opportunities from mining would be able to propel the state forward.

By the late 1990s, however, a local non-governmental organization, the Lawyers Environmental Action Team (LEAT), had begun investigating issues in the gold mining sector and alerting the public and the government that all was not well (LEAT 2008).[10] Initially LEAT's critiques were brushed off. When LEAT members alleged human rights

---

eleven year stay in East Africa, five of it in Tanzania but many of her informants were in their 50s and 60s. To ascertain whether younger Tanzanians would agree, a prominent environmental lawyer, Rugemeleza Nshala (age 41), was queried. He was in full agreement with his elders on how important national service, being sent to secondary school outside of his region and having Kiswahili as the national language were to this sense of Tanzanian identity. Interview by author, October 10, 2007.

10 LEAT is a public interest environmental and legal advocacy organization established in 1994 by University of Dar es Salaam graduates. They were one of the earliest successful NGOs in criticizing the government on various issues and have fared remarkably well. This demonstrates the gradual opening of political space for civil society in Tanzania over the last two decades. Information and documents published by LEAT are accessed April 21, 2008. (www.leat.or.tz/)

abuses of mine workers, the NGO's offices were searched by the police; one lawyer was briefly detained, and two were charged with sedition for claiming that a foreign-owned mine had buried miners alive while excavating.

LEAT's and the media's concerns did not go unnoticed by the GOT which decided to investigate the gold mining sector (Ministry of Energy and Minerals 2006). The GOT report concluded that "the mineral sector has not been contributing adequately to the socioeconomic development of the state...no one has started paying corporate tax to date...they claim to have accumulated heavy losses, despite a steady increase in the world market gold price since 2002. Although there has been an impressive increase in export values, the same has not been reflected in the actual export earnings of the state (Ministry of Energy and Minerals 2006). This report made several recommendations for reform. The most significant are: 1) removal of the 15 percent additional capital allowance since it had no legal basis and was one of the prime reasons for non-payment of corporate tax by mining companies; and 2) that new mining investments should fall under the Income Tax Act of 2004 in order to provide more revenue to the government.

Further, the report called for the Tanzania Revenue Authority (TRA) to be strengthened in order to respond when companies fail to file properly and to collect back taxes owed. As a member of the East African Community, Tanzania abides by a common external tariff, which did not apply at the time of the signing of the early contracts. This must be considered when contracts are renewed along with a host of other tax provisions overly favorable to the mining companies.

Based on their own report and calls from LEAT and the public on the need to re-examine the mining sector, the GOT decided that public debate would be encouraged and no mining contracts would be extended or new ones signed until a decision was made on appropriate new terms. Nonetheless, the Minister of Minerals and Energy secretly signed some contracts. This resulted in a public outcry, and, along with eight other ministers accused of corruption, he was removed in January 2008, just prior to Tanzania's signing of a compact agreement with the U.S. Millennium Challenge Corporation (Africa Confidential 2008; MCC 2008). Furthermore, in November 2007 the GOT established a committee of individuals with excellent credentials to review all mining contracts (Africa Mining Intelligence 2008).

In March 2008, a report published jointly by the Christian Council of Tanzania, the National Council of Muslims in Tanzania and the Tanzania Episcopal Conference, and funded by Norwegian Church Aid and Christian Aid, called for major reforms. The foreword states, "We have a role as leaders in Tanzanian society. ... We need a mining industry that puts life as the foremost point of reference against the economic gains...We certainly found that mining for profit is not enough; we need mining for life" (Curtis and Lissu 2008). Contrast this with the history of violence on the continent associated with mining and minerals resource extraction (Lind and Sturman 2002). This report particularly took issue with the dislocation of local communities and the loss of livelihoods for about 400,000 artisanal miners when the international companies became fully operational (Curtis and Lissu 2008).

One scholar-activist suggests even more radical steps than either the GOT or religious leaders. Rugemeleza Nshala proposes some interesting research avenues and legal steps that could be taken to gain greater revenue from mining for the people of Tanzania (Nshala n.d.).[11] Nshala argues that, with the exception of Botswana, which renegotiated early unfavorable contracts with DeBeers and others, no African states have sufficiently benefited from their mineral endowments. He objects to the insignificant contributions of gold mining to the GDP compared to export values. He concurs with the GOT's concern that almost all profits are

11 Nshala, Rugemeleza, The Extractive Industry in Africa: A Hard Look at Regulatory and Tax Law Reforms introduced by the World Bank in Sub-Saharan African States. (Cambridge, MA.: Harvard University n.d.). Nshala was a founding member of LEAT, its Executive Director for many years, and one of the lawyers charged with sedition.

expatriated, while few new business opportunities have been generated on the local economy.

According to Nshala, in common with the constitutions of many other African states, Tanzania claims permanent sovereignty over natural resources with the government acting on behalf of the people (United Republic of Tanzania 1997). Nshala plans to explore the constitutional and legal obligations of the GOT for the appropriate management of natural resources to benefit the citizens of Tanzania and to examine new international literature challenging the sanctity of contracts to determine possible applicability to Tanzania.

Elsewhere in Africa, metals and minerals are used to fuel conflicts.[12] That religious leaders, activists, and the GOT have all identified the need for the citizens of Tanzania to benefit more from its precious resources illustrates a commitment to human security not seen many other places on the continent. One can argue as well that Nyerere's vision of a politically just and socially equitable society remains.

The Future of Gold Mining in Tanzania

Gold prices at the end of 2008 are at a near all-time high of $833.67 (as of December 15, 2008). According to Curtis and Lissu (2000), Tanzania has exported gold worth more than $2.5 billion over the last five years with the government receiving on average only $21.7 million per year in royalties (3 percent) and taxes on these exports, or 10 percent of the total value exported. They also note that over one third of the population live in dire poverty—less than $1 per day—and that Tanzania is one of the ten poorest states in the world. Curtis and Lissu and the GOT provide detailed analyses comparing revenue streams to the government if royalties were increased and the tax code was modified. The United States Geological Service notes that the cash cost of gold was $384 in 2005 from the open pit Buhemba Mine, highest of all costs they cite (USGS 2005). More and

---

12 For instance in Liberia, Sierra Leone, Democratic Republic of Congo.

more Tanzanians are beginning to notice that, at current prices, the state is not benefiting sufficiently, especially when known gold reserves will run out within the next ten to twenty years.

A confluence of interests — the GOT, religious leaders, environmental activists, the media, the public and even international NGOs and donors — are beginning to question whether the excess profits international mining companies are making from Tanzania's resources at current gold prices are appropriate. Nshala is blunt: "It is clear that the World Bank-inspired regulatory and tax regimes, if left as they are, will bleed the African states' economies to death and lead to serious economic, social and political unrest" (Nshala n.d.). That one of the state's top activists is suggesting there may be internationally legal ways to challenge the agreements in place indicates a sophisticated understanding of non-violent confrontation rarely seen on the continent.

Tanzania is unlikely to descend rapidly into violence and chaos for its leaders continue to practice Nyerere's concept of humanism or "humane governance" (Helleiner 2002). The GOT's report recommended changes to mining contracts to derive greater revenues on behalf of Tanzanian citizens, indicating that, at a strategic level, the government is focused on human security as an important element of national security. Unlike his predecessors, as evidence mounted of high-level corruption–some related to natural resource extraction, President Kikwete took action, firing about one-third of his cabinet. This shows some responsiveness, but only if mining contracts are cancelled or amended will good governance and real concern about human security be demonstrated.

Tanzania has charted a unique sociopolitical and economic path since independence. From the beginning, President Nyerere wished to ensure that his citizens benefited equitably from the resources in the state, demonstrating an early understanding of the concept of human security. Unfortunately, many of his policies only reinforced poverty. Subsequent leaders have tried to maintain his vision while embarking on economic reforms to increase wealth generation. This has resulted in mining contracts that bring too few benefits to the state. Hopefully, the GOT and the international mining companies can come to a compromise, as occurred in Botswana, with a more equitable sharing of the mining profits. A Maasai proverb talks about progress taking a zigzagged path. It would be unfortunate if the GOT felt pushed to adopt Nyerere's extreme measure of nationalization in order to secure greater benefits for its citizens in the interest of human security.

Dr. Diana B. Putman is a career Foreign Service Office with the United States Agency for International Development, currently on detail to the United States Africa Command. She has served in Asia and the Middle East, and has spent over twenty years doing research and development work in Africa. Dr. Putman holds graduate degrees in Anthropology and Strategic Studies.

References

Africa Confidential. 2008. February 15.

Africa Mining Intelligence. Who will Review Mining Contracts? http://www.lexisnexis.com/us/Inacademic/frame.do?tokenKey=rsh20.706615.979472871 (accessed April 20, 2008).

Associates in Rural Development. 1999. *Tanzania Flashpoints Study*. Washington, DC: ARD.

Associates in Rural Development. 2003. Democracy and Governance Assessment: Transitions from the Single-Party State. Burlington, VT: ARD.

Cutter, Charles H. 2007. *Africa 2007*. Harpers Ferry, WV: Stryker-Post Publications.

Curtis, Mark and Tundu Lissu. 2008. *A Golden Opportunity: How Tanzania is failing to Benefit from Gold Mining.* Dar es Salaam, Tanzania: Colour Printing.

Gold Mining in Tanzania. http://www.tanzaniagold.com/index. html (accessed April 21, 2008).

Helleiner, Gerry. 2002. An Economist's Reflections on the Legacies of Julius Nyerere. In *The Legacies of Julius Nyerere: Influences on Development Discourse and Practice in Africa*, ed. David A. McDonald and Eunice Nyeri Sahle. Trenton, NJ: Africa World Press.

Johnson, R.W. 2000. Nyerere: A flawed hero. *The National Interest* 60 (Summer).

Kaplan, Irving, ed. 1978. *Tanzania: A State Study.* Washington, DC: The American University.

Lawyers Environmental Action Team (LEAT). www.leat.or.tz/ (accessed April 21, 2008).

Lind, Jeremy, and Kathryn Sturman, eds. 2002. *Scarcity and Surfeit: The Ecology of Africa's Conflicts.* Pretoria, South Africa: The Institute for Security Studies.

Lofchie, Michael. 2007. Interview by author. October 10.

Lupogo, Herman. 2008. Tanzania: Civil-Military Relations and Political Stability. *African Security Review* 10, no. 1.

Millennium Challenge Corporation. http://www.mcc.gov/ (accessed April 22, 2008).

Ministry of Energy and Minerals, the Government of Tanzania. 2006. *Review of Mining Development Agreements and Fiscal Regime for the Mineral Sector.* Dar es Salaam, Tanzania: GOT.

Ministry of Energy and Minerals. 2006. *Review of Mining Development Agreements and Fiscal Regime for the Mineral Sector.* Dar es Salaam, Tanzania: The United Republic of Tanzania.

Nshala, Rugemeleza. 2007. Interview by author. October 10.

Nshala, Rugemeleza. n.d. The Extractive Industry in Africa: A Hard Look at Regulatory and Tax Law Reforms introduced by the World Bank in Sub-Saharan African States. Cambridge, MA: Harvard University.

Nyerere, Julius K. 1968. *Freedom and Socialism: Uhuru na Ujamaa.* London: Oxford University Press.

Pratt, Cranford. 2002. The Ethical Foundation of Julius Nyerere's Legacy. In *The Legacies of Julius Nyerere: Influences on Development Discourse and Practice in Africa,* ed. David A. McDonald and Eunice Nyeri Sahle. Trenton, NJ: Africa World Press.

Revenue Watch Institute. 2008. *State Report: Tanzania.* http://www.revenuewatch.org/our-work/countries/tanzania.php (accessed December 16, 2008).

United States Department of State, Bureau of African Affairs. 2008. *Background Note: Tanzania.* http:/www.state.gov/r/pa/ei/bgn/2843.htm.

United States Geological Survey. 2005. *Tanzania 2005 Minerals Yearbook.* http://minerals.usgs.gov/minerals/pubs/country/2005/tzmyb05.pdf (accessed December 16, 2008).

United Republic of Tanzania. 2000. *The United Republic of Constitution of 1977.* Dar es Salaam, Tanzania: GOT.

Williamson Diamond Mine. http://en.wikipedia.org/wiki/Williamson_diamond_mine (accessed May 25, 2008).

African Traditional Religions Today

Megan Stallings

Key Points

- The religious diversity within Africa is immense. Where different religions meet, there is conflict, syncretism or both.

- African traditional religions have no holy book and no sacred written work of scripture; but religion is central to all African traditional societies and the communities are based on it.

- African traditional religions will continue to decrease in number and size because they are religions that contract, and are not universalizing. However, pieces of the African traditional religions will continue to survive through the process of syncretism.

African traditional religions are alive and well. However, it is also different than it was 100 or 200 or 2000 years ago. Traditional religions constantly change and evolve as the African people come in contact with believers from other religions. Syncretism, or "the combination of different forms of belief or practice," is continual (Merriam Webster 2008). The religious diversity within Africa is immense; there are innumerable religions and it is impossible to know all of them. What is known is that where those religions meet, there is conflict, syncretism or both.

African traditional religions have been present for longer than any written account can capture. "Africa has been a religious continent, if we define religion as the imposition of special rules of conduct, intense imaginative reaching toward the intangible and an appetite for the supernatural" (Welch 1965, 11). No other part of the world has practiced so many different religions, whether indigenous or imported

(Welch 1965). This chapter however, will primarily focus on the relatively recent changes to African traditional religions in the last 1500 years. In addition, this chapter cannot attempt to dissect all African traditional religions, or provide all the facets of the beliefs. Instead, it will focus on the main beliefs of the preponderance of religions from ancestral Africa. This obviously leaves a great degree of ambiguity. And while the numerous religions of the world have all played a part in shaping the religions and beliefs of Africa today, this chapter will focus on the changes caused by the two primary universalizing religions, Christianity and Islam, which have the objective to convert non-followers. The chapter will not attempt to explain the doctrine or teachings of any one religion, only some of the major avenues along which they connected.

Background on African Traditional Religion

African traditional religions have no holy book and no sacred written work of scripture. Therefore it is exceedingly difficult to garner understanding of the religions. Knowledge is passed down primarily through word of mouth and unifying practices, then further through dances, paintings, sculpture, music festivals, and archeological discoveries. Additionally, there are some writings but their validity and bias are unknown (Moyo 2001; Parrinder 1969). Therefore the accuracy of the knowledge is questionable. However, since this is the only method of learning, we must understand its limitations and use it for its value.

Religion is central to all African traditional societies; it is both social and political and the communities are based on it. Even atheists within African societies subject themselves to religion because communities are cultural hearths, and the communities base themselves in religion (Moyo 2001). Religion cannot be separated as one element of life because African traditional societies are a sacral, not secular society (Ferkiss 1967). However, religion does not unite disparate communities; the religions are decentralized, do not evangelize, and do not have professional clergy

(Moyo 2001; Ferkiss 1967). Yet, it is amazing how so many communities have similar beliefs and share the same basic tenets and practices. Therefore, even though there are an unknown number of African traditional religions, this chapter groups them together to cover the primary tenets.

There are five basic beliefs upon which the majority of African traditional religions base their premises: the belief in supreme beings; the belief in spirits and divinities; the belief in life after death; the establishment of religious personnel and sacred places; and the belief in witchcraft, and magic (Moyo 2001). The Supreme Beings can have many names but are commonly referred to as God and can be either male or female. Other common names reflect relationships the followers have with the supreme being, such as creator, source of water, source of power, or giver of rain or light. The names are not abstract, but rather show the Supreme Being's practical relation to the lives of the followers (Moyo 2001; Parrinder 1969). There are also celestial pagan qualities connected to God, such as lightning, rainbows, and the moon (Parrinder 1969; Welch 1965).

Spirits and divinities also play a great role. The supreme being is actually surrounded by them, as they serve lesser functions such as servants or messengers to God. Some scholars question whether God is actually worshipped, or if the followers worship their ancestors' spirits first. Most research indicates the followers categorically state that they just revere and respect their ancestors immensely and worship God through them (Moy 2001). Furthermore, some inquiry posits that there were no temples to God, yet there were temples to items in nature, leading to the idea of polytheism (Parrinder 1969). Animism, indicating a soul within everything, is also very important to some African traditional religions. However, it is incorrectly assumed to be the sole basis of all African traditional religions (Parrinder 1969; Ferkiss 1967).

Life after death is a relatively new addition to the African traditional beliefs. Followers believe life was originally intended to go on forever, with periods of rejuvenation. However, there was an intervention or disobedience that led to death as a part of life. Along with reincarnation, a common belief is that the dead can punish those who wronged him/her (Moyo 2001; Parrinder 1969).

There are three main types of religious leaders within the African traditional religions that are generally used for positive acts. There are religious officials that preside at shrines. Second, there are spirit mediums who communicate with family ancestors. These mediums can play a significant part in mobilizing the community; they were an important piece to the unity of the movement for liberation from colonialism in several locations. Third, there are diviners who communicate with the spirit world for solutions to problems. The religious leaders can use a variety of places to conduct their worship but there is usually an elevated room in each home for this purpose. In addition, caves, stones, burial places, and mountains are especially sacred places of worship (Moyo 2001).

Converse to the positive beliefs discussed above, witchcraft and magic tend to be negative forces within the African traditional religions. Witches and sorcerers use their power to destroy life through curses or poisons. Believers also use magic for protection and/or harm, often to ward off consequences of superstitious beliefs (Moyo 2001; Parrinder 1969).

The Introduction of Christianity

Religion is not static. Life events bring change, and contact with other beliefs also brings change. African traditional religions primarily changed when they came in contact with Christianity and Islam. Figure 1 shows the gradual disappearance of pure African traditional religions as a result of this contact (Religion in Africa 2008). Christianity and Islam are both universal religions, and two of the three "book religions" (Judaism being the third). Even though this chapter will not discuss Judaism due to its ethnic nature, it is important to note that Judaism presented Africa with its first contact with a religion that did not depend on elements of nature or idols. Judaism was the first monotheistic religion in Africa that solidified members together even when separated geographically (Welch 1965).

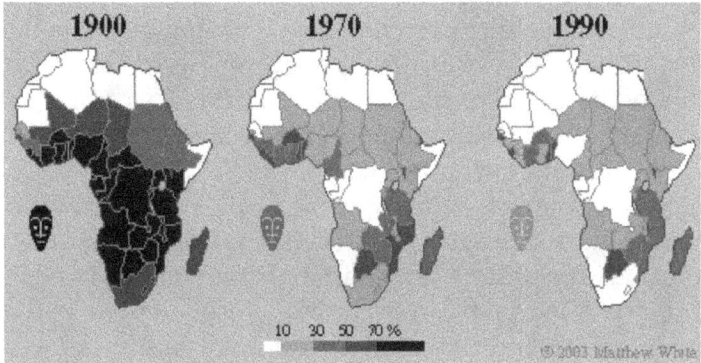

Figure 1. Percentage of Population Practicing an African Traditional Religion (Religion in Africa 2008)

Christianity in Africa dates back to the 1st century when it was introduced in Egypt. There was extremely strong support and a majority of Egyptians followed the religion. However, Egypt was subsequently conquered by Muslims during the 7th century which did not kill, but quelled, the Christian faith. In addition, Christianity had a strong hold on the North African countries of Tunisia, Morocco, Libya, and Algeria until the Muslim conquests of the 7th century. Traveling from Egypt, Christianity diffused to Ethiopia during the 4th century, where it is still strong today. The spread of Christianity almost ceased between the 7th and 15th centuries due to Muslim rule and polytheistic Romans. Christianity was not present south of the Sahara until the Portuguese missions which followed traders during the 15th century (Moyo 2001; Parrinder 1969). Christianity greatly spread in both Sierra Leone and Liberia in the 19th century, as these countries were inhabited by freed slaves from Britain and the United

States. Christianity was an important aspect of culture that relocated with colonization. Some of the African traditional religions already had the idea of the Trinity, the concept that God is one being but three persons (God the Father, God the Son, and God the Holy Spirit). Holding this idea, before the missionaries arrived, made the acceptance of that belief easier (Moyo 2001). Missionaries discovered they did not have to convince the Africans of the belief in one God or in life after death, as those were already main components of their traditional religion (Parrinder 1969). These few similarities made the acceptance of Christianity easier within the communities.

The impact of Christianity on African traditional religions can primarily be seen in the adjustment to traditional practices. The Christian movement in Yoruba county of Nigeria is an example of syncretism between the Christian and African Traditional faiths, as is the Aladura or "praying people" (Parrinder 1969). The African Independent Churches are some of the more prevalent examples seen today.

The most common forms of Christianity in Africa today are the African independent churches. They are denominations which separated from the European dominated churches for a variety of reasons. First, Africans wanted African symbols, images, costume, and music in their religion; the missionary churches did not include these pieces. Second, most missionary churches did not make any attempt to understand African traditional practices which Africans wanted incorporated, such as speaking in tongues and faith healing; they immediately called them "heathen" or "superstitious." Third, many missionaries came with the colonists, who practiced racial discrimination, paternalism, and ethnocentrism in the form of separate church entrances and sanctuaries, which were customs contrary to the philosophy that Christianity preached. Fourth, once the Bible was translated into African languages, Africans saw some of the stories in a clearer capacity. One, many Africans interpreted the Bible to communicate that both Abraham and David were polygamists; and second, they deduced that the fifth commandment called all believers to honor their parents. These revelations were grounds for Africans to continue some traditional practices such as polygamy and ancestor worship. The final reason for separation from the European dominated churches was that Africans wanted indigenous leadership (Moyo 2001).

Today, African independent churches generally follow the same doctrine and use the same Bible, prayers, and hymns; but they have African leadership as a symbol of their independence from the missions. The first independent churches began in west and south Africa, and then spread to east and central Africa (Moyo 2001; Parrinder 1969). There are differing opinions on how the independent churches began. Some sources indicate the beginning of the churches was Donna Beatrice in the 16th century. She claimed to be possessed by the spirit of St Anthony and stated Christ and the apostles were black; therefore, how could a white Christ help suffering Africans (Moyo 2001). Other sources infer the first independent movement was sparked by Edward Blyden. A missionary from the Dutch West Indies, he was ordained in the Presbyterian church in 1858 and spread the message of his strong rejection of Negro inferiority (Parrinder 1969).

Regardless of the beginning, by the 1960s, the time of state independence in Africa, there were between 4,500 and 6,000 independent churches, of which approximately 90 percent have survived from their inception (Moyo 2001; Parrinder 1969). Non-African Christians have been fairly open to the independent churches because they realize it is the most effective means of spreading the Christian message in Africa (Parrinder 1969). In addition, they know traditional Christian churches are associated by the African people with colonialism and therefore have difficulties dealing with the state (Welch 1965).

There are numerous types of independent Christian churches, but the two which primarily Africanized the Christian faith are the Ethiopian type and the Spirit type.

The Ethiopian type is mainly in protest to white colonist power and started in the late 19th century in south and east Africa. They follow the same Christian doctrine but have African leaders. The Spirit type is commonly called Zionist and expresses itself through singing and dancing. Zionist principles emphasize speaking in tongues and faith healing, where the Holy Spirit is interpreted through mediums and diviners. They forbid any use of African traditional religions. Many of these new churches are fundamentalist and authoritarian; they discourage critical thought and can lead to extremist religious movements. The independent churches within Africa are currently being challenged by the Pentecostal and Evangelical churches, which are drawing followers because of the opportunity for employment and money, as they have ties to the international community (Moyo 2001).

The Introduction of Islam

Islam was founded and came to the African continent three centuries after Christianity. Islam moved to Egypt directly after its founding in 640 AD, and then continued by conquest to the remainder of North Africa. Islam was largely successful in these areas due to the great schisms and persecutions that resulted from Christianity (Welch 1965). The conquerors placed Christians as second class citizens, but allowed Christians (and Jews) to continue following their faith because they deemed them true believers in God (Moyo 2001; Parrinder 1969). By the tenth century, many states in west Africa were established Muslim territories. Islam attracted elites because it was associated with the revered Arab civilization and because it allowed some traditional African practices, such as polygamy, circumcision, magic, and ancestor worship, to continue (Parrinder 1969). Islam was also brought by conquerors, not a defeated people who had come to Africa in exile or as slaves (Welch 1965). However, many of the converted west Africans were not truly Islamic; they often observed some of the five pillars but marginalized Islamic sharia law and dress codes. For example, they would attend mosque on Friday, but on Sunday would dance to the beliefs of old river spirits. In the 16th and 18th centuries, Islam spread to the masses by way of jihad. In the 19th century, Islam spread again as a uniter among Africans who resisted European colonialism (Moyo 2001; Parrinder 1969). Overall however, Islam spread slowly and steadily throughout Africa, except during the jihads when expansion was rapid. It was also difficult to spread into Ethiopia because of the strong Christian support (Parrinder 1969).

Today, most folk Islamic African groups incorporate these traditional practices, such as ancestor worship, the wearing of amulets, and witchcraft, into their Muslim beliefs (Moyo 2001). Orthodox and extremist Muslim groups do not allow traditional practices (Lobban 2008). Combining both beliefs, the folk Islamic groups may have verses of the Koran wrapped in amulets around their necks. However, many Muslims worldwide are growing concerned with the lackadaisical practices of folk African Islam, when in the past they had been tolerant (Parrinder 1969). There are also some African Muslims seeking to rejuvenate orthodox Muslim beliefs, which can lead to fundamentalism. But those attracted to fundamentalism are a small, distinct group, generally college students and intellectuals who are intrigued by the idea of an Islamic state (Moyo 2001).

If not allowed to continue their practices, African Muslims may spawn a separatist movement similar to the move made by the African Christian independent churches. Christians have always opposed African traditional practices, which spawned the independent churches. A new zeal by worldwide Muslims to oppose the syncretized African Muslim faith may push Africans to start a similar Islamic movement, as is already beginning in Sudan, northern Nigeria, Algeria, and Egypt (Lobban 2008).

Even though Muslim conversion was plentiful between the 7th and 18th centuries, Christian missionaries in the 19th and 20th centuries were primarily responsible for the resurgence of Christianity due to their ability to provide Western education, which was popular in Africa. Even in traditional Muslim areas, children would go to Koranic school for a year or two and then transfer to a Western school which was usually taught in English or French (Parrinder 1969). This produced a wealth of educated Christians who typically dominate political life in the African states (Welch 1965). However, colonialism and missionaries did not entirely halt Islam. Many colonial rulers allowed Muslim leaders to stay intact because they had a conservative control over the people. In addition, European racism strongly contradicted with the Muslim belief of equality and was a reason for the continued Muslim hold (Moyo 2001).

African traditional religions were not the only belief systems to change. Christianity and Islam also syncretized, to a lesser degree, due to contact with each other and the African traditional religions. Western education and governments forced some Islamic states to move away from some old Islamic ways, mainly due to human rights issues. And conversely, in some colonialist holdings, western governments forced a change on Christian missionaries to adopt a rule of protection against Islam. This rule however, was mostly for political reasons and not religious (Parrinder 1969).

Conflict

In many locations peaceful syncretism did not occur. In particular, many of today's conflicts are at the intersection of Christian and Muslim areas. The main dividing line between Christianity and Islam is relatively clear and can be seen in Figure 2, which shows the spatial pattern of major African religions. Current events clearly show conflict along this same line, especially across the Sahel and the Horn of Africa. Even though Christianity and Islam have brought many positive aspects to Africa, their differences, as well as competitive natures, have brought the potential for destruction. And while African traditional religions are not without conflict, the religion is more of a social, rather than personal, practice. African traditional religions deal with shame, not guilt or sin, and therefore do not often cause personal conflict (Welch 1965).

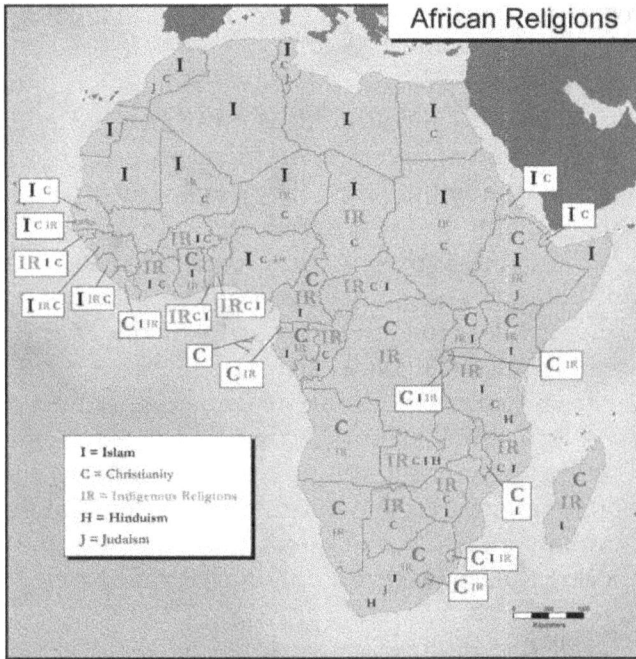

Figure 2. Distribution of Religion (size of character indicates relative prominence) (Reveron 2007).

Conclusion

As folk cultures decrease in size and number, adherents of African traditional religions will also continue to decrease. However, pieces of the African traditional religions will continue to survive through the process of syncretism.

Missionaries and colonists wielded the potential power to destroy African culture and religion; but ironically, that power is also what caused the forced continued practice of African traditional religions (Moyo 2001; Parrinder 1969).

The Africans have been relatively receptive to new ideas, while still retaining a hold on their old ways. With so many conquests over time, traditional Africa has been altered, but not lost (Welch 1965). In fact, enough traditional ideas have held on that Africans may see a revival in traditional practices as an attempt to bring order and stability back to their lives.

All religions around the world change and evolve; it is inevitable. They will split, reform, merge, and split again. With the great diversity of religions, it is impossible to escape contact among them. "Schism is a recurring factor in the historic church" (Parrinder 1969, 162). As people relocate and travel, to conduct trade or business, cultures inevitably interact and sometimes collide. This has never been more prevalent than in today's globalizing world with the shrinking distance between places. Even in Africa, religion seems to have the ability to transcend ethnicity and class. The future will see much more syncretism, until all facets of culture, including religion, are melded into various forms barely resembling their original character. In a perfect world humans embrace that syncretism, at the same time remembering their own traditional roots and history.

Major Megan B. Stallings is a personnel officer in the United States Army. Previously, she served as an Assistant Professor of Geography at the United States Military Academy where she taught and researched in the areas of physical geography and land use planning. She holds graduate degrees in Geography, National Security and Strategic Studies, and Human Resources Development.

References

Ferkiss, Victor. 1967. Religion and Politics in Independent African States: A Prolegomenon. In: *Boston University Papers on Africa: Transition in African Politics*, ed. Jeffrey. Butler and A.A. Castagno. New York: Praeger.

Lobban, R. 2008. Personal communication, February 5.

Merriam-Webster Dictionary. 2008. http://www.m-w.com (accessed January 20, 2008).

Moyo, Ambrose. 2001. Religion in Africa. In *Understanding Contemporary Africa*, ed. April Gordon and Donald Gordon. 3rd ed. Boulder, CO: Lynne Rienner Publishers.

Parrinder, Geoffrey. 1969. *Religion in Africa*. London: Pall Mall Press.

Religion in Africa Map. 2008. http://users.erols.com/mwhite28/afrorelg.htm (accessed January 20, 2008).

Reveron, D. 2007. PowerPoint Slides from Classroom Discussion. US Naval War College. Newport, RI.

Welch, Galbraith. 1965. *Africa: Before They Came*. New York: William Morrow & Company.

Africa's Youthful Population Age Structures and its Security Prospects

Richard P. Cincotta and Laurel J. Hummel

Key Points

- While the North and southern African regions have experienced significant fertility declines, fertility rates in West, Central and East Africa are the highest of all UN-recognized geographic regions.

- Due to persistently high fertility, most sub-Saharan African countries are expected to experience youthful age structures and significant levels of population growth well beyond 2025.

- Substantial political and economic progress could occur among North African states by 2025, whereas most of West, Central and East African states are likely to struggle to contain instability and political violence. In the southern region, the severity of AIDS mortality and the persistence of significant rates of HIV infection inject uncertainty into the future.

- Eventual progress through the demographic transition will likely initiate politically consequential ethnic shifts in numerous countries. Unless ethnic tensions are eased, the pathway out of sub-Saharan Africa's youthful demographic condition could be difficult.

- Young men attract the bulk of policy attention for jobs and training; however, the key to ultimately changing age structure lies in policies that elevate women's educational, social, economic, and legal status and provide adequate access to contraception.

During the late 1960s and early 1970s, a handful of East Asian and Caribbean governments purposefully set their sights on a demographic path that, in less than a generation, would reconfigure their states' *age structures* — the distribution of population among age groups — and indelibly alter the household economics of their citizens. Within the short span of two to three decades, these subtle changes contributed to profound shifts that rippled through the national economic, social and political systems in these regions. By the mid-1980s, most Latin American and South Asian states had joined this demographic path, and by the 1990s the *total fertility rate* (TFR) — an estimate of lifetime childbearing expressed as the average number of children born per woman — of states in North Africa, and of some in the Middle East and southern Africa, began to ebb toward smaller family size. Yet for most of Africa's sub-Saharan states, from those in the continent's Sahelian and coastal western reaches, across its densely forested central region, and along its drier eastern flank, this demographic journey remains in its early stages. In fourteen African states, fertility has barely fallen from very high levels (TFR of 5.5 or more children per woman) over the past half-century, and in another six this measure has stalled (declined by less than 1 child over the past 15 years) following a short period of decline (Figure 1).

Atop these trends, the age structures of many of sub-Saharan Africa's states are influenced, to some degree, by the persistence of strains of the *human immunodeficiency virus* (HIV) and their toll of adult and child mortality associated with *acquired immune deficiency syndrome* (AIDS). Epidemiologists consider these states to be experiencing a generalized epidemic, where adult HIV prevalence among the general adult population is at least 1 percent and transmission is mostly due to unprotected heterosexual contact. So far, AIDS has left its deepest social and demographic impression on the states of Africa's southern and eastern regions. Indeed, the world's most seriously AIDS-affected states — each of which currently exhibits an HIV prevalence among reproductive-age adults over 15 percent — are in southern Africa (UNAIDS 2008).

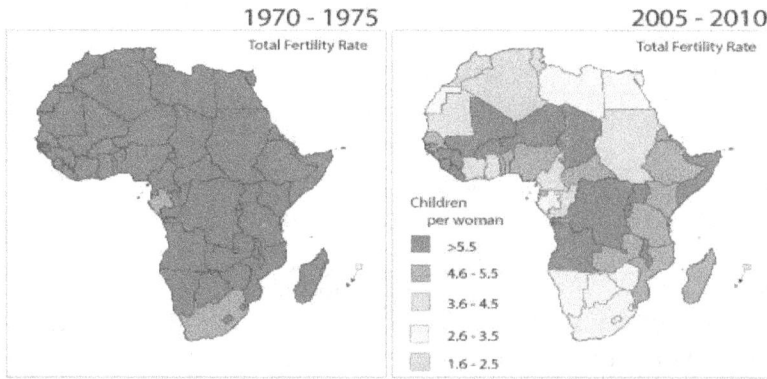

Figure 1. Total Fertility Rates of African States, 1970-75
and 2005-10 (United Nations Population Division 2007)
Map by Richard P. Cincotta.

What do these demographic conditions and trends mean for Africa's present and future security environment? To political demographers, those who probe the demographic characteristics of states for clues to their political and economic behavior, and to geo-demographers, those who study the impacts of demographics on place and space, they portend a great deal. In this chapter we apply some of the political and geo-demographer's tools to gauge Africa's political environment, now and in the future, and we discuss the limits and uncertainties of these interpretations.

This chapter employs an age structural typology to track the progress of a state's population through the *demographic transition* — the shift from large families and short life expectancies, to small families and longer lives. Before we describe this typology and discuss the political significance of age structural change, it will be helpful to briefly review this momentous demographic process.

A Quick Trip Through the Demographic Transition

The demographic transition is, itself, composed of two component transitions: a death rate transition, and a later birth rate transition (Figure 2). Nearly all societies are assumed to have endured a pre-transition past, during which they experienced high death and birth rates, and low resultant rates of population growth (see Figure 2, stage 1). Relatively low-cost interventions in public health and improvements in sanitation, which became state projects in 18th century Europe, triggered sharp declines in death rates — particularly childhood death — as they spread globally. As the rate of childhood death decreased, the frequency of childbearing hardly budged at first, opening a gap between death and birth rates that spawned rapid population growth (stage 2). In a majority of states, a later decline in the birth rate has significantly narrowed that gap, slowing population growth (stage 3). In the following stages of the transition (stages 4 and 5), death rates tend to rise again as seniors (over 65 years of age), who face an increasingly elevated risk of death as they age, become an increasingly larger proportion of the age structure. While in most industrialized states birth and death rates are now roughly equal (stage 4), in a few (mostly Eastern) European states death rates have climbed conspicuously higher than birth rates (stage 5), reflecting these populations' very low levels of fertility (below 1.5 children per woman), a relatively small number of women in the prime reproductive years (age 20 to 29), and large proportions of seniors (age 65 years and older).

This "dance" between the death rate and birth rate during the demographic transition drives population age structures through a successional sequence of complex forms. We characterize the age structures that result from this successional sequence by employing the following typology.

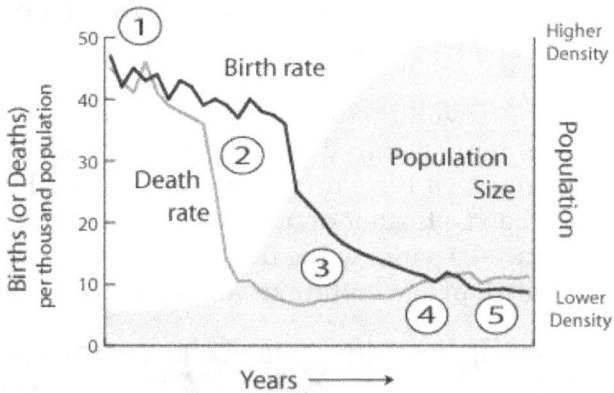

Figure 2. A model of the demographic transition process showing idealized death rate and birth rate transitions, and relative changes in population. Five stages are depicted: (1) pre-transition, (2) early transition, (3) middle transition, (4) late transition, and (5) advanced transition. While declines in the death rate have typically preceded declines in the birth rate, historically the pace and timing of these component transitions have varied. Almost all African states are reflective of stage 2. Graphic by Richard P. Cincotta.

Population Age Structures: A Typology

Built on earlier published efforts (Cincotta and Leahy 2007; Leahy et al. 2007), this age structural typology identifies three general *transitional age structure types* — T1, *youthful*; T2, *intermediate*; and T3, *mature* — each produced primarily by declines in fertility and infant mortality, and by longer lifetimes. Formally, each population can be fit into one of these transitional types on the basis of its median age (Table 1). This typology remains consistent with a previously published method (Leahy et al. 2007) which classified age structures based on two population components: the proportion of people below 30 years of age, and the proportion of seniors (65 and older). Graphing the populations of states using these two components illustrates the successional sequence of age structures that has emerged as a result of demographic transition (shown later in this chapter in Figure 5).

Table 1. An age structural typology. Ranges for age structural types featured in this chapter. Each type is associated with a 10-year span in median age. Each of these types can be further divided into two subtypes, early and advanced, spanning the first and second 5-years of median age in the age structural type.

		Typical Age Structure			
Type	Median Age	Younger than age 30	Age 65 and older	Subtype	Subtype range Median age (years)
T1	>15 to 25	≥60%	–	T1a T1b	>15 to 20 >20 to 25
T2	>25 to 35	< 60%	<10%	T2a T2b	>25 to 30 >30 to 35
T3	>35 to 45	–	≥10%	T3a T3b	>35 to 40 >40 to 45
T4	>45 to 55	–	≥22%	T4a T4b	>45 to 50 >50 to 55

Transitional types can also be associated with stages of the demographic transition. For example, youthful age structures (T1) arise within stage 2 (see Figure 2) of the demographic transition (no state-level populations remain in stage 1, the pre-transition stage). Intermediate age structures (T2) typically arise within the demographic transition's stage 3, as death rates hit very low levels and the gap between death and birth narrows. Mature age structures (T3) are associated with movement toward the convergence of birth and death rates (stage 4). A fourth group of *post-mature* age structures (T4) are projected to emerge among those states that advance more deeply into the demographic transition's stage 5.

The forces exerted by the demographic transition— declining fertility and infant mortality, and extended life expectancy — are not the only demographic influences on age structure. Other demographic forces, denoted in this typology as *extra-transitional influences* (a classification series beginning with "X"), today regularly impose subtle modifications on numerous age structures, and wholly reconfigure a few. Those "X-influences" of current importance are immigration (temporary labor, X1; permanent residence, X2), premature adult mortality (AIDS-related, X3; in middle age, X4), and sex-selected abortion (X5). In the not-too-distant past, age structures more regularly were reconfigured by war (such as the dramatic effect of World War II on Russia's population) and famine (the Great Leap Forward's effects on China's population). In addition, the politics of states is often influenced by distinct ethnic and regional populations (such as the Shi'ia of Lebanon and the Haredim of Israel) whose *compositional influences* (C-influences) — group growth rates and age structural differences — are locally apparent, but difficult to discern from state-level data. With only a handful of exceptions, however, sub-state ethnic and regional demographic data are inaccessible to most researchers, making it difficult to identify politically meaningful trends on small spatial scales.

Today, Africa is dominated by youthful (T1) age structures. In fact, 51 of Africa's 53 states — all but Tunisia and Mauritius — have youthful age structures. Moreover, about half of the world's T1 states are located on the continent. Africa features an additional defining characteristic — the influence of high levels of AIDS-related mortality (X3), which is principally discernable in the age structures of the most seriously AIDS-affected states: Botswana, Lesotho, Namibia, South Africa, Swaziland, Zambia and Zimbabwe. In these southern African states, roughly 15 to 28 percent of people age 15 to 49 are HIV positive, as compared to 0.8 percent of the same age group worldwide (UNAIDS 2008).

In AIDS-affected states across the continent, the spread of HIV has exacted a heavy toll on individuals, families and communities, reaching across educational and income-class boundaries that, during the course of other generalized epidemics, buffered elites from infection. A recent analysis by UNAIDS (2008) estimates that of the 33 million people presently living with HIV/AIDS, about 22 million are in Africa, almost all of them residing south of the Sahara (Figure 3). In 2007, roughly 1.7 million Africans were newly infected by HIV, significantly below the 2001 estimate of 2.2 million, but again representing the greatest incidence, by far, of infection around the world.

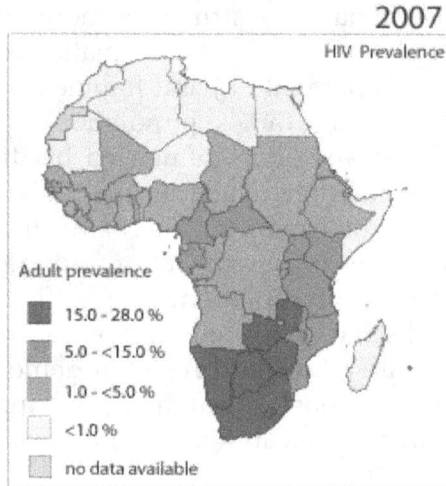

Figure 3. HIV Prevalence in African States Among Reproductive-age Adults (age 15 to 49 years), 2007 (UNAIDS 2008) Map by Richard P. Cincotta.

Implications of Age Structural Types

To peer into Africa's political future (our pursuit in the following sections) requires a brief review of the basics of an *age structural theory of state performance* and an acknowledgement of its limitations and uncertainties. State age structure theory is a line of reasoning that grew out of the basic observation that particular age profiles are more likely than others to enhance the ability of states to manage their population's political, economic and social environment. Put simply, this theory implies that youthful age structures

(T1) tend to be unfavorable to states, producing a set of challenges that deter or threaten their stability. As an age profile matures (T2, T3), its ratio of workers to dependents climbs—a condition tending to present states with more opportunities to strengthen their legitimacy and economic strength than challenges that could undermine it. As age profiles reach advanced maturity (T4), obtaining substantial proportions of seniors (age 65 and older), their favorability gives way to new economic and political challenges, among them the need to balance funding for elderly support against other domestic priorities and foreign policy concerns.

This swing from unfavorable, to favorable, back to a less favorable profile during the course of the demographic transition follows the general trend of the support ratio (Figure 4) — the proportion of working-age people (age 15 to 64 years old) to the sum of childhood (less than 15 years) and old-age (65 and older) dependents in the population. For example, a state with a support ratio of 2.0 has two working-age people for each person either below age 15 or above 64; a support ratio of 1.0 means that there is one working-age person for each dependent, either young or old. The figure thus shows that T2 and T3 population structures have a higher ratio of (potential) workers to dependents than T1 and T4 structures.

The outcomes associated with the ups and downs of the support ratio are not a foregone conclusion. Instead, the age structural condition exposes states to risks and opportunities that can be expressed as statistical likelihoods of potential outcomes. Like a card game, outcomes of being exposed to age structure-related risk depend both upon what is "in the cards," and who is playing. The outcomes that are associated with favorable or unfavorable age profile-related conditions depend on the ability of the state—its government's leadership and institutions—to manage them. Realistically, outcomes also can be influenced by other internal and external conditions.

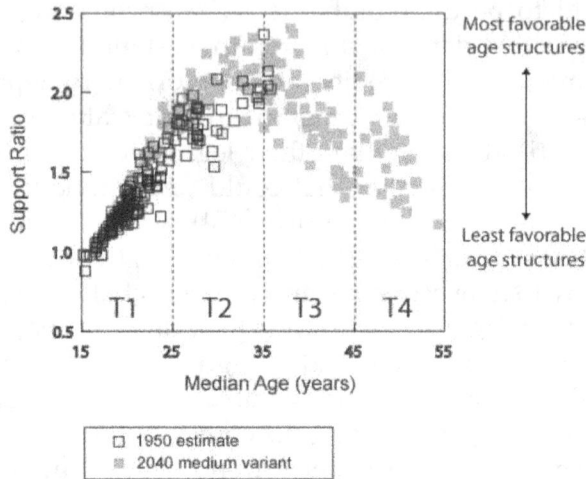

Figure 4. Estimates of the support ratios (the working-age population divided by the sum of childhood and senior populations) of the world's states in 1950, and projections of that indicator for 2040, showing the relationship to the population's median age. The successional sequence of profile types (T1, T2, T3, T4) is indicated along the lower axis. This arc, spanning 1950 to 2040, depicts the trajectory of the support ratio through the course of the age structural transition—from low support when children represent a large proportion of the population (T1), to high support when those in the working-age dominate (T2, T3), and then again to low levels of support as seniors assume a large proportion of the population (T4) (UN Population Division 2007). Graphic by Richard P. Cincotta.

Profiles and Their Subtleties

To help identify more subtle differences and dynamics along the age structure transition, each type has been divided into two phases, an early (a) and advanced phase (b), yielding in 2005 a world of six basic state-level *age profiles*—T1a, T1b, T2a, T2b, T3a, and T3b. The most prevalent age profile on the African continent is currently the "youngest" of all profiles, T1a (Figure 5), the early youthful profile (in 35 states out of 43 worldwide assessed as T1), followed by T1b, the advanced youthful profile (in 16 African states).

As noted above, only two states have acquired an intermediate profile: Tunisia, classified as T2a, and *early intermediate profile*, and the small island state of Mauritius in the Indian Ocean, east of Madagascar, classidied as T2b, an advanced *intermediate profile*. Demographic transitions in both Tunisia and Mauritius resembled those of populations in East Asia in pace and timing, and involved well-funded governmental family planning programs and policies aimed at raising women's age at marriage (Metz 1994; Leahy et al. 2007). A *mature profile*, T3a, is a projected to emerge in both Tunisia and Mauritius by 2025 (Figures 5 and 6), assuming that changes follow those projected by the United Nations Population Division's medium variant (2007).

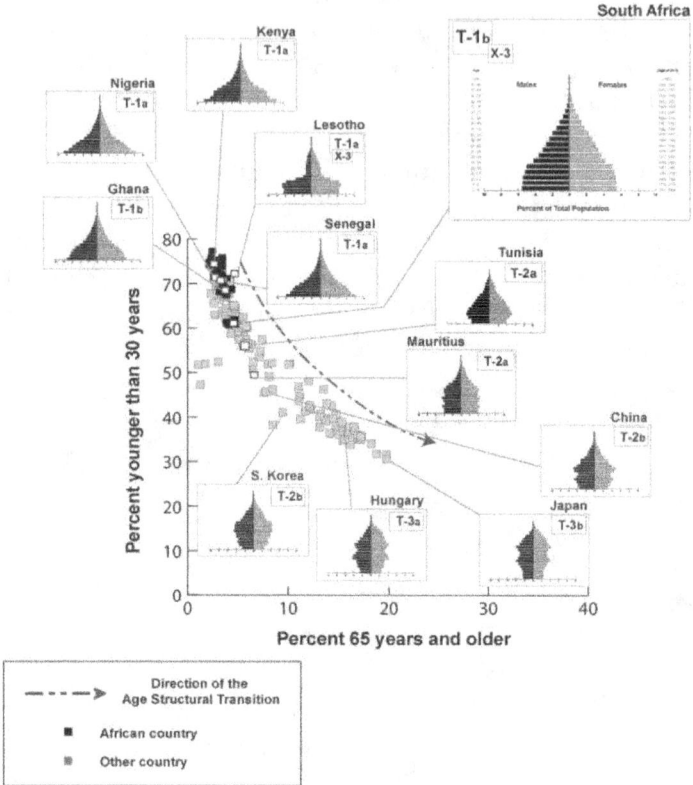

Figure 5. Profiles of the present array of Africa's age structural types, 2005. African states are overwhelmingly youthful (high on the Y axis, low on the X axis) (UN Population Division 2007). Graphic by Richard P. Cincotta.

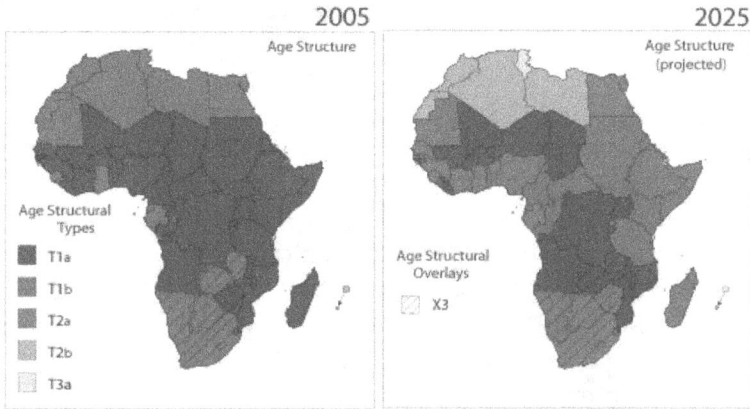

Figure 6. The Geographical Distribution Africa's Age Structural Profiles in 2005, and Projected Age Structural Profiles to 2025 Using the UN Medium Variant. (UN Population Division 2007). Map by Richard P. Cincotta.

Interpreting Africa's Age Profiles

Early youthful profiles (T1a, median age ≤20 years) are characteristic of populations with high stable fertility, declining infant mortality, and rapid population growth. This pyramidal profile shown graphically within Figure 5 is currently a feature of 35 African states, the vast majority of which are in West, Central and East Africa, with a few scattered within the continent's southern region. Distribution of age structure types by state is shown within Figure 6. Stocked with young children and adolescents, and therefore unlikely to mature substantially for several decades, T1a profiles can be termed "chronically youthful age structures."

Next in this successional series are the advanced youthful profiles (T1b, median age between 21 and 25 years). Alternatively described as "acutely youthful age structures," and typified by substantial declines in fertility and smaller cohorts of children, the T1b profile is a feature of 16 African states, most located either in North Africa or in the continent's southern region.

Both T1 profiles (T1a and T1b) embody the demographic qualities of a *youth bulge*—a large proportion (>40 percent) of young adults, ages 15 to 29, in the working ages, and rapid rates of workforce growth (≥3 percent per year). Youth bulge states typically endure a political environment influenced by an ideologically experimental and often volatile youth culture, and strain to manage a social environment in which relatively large and growing numbers of young men vie for an inadequate number of jobs. In such environments, the political mobilization and recruitment of young men, either by state or non-state actors, tend to be easy, and the ability of governments to thwart the rise of exploitive and disruptive organizations limited. Understandably, states with T1 profiles have been found to carry elevated risks of the emergence of a civil conflict—either of low or high intensity—within a decade (Cincotta and Leahy 2007; Leahy et al. 2007), and to bear additional risks of other types of political violence and domestic terrorism (Urdal 2006).

The next more mature profiles in the series, intermediate profiles (T2a, median age between 26 and 30; and T2b, median age 31 to 35), are transient types; they quickly mature, and together typically last only about two decades. States having this profile experience a *demographic dividend*: an increasingly favorable ratio of workers to children, falling rates of workforce growth, a decline in the numbers of children due to enter school, and—in a surprising number of cases—unusually high rates of accumulated savings. Each of these, if acted upon, can catalyze economic growth and development (Lee and Mason 2006; Williamson 2001; Bloom et al. 2002).

Transitions from youthful to intermediate profiles have also been associated with consequential political shifts. During the prior three decades, the likelihood of achieving and maintaining liberal democracy has been three to four times higher among states with intermediate profiles than those with youthful profiles (Leahy et al. 2007). A recent analysis attributes this increased likelihood of liberal democracy to the dissipation of political volatility associated with a youth bulge and the economic opportunities that the demographic dividend avails states (Cincotta 2008; Cincotta in press). And while T2 states typically bear significantly lower risks of the emergence of armed civil conflict and other domestic acts of political violence, these instabilities have often persisted or reemerged from the past, despite this transition.

AIDS-related Mortality

Early in the course of the pandemic, analysts found cause to predict that the high rates of premature death and illness associated with AIDS would ultimately lead to increasing levels of economic and political dysfunction in the worst affected African states. The contributing factors to these hypothesized breakdowns were drawn from a long list of the disease's known impacts, including losses of educated and specifically-skilled individuals; escalating costs of healthcare, disability coverage and worker training; the toll on parenting and the growing ranks of orphans; high proportions of young people relative to working-age adults (a large youth bulge); and deficiencies in the operational readiness of military and police forces (ICG 2001).

Instead, there is evidence of state progress and economic development in African societies hit hard by AIDS, despite the extraordinary hardships endured by families and communities. For example, among the most seriously AIDS-affected states of southern Africa are four (Botswana, Lesotho, Namibia, and South Africa) categorized by Freedom House (2008) as "free," a rating that analysts regard as indicating a liberal democracy. And three of these (Botswana, Namibia and South Africa) are among Africa's six wealthiest states, measured in per capita gross domestic product adjusted for differences in purchasing power (World Bank 2007).

Analysts appear to have over-estimated the power of AIDS-related financial costs and human hardships to penetrate the state apparatus, and under-estimated the ability of state institutions, economies and communities to adjust. Recent reviews (de Waal 2006; Barnett 2006) argue that these analyses largely misjudged the impacts of labor losses in African societies where low-skill labor is abundant, and unreasonably fretted over the operational readiness of militaries in places where the military's role in political stabilization has historically been ambiguous (also, see the chapter on African militaries). Just as important, analysts failed to recognize how low citizens' expectations remain in most African states and they were unable to gauge the degree to which AIDS issues would lack political traction.

An analysis by UNAIDS (2008) concludes that many states recently have made major progress in lowering the rate of AIDS-related death and preventing new infections. The report credits some of the slowdown in the epidemic's momentum to the six-fold increase in financing that HIV programs in low- and middle-income states have experienced over the past decade—including funding through the United States President's Emergency Plan for AIDS Relief (PEPFAR), begun in 2003. UNAIDS also notes documented changes in sexual behavior in some (mostly East) African states, and the stabilization of HIV prevalence in southern Africa, albeit at very high levels. Recent leadership changes in South Africa's government bode increased dedication to programs consistent with scientific evidence concerning modes of HIV transmission and effective prophylactic measures, and are likely to pave the way for more effective dissemination of anti-retroviral treatment (ARTS) and the expansion of prevention programs in that state.

Africa in 2025

North Africa. Declines in fertility that have already occurred in the Mediterranean coastal states of North Africa have set in motion a reshaping of state-level age profiles that, over the next 25 years, will demographically differentiate them from those in African regions south of the Sahara, as well as from much of the Middle East. Today, the use of modern contraception by married women in North Africa has reached relatively high levels in Algeria (52 percent), Egypt (57 percent), Morocco (55 percent), and Tunisia (53 percent), as compared to 68 percent in the United States (estimates of modern contraceptive prevalence published by the Population Reference Bureau (2008) from various primary sources). Fertility trajectories in North Africa reinforce a consensus already established among demographers: that most modern interpretations of Islam are neither inconsistent with widespread contraceptive use nor with the achievement of a small family norm—a consensus that evolved as Iran, Turkey, Lebanon, Albania, Bosnia and Herzegovina, and Indonesia passed through similar transitions (Weeks 2008).

If the behavior of the coastal North African states evolves in a manner consistent with the recent history of states in Asia, the Caribbean, and Latin America that passed through similar stages of demographic maturity during the past three decades, then we can expect North Africa to experience a diminishing likelihood of civil conflict by 2025. This pattern of age structural change is scheduled to advance fastest across the Maghreb states (Tunisia, Algeria, and Morocco) and then spread to Libya and then Egypt. According to recent analyses (Cincotta 2008; Cincotta in press), the dissipation of North African youth bulges over the next decade will increase the likelihood of liberal democracy being established in one or more of these states—though determining which ones will liberalize and precisely when this will occur are beyond this model's purview.

East, West and Central Africa. Across the waistline of Africa, the security and developmental prognosis is less promising. Age structures remain youthful, population is growing rapidly, the investment picture is poor, women's legal and educational status is generally low, and fertility

273

remains high. While West Africa's emerging liberal democracies—Ghana, Benin, Senegal and Mali (Freedom House 2008)—may continue to successfully stave off authoritarianism, a recent age-structural analysis gives these liberal regimes minimal chances of maintaining democracy at such high levels over the coming decade (Cincotta in press). Meanwhile, the toxic combination of Nigeria's chronically youthful age profile (T1), its deeply divided ethnic politics, and difficult-to-govern regions, suggests the possibility of this state's emergence by 2025 as an "African Pakistan"—a state that may not be reluctant to allow its internal conflicts to drift into the regional neighborhood, rather than face the dangerous and politically risky task of suppressing them internally.

The demographic signals of Nigeria's distress are unmistakable. UN demographers estimate that state's fertility has dropped by just one child per woman over the past six decades—from 6.9 to 5.9 children per woman (UN Population Division 2007). During that period Nigeria's population grew from less than 35 million to nearly 155 million today (in 2009), and is now increasing by about 3.5 million people annually. Current projections suggest that Nigeria will reach the 200-million-person mark around 2025 (UN Population Division 2007; US Census Bureau, International Program Center 2008). Nigeria's currently low rate of modern contraceptive use among married women (8 percent) is apparently constrained by several factors, some reflecting women's low social and legal status, others pointing to failures of governance. The most commonly cited are poor access to contraception and limited reach and effectiveness of maternal health services, low educational attainment among women (less than one-third attend secondary school), and high child mortality (nearly 1 in 5 die before age five) (UN 2008).

Alarmingly, some demographers have recently hinted that fertility projections recently published by the United Nations (2007) for West, Central and East Africa may be overly optimistic. In Ghana (TFR for 2005-10 of 3.8

274

children per woman), Senegal (TFR 4.7) and Kenya (5.0), where attention to family planning and girls' education appeared to have inspired significant fertility declines in the 1990s, recent surveys show that this trend has stalled (Bongaarts 2006). Meanwhile other countries — Burundi (TFR 6.8), Guinea-Bissau (7.1), and Niger (7.2) — remain virtually at the dawn of their fertility transition. For states with water-scarce or labor-saturated rural economies, the switch to job-intense industrial development is becoming imperative. Yet the levels of infrastructure, institutional capacity, and education are largely insufficient to support this shift, and political and financial environments have yet to attain the degree of stability necessary to instill confidence in potential investors, even investors in African diaspora communities.

Ultimately, as African populations advance through the demographic transition, fertility is likely to decline as it has elsewhere: first among the most urbanized, most secular, and most educated populace, and then among others. The most rural, most religious, and most economically disadvantaged ethnicities — particularly those where women's status is lowest — generally lag in this transition. Typically politically marginalized, such minorities tend to grow in relative size and remain youthful and politically volatile as the more urban, educated and economically advantaged populations — those controlling the state — decline in relative size (Leuprecht 2006). The unfolding of this "ethnodemographic power paradox" could further exacerbate ethnic tensions in some of the more deeply divided societies of West, Central and East Africa.

Southern Africa. Given the failure of dire predictions that analysts cast during the early decades of Africa's AIDS epidemic, and the novel demographic qualities and social environments associated with the most affected countries, it is wise to be cautious in discussing the future of these states. In the most seriously AIDS-affected states of southern Africa, the epidemic has produced atypical youth bulges — youthful age structures (T1/X3) with relatively slow rates of growth (around 1 percent annually) in the working-age population due to adult mortality, and a young adult population with an uncommon vulnerability to mortality and an high degree of dependence on government-supplied or externally-funded services. Sub-Saharan Africa is expected to continue to bear high human and financial costs from HIV/AIDS through 2025, and to request assistance from donor states as well as supranational and non-governmental organizations to weather these growing burdens.

For decades, southern African states have exceeded their northern neighbors in providing basic education and health services, including family planning, to their citizens. During the late 1980s — before HIV's rapid rise to extraordinary levels of prevalence in the region — modern contraceptive use rose from very low levels and fertility began its decline. These trends have held, as contraceptive use among married women has reached moderate levels in Botswana (42 percent), Namibia (43 percent), and Swaziland (48 percent), and relatively high levels in South Africa (60 percent) and Zimbabwe (58 percent) (Population Reference Bureau 2008).

Meanwhile, HIV continues to challenge medical science and frustrate public health practitioners. Neither an effective HIV vaccine nor a self-administered microbicide, even if developed and tested soon, will likely be widely disseminated in the near term. Nonetheless, analysts expect ongoing prevention efforts and local behavioral changes to continue to depress HIV infection rates. By 2025, the majority of Africans living with HIV will likely have access to life-extending anti-retroviral therapies (ART). However, Africa's ART delivery systems will face challenges from service dysfunction, immature transportation infrastructure, disruptions related to political instability, and the mounting economic and social costs of the growing number of AIDS survivors. According to one set of recent projections (Stover 2008), augmented prevention programs — rapidly scaled up to universal access by 2015 — could reduce by one-third the number of Africans requiring life-extending ART by 2025.

Policy-relevant Conclusions

From the perspective of political and geo-demography, Africa's security future is captured in a phrase: the good, the bad, and the uncertain. Based upon North Africa's changing age structures, the futures of its Mediterranean coastal states appear relatively bright. From the same perspective, however, sub-Saharan Africa's chronically youthful age structures—reinforced by low levels of secondary education and the low legal and social status of women—signal decades of political instability and sporadic conflicts to come, putting pressure on regional powers and multi-lateral organizations to ramp up their commitments to conflict mediation and peacekeeping operations. And then "the uncertain": a demographic consideration of the future of states in Africa's southern region, where age profiles have been reworked by AIDS-related mortality, leaves us puzzled. Demographically, this is uncharted territory—and it is shifting as AIDS treatment programs take hold.

What can be learned from Africa's increasingly variable landscape? In North Africa's states, the foundations for fertility decline were laid, over decades, by policies and programs that are improving women's status by increasing girls' educational attainment, establishing women's rights through secular law and civil courts, guaranteeing access to a wide range of contraception, and improving women's mobility in the workplace. Similar lessons have been learned more recently in southern Africa, where women's rights organizations have been pivotal in securing these reforms.

To most analysts, the relationship between women's status and political stability seems much less than intuitive or, if understood, women's status appears too bound by cultural inertia to be a practical lever for altering domestic political conditions. This disconnect is the source of the *youth bulge policy dilemma*: because of their potential roles in political violence (potentially an imminent danger), young men necessarily draw the bulk of policy attention and funding for jobs and training. However, the ultimate key to changing age structure, and thus subduing the youth-bulge-induced demand for jobs and services, lies in policies that improve women's status. Besides its role in driving age structural change, there are other reasons to consider this factor important. The United Nations recognizes improvements of women's status to be a keystone to increased quality of life — a perspective well-reflected in the eight UN Millennium Development Goals, which directly target women's status as a means to eradicate poverty and hunger, and to reduce disparities in education, and in maternal and child health (UN 2008). As well, the UN Development Fund for Women (UNIFEM) considers gender inequality to be a fundamental impediment to ending trafficking and violence against women, and likewise identifies improvements in women's status in African states as critical to achieving broad progress in economic, social and political development (UNIFEM 2008).

While stressing the critical importance of advancing sub-Saharan Africa's populations through the demographic transition, we caution that unless aspects of minority development and integration are addressed, disadvantaged ethnic groups with persistently high fertility could ultimately emerge as a larger and relatively more youthful proportion of the population when the age structure of more advantaged groups matures. More equitable economic development and better access to services for minorities, greater political inclusiveness, and programs that focus on improving the legal and social status of minority women could minimize the deleterious impact of these shifts.

A candid analysis must acknowledge that the AIDS epidemic has not, to this date, destabilized African governments and that its identification as a threat to state security in Africa, generated in the course of mobilizing an international response, may have been overstated. That said, the enormous toll of suffering associated with HIV/AIDS continues to warrant a focused health and humanitarian response, including high levels of assistance from international sources and the attention of international health research. Analysts argue that increasing the focus on effective prevention methods, alongside ART treatment, could reduce the future financial and human costs that African states and international donors will someday assume (Potts et al. 2008).

While demographic projections and their interpretations can provide only a cloudy window to the future, they signal a reasonable warning over the future of West, Central and East African regions, which today (in 2009) collectively comprise a population of more than 750 million. By 2025, these regions are projected to be home to over one billion people, and could find themselves the world's last regional bastion of generalized poverty and high fertility. Freeing much of sub-Saharan Africa from the cycle of low women's status, high fertility, political instability, and poverty looms as one of the most formidable foreign policy challenges of the 21st century.

Dr. Richard P. Cincotta is the Demographic Consultant to the Long Range Analysis Unit of the National Intelligence Council in Washington, DC. His research has focused on the demographic transition and its relationships to natural resource dynamics and to the political dynamics of states. He has participated in field research in China, India, and Morocco, and served in an intelligence field in the U.S. Navy.

Colonel (Dr.) Laurel J. Hummel is an Academy Professor and Director of the Geography Program at the United States Military Academy. A former Army intelligence officer, she has taught a variety of physical and human geography courses and has researched in the areas of military geography, geodemographics, and geography education. She holds graduate degrees in Geography, Educational Leadership, and Strategic Studies.

References

Barnett, Tony. 2006. A Long-wave Event. HIV/AIDS, Politics, Governance and "Security": Sundering the Intergenerational Bond? *International Affairs* 82, no.2: 297-313.

Bloom, David E., David Canning, and Jaypee Sevilla. 2002. *The Demographic Dividend: A New Perspective on the Economic Consequences of Population Change.* Santa Monica, CA: RAND.

Bongaarts, John. 2006. The Causes of Stalling Fertility Transitions. *Studies in Family Planning* 37, no.1: 1-16.

Cincotta, Richard P. 2008. How Democracies Grow Up: Countries with Too Many Young People May Not Have a Fighting Chance for Freedom. *Foreign Policy* 165: 80-82.

Cincotta, Richard P. *in press*. Half a Chance: Youth Bulges and Transitions to Liberal Democracy. *Environmental Change and Security Project Report* 13.

Cincotta, Richard P., and Elizabeth Leahy. 2006. Population Age Structure and Its Relation to Civil Conflict: A Metric. *Environmental Change and Security Project Report* 12: 55-58.

de Waal, Alex. 2006. *AIDS and Power: Why There Is No Political Crisis -- Yet.* New York: Zed Books.

Freedom House (FH). 2008. *Freedom in the World, 2007: The Annual Survey of Political Rights and Civil Liberties.* New York: FH, Rowman & Littlefield.

International Crisis Group (ICG). 2001. HIV/AIDS as a Security Issue. Washington, DC and Brussels, Belgium: ICG.

Leuprecht, Christian. 2006. The Demographic Security Dilemma. Presented at the Annual Meeting of the American Political Science Association, Philadelphia, PA. Aug 31.

Leahy, Elizabeth, Robert Engelman, Carolyn Gibb Vogel, Sarah Haddock, and Tod Preston. 2007. *The Shape of Things to Come: Why Age Structure Matters to a Safer, More Equitable World.* Washington, DC: Population Action International.

Lee, Ronald D., and Andrew Mason. 2006. What is the Demographic Dividend? *Finance and Development* 43, no. 3: 16-17.

Metz, Helen Chapin. 1994. *Mauritius: A Country Study.* Washington, DC: Government Printing Office for the Library of Congress. http://countrystudies.us/mauritius/ (accessed November 18, 2008).

Population Reference Bureau (PRB). 2008. *World Population Data Sheet.* Washington, DC: PRB.

Potts, Malcolm, Daniel T. Halperin, Douglas Kirby, Ann Swidler, Elliot Marseille, Jeffrey D. Klausner, Norman Hearst, Richard G. Wamai, James G. Kahn, and Julia Walsh. 2008. Reassessing HIV Prevention. *Science* 320, no. 5877: 749 -750.

Stover, John. 2008. *Personal communication.* Projections accessed with permission. HIV/AIDS Projections. Danbury, CT: Futures Institute.

UNAIDS (Joint United Nations Programme on HIV/AIDS). 2008. *Report on the Global AIDS Epidemic.* Geneva: United Nations.

UNIFEM (United Nations Development Fund for Women). 2008. *Gender Equality Now: Accelerating the Achievement of the Millennium Development Goals.* New York: UNIFEM.

United Nations (UN). 2008. *The Millennium Development Goals Report, 2008.* New York: UN Department of Economic and Social Affairs.

United Nations Population Division. 2007. World Population Prospects: The 2006 Revision. New York: UN Dept. of Economic and Social Affairs.

US Census Bureau, International Program Center. 2008. International Data Base. http://www.census.gov/ipc/www/idb/ (accessed December 1, 2008).

Urdal, Henrik. 2006. A Clash of Generations? Youth Bulges and Political Violence. *International Studies Quarterly* 50: 607-629.

Weeks, John R. 2008. *Population: An Introduction to Concepts and Issues, Tenth Edition*. Belmont, CA: Thomson Wadsworth.

Williamson, Jeffrey G. 2001. Demographic Change, Economic Growth, and Inequality. In *Population Matters: Demographic Change, Economic Growth, and Poverty in the Developing World*, ed. Nancy Birdsall, Allen C. Kelley, and Steven W. Sinding. Oxford: Oxford University Press.

World Bank (WB). 2007. *World Development Indicators Online*. Washington, DC http://publications.worldbank.org/WDI/ (accessed November 28, 2008).

Sub-Saharan Africa's Urban Geography

James Farrell Chastain and Steven Oluic

Key Points

- Sub-Saharan Africa is the most rapidly urbanizing region in the world and provides a distinctive "African Urbanization."

- Nearly all of the future population growth in sub-Saharan Africa will take place in urban areas.

- The colonial past influences the present and future nature of African urbanism.

- African urban places are largely *overurbanized;* they have more urban residents than the economies and infrastructure of cities can sustain.

- Urbanization in sub-Saharan Africa will provide challenges and opportunities for increasing human security in that region.

Introduction

In 2008 the world passed a significant threshold; for the first time in the history of humankind the majority of us are living in urban places (United Nations 2007b). This change occurred largely over the 20th century. It is estimated that in 1900 10 percent of the world's population lived in cities, growing to 45 percent by 2000 (United Nations 2007b). To better understand what these percentages actually represent in terms of aggregate numbers, consider the urbanization in tandem with population growth, as illustrated in Figure 1. In 1950 the world's total population was more than two billion. By the beginning of the 21st century the earth was supporting triple that number. Thus, the increase of people living in urban places is related to the rapid world human population increase. The future condition of human

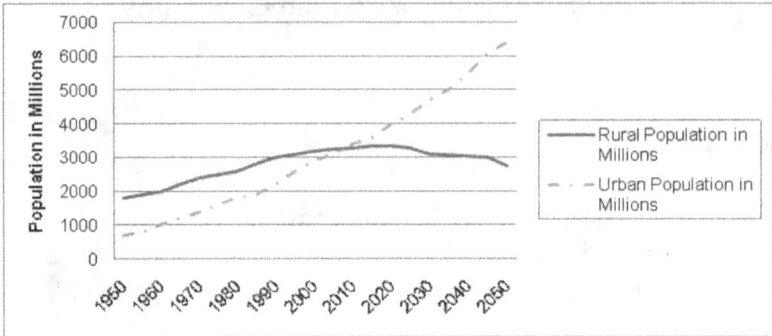

Figure 1. World Rural Versus Urban Population Trends
1950-2050 (United Nations 2007a) Graphic by James F.
Chastain.

Urbanization has not taken place uniformly across
the globe. Since 1950, the majority of urban growth is in
the developing world. Figure 2 expresses this dichotomy
between the more developed and less developed (also
known as developing) regions.

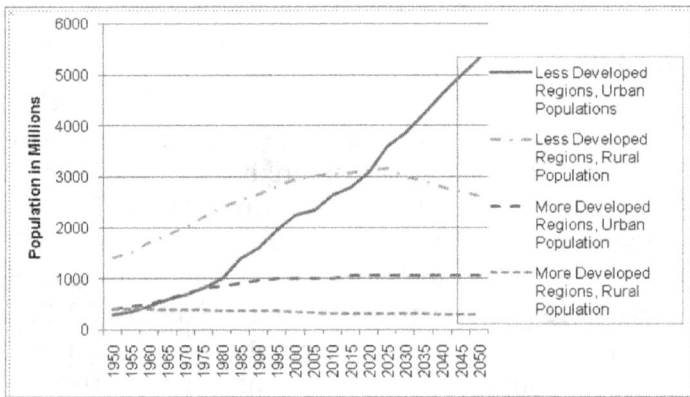

Figure 2. More Developed versus Less Developed Regional
Population Settlement Change 1950-2050 (United Nations
2007b) Graphic by James F. Chastain.

Sub-Saharan Africa is a prominent region in the developing world. No other region has experienced the high rates of urbanization that has taken place here over the last fifty years. Africa is primarily a rural continent, with many people living in the countryside eking out a hardscrabble existence through subsistence farming. Even so, Africa's urban populations are growing faster than its overall average 4 percent annual growth rate. If this continues unabated, Africa's urban population will triple by 2050 (United Nations 2007a). This means African issues are and will be increasingly tied to urban places.

Many Africans and African urban centers will be fundamentally challenged and affected by a range of vulnerabilities and hazards as they interact with and adapt to new urban realities. African urbanization patterns have not modeled those experienced in the West. The age of industrialization led to the rapid growth of Western manufacturing centers. The rapidly industrializing West drew thousands from the countryside into the manufactories in the urban centers. This is not the case in sub-Saharan Africa. Therefore, a better understanding of African urban development will help inform policy makers in the 21st century. This chapter presents an overview of pre-colonial, colonial, and post-colonial urban development with the purpose of situating present and future urban trends in sub-Saharan Africa. North African urbanization is more similar to Middle Eastern urbanism and is not our focus. We discuss sub-Saharan African urbanization and suggest its form as more distinctive in terms of an "African" process and situation.

Legacies of the Past: Sub-Saharan Africa's Urbanization

There have been several typologies of African cities developed by scholars in order to explain urban development and morphology. O'Connor (1983) developed six types of African cities, which describe the structure of the cities as a function of their indigenous founders as opposed to foreign or colonial influences. Given Africa's historical experience, it may be more useful to discuss the urban development of sub-Saharan African cities as hybrid cities (Aryeetey-Attoh 2003). Coquery-Vidrovitch (2005) outlined four periods that encompass African urbanization and incorporate transitions and interaction between various urban models and temporal succession. These are: 1) Ancient cities, pre-1450, 2) Islam & Arab contact, 3) Portuguese-European impacts, and 4) European Colonialism. However, based on the objectives of this book we will generalize the urban types and eras into only three periods: pre-colonial, colonial, and post-colonial.

Modern scholars have tended to under appreciate sub-Saharan Africa's pre-colonial urban heritage (Stock 2004; Murray and Myers 2006; Kaplan et al. 2008). Unfortunately, it took many years to understand indigenous African urban sites and patterns. This is attributable to prevailing racist attitudes among most 19th and 20th century colonial administrators and academics, the lack of indigenous written histories describing the sub-continent's past, and the destruction of archeologically significant places by colonial economic exploitation (Shillington 1995). In actuality, Africa's rich pre-colonial urban legacy reflects the impacts of both indigenous and external urban influences.

Sub-Saharan Africa's pre-colonial urban patterns primarily consist of a central palace and shrine compounds surrounded by high walls, usually along an intra-regional trade route. The site and growth of these cities reflected their political, economic, and social role in society. The proximity of the palace and shrine served as a symbol of the ruler's base of power; the compounds served to separate the social elite from the common elements of this pre-colonial society. The outer wall functioned as a protective barrier for the local population, which undergirded the ruler's place as the guarantor of local security. Southern Africa's Great Zimbabwe period (11th through 15th centuries) is an example that illustrates a highly advanced pre-colonial indigenous urban site. Great Zimbabwe's ruling class resided on a relatively high, centrally located hill surrounded by a valley containing approximately 20,000 people. Great Zimbabwe's central edifice is known as "The Great Enclosure." It served as the focal point for the area's religious and political activities, and is the largest pre-colonial structure in sub-Saharan Africa. Early colonial administrators attributed the Great Zimbabwe's construction technology to Arab or Phoenician builders, again reflecting the deep-seated and incorrect notion of black African inferiority (O'Connor 1983; Shillington 1995; Stock 2004). However, Arabs did significantly influence many pre-colonial African urban places.

Early Arab-Islamic traders influenced pre-colonial sub-Saharan African cities centering them on a permanent market, mosque, public baths, and access to trade networks. Examples are the Sahel trade route cities of Kano, Zaria, and Sokoto, but they can also be seen in the East African cities of Mogadishu and Kilwa. Residential land use was compact, with open courtyards and cellular urban structures. The construction of these cellular structures protected familial and gender privacy by using the familiar Middle East building "L" shaped entrances, windowless walls, and narrow alleyways to create visual blind spots (O'Connor 1983; Stock 2004).

The advent of the European colonial period in Africa brought new influences to both existing urban places and the new cities established in sub-Saharan Africa. Two types of urban forms are generally associated with this era: the colonial city and the European city. Outside the scope of this chapter, but relevant to symbolic places in several port cities is the sinister legacy of the slave trade that left relict slave trade center prisons in these ports.

The colonial cities were the administrative and trade centers of the European colonial powers. To facilitate communications and commerce most colonial cities were located on the ocean, rivers or eventually along railway lines. The colonial city served to control resource extraction from the hinterlands of sub-Saharan Africa to European industrial cities. This fact dominated urban spatial patterns and linkages; roads and railroads did not connect Africa's major cities but were built to facilitate the extraction of Africa's rich resources to the coast for export. Moreover, the Colonial City served as *entrepôts* for the importation of European finished industrial goods — whose raw materials had probably originated as exports from the region (O'Connor 1983; Stock 2004).

Colonial cities were characterized by the social, spatial, and functional segregation of people and land use. Indeed, colonial African cities "were designed to distribute scarce resources in such a way as to promote an exploitative emphasis on economic relations, to facilitate control and domination by a non-indigenous colonial elite, and to solidify a condition of dependency..." (Soja and Weaver 1976, p. 201). The colonial city is an enduring physical symbol and manifestation of the industrial age's drive for empire building and resource exploitation. A few examples of colonial cities are Dar es Salaam, Tanzania; Dakar, Senegal; Conakry, Guinea; Kinshasa, Democratic Republic of the Congo (O'Connor 1983; Stock 2004).

European cities differ from colonial cities based on whom the cities were designed to be occupied by. The European city was developed for European settlement. These settler-designed cities were established by the colonial rulers and were used solely by the European administrators, military, and merchants. No provision was made for the black African population, except for servants and domestic workers. These cities were a completely new urban form in sub-Saharan Africa. They exhibit clear European urban planning principles and patterns. These cities segregated and controlled non-European access and residence within and around them (Njoh 2008). The modern European grid-like block and street patterns clearly outline the central city area. This is where European marketplaces and even some small-scale manufacturing were located. These cities tended to be more expressive of European design principles and settlement patterns as they were designed, implemented, and enforced by a more authoritarian governmental apparatus (O'Connor 1983; Njoh 2008). The Asian "colored" merchants were located on the margins of the city area, allowing them to act as a social and economic intermediary between the central "white" areas and the growing "black" African settlements outside the margins of the planned urban space. The growing peripheral settlements, densely settled by large numbers of migrant workers farther from the margins of the nascent cities, were not planned but reflected the possible economic opportunities available to black Africans (O'Connor 1983). Several examples of European cities include Harare, Zimbabwe; Lusaka, Zambia; Windhoek, Namibia; and Nairobi, Kenya. The European nature of these cities is often still displayed on maps using colonial city and state place names. An example of an anachronistic place name is Salisbury, Southern Rhodesia, the colonial name of Harare, Zimbabwe.

Post-colonial urban growth typically included two characteristics of the existing developed cities and is the most likely city form encountered in sub-Saharan Africa. Their "hybrid" nature reflects the enduring legacy of the indigenous, Arab-Islamic, colonial, and European influences on the social and economic history of sub-Saharan Africa. However, over the past forty years, the rapid growth of these cities, coupled with uncontrolled migrant inflows and corrupt and inept city governments, has resulted in extensive slums or shantytowns surrounding them which defy any clear spatial pattern. This concise overview of sub-Saharan urbanism helps to situate our understanding of the region's rapid urbanization and its inherent challenges.

Urban Patterns & Spatial Characteristics

Figure 3 displays several distinct urban patterns in Africa. In 1950 the majority of sub-Saharan Africa's forty-eight states were primarily rural. Only South Africa had an urbanization level above 50 percent. By 1965 the post-independence era was in full motion and Africa started to experience uncontrolled urbanization as colonial restrictions on black African urban settlement ended. By 1990 almost

all of sub-Saharan African urbanization rates were above
20 percent. By 2010 only Niger, Uganda, Rwanda, Burundi,
and Lesotho are projected to have urbanization levels below
20 percent. Sub-Saharan Africa's recent past and future
illustrates unprecedented rates of urban growth over such
a short period of time (United Nations 2007a; World Bank
2008).

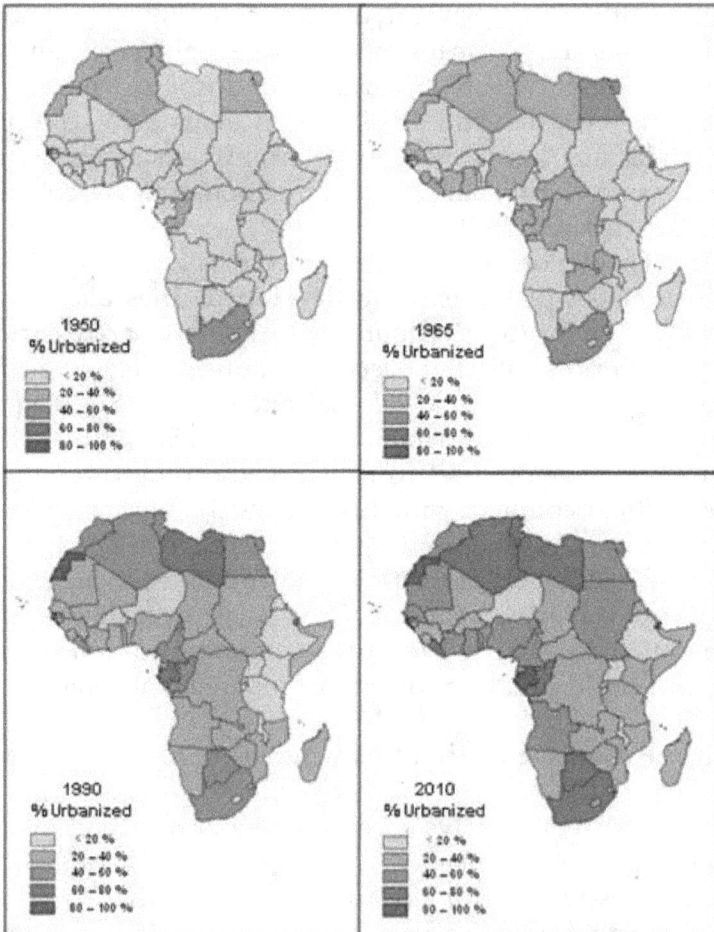

Figure 3. African Urbanization 1950, 1965, 1990, 2010
(United Nations 2007a) Graphic by James F. Chastain and
Steven Oluic.

There are three relatively large urban agglomerations in sub-Saharan Africa today (see Figure 4). The southernmost agglomeration is centered on Johannesburg, South Africa-- sub-Saharan Africa's largest city in 1950. Moving northeast from Johannesburg the next large agglomeration rests in the East Africa cities of Dar es Salaam, Tanzania; Mogadishu, Somalia; Nairobi, Kenya; and Addis Ababa, Ethiopia. The largest sub-Saharan African urban cluster occurs in the West African region between Abidjan, *Cote d'Ivoire* and Lagos, Nigeria. Other major sub-Saharan towns are dispersed across the continent and are relatively isolated from one another based on the lack of road and railroad transportation links (Shillington 1995). This is one of the major obstacles to regional development as many national markets anchored in colonial cities are sequestered from each other with little to no cross-border traffic of people, or commodities between them. In fact, most of these larger post-colonial cities are apt to have more connections with their former European patrons when measuring linkages by airplane travel and trade (Stock 2004). This external urban orientation is further geographically illustrated by the continent's coastal-peripheral urban sites (Figure 4). To better appreciate what these patterns mean we must define urban and urbanization.

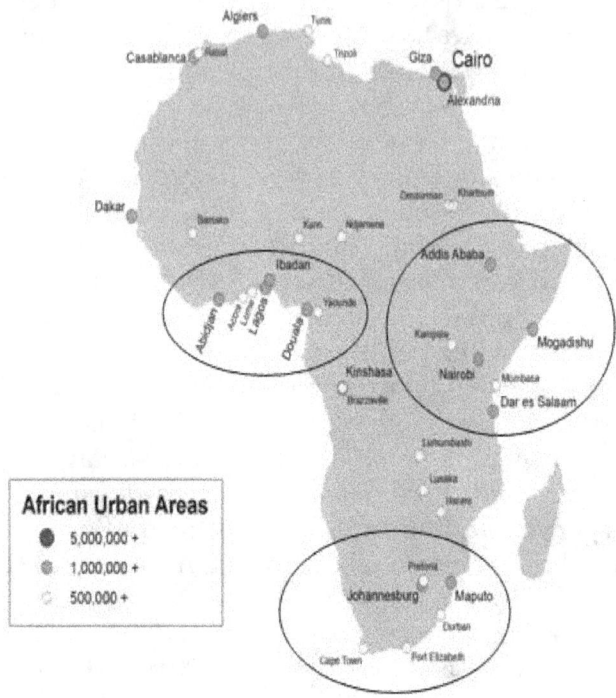

Figure 4. Major African Urban Populations (United Nations 2007a) Graphic by James F. Chastain and Ian Irmischer.

The terms urban and urbanization have been defined and used in several ways. A contemporary urban place is defined as a densely settled non-agricultural human settlement (Kaplan et al. 2008). This definition implies a large number of people living closely together and connected primarily by their shared economic relationships. Historically, urban places have been locations of great economic growth, the age of industrialism being the precursor to most Western cities. Cities facilitate economic activity efficiently by locating administration, labor, markets, production, and transportation networks in spatial proximity (Mumford 1961). Through this proximity, varied functions, and symbiotic relationships an urban place produces economic growth which is both cumulative and causative of future urban growth (Pred 1966). This economic growth normally results in cities in which the majority of the population is better-off economically, have smaller families, better access to government services, and generally live at a higher standard of life than their rural counterparts (UN 2007b; World Bank 2007). This may be applicable in the developed world; however, sub-Saharan Africa's urbanization patterns are quite different.

Urbanization is defined as an increase of people living in urban areas relative to rural places. Rural-to-urban migration and natural population increase account for most of this growth (United Nations 2007b). Of course, the migration can be international or domestic, as the result of amenities such as economic attraction or disamenities like civil upheaval in neighboring states. Of these two processes in urbanization, domestic rural-to-urban migration accounts for the greatest amount of sub-Saharan Africa's urban growth. Rural African populations are influenced by a host of real and perceived pressures and prospects. We can simplify the range of influences into geographical categories termed "push" and "pull" factors.

Push factors are those conditions that compel rural residents to seek a new life in urban places. High fertility rates are a cultural norm in most rural societies as the available family members are a ready labor source on the farms. Moreover, larger rural families provide support to aging parents, as any other form of social security is largely absent from these societies. Another aspect of high fertility as a cultural norm is the social prestige associated with larger families. However, generational rural demographic increases eventually provide unused excess labor as communal and family farm plots cannot sustain further subdivision nor sustain the increased demand for food (Stock 2004).

As Africa's large child-aged cohorts mature into adults and seek employment, they depress local wages and strain the productive capacity of land. The subsistence nature of sub-Saharan rural economies provides little employment opportunity, and these places often lack many governmental and private services such as access to education, health care, or training programs. The failure of agricultural policies including poor marketing services, pressure on the land through population growth, climate variation and change, the failure of true land reform, and the increasing number of regional and civil conflicts tend to "push" rural male youths to urban places in search of jobs to provide remittances back to their families (Tibaijuka 2004).

Cities are often seen as the only mechanism to escape poverty and offer a variety of economic and education opportunities. These prospects — real and perceived — for a better life act to "pull" rural migrants to the city from the hinterlands. The potential for higher wage employment and a brighter future is a powerful impetus to move and drives most migration to urban centers. However, these perceptions are not the reality as urban unemployment has often reported to be well above 50 percent in most sub-Saharan African cities (Stock 2004). Additionally, many of the educational, training, and services believed to exist in municipalities do not often materialize for migrants.

Although rural to urban migration is often credited as the leading determinant of a society's rapid urbanization, this is not the general rule in sub-Saharan Africa. Typically sub-Saharan African cities grow by high rates of natural increase with rural-to-urban migration a close second (United Nations 2004; United Nations 2007b).

As also experienced in Western societies, urbanization leads to reduction in fertility rates (Caldwell 1982; Kalipeni 1995). While this is also true for most of sub-Saharan Africa, urban fertility rates are still much higher than most other urbanized and urbanizing societies in the world. High urban natural increase combined with higher rural natural increase and their concomitant rural to urban migrations put an inordinate pressure on the capacity of urban economies to generate jobs, provide education, and healthcare. Most government services depend on tax revenues for financing their operations. Without large-scale employment opportunities, cities are not able to fund present or future services leading to rampant unemployment, little or decrepit infrastructure and exploding crime rates. The failure of sub-Saharan African cities to employ and provide services to its newcomers is often referred to as *"overurbanization."* Overurbanization denotes a condition of urbanization where urban growth outstrips a city's potential to adequately provide all of the services necessary to support the population and protect civil society (Knox and McCarthy 2005; United Nations 2007b).

The endemic problems of corruption and nepotism further complicate the urban areas of sub-Saharan Africa. Although many African states' lands are often rich in natural resources, much of the profits and tax revenues are skimmed off by corrupt leaders and businesspeople, and rarely reinvested in African economies. Those states less well-off have been the recipients of billions of dollars of international aid in the post-colonial era that makes little impact on the plight of urban and rural citizens. This culture of corruption only exacerbates Africa's overurbanization phenomenon (Stock 2004).

Overurbanization in most sub-Saharan African cities has created a range of challenges that weaken the role of cities as engines of economic growth. Pervasive poverty, inadequate housing, lack of urban services, transportation problems, and environmental degradation all contribute to dreadful living conditions for many urban dwellers. Thus, African overurbanization should be understood as a process of interrelated changes that are mostly detrimental to how people live. Accordingly, many African urban areas are much more than places where people live. They are also a potentially insalubrious context for social-economic-political relations. The complex interaction of the challenges of urban life may be generally simplified into two outcomes to people: poverty and housing (Kaplan et al. 2008).

Overurbanization Challenges in Sub-Saharan Africa's Future

Many Africans and African urban centers will be fundamentally challenged by a range of vulnerabilities and hazards as they interact with and adapt to new urban ways of life and a changing global economy. The informal sector of the economy is unregulated. Illicit employment is often practiced by the most vulnerable segments of urban society: migrants, women, and children. As the formal sector of the economy represents legal and recognized employment, these jobs produce tax revenue for local and state governments as well as for urban infrastructure and services. As urban populations grow in many large sub-Saharan cities, the urban economy is unable to provide formal sector employment, forcing many urban dwellers to work in the informal, or "gray," sector of the economy. Typical informal sector jobs are street traders, artisans, food vendors, drug traffickers, smugglers, thieves, and prostitutes. Although some seem less noisome than others, they all disadvantage urban governance by denying potential tax revenues and flouting the rule of law (Stock 2004; World Bank 2007). It is estimated that more than half of sub-Saharan Africa's urban jobs are in the informal sector, and that this sector is growing ten times faster than formal sector employment. That means that these jobs will support the vast majority of sub-Saharan Africa's estimated 900 million urban populations by 2050 (UN 2007a; World Bank 2008).

The lack of revenues to maintain and improve infrastructure has directly affected the levels of foreign aid and international investment. In the majority of urban centers public buildings are in a state of disrepair, roads lay unrepaired, airport modernization and upgrades are nonexistent which in turn threatens the loss of certification for air travel safety. As well, railroad lines and yards, seaport piers, and cargo terminal handling facilities are in such disrepair due to mismanagement and corruption that international firms are looking elsewhere for investment.

For several states this urban disaster has led to former patron states leaving the region or neocolonial economic ties being cut (Waldon 2007).

The resulting contrast in geographic space of the formal and informal sectors of the economy is quite evident in the urban environment. Extravagant homes and modern office buildings represent the small formal sector that offers well-paid jobs and opportunities; these contrast sharply with the slums and squatter settlements of individuals employed in the informal sector, which are disadvantaged by a lack of education, formal training, and gender inequality. Increasingly, many disadvantaged youths are turning to income redistribution measures through crime and other antisocial behavior. Urban centers may predictably become a source for the "child soldier" phenomena plaguing sub-Saharan Africa (Hanson 2008; Knox and McCarthy 2005).

Overurbanization of the largest cities has not only led to a large informal sector; it has also produced some of the world's most expansive slum housing quarters in sub-Saharan African cities. Over 300 million Africans live in sub-Saharan African cities and over 400 million more will be added by 2050. Housing the urban poor is and will continue to be a significant challenge as some assert that over 60 percent of city residents will live in slums (United Nations 2004; United Nations 2007b). There is a wide gap between housing needs and supply. A stark example is the housing situation in Nigeria, a relatively well-off state given its abundant oil resources, which is only able to supply 10,000 housing units while there is a backlog of over four million housing units (Tibaijuka 2004).

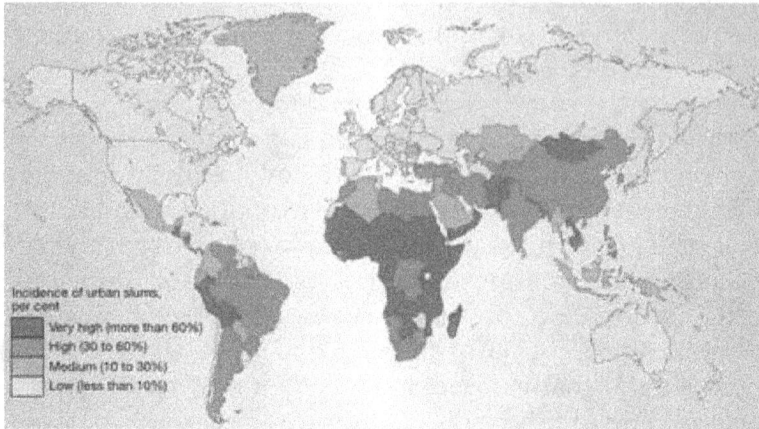

Figure 5. Global Urban Slum Incidence
(United Nations 2004)

Slums occur world-wide, but have a concentration in Africa (Figure 5). The urban location of many slums in sub-Saharan Africa is a legacy of the colonial-European city. Colonial-European city zoning and land use patterns served to isolate the majority of indigenous Africans in rural areas where their labor was used to exploit natural resources and provide agricultural products from plantations to the imperial economies. The small number of Africans allowed working in urban areas occupied peripheral settlements away from European housing and businesses in the central city. This served to control African access to urban places. After independence, African elites displaced the Europeans and occupied the central city, perpetuating the divide (Coquery-Vidrovitch 2005; Njoh 2008). Lacking entry credentials, new migrants to the city were forced to perch on the urban fringes. As the rapid urbanization of regions has outstripped the supply of affordable private or public housing in cities, the housing supply for the majority of sub-Saharan urbanites is and will continue to be slum settlements at the periphery of urban society and infrastructure (O'Connor 1983; Knox and McCarthy 2005). Sub-Saharan African urban slum population statistics are listed in tables 1 and 2.

Table 1. Comparison of African to World Urban Slum Dwellers (United Nations 2004)

Region	Urban Population (000)	Urban Pop as % of Total Population	% Slum Dwellers in Total Population
Sub- Saharan Africa	231,052	34.6	71.9
Northern Africa and the Middle East	145,624	57.7	29.5
Advanced economies	676,492	78.9	5.8
World average	2,923,184	47.7	31.6
Developing states	2,021,665	40.9	43

The vast majority of the new urban dwellers are unemployed or employed at low wage within the informal labor market. The nature of these squalid housing settlements provides an unsanitary and dangerous environment. The majority of these homes or shelters are not connected to the local electrical grid and lack plumbing for fresh water supply or sewage disposal. The safety and access of the urban drinking water supply is an acute problem for many sub-Saharan African cities. Less than 20 percent of these houses have a water connection; most residents depend on one tap, with an irregular water flow of dubious quality, to serve more than one hundred people. In effect, millions of African urbanites have, at best, limited access to one of life's basic necessities; and in many cases the available water will be a source of disease. The poor availability of potable water will likely worsen as squatter settlements expand; this will further exacerbate already strained medical infrastructure and services (United Nations 2004; USAID 2005; United Nations 2007b; World Bank 2008).

Table 2. Select African State Urban Slum Populations
(United Nations 2004)

State	Slum Dwellers as % of Urban Population
Sierra Leone	96
South Africa	33
Lesotho	57
Cameroon	79
Kenya	67
India	55
Central African Republic	92
Morocco	33
Ghana	70

These residents' housing will be substandard, in violation of local building regulations, and largely over-crowded. These nonpermanent makeshift houses will be built illegally on neither land that people own nor rent. Thus, lack of land tenure limits the potential of capital accumulation in homes. This housing will be located on unpaved streets in the least desirable locations — derelict sites, poorly drained land, and waste dumps. They will usually coexist with open sewers on denuded, uneven land. This will further lessen resiliency of slum dwellers when dealing with natural disasters such as mudslides. Diseases such as cholera, tuberculosis, and HIV/AIDS will grow due to the nature of these urban settlements. Outside of international aid organizations, there is little that the social services and medical infrastructure of most sub-Saharan African cities and states can do (Stock 2004; Bennhold 2008).

Household strategies for dealing with this urban environment may include having more children to help increase household resources, while limiting education and training opportunities for these children working in the informal sector. This type of reaction would worsen an already difficult situation. It is important that we understand that African security will be increasingly realized or threatened in urban places.

A Dismal Urban Future or Hidden Opportunities?

Urban places are typically the engines of growth and revenues, however in sub-Saharan Africa they are a severe drain on state economies. The overurbanization of most sub-Saharan cities is a tremendous disadvantage to African states competing in an increasingly integrated global market. The boom and bust economic cycles that ravage African economies, the endemic corruption, incompetent and nepotistic ruling elites, high birth rates, and lack of educational opportunities, employment, and medical care will retard any national progress.

Increasingly frustrated populations living in absolute squalor while their state's resources are exploited by political leaders and transnational corporations will likely lead to more civil strife. Urban centers are becoming increasingly dangerous as illustrated by South Africa, once the leading state in Africa; it now boasts the highest murder rates in the world. Those who have skills and professions are seeking their fortunes elsewhere, typically in Western countries. This contributes to the region's "Brain Drain" phenomenon (Tibaijuka 2004; Kaplan et al. 2008).

This increasing instability may provide a fertile environment for a restive population to be exploited by local opposition leaders, organized crime networks and local warlords. The weakened African state will not have the capacity to regulate conflict any longer. The current (2009) global economic contraction means less resource demand, leading to decreased investment in Africa. However, opportunities may also be found in sub-Saharan African twenty-first century urbanization.

Urban places do create efficiencies in the distribution of goods and services to people. By understanding the future growth potential in sub-Saharan Africa's urban places, governments can plan for the cost-effective and equitable provision of water, sewers, schools, to newly urbanized populations. If these migrants were to stay in rural places, governments would be hard pressed to efficiently provide these services to their citizens. Thus, urban places may also be developed as spaces of hope for improving human security on the continent. The most significant issue will not be the planning and identification of issues inherent with rapid urbanization, but providing the financial capital to pay for simple urban necessities needed now like paved roads, clean water access, and regular trash disposal. Early and consistent investment in African municipalities may be the most cost effective strategy to maintain security on the continent. Urban places provide an ideal target for this investment.

Major James Farrell Chastain is an Assistant Professor of Geography at the United States Military Academy. He has taught courses in Military Geography, Urban Geography, American History, World History, Physical Geography, Cultural Geography, Latin American Geography, and the Geography of the Middle East and Africa. His research focuses on North African immigration into France and African urbanization. MAJ Chastain holds a graduate degree in Geography.

Lieutenant Colonel (Dr.) Steven Oluic is Associate Professor of Geography, and has taught courses in Urban Geography, Physical Geography, World Regional Geography and European and Russian Regional Geography. His research focuses on radical Islam in southeastern Europe and radicalism among the Balkan Muslim Diasporas in the US and Europe. He is the author of one book, numerous book chapters and articles, and is the recipient of several research grants. LTC Oluic holds graduate degrees in Environmental Science and Geography.

References

Aryeetey-Attoh, Samuel. 2003. *Geography of Sub-Saharan Africa.* 2nd ed. Upper Saddle River, NJ: Prentice Hall.

Bennhold, Kristin. 2008. Annan urges rich nations not to drop aid to Africa. *International Herald Tribune.* November 17.

Caldwell, John. 1982. *Theory of Fertility Decline.* New York: Academic Press.

Coquery-Vidrovitch, Catherine. 2005. *The History of African Cities South of the Sahara.* Princeton: Markus Wiener Publishers.

Hanson, Stephanie. 2008. Council on Foreign Relations website. Urbanization in Sub-Saharan Africa. http://www.cfr.org/publication/14327/urbanization_in_subsaharan_africa.html#2.

Kalipeni, Ezekiel. 1995. The Fertility Transition in Africa. *The Geographical Review*85, no. 3: 286-300.

Kaplan, David, James Wheeler, and Steven Holloway. 2008. *Urban Geography.* 2nd ed. Hoboken, NJ: John Wiley & Sons.

Knox, Paul, and Linda McCarthy. 2005. *Urbanization.* 2nd ed. Upper Saddle River, NJ: Prentice Hall.

Mumford, Lewis. 1961. *The City in History.* New York: Harcourt.

Murray, Martin J., and Garth Myers, eds. 2006. *Cities in Contemporary Africa.* New York: Palgrave MacMillan.

Njoh, Ambe. 2008. The segregated city in British and French colonial Africa. *Race Class* 49: 87-95.

O'Connor, Anthony. 1983. *The African City.* New York: Africana Publishing Company.

Pred, Allen. 1966. The *Spatial Dynamics of Urban Industrial Growth.*

Cambridge: MIT Press.

Shillington, Kevin. 1995. *History of Africa*. Oxford: Palgrave Macmillan.

Soja, Edward. and C. Weaver. 1976. Urbanization and underdevelopment in East Africa. In *Urbanization and counter-urbanization*, ed. B.J. Berry. Beverly Hills, CA: Sage.

Stock, Robert. 2004. *Africa South of the Sahara*. 2nd ed. New York: The Guilford Press, 2004.

Tibaijuka, Anna K. 2004. Africa on the Move: an urban crisis in the making. Report submitted to the UN-Habitat Commission for Africa.

United Nations. 2004. *The State of the World's Cities*. London: Human Settlements Programme.

United Nations. 2007a. World Urbanization Prospects: 2007 Revision, Department of Economic and Social Affairs/Population Division.

United Nations. 2007b. State of World Population 2007: Unleashing the Potential of Urban Growth.

United States Agency for International Development. 2005. Congressional Budget Justification - FY 2005, Annex I: Africa. http://www.usaid.gov/policy/budget/ cbj2005/afr/za.html.

Waldon, Pablo. 2007. Experts Question G8's Emphasis on Africa. Deutsche Welle News Service, May 18. http://www.dw-world.de/dw/article/ 0,2144,2516406,00.html.

World Bank. 2008. Africa's Urbanization for Development. http://www.worldbank.org/external/default/WDSContentServer/WDSP/IB/2008/09/10/000334955_200 80910063642/Rendered/PDF/452980WP0Box3311Urbanizat ion1Report.pdf.

Africa's Medical Geography

Jon C. Malinowski

Key Points

- Diseases are a serious threat to the lives of Africans.

- HIV infection rates are higher in Africa than anywhere in the world.

- Healthcare for millions of Africans is poor and providing care for the general public is a difficult challenge for governments and other organizations.

Introduction

Africa is profoundly and tragically affected by disease. Poverty, political chaos, and geographic conditions have made the continent a crucible for disease rates that are rare in most other parts of the globe. Disease in Africa does not just kill humans. It weakens them, takes them away from productive activities, and makes them more susceptible to other stresses.

Disease morbidity (sickness) and mortality (death) statistics for Africa are astounding. For example, it is estimated that 1 million Africans (approximately 1 in 967) die per year from malaria (UNICEF 2007). In the United States, the same disease kills less than 10 people annually. Over 24 million people in sub-Saharan Africa have HIV/AIDS (approximately 1 in 40), including about 2 million children, and government health expenditures per person in some African states are below $20 per person per year according to the World Health Organization (UNAIDS 2008a; World Health Organization 2007a). In the United States, there are about 250 physicians for each 100,000 people. In Niger, there are only two (World Health Organization 2007a). To understand Africa's challenges, health and disease must be considered.

Medical Geography

Given the scope of this book, an introduction to the field of medical geography is impossible, but it is important to keep the basic tenets of the discipline in mind when contemplating health in Africa. In short, medical geographers tend to focus on two broad areas related to health and disease. First, they consider the distribution and spread of diseases or other health-related issues, including studying the factors that may help or hinder diffusion. Second, medical geographers focus on access to healthcare and the availability of medical care.

Human health can be affected by numerous stimuli, including chemical, physical, infectious, and psychosocial insults (Meade and Earickson 2000). In Africa, for example, a chemical impact on health might be low iron levels in the blood caused by malnutrition. Negative physical stimuli might include broken bones or other traumas. Infectious insults can be caused by viruses, bacteria, flukes, protozoa, etc. Malaria and sleeping sickness (trypanosomiasis) are just two examples. Finally, health can be affected by psychosocial factors such as war, crowding, or cultural attitudes. Female genital mutilation, practiced in some parts of Africa, is an example of a cultural tradition that often has profound negative effects on the health of women.

Meade and Earickson (2000) summarize the state of health in a population with what they call a triangle of ecology. In short, they emphasize that health is a function of the population, the habitat they live in, and their behavior. For example, a population that is older might be more susceptible to mortality from the flu. A population that lives in a tropical habitat will be more likely to contract particular diseases than desert dwellers. And finally, a population's beliefs and social structure can also affect overall health. Thus, as we highlight some of Africa's major health challenges, it is necessary to consider the multiple factors affecting morbidity or mortality.

An analysis of a population's health has numerous geographical components. Consider a sick child suffering from malaria in a tiny West African village. At the local level, the child might be affected by the absence of a healthcare clinic or proper medicine. At the state level, the child may be affected by political chaos that focuses government resources elsewhere. At the regional level, the child is affected by the climate and vegetation patterns that encourage the spread of the mosquitoes that carry malaria. And at the international and global levels, the child is affected by an economic system that, whether right or wrong, has contributed to Africa's economic marginalization. Thus, it is important to consider factors at various geographic scales when attempting to understand positive or negative changes in a population's health.

Selected Major Diseases of Africa

Numerous serious diseases affect large numbers of Africans and severely tax the economic resources of state governments and international aid groups. While some, like malaria, are eons old, others, like HIV, are creating new and unique challenges for the continent.
We offer a discussion of the diseases which are most problematic to Africa.

HIV/AIDS

HIV/AIDS is the number one killer in Africa, killing 2.1 million in 2006 alone. In 2008, roughly 67 percent of all HIV-infected persons worldwide lived in Sub-Saharan Africa, a total of about 22 million people. Geographically, the infection is most severe in central and southern Africa, where the disease is devastating populations. As shown in Figure 1, some states now have nearly a quarter of their population infected. Swaziland, Botswana, and Lesotho each have infection rates of over 23 percent (UNAIDS 2008a; Population Reference Bureau 2008).

Approximately 61 percent of all Africans infected with HIV are women. Women, and especially young girls, are biologically more susceptible to contracting HIV, but biological factors alone do not explain why young women are the face of AIDS in Africa. The disparity between status of men and women highlights the discrimination and abuse that affects women in many parts of the continent. In some African states, women have little or no say in a sexual relationship or marriage and are thus often prevented from accessing HIV/AIDS information or demanding that a husband or partner use a condom. In some Kenyan communities, when a woman's husband dies she is forced out of her home and her property can be taken, thus thrusting her into poverty (Human Rights Watch 2008). In addition, girls are less likely to receive education equitable to boys and have a harder time accessing economic resources in their communities when it comes time to earn a living or pay for healthcare. Because of this, many girls seek older, economically stable males for relationships, but older men are more likely to be infected by HIV (Poku 2006). Rape, forced marriage at a young age, and the sexual exploitation of women during times of conflict are also factors in some African states (UNAIDS 2008b). In short, the poor status of women in many regions of Africa can be equated with high HIV/AIDS rates for females, especially among women who are 15 to 24.

Swaziland	26.1
Botswana	23.9
Lesotho	23.2
South Africa	18.1
Namibia	15.3
Zimbabwe	15.3
Zambia	15.2
Mozambique	12.5
Malawi	11.9
Kenya	7.8
Central African Republic	6.3
Tanzania	6.2
Uganda	5.4
Cameroon	5.1
Cote d'Ivoire	3.9
Congo	3.5
Nigeria	3.1
Rwanda	2.8
Angola	2.1
Ghana	1.9
Liberia	1.7
Sierra Leone	1.7
Burkina Faso	1.6
Mali	1.5
Congo, Dem. Rep. of	1.4
Senegal	1.0
Algeria	0.1
Morocco	0.1

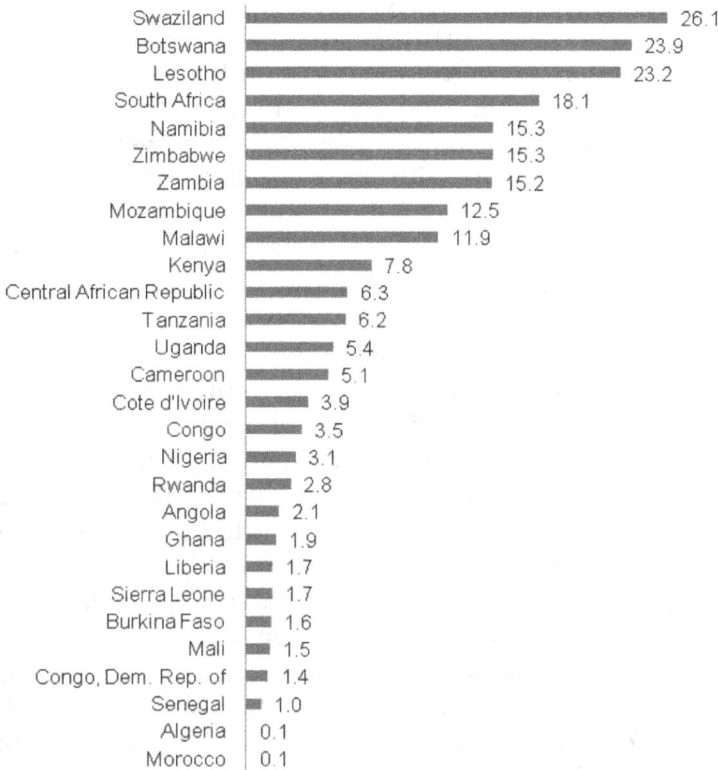

Figure 1. Percent of Adults (ages 15-49) in Selected African States Infected with HIV, 2007 (UNAIDS 2008a; chart by author)

AIDS has a catastrophic effect on Africa's health. One-third of all HIV-infected infants die in their first year if not treated. Life expectancies, which had been rising in many places, have taken a downturn in areas where HIV rates are high. The average life expectancy in Lesotho has dropped to 36 from a high of 60 just 10 years ago according to the Population Reference Bureau (2008). Because of high death rates among young adults, workforces are also affected and thus a state's economic productivity can be reduced significantly. For example, AIDS has killed many teachers in Africa, making it harder to provide even basic education in some areas (UNAIDS Inter-Agency Task Team 2008). Poor education in turn often perpetuates a downward spiral of higher AIDS rates in addition to lower economic productivity and ability to compete in the global economy. Societies must also come to grips with the estimated 12 million AIDS orphans who have lost both parents to the disease. AIDS also has led to increased prevalence of pneumonia and tuberculosis in areas with high infection rates (Bulletin of the World Health Organization 2008; Skolnik and Carter 2007).

Because transmission of the disease in Africa is primarily through sexual contact, prevention measures are mostly directed to sex education programs. Abstinence, delayed sexual activity, monogamy, condom use, counseling, and testing are all emphasized. But as noted, education systems have also been affected by AIDS deaths and even when education is available, girls often have unequal access. In addition, myths and misunderstandings about AIDS and sex often work against health education. Myths about AIDS in some areas of Africa have included the notion that sex with a virgin will cure the disease or that HIV does not even exist and is actually an old disease that has been around for a long time (Bateman 2007). As an extreme example of the effects of these attitudes, a recent study estimated that over 330,000 lives were lost in South Africa due to the government's rejection of donated antiretroviral (ARV) drugs and denial that HIV was the cause of AIDS (Chigwedere et al. 2008). Because many states have few resources for health care anyway, HIV/AIDS presents a formidable challenge (Cohen et al. 2008).

Malaria

Malaria is caused by parasites of the genus *Plasmodium* and is spread to humans by the bite of infected Anopheles mosquitoes. Thus, in terms commonly used by medical geographers, the *Plasmodium* parasite is the agent of the disease, the human is the host of the disease, and the mosquito is the vector by which the disease is transferred to the host. There are four types of *Plasmodium* parasites that can infect human populations, but the most deadly is *Plasmodium falciparum*, alone responsible for 90 percent of the world's malaria deaths (World Health Organization 2007c).

When a person is bitten by an infected mosquito, the parasite quickly infects the cells of the liver and asexually reproduces for one to two weeks. When the hepatocyte cells of the liver rupture from the infection, red blood cells are infected. Further reproduction of the parasites occurs in the red blood cells and in time, more and more blood cells become infected. Because the parasite is primarily in liver cells and red blood cells, it remains relatively hidden from the body's immune system. Some of the parasites also remain dormant for a period of six months to three years. Thus, a person infected may have recurrent bouts with the disease years after infection if untreated (Greenwood et al. 2008).

Typical malaria symptoms include fever, chills, vomiting, and headaches and generally manifest themselves approximately 10-15 days after infection. In many cases, the disease can be fatal if untreated. Treatment generally includes the use of antimalarial drugs. Historically, one of the cheapest and thus most commonly used drugs was chloroquine, but in recent decades *Plasmodium falciparum* has grown resistant to chloroquine, prompting the use of other drugs.

Geographically, malaria is associated with water because mosquitoes lay eggs in water. Thus, in areas with high rainfall year-round or near stagnant or slow-moving water, malaria may be endemic (i.e. always present to some degree within the population). In areas that are primarily affected by periodic rainfall, the disease may only be seasonal. Historically, the draining of wet areas was a common form of malaria control. Today, efforts are centered on controlling mosquito populations through the use of indoor residual spraying (IRS) and the use of long-lasting insecticidal Nets

(LLINs). IRS involves spraying interior walls of a building with insecticides because mosquitoes often rest after biting a victim. Thus, if they bite one person in a household and then land on a treated surface, they will die before they can infect someone else. The nets operate in a similar way and are quite cost effective at only a few dollars per treated net. When combined with local efforts to reduce the places where mosquitoes can breed, malaria often can be controlled. The chemical DDT was commonly used in the past as a cheap insecticide for IRS, and still is used at times, but there are a whole range of other alternatives currently available, although at higher cost. The use of prophylactic drugs is rarely practical for residents in malarial areas and is more commonly used by travelers. No cheap and totally effective vaccine for malaria has been developed to date (Greenwood et al. 2008).

Malaria is a global problem, with about 40 percent of the world's population at risk and more than a half billion cases of sickness annually. The vast majority of cases and deaths, as many as a million a year, are in sub-Saharan Africa, where the disease is endemic (CDC 2007a; see Figure 2). It is estimated that a high prevalence of malaria causes an average decline of 1.3 percent in a state's annual economic growth, which over the years has led to a poverty gap between counties where malaria is and is not common (World Health Organization 2007c). In poor families, malaria reduces the ability of productive workers to earn a living and diverts potential savings to healthcare and treatment. The World Health Organization estimates that malaria alone accounts for 40 percent of public health expenditures, up to half of all admissions to hospitals or clinics, and up to 60 percent of outpatient visits. Infected children often miss school as well, reducing their future ability to earn a productive living.

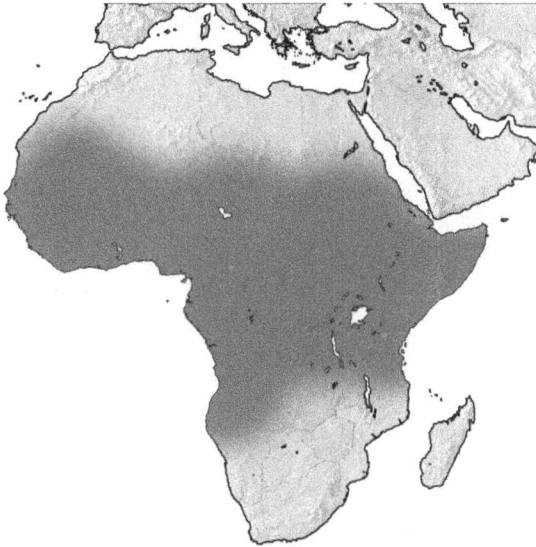

Figure 2. Distribution of Malaria (CDC 2004; map
by author)

Yellow Fever

Yellow fever is a mosquito-transmitted viral disease
that causes an acute hemorrhagic fever. In the most severe
cases, which account for about 15 percent of all infections,
internal hemorrhaging occurs followed often by coma and/
or death (Centers for Disease Control 2007b). The disease
remains common in Africa despite an effective vaccine. In
the 1960s Yellow Fever was almost wiped out, but many
states stopped immunizing children and in recent decades
the disease has returned. As shown in Figure 3, over 30
African states are considered at-risk. Immunization rates of
60-80 percent are needed to contain the disease, but many
states do not exceed vaccination rates of even 30 percent
(Canadian Medical Association Journal 2008).

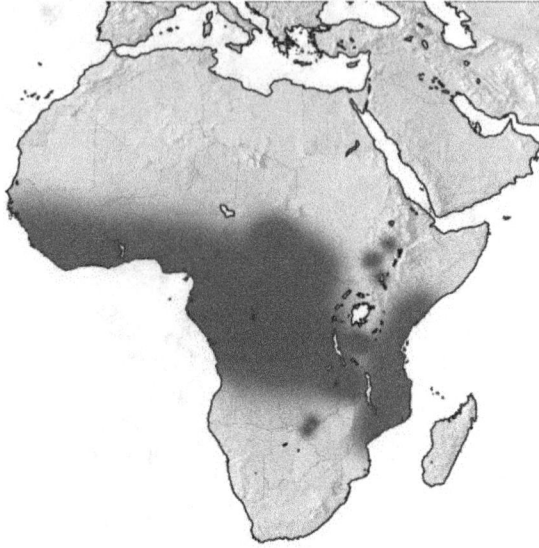

Figure 3. Distribution of Yellow Fever (Centers for Disease
Control and Prevention 2007b; map by author)

Sleeping Sickness (Trypanosomiasis)

Sleeping sickness, the common name for human
African trypanosomiasis, is a fly-vectored parasitic disease
that is fatal if left untreated. The disease, which has two
major forms (*gambiense* and *rhodesiense)*, is endemic in
much of sub-Saharan Africa. Sleeping sickness is spread
by large, biting tsetse flies (Figure 4), which live on the
blood of humans and animals. The parasite, a single-celled
protozoa, causes fever, joint pain, headaches, and swollen
lymph nodes in the early stage of infection. If untreated, the
disease breaks down the immune system and can lead to
cardiac, endocrine, and kidney disorders as well as anemia
(Simarro et al. 2008). Delirium and coma are common
in advanced stages. Eventually, without treatment, 100
percent of infected persons will die. In addition to infection
from tsetse flies, sexual contact and blood transfusions can
also spread the disease.

In 2000, the World Health Organization estimated that up to 60 million people in Africa were at risk of being bitten by a tsetse fly and that 300,000 Africans were infected. The World Health Organization reported just over 16,000 new cases. Africans most affected by sleeping sickness are those who live, farm, fish, or hunt in areas where the tsetse fly is common (World Health Organization 2008b). Because the tsetse fly inhabits areas that otherwise would be excellent agricultural land, trypanosomiasis has a detrimental effect on the economy of the states infected. Sleeping sickness also affects cattle and other animals and therefore reduces the human population in some parts of Africa because farmers cannot raise cattle in areas where tsetse flies are common. The disease is known as *nagana* when it infects animal populations. Animals also serve as a reservoir (source population) for the parasite, allowing it to survive in areas even if the human infection rate is low.

Efforts to control the disease are multifaceted. Vector control efforts using insecticide to kill tsetse flies or traps to reduce their numbers are common, but expensive. Insecticides can be sprayed in endemic areas or even poured onto livestock on which flies feed. Traps are inexpensive, but are not useful over large areas. A successful but expensive technique is the sterile insect technique (SIT) that involves releasing sterile male flies into the environment to compete with regular males. This reduces the number of offspring that female files produce, but the cost is quite expensive and beyond the reach of most states. Drug treatments for the disease are available, but many are costly, require multiple doses, or have significant side effects. Some drugs are also not effective for patients in the latter stage of the disease. Another focus of control efforts revolves around better identification and monitoring of infected areas and populations. This can be difficult given the political turmoil and poor communications infrastructure across much of the continent (Simarro et al. 2008).

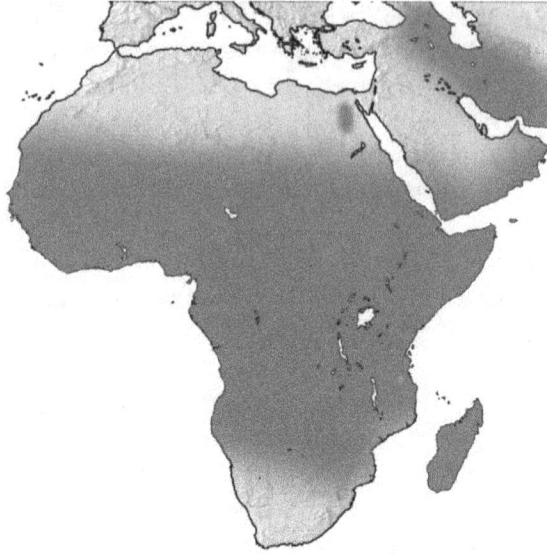

Figure 4. Areas Infested by Tsetse Flies (FAO 2002; map by author)

River Blindness (Onchocerciasis)

Onchocerciasis, or river blindness, is a parasitic disease spread by the bite of certain black flies. The parasite (*Onchocerca volvulus*), causes worms to grow in the human body, which initiates a strong immune response and causes severe itching. The worms can live up to 15 years with each female worm typically laying 1000 to 3000 eggs per day. Small larvae hatched from the eggs can get picked up by black flies when they bite, thus potentially carrying the larvae to the next human a fly bites. In many infected humans, microfilariae migrate to the surface of the cornea, and over time, the cornea becomes permanently opaque (World Health Organization 2008c).

As shown in Figure 5, river blindness is most common in West and Central Africa, where an estimated 18 million people are infected by the parasite. Of those affected, approximately 300,000 to a half million are permanently blind because of the disease. River blindness can significantly reduce economic productivity because infected or blinded persons cannot work and must be cared for by others in the community. These caregivers are often children who in turn cannot attend school. Some infected areas, often locations with good soil fertility, are totally abandoned. Prevention efforts focus on controlling black fly populations, but the drug Mectizan® is now used at a cost of about $1.50 per dose. A single injection per year helps keep the disease in check and reduces the itching that goes with infection (Mectizan Distribution Program 2006).

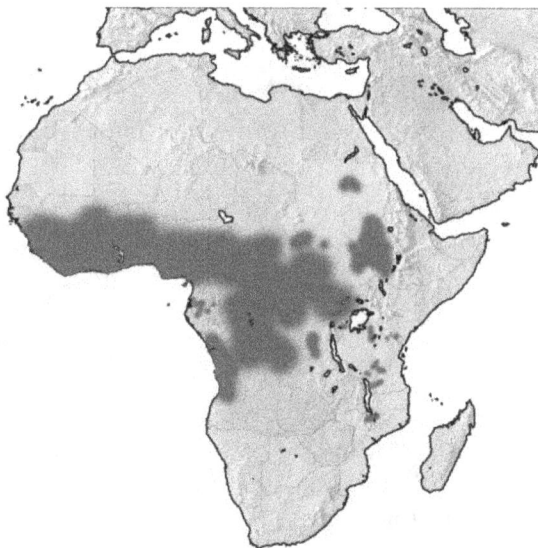

Figure 5. Distribution of River Blindness (Mectizan Donation Program 2006; map by author)

Dengue Fever

Dengue fever is an infection spread by the bite of a mosquito to humans. It is endemic in 100 states around the world, including many in Africa (Figure 6). The disease is on the rise globally and approximately 40 percent of the world's population is at risk. Increased urbanization is largely to blame because humans often create small pools of water in trash heaps and around residences, providing perfect breeding grounds for mosquitoes. Because of this, populations in urban and suburban areas of the tropics are most at risk, which may explain the disease's continuing prevalence in Africa, where cities have grown tremendously in the past half century. In 1950, Africa was only 15 percent urbanized, but by 2007 that number had increased to 37 percent and continues to rise (Population Reference Bureau, 2007b). Dengue causes a flu-like condition, but in some patients can progress to what is known as dengue hemorrhagic fever that manifests with very high fever, enlargement of the liver, and often, death. There is no approved vaccine, so control methods focus reduction or elimination of mosquito populations, a difficult task in urban areas with countless small pools and puddles of rainwater, wastewater, and the like (World Health Organization 2008a).

Ebola

Ebola is a horrific virus that causes death in up to 90 percent of all humans infected. Fever, weakness, aches, and sore throats may be followed by vomiting, diarrhea, kidney and liver impairment, and in the worst cases, internal and external bleeding as the body's cell membranes fall apart. Because Ebola kills quickly, (two days to two weeks) and because transmission requires direct contact with the blood or bodily fluids of an infected person, the disease has not affected a wide area. But given the deadliness of the virus, and the reality that humans can travel around the world in just hours, health officials are naturally concerned about Ebola (World Health Organization 2007b).

The disease was first identified in 1976 and has caused over 1200 known deaths since. The reservoir for Ebola is not known. There are cases of transmission from primates to humans, but it is believed that primates are infected from some other source. Contact with other animals has also been linked to cases in humans. Ebola is found in Africa and parts of the Western Pacific. There are four subtypes, including Zaire, Sudan, Côte d'Ivoire, and Reston, which has not caused illness in humans and may have originated in Asia; it was found in a group of monkeys imported from the Philippines to Reston, Virginia in 1989 (World Health Organization 2007b).

Marburg Hemorrhagic Fever

Marburg is caused by a virus of the same family as Ebola. It presents itself in such a way that it is almost indistinguishable from Ebola. At the onset, patients have severe headaches, fever, and body aches. After several days, diarrhea, vomiting, and bleeding from body orifices destroys the body, and death usually occurs between five and eight days after symptoms begin. In Africa, cases of the disease have been recorded in Kenya, South Africa, Democratic Republic of Congo, and Angola. Cases were also reported in Yugoslavia and Germany in 1967 from contact with an African green monkey imported for research purposes from Uganda (World Health Organization 2005).

Dracunculus / Guinea Worm

The guinea worm (*Dracunculus medinensis*) is a roundworm that infects humans when contaminated water is ingested. The larvae of the worm live in freshwater copepods, often referred to as water fleas, of the genus *Cyclops*. When humans drink contaminated water, the infected copepods get into the stomach and then are destroyed by stomach acid, allowing the larvae to get into the human system. Over time, generally about a year, female worms mate and grow to 2-3 feet long and eventually begin to emerge from the body, usually from the legs. At the point where the worm begins to emerge, a painful blister forms. Humans often try to relieve the pain of the blister by submerging it in water. When this happens, the blister can rupture, and when it does, the female worm releases thousands of larvae, which then can be ingested by the copepods to continue the disease cycle. The worm eventually, and slowly, works its way out of the ruptured blister. The pain of this process has given the worm the nickname "the fiery serpent" in some areas (World Health Organization 2008d).

Eradication of the guinea worm is one of the great successes of the global public health community. Twenty years ago there were approximately 3.5 million cases worldwide. In 2006, just over 25,000 cases were reported and by 2007 cases were just under 6,000, a dramatic decline in just one year. Nearly all of these were in Sudan. Other remaining cases are in Mali, Niger, and Nigeria. Some estimates suggest that the disease may be eradicated by 2009, making it the first successful global eradication of a health risk since smallpox three decades ago. The success has largely come due to the distribution of drinking tubes with gauze at one end that block the copepods from being taken in by humans when drinking from ponds or streams. Treatment of water sources has also contributed to the decline. This success is an excellent reminder that disease can be treated by addressing the agent (parasite, virus), the vector (copepod, mosquitoes) or the host (humans) (World Health Organization 2003).

Malnutrition

A lack of proper nutrition for many Africans complicates efforts to combat other diseases and health conditions. The Population Reference Bureau reports that as of 2008, 26 percent of all Africans are undernourished (Population Reference Bureau 2008). The number rises to 31 percent in sub-Saharan Africa. In some states or in local areas, the numbers can be even higher. For example, over 50 percent of people in war-torn Liberia and Sierra Leone do not receive adequate nutrition. This means they do not even have adequate energy intake to carry out light physical activity. It is estimated that malnutrition contributes to half of child deaths before age 5 worldwide. Undernutrition is particularly dangerous to a population's health because it weakens people and thus makes them more susceptible to disease or less able to fight a disease once contracted. In addition, nutritional deficiencies, such as not enough iron in a child's diet, can retard proper physical or mental development. Nearly half of Ethiopia's children are malnourished, growing up "stunted and sickly, weaklings in a land that still runs on manual labor...shorn of as many as 15 IQ points, unable to learn or even concentrate, inclined to drop out of school early" (Wines 2006).

Healthcare

A discussion of healthcare on the continent is well beyond the scope of this chapter, but it safe to say that access to healthcare for millions of Africans is poor. Some states are only able to, or willing to, spend just a few dollars a year on healthcare per citizen. Poor states have numerous demands on limited budgets; schools must be built, borders or state sovereignty must be defended, roads must be constructed. As shown in Table 1, per capita health expenditures from all sources (private and public) are quite low when compared to over $5,667 per person in the United States. In addition, the number of physicians per capita is also startlingly low compared to the U.S. (2.4 per 1000 population in 2004), and the average (3.0 per 1000) for the 30 member states of the OECD (OECD 2006).

Table 1. Selected Healthcare Indicators for Selected African States

State	Per Capita Spending on Healthcare[1] (2006 $US)	Physicians per 1000 people[2] (2004)
South Africa	$ 437	.770
Namibia	$165	.297
Botswana	$362	.398
Nigeria	$27	.282
Senegal	$38	.057
Mali	$28	.079
Burkina Faso	$27	.059
Chad	$22	.039
Ethiopia	$6	.027

[1] Total of public and private spending per person. United States was $5,667 for the same period. World Bank 2007.
[2] Africa Health Workforce Observatory 2007.

Even when money is available for healthcare, deciding how to spend it is not always easy. Should a government target a specific disease or health problem that plagues its citizens, or should resources be divided evenly to improve overall health? Furthermore, should a state invest in high technology devices that might only benefit a few in the capital city, or should resources be invested in simpler technologies that can be distributed widely? Resources also affect the availability of pharmaceuticals, which frustrates aid workers who know that many diseases could be controlled or eliminated if the sick had access to even basic drugs (Stock 1995).

Geographically, rural areas are often in dire need of access to health clinics or doctors, but poor roads make the implementation of rural health strategies quite difficult. And even if a small, primary care facility is available, it might still be a day's journey for a poor, rural African. Thus, although a sick person may have access to healthcare, the frequency of treatment may be low and follow-up appointments or treatments rare.

Dr. Jon C. Malinowski is Professor of Geography at the United States Military Academy, West Point, New York. He has taught a variety of world regional geography courses, including Geography of the Middle East and Africa. In addition to academic articles in the field of Behavioral Geography, Dr. Malinowski is a co-author of or contributor to several textbooks.

References

Africa Health Workforce Observatory. 2007. Africa Health Workforce Observatory. http://www.afro.who.int/hrh-observatory/index.html (accessed December 14, 2008).

Bateman, Chris. 2007. Paying the Price for AIDS Denialism. *South African Medical Journal* 97, no.10: 912-914.

Bulletin of the World Health Organization. 2008. HIV drives children's pneumonia in sub-Saharan Africa. *Bulletin of the World Health Organization* 86, no. 5: 324-325.

Canadian Medical Association. 2008. US$58 million grant to fight yellow fever in Africa. *Canadian Medical Association Journal* 177, no. 9: 1017.

Centers for Disease Control and Prevention (CDC). 2004. Malaria: Geographic Distribution. Atlanta. GA: Centers for Disease Control and Prevention. http://www.cdc.gov/malaria/distribution_epi/distribution.htm (accessed December 14, 2008).

Centers for Disease Control and Prevention (CDC). 2007a. Malaria Facts. Atlanta. GA: Centers for Disease Control and Prevention. http://www.cdc.gov/malaria/facts.htm (accessed December 14, 2008).

Centers for Disease Control and Prevention (CDC). 2007b. Yellow fever fact sheet. Atlanta, GA: Centers for Disease Control and Prevention.

Chigwedere, Pride, George Seage, Sofia Gruskin, Tun-Hou Lee, and M Essex. 2008. Estimating the Lost Benefits of Antiretroviral Drug Use in South Africa. *Journal of Acquired Immune Deficiency Syndromes* 49, no.4: 410-415.

Cohen, Myron S., Nick Hellmann, Jay A. Levy, Kevin DeCock, and Joep Lange. 2008. The spread, treatment, and prevention of HIV-1: evolution of a global pandemic. *The Journal of Clinical Investigation* 118, no. 4: 1244-1254.

Food and Agricultural Organization of the United Nations (FAO). 2002. Fighting tsetse -- a scourge to African farmers. http://www.fao.org/english/newsroom/news/2002/4620-en.html (accessed December 13, 2008).

Greenwood, Brian M., David A. Fidock, Dennis E. Kyle, Stefan H.I. Kappe, Pedro L. Alonso, Frank H. Collins, and Patrick E. Duffy. 2008. Malaria: Progress, perils, and prospects for eradication. *Journal of Clinical Investigation* 118: 1266-1276.

Human Rights Watch. 2008. Women and HIV/AIDS. http://www.hrw.org/women/aids.html (accessed June 15, 2008).

Hunter, Lori M. 2007. Understanding how HIV/AIDS, agricultural systems, and food security are linked. Washington, DC: Population Reference Bureau.

Hunter, Lori M. 2008. HIV/AIDS and the natural environment. Washington, DC: Population Reference Bureau.

Meade, Melinda. and Robert Earickson. 2000. *Medical Geography*. 2nd ed. New York: Guilford Press.

Mectizan Donation Program. 2006. Distribution of Onchocerciasis worldwide. Decatur, GA: Mectizan Donation Program.

Organisation for Economic Co-operation and Development (OECD). 2006. OECD Health Data 2006: How Does the United States Compare. http://www.oecd.org/ dataoecd/29/52/36960035.pdf (accessed December 12, 2008).

Poku, Nana. 2006. *AIDS in Africa*. Cambridge: Polity Press.

Population Reference Bureau. 2007a. 2007 World Population Data Sheet. Washington, DC: Population Reference Bureau.

Population Reference Bureau. 2007b. World Population Highlights, 2007. Washington, DC: Population Reference Bureau.

Population Reference Bureau. 2008. 2008 World Population Data Sheet. Washington, DC: Population Reference Bureau.

Regional Committee for Africa. 2005. Control of human African trypanosomiasis: a strategy for the African region. Geneva: World Health Organization Regional Committee for Africa.

Simaro, Pere P., Jean Jannin, and Pierre Cattand. 2008. Eliminating human African trypanosomiasis: where do we stand and what comes next? *PLoS Medicine* 5, no. 2.

Skolnik, Richard, and Joanne Carter. 2007. TB anywhere is TB everywhere. Washington, DC: Population Reference Bureau.

Stock, Robert. 1995. *Africa South of the Sahara*. New York: The Guilford Press.

UNAIDS (Joint United Nations Programme on HIV/AIDS). 2008a. *Report on the Global AIDS Epidemic*. Geneva: United Nations.

UNAIDS (Joint United Nations Programme on HIV/AIDS). 2008b. HIV/AIDS and gender fact sheet. New York: UNAIDS Interagency Task Team on Gender & HIV/AIDS.

UNICEF. 2007. Africa malaria day 2007.http://www.unicef.org/ media/media_39453.html (accessed December 14, 2008).

Wines, Michael. 2006. Malnutrition is Cheating Its Survivors, and Africa's Future. *New York Times*. December 28.

World Bank. 2007. *World Development Indicators, 2007.* Washington, DC: World Bank.

World Health Organization. 2003. Action against worms. *PPC Newsletter* 2003, no. 1. Geneva: World Health Organization.

World Health Organization. 2005. Marburg hemorrhagic fever (fact sheet). Geneva: World Health Organization.

World Health Organization. 2007a. Core Health Indicators 2007 Database. Geneva. http://www.who.int/whosis/database/ (accessed December 14, 2008).

World Health Organization. 2007b. Ebola hemorrhagic fever (fact sheet number 103). Geneva: World Health Organization.

World Health Organization. 2007c. Malaria fact sheet. Geneva: World Health Organization.

World Health Organization. 2008a. Dengue and dengue hemorrhagic fever (fact sheet Number 117). Geneva: World Health Organization.

World Health Organization. 2008b. Human African trypanosomiasis. Geneva: World Health Organization.

World Health Organization. 2008c. Priority eye diseases. Geneva: World Health Organization.

World Health Organization. 2008d. What is guinea worm? Is it a real worm? Geneva: World Health Organization.

Yin, Sandra. 2007. Misconceptions about attitudes toward AIDS in Africa. Washington, DC: Population Reference Bureau.

Environmental Security in Africa

Luis A. Rios and Amy Richmond Krakowka

Key Points

- Interrelationships between human and natural processes can lead to destabilizing human security.

- Environmental security in Africa can be viewed in terms of many complex and non-linear interactions.

- Environmental security in the Sahel region of Africa centers on climate variability and change.

Many areas of the world struggle on a daily basis with a multitude of environmental stressors ranging from day-to-day inconveniences to outright disasters threatening life and livelihood. The field of environmental security attempts to understand how the interrelationships between human and natural processes destabilize the environment and undermine human security. Indeed the cyclical relationship between resource depletion, poverty, and conflict has the ability to push societies to the brink of disaster. Environmental security is one component of human security, defined by the United Nations in 1994 as the intersection of economic, food, health, environmental, personal, community and political needs (Nyong 2005).

This chapter delves into the ideology behind the often convoluted and relatively new idea of environmental security. Only after realizing the complexity of these relationships can one make informed, nuanced judgments about a particular geographic domain and the spatial challenges that dominate it. We will discuss environmental security and how it pertains to Africa as a whole, and end the chapter using the Sahel region as a specific example of a place that is challenged.

What is Environmental Security?

Soon after the Cold War ended and decades of Soviet geopolitical influence abated, it became quite clear that the notion of security was about to dramatically shift to something entirely new. The dominance of bilateralism was replaced by multilateralism and, further, the natural environment began to be viewed as one of many increasingly important non-state actors. Since the mid-to-late 1980s policy-makers have struggled with the idea of linking the environment, environmental degradation, military operations, and conflict (Allenby 2000; Graeger 1996).

The concept that environmental stress can induce human insecurity is not new and countless examples exist throughout history (warfare in ancient China and the collapse of Native American population centers in present day southwestern United States are just two). The post-Cold War era saw a refocus towards environmental concerns when actors such as India, China, various African states, the "new" Russia, and the European Union (EU) began to emerge and assert their newly-found influence on the world stage. In the U.S., one of the first manifestations of this new environmental security paradigm (as state policy) dates back to the first Clinton administration when concerns about military-induced environmental degradation rose to prominence. As a matter of execution, Clinton administration concerns centered on the prevention, remediation and mitigation of significant environmental problems related to military installations and efforts therefore were budgeted and staffed to meet these particular goals. The definition continued to evolve in time through the late 1990s to take on a more international flavor as the enormity, complexity, and interrelatedness of environmental malfeasances began to be realized throughout the developed and lesser developed areas of the world.

The notion that the environment was critical to security strategy made its formal U.S. policy debut in the National Security Strategy of 1991. This document outlined the four principle threats to U.S. national security, one of which was "environmental dangers." In 2005, environmentally related instability was emphasized as a fundamental strategic concern and a key player in contemporary conflicts by the Department of Defense (DoD) (DoD 2005).

The idea of environmental security is difficult to codify, but boils down to a state's perspective and end goal. For example, the perspective can be one of ecological security if the sole goal is to address environmental concerns for the sake of the welfare of the environment—this is the crux of environmentalism. This ideology does not take into account the possibility of conflict stemming from environmental disturbances nor does it acknowledge that the environment is inextricably tied to human populations.

Another more complex perspective is a state-centered approach where actors behave solely in their own self interest. This approach is easier to implement if the state has complete control, but it often pits a state in a confrontational "us versus them" frame of mind. The state-centered approach has several glaring pitfalls. First, this method often ignores some very obvious and key trans-border considerations related to many environmental problems. It can also be quite militaristic as it reduces most environmental aspects to a conflict-driven set of problems between the state and its enemies. As a result, this narrow approach has a weak effect on diplomatic policy, mutually-derived security arrangements with other states, and the proper use of military lands, since everything about it is rather one-sided (Graeger 1996).

A broader and more helpful perspective involves looking at environmental security matters in a supranational way. Here, the key is multi-state cooperation when security and the environment coincide, acknowledging the potential and far reaching impacts of environmental issues that are important to other states (Graeger 1996). Modern-day examples of this include the 1989 Montreal Protocol banning the production of dangerous chemicals responsible for atmospheric ozone depletion, the 1997

Kyoto Protocol addressing climate change policy matters, and the more encompassing United Nations-driven Intergovernmental Panel on Climate Change (IPCC) which directs climatic research in an effort to provide policy-ready recommendations to states around the globe. Each of these supranational agreements has taken scientific data to generate suggestions for policy makers worldwide to consider, debate, and perhaps adopt. The implications and complexity of such supranational constructs are clear in terms of potential gain, yet fraught with inherent pitfalls as states often choose to act in their own economic self interest. Such was the case when the U.S. and Australia signed but failed to ratify the Kyoto Protocol, citing dire economic consequences and protesting the exemption of India and China. Here both states acted in their own economic self interest, essentially rendering the protocol impotent and moot.

In 1996 the United Nations (UN) took on the subject of environmental security by establishing a panel under its larger Millennium Project umbrella. The UN gathered experts in many fields in an attempt to adopt a single definition from a set of varied ones. After contentious debate the panel settled on a Millennium Project-approved definition of environmental security as "environmental viability for life support," with three sub-elements (Millennium Project 2008):

- preventing or repairing military damage to the environment

- protecting the environment due to its inherent moral value

- preventing or responding to environmentally caused conflicts

If one generally accepts that the environment can act as a trigger or exacerbating force for conflict, and that both social and economic instability are related to the quality of the environment, the definition can be further refined as freedom from social and economic instability due to environmental stressors and degradation (Glenn et al. 1998). This definition has been widely adopted due to its succinct approach.

Environmental Security in Africa

Unlike more developed regions of the world, environmental security—or insecurity—in Africa can be viewed in terms of many complex and non-linear interactions. Such interactions include the instability brought on by large populations, poor infrastructure, existing conflict, the prevalence and widespread nature of endemic diseases, fragile ecosystems, weak governance, and the developing and highly uncertain specter of climate change and climate variability. As stated by the UN's Environmental Programme (UNEP), in general there continues to be a downward spiral with decreases in quality and quantity of environmental goods and services that places serious constraints on economic development and human well-being (UNEP 2006).

The African continent is geographically diverse in every sense of the word. It is easy to forget that the continent of Africa is larger than China, the United States, Argentina and Western Europe combined, totaling over 18.7 million square kilometers (African Studies Center 2008). Africa consists of seven distinctive climates as defined by the Koppen climate classification system, each with different precipitation patterns, soil regimes and vegetation types. Africa's human diversity is also great—the continent is home to 53 sovereign states, 900 million inhabitants, and over 2000 languages. There are countless tribes and ethnicities upon which Western colonists imposed their ideologies, resulting in a complex and often intertwined cultural geography. Hence, environmental security in Africa is wide ranging, complex and multi-faceted. If managed correctly Africa's vast resources offer huge potential for development; however, wise management has not often been the case.

One of the key elements of environmental security is food security. Environmental security and food security are intricately linked and are influenced by many of the same factors such as corruption, absence of human rights, fresh water resources, and climate. Food supply can be reduced by overpopulation, ethnic conflict, weak or ineffective government, and environmental degradation (Marsh and Grossa 2005).

Seventy percent of Africans depend on agriculture as their means of livelihood; hence African states can largely be considered rural economies. Yet for reasons cited above, over 35 percent of the people in Africa are considered hungry (Sanchez 2005). Globally, there is enough food produced to adequately feed all of humankind; however, allocation and distribution inequities occur resulting in millions of poorly nourished people (Marsh and Grossa 2005). The poor face starvation, as they do not have the means to purchase or produce their own food. Regarding rural agriculture, overpopulation forces people into less productive marginal lands resulting in short-term production gains; these gains are unsustainable in the long term. Also, ethnic conflict and ineffective governments magnify the problem by slowing or preventing food distribution to hungry people. The poor and hungry in Africa are frequently those who live furthest from roads. The lack of road networks drives up the time and cost of distributing food; consequently further worsening hunger among the poorest communities. Thus, these factors combine to form hunger 'hotspot' regions within Africa (depicted in Figure 1). The UN Millennium Project Task Force on Hunger identified tropical sub-Saharan Africa as the region facing the greatest challenges in reaching the UN Millennium Development Goal of reducing the proportion of people who suffer from hunger by half between 1990 and 2015. Of those who are hungry, 50 percent are farmers (Sanchez 2005). This is primarily due to poor agricultural yields, mostly as a result of declining soil fertility.

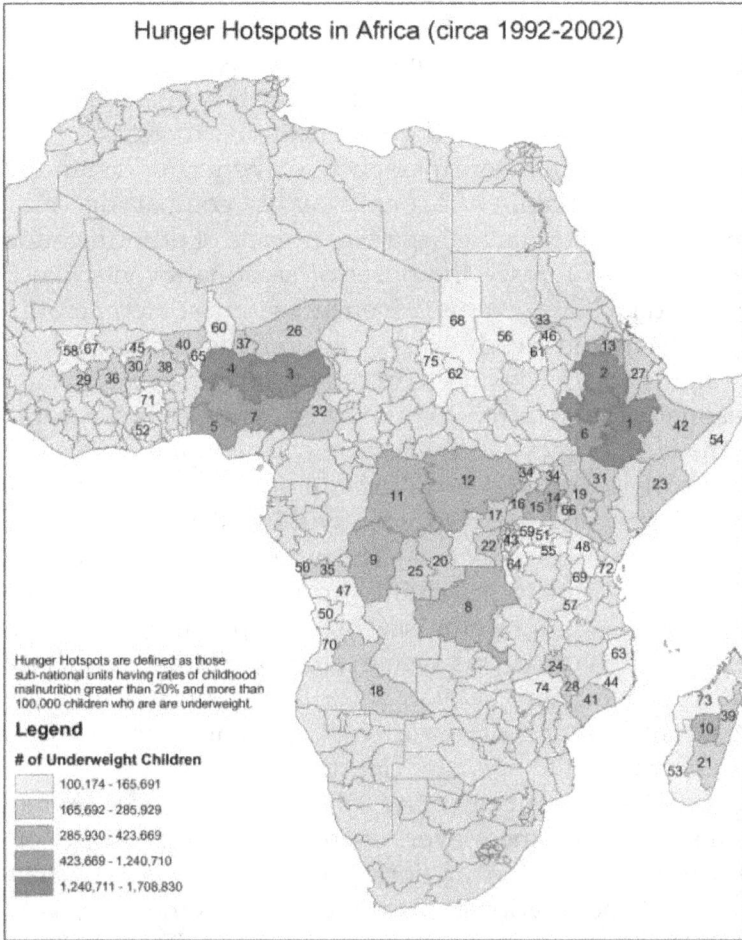

Figure 1. Hunger Hotspots in Africa (CIESEN 2008)

Desertification is to blame for much of Africa's poor soil. Desertification was defined by the UNEP in 1992 as land degradation in arid, semi-arid and dry sub-humid areas, which results from various factors including climatic variations and, most importantly, human activities. Simply, it is the process of degrading dry land primarily by human activity when those activities use the land beyond its carrying capacity, thus affecting human welfare (Hulme

1993). Desertification in Africa is worsening for two reasons. First, overuse of the land and poor irrigation practices have created salinized soils which contain too much salt for vegetation to grow. Second, drought has intensified hot, dry climates and hastened desertification processes.

From a short-term perspective, a better understanding of climate variability is one way to combat the most immediate and tangible negative impacts of desertification. The ability to foresee the onset of seasonal events like El Niño and La Niña (events driven by sea surface temperature anomalies) and ready access to remote sensing data/ technologies afford ways to mitigate and persevere through seasonally tough farming conditions. A program developed by the U.S. Agency for International Development (USAID) as an early warning system for famine and for the strategic deployment of food resources within Africa is aimed at accomplishing this very task. The program is three-pronged: integrating climate variability forecasts, monitoring the progress of each growing season, and planning near-term response activities. This system allows relief agencies, local states, and farmers to plan accordingly, thus minimizing the possible impact of desertification events that stem from climate variability episodes (Hastings 2005).

The current inability of many Africans to feed themselves becomes ever more important when one recognizes that the majority of African states have increasing populations. Rwanda, an extreme case, is on track to double its population in 17 years (US Department of State 2008). Rwanda is one of the world's most densely populated states so overpopulation there is one of the most critical environmental stressors. In Rwanda, population growth was enabled by myriad factors including improved sanitation, healthcare, and relatively successful agricultural yields driven by fertile volcanic soils and two rainy seasons. However, overpopulation coupled with environmental degradation resulted in a reduced food supply. In an attempt to remedy this situation, agriculture was expanded into marginal lands, resulting in the further degradation of land including, erosion, further soil exhaustion, decreased water supply and, in turn, a lower agricultural yield. This cycle caused the migration of people from farms to cities ill-equipped to support them, which served to perpetuate an existing poverty cycle. This precarious situation can be exacerbated by climate change and climate variability episodes. In Rwanda unsustainable farming practices, drought, migration, and population growth led to insufficient food supplies and consequently transformed it from a leading food producer per capita in the region in the 1980s to one of the worst in the 1990s (Diamond 2005). The combination of these factors resulted in a dangerous strain on the Rwandan population that served as a catalyst for the 1994 genocide.

A key element to both food supply and human survival is access to fresh water. Fresh water stress is expected to increase in future years (Figure 2). Fresh water is also a critical component of mining, hydro power generation, tourism, and livestock production, all of which are important to healthy African economies. Parts of Africa are endowed with large fresh water reserves; however in 2005 only about 5 percent of the development potential of this resource was realized due to poor infrastructure and a lack of money to invest in development projects (UNEP 2006). Africa's fresh water supply is not evenly distributed and in many places, evaporation exceeds precipitation more than six months of the year (Love et al. 2006). Consequently, in many African states fresh water is threatened by overuse, poor management, and stresses caused by climate variability and change. Droughts of varying intensity are common in Africa, and the continent has suffered eight serious droughts since World War II (Zerbe 2004).

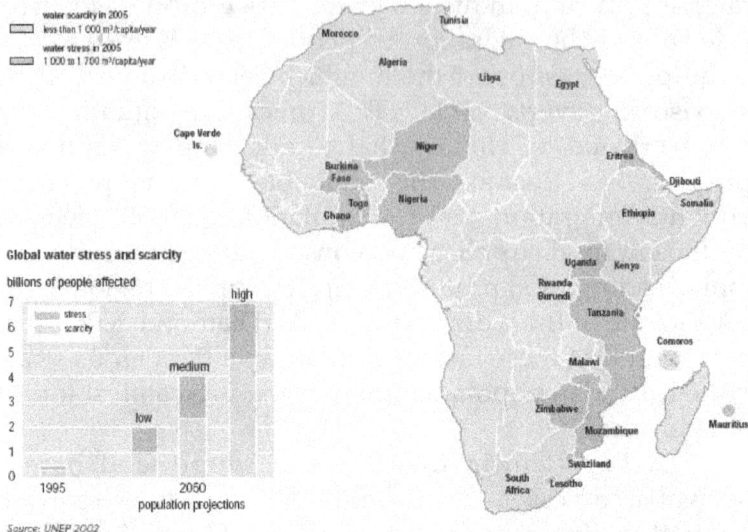

Figure 2: Freshwater stress and scarcity by 2025

water scarcity in 2005
less than 1 000 m³/capita/year
water stress in 2005
1 000 to 1 700 m³/capita/year

Global water stress and scarcity

billions of people affected

Source: UNEP 2002

Figure 2. Freshwater Resources in Africa
(UNEP 2002)

The combination of increasing populations, degraded soils, inconsistent access to fresh water, and changes in climate build the foundation for environmental security concerns in Africa.

Case Study: Environmental Security in the Sahel Region

Scientific research including numerical (computer) modeling predictions are ongoing regarding the severity of climate change and variability scenarios affecting the Sahel. All serious discussions tend to center along the argument that the future of the African climate system (including the Sahel) is likely to have severe consequences and impacts on human populations. This section will look at the Sahel region of Africa by focusing on the intersection between physical and cultural settings and juxtaposing these against climate change and variability considerations. The idea of climate change and variability is especially troublesome here because it threatens to unravel a precariously balanced and volatile region of the continent, likely affecting each of the factors that comprise human security.

The Physical Setting of the Sahel

The area of Africa known as the Sahel is a strip of tropical savanna wedged between the Sahara Desert to the north and the tropical rain forests of Central Africa to the south. This is a region dominated by a contrast in climatic regimes delicately balanced between wet and dry seasons. In this region, countries like Mali, Niger, Chad and Sudan have approximately 80 percent of land area classified as true deserts with a small area that is marginal, at best, for agricultural production and economic potential. Niger, especially, is affected by the aforementioned delicate balance of wet and dry seasons. Figure 3 shows graphical depictions of climate data (temperature and precipitation) for three cities in Niger: the capital city of Niamey in the southwest, and Agadez and Bilma to the northeast. Note that each graph shows a precipitation maximum centered during the July-August timeframe, highlighting limited and seasonal potential of agricultural activities in this part of the continent. In the southern third of the Sahel, for example, precipitation totals support marginal agricultural yields in the vicinity of Niamey while practically uninhabitable conditions dominate Bilma, which is well to the northeast and within the Sahara Desert. It is clear from this simple map that the shift in seasons governs the ebb and flow of life in the Sahel, and that the area is intricately connected to its rainfall pattern.

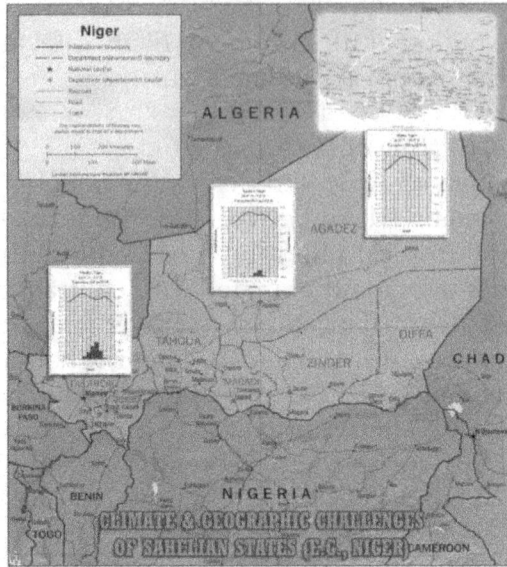

Figure 3. Graphical depiction of climate data across the Sahelian state of Niger. Climate data graphed by month. Precipitation totals provided in centimeters and temperature data provided in degrees Celsius. (University of Texas at Austin online map library)

Another aspect of the Sahel's physical geography is its access to water. More than any other physical factor and natural resource, access to clean water is paramount to a people's ability to survive and thrive. The Sahel is home to the Niger River (Figure 4), an arc-shaped stream channel with its origin in the higher elevations of Guinea and which meanders though Mali and Niger before finally flowing to the Atlantic Ocean through its delta in southern Nigeria. When it comes to this major source of water, relative location is everything. In Niger or Mali, for example, the river traverses a true desert, with much less flow than in places benefiting from a wetter climate (Nigeria and Benin, for example). Competition and usage of this vital resource is a potential catalyst of conflict if not managed cooperatively among states that share it. The Niger is quite likely to come under increasing pressure as climate variability episodes and longer-term climate change events manifest themselves in yet-unknown ways.

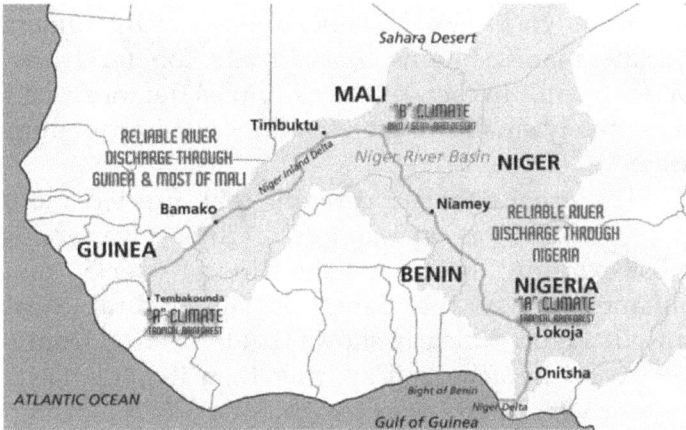

Figure 4. Niger River With Respect to the Western Half of the Sahel (Wikimedia.org 2007)

The Cultural Setting of the Sahel

Many problems in Africa are people-centered—whether clans in Somalia, rebel groups in Darfur or the constant struggle between nomadic pastoralists and subsistence farmers in Northern Africa and the Sahel. This is especially meaningful when one considers that the very complex pattern of tribal religions, languages, and cultures encountered in sub-Saharan Africa does not really fit the modern post-colonial construct of geopolitical boundaries. In the Sahel, poverty is a key component of environmental degradation as people frequently adopt practices that degrade the environment because their most immediate goal is daily survival rather than long-term sustainability (Nyong 2007).

The Impact of Climate Change and Variability on the Sahel

Evolving from a loosely regarded idea in the early 1980s to *the* environmental issue of the 21st century, the causes, societal impacts, and complex interactions of short-term climate variability and concerns about longer-term climate change have certainly taken center stage in many of today's meaningful scientific endeavors and discussions. Areas of the world like the Sahel are especially vulnerable to climate manifestations that deviate too far from the expected norm. In fact, recent examples demonstrate that even relatively small climate variations can impact humans greatly.

The great Sahelian drought that affected the area from 1968 to 1993 is an example of climate variability at its most extreme. It affected the lives of over 50 million inhabitants across the Sahel as agricultural systems collapsed. Figure 5 clearly shows that the period from 1968 to 1993 was characterized as drier than the standardized norm for every single year except for 1976, when rainfall was about the average (Dore 2005). A significant percentage of agriculture in this area is rain-fed (over 40 percent in Niger, for example) so the implication of drought to human security is clear, especially in light of sparse or immature irrigation systems.

The IPCC, the UN chartered organization charged with the daunting task of compiling the body of work on climate change and its many implications, argues that continued changes affecting the African continent will be wide-ranging and likely severe. The observed record across the region shows that during the 20th century, the temperature across the Sahel rose 0.7°C (IPCC, 2007). Although climate models suggest a warmer planet and warmer oceans, the attendant increase in evaporation and rainfall that will follow in some places does not translate to increased rainfall for the Sahel. Some models suggest a 0.2°C to 0.5°C rise per decade or 1.5°C to 4.5°C by the year 2100, with drier conditions throughout the Sahel and northern Africa (Saharan Africa) and a net decrease in precipitation of between 10 percent and 30 percent of current norms. IPCC scientists, however, caution that the mechanisms, responses and climatic forcing factors that will drive changes in the

21st century are still not well understood. Some models, for example, indicate a modest moistening of the area, pointing to a disparate and often perplexing set of results that highlight the problematic nature of accurate climate forecasting. As a general rule climate scientists run a series of computer models that take into account not only greenhouse gas emissions and solar/terrestrial energy budgets, but factors such as the complex and non-linear atmosphere-ocean linkages in order to assess the future of the global climate system. Climate scientists often "back" forecast past climates in order to see if a particular model handles already observed phenomena (such as droughts and other climatic variations), thus gaining (or losing) confidence in a particular model. In the end, it is a process of learning and re-learning that continually hones and sharpens the overall predictive skill (Christensen et al. 2007).

Hulme et al. (2005) argue that the robustness and reliability of long-term climate change predictions over tropical regions of the world (such as tropical Africa) are especially unreliable and problematic. Poor numerical representations of key variables such as land cover-atmosphere interactions, tropical sea surface temperatures, overall areal coverage of vegetation, and the impact of dust and aerosols are often cited as examples of how little understanding there is about the mechanisms that drive prolonged desiccation episodes in the Sahel (Hunt 2000; Leblanc et al. 2007). Furthermore, the importance of properly depicting tropical sea surface temperatures, an integral driver of climate in the Sahel, and merging these data with the aforementioned land cover construct, makes understanding of climate forcing mechanisms in this area of the world especially difficult (Leblanc et al. 2007).

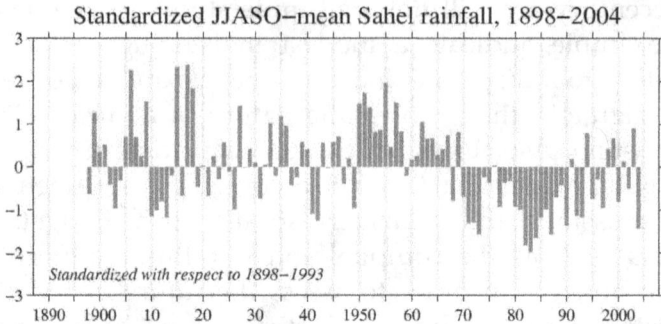

Figure 5. Sahelian Rainfall Deviations from Standardized
Means for June, July, August, September and October
(JJASO). The box highlights the 1968-1993 drought
years. (note: data averaged for the entire Sahel Region)
(Tschakert 2006)

While is it critical to systematically improve the reliability and knowledge base about these large-scale numerical models, Hastings (2005) points to the idea of human populations adapting to shorter-term variability episodes as a legitimate and pragmatic way of dealing with climate-driven calamities. The 20th century saw several of these severe multi-year/multi-decadal events throughout Africa so "...lessons from adaptation to short-term climate variability would build capacity to respond to incrementally longer-term changes in local and regional climates" (Hastings 2005). In the end, it is clear that these multi-faceted problems faced by the Sahel are compounded by the looming and ever-growing threat of climate uncertainty. Even if the science of forecasting the future state of the climate system is inexact and problematic, it is fortunate that the inhabitants of this region are exceptionally adaptive and innovative, and they have the attention of multinational organizations and governments. Since the effects of climate change may indeed be dire, it is imperative that action be taken in a cooperative sense, as inaction may prove far more devastating and difficult to deal with as time goes on.

Conclusion

Throughout the world, but especially in the lesser developed areas of the globe, environmental security plays a dominant role in the human security of states and how these states behave: as single actors or as members of the larger global stage. Although the concept of enviromental security is relatively new and often contentious, given its many definitions and perspectives, it is clear that it influences human security. Increasingly the idea of environmental security has become a necessary tool to understanding conflict, the potential for conflict, and by contrast the prospect for stability. Multi-state efforts like the Kyoto Protocol and the increasingly powerful influence of the IPCC confirms the importance of the environment in policy making.

Whether conflict arises from environmental stressors or the other way around, this multi-faceted notion within the Sahel region of Africa affects the lives of millions of Africans on a daily basis, threatening life and livelihood in tangible ways. Within this part of Africa, climate is a daily and dominant influence in the lives of its residents. The fact that the Sahel is wedged between two vastly different climate zones implies that everything about daily life is governed by how much precipitation falls, when it falls, and what can be done with it. Given the lack of sophisticated irrigation systems and the myriad other stressors within the region, climate is often the catalyst that tips a state in a negative direction, exacerbating population pressures, existing medical problems, weak governance, and the over-reliance on organizations providing aid.

The Sahel is one example of how the environment influences human security, but many places in Africa face the same challenge. Continued degradation of environmental resources coupled with population growth and weak governance position many African states to be vulnerable to environmental stresses. This vulnerability is only increased with the potential of climate change. The future security of many African states will need to address these relationships: geography offers a unique vantage point from which to understand the dynamics of environmental security.

Lieutenant Colonel Luis A. Rios is an Assistant Professor of Geography at the United States Military Academy. An Air Force weather officer, his research interests include environmental security, military geography, climate and climate change impacts on national policy, and natural disaster response and mitigation. He teaches Physical Geography, Meteorology,Cclimatology and Environmental Security courses and holds undergraduate and graduate degrees in Meteorology and Tropical Meteorology.

Dr. Amy Richmond Krakowka is an Assistant Professor of Geography at the United States Military Academy. Her research focuses on valuing ecosystem goods and services, energy security, and environmental security. She has published articles in journals such as 'Ecological Economics' and 'The Energy Journal.'

References

African Studies Center, The University of Pennsylvania. 2008. http:// www.africa.upenn.edu/ (accessed December 10, 2008).

Allenby, Braden. 2000. Environmental security: concept and implementation. *International Political Science Review* 21: 5-21.

CIESIN Columbia University. 2008. Africa Hunger Hot Spots. www.sedac.ciesin.columbia.edu/wdc/map_gallery.jsp (accessed July 27, 2008).

Christensen, Jens H., B. Hewitson, A. Busuioc, A. Chen, X. Gao, I. Held, R. Jones, R.K. Kolli, W.-T. Kwon, R. Laprise, V. Magaña Rueda, L., Mearns, C.G. Menéndez, J. Räisänen, A. Rinke, A. Sarr and P. Whetton, 2007. Regional Climate Projections. In *Climate Change 2007: The Physical Science Basis. Contribution of Working Group I to the Fourth Assessment Report of the*

Intergovernmental Panel on Climate Change, ed. Solomon, S., D. Qin, M. Manning, Z. Chen, M. Marquis, K.B. Averyt, M. Tignor and H.L. Miller . Cambridge: Cambridge University Press.

Department of Defense (DoD). 2005. *The national defense strategy of The United States of America.* Washington, DC: U.S. Government Printing Office.

Diamond, Jared. 2005. *Collapse.* New York: Penguin Books.

Dore, Mohammed H.I. 2005. Climate change and changes in global precipitation patterns: what do we know? *Environment International* 31: 1167-1181.

Glenn, Jerome C., Perelet, Renat, and Theodore J Gordon. 1998. *Environmental security-emerging international definitions, perceptions and policy considerations.* American Council for the UN University Millennium Project, for the Army Environmental Policy Institute.

Graeger, Nina. 1996. Environmental security? *Journal of Peace Research* 33: 109-116.

Hastings, David A. 2005. Africa's climate observed: perspectives on monitoring and management of floods, drought and desertification. In *Climate Change and Africa,* ed. Pak Sum Low. Cambridge: Cambridge University Press.

Hulme, Mike. 1993. *Exploring the links between desertification and climate change – research on the Sahel region of Africa.* Climatic Research Unit at the University of East Anglia in Norwich, England. Heldref Publications.

Hulme, Mike, Ruth Doherty, Todd Ngara, and Mark New. 2005. Global warming and African climate change: a reassessment. In *Climate Change and Africa,* ed. Pak Sum Low. Cambridge: Cambridge University Press.

Hunt, B. G. 2000. Natural Climatic Variability and Sahelian Rainfall trends. *Global and Planetary Change* 24: 107-131.

345

Leblanc, Marc, Guillaume Favreau, Sylvain Massuel, Sarah Tweed, Maud Loireau, and Bernard Cappelaere. 2007. Land clearance and hydrological change in the Sahel: SW Niger. *Global and Planetary Change (2007).*

Love, David, Steve Towomlow, Walter Mupangwa, Pieter van der Zaag, and Bekithemba Gumbo. 2006. Implementing the millennium development food security goals–Challenges of the southern African context. *Physics and Chemistry of the Earth* 31: 731-737.

Marsh, William and John Grossa. 2005. *Environmental Geography.* Hoboken, NJ: Wiley & Sons, Inc.

Sanchez, Pedro, and Monkonbu S. Swaminathan. 2005. Hunger in Africa: the link between unhealthy people and unhealthy soils. *Lancet* 365: 442-444.

The Millennium Project: Global Future Studies and Research. http://www.millennium-project.org/millennium/es-2def.html (accessed September 15, 2008).

National Aeronautics and Space Administration (NASA). Earth Observatory Web Site. http://earthobservatory.nasa.gov/Study/Desertification/Images (accessed September 18, 2007).

Nyong, Anthony. 2007. Resource and Environmental Security. In *Too Poor for Peace? Global Poverty, Conflict, and Security in the 21st Century*, ed. Lael Brainard and Derek Chollet. Washington, DC: Brookings Institution.

Tschakert, Petra. 2006. Views from the vulnerable: understanding climatic and other stressors in the Sahel. *Global Environmental Change* 17: 381-396.

United National Environment Programme (UNEP). 2002. *Freshwater resources in Africa.* New York: United National Environment Program.

United National Environment Programme (UNEP). 2006. *Africa Environment Outlook, Our Environment, our wealth.* New York: United National Environment Program.

United States Department of State. 2008. *Rwanda.* http://www.state.gov/r/pa/ei/bgn/2861.htm (accessed December 10, 2008).

University of Texas at Austin Map Library. http://www.lib.utexas.edu/maps/africa/niger_2000_pol.jpg (accessed September 15, 2007).

Wikimedia (via Google Images). http://upload.wikimedia.org/wikipedia/commons/0/0d/Niger_river_map.PNG (accessed September 19, 2007).

Zerbe, Noah. 2004. Feeding the famine? American food aid and the GMO debate in Southern Africa. *Food Policy* 29: 593-608.

China and Natural Resource Competition

Kent Hughes Butts & Brent Bankus

Key Points

- China's economic growth has exceeded its domestic resource base and has made it dependent upon imports for critical supplies of fuel and minerals.

- China's quest for resources is driving its significant presence in Africa. China does not trust the free market to provide a secure supply of resource imports and is purchasing equity ownership of mineral deposits and mining companies .

- A natural ally of African states as leader of the developing world, China is using debt forgiveness, development aid and participation in African Peacekeeping Operations to gain influence and access to resources.

- It is unlikely that China's influence will exceed that of centuries old colonial economic and military ties.

- China's presence creates the potential for cooperation with the U.S. on stabilizing capacity building and development activities.

Introduction

Africa is a vast continent with diverse geographic patterns and a relatively limited population. The resource base of Africa is enormous, with powerful rivers, world leading concentrations of strategic minerals, and important petroleum and uranium deposits. Nevertheless, it is comprised mainly of developing states, with limited capacity and infrastructure. Western development strategies have failed miserably in Africa, falling victim to Cold War politics, cultural differences and Africa's colonial heritage. Long a friend of Africa in its self-declared role as leader of the developing world, China is in the midst of a resurgent African initiative based on a "politics free" development model aimed at securing access to Africa's resource supplies. This chapter examines China's African strategy, offers an assessment of its implications for United States (U.S.) national security, and suggests a proactive, interest based approach for dealing with this phenomenon.

The strategic landscape of Africa is defined by its geography. Africa's topography ranges from 5800 meter (about 19,000 feet) volcanic peaks with year-round ice fields to scorching deserts that limit settlement and commercial transportation, to brutally hot and humid river valleys teaming with malaria and other waterborne diseases, to resource rich coastlines swept by cold and nutrient rich currents. Within this enormous continent exist large numbers of social and ethnic groups characterized by unique cultural values and languages. The cultural geography of the continent has, like the sand dunes of the Sahara, been swept by waves of cultural penetration—from Arab slave traders bringing the Muslim religion, to Western colonial exploitation that bifurcated nations and clans, and through the establishment of artificial political borders. This has generated a backwash of African socialism.

The economic geography of Africa has been defined by transportation and in particular, the seaborne movement of cargo and the penetration of the interior by railroads. Transportation established functional regions bound together by economic linkages that brought not just mineral cargoes and the resultant foreign exchange earnings, but also new ideas, expectations, and disease. The environment has been altered by these processes. Renewable resources have been exploited beyond recovery, and mineral exploitation has generated significant pollution that has rendered agricultural land infertile and given rise to social protest in a loss of governmental legitimacy. Stability in Africa can only be achieved by addressing these geographic variables through a process of cooperation between internal and external actors that recognizes this geographical diversity and its implications for governance. The most interesting external actor from the perspective of U.S. national security is China.

Emerging trends have the potential to further destabilize African countries. They include environmental security and climate change; urbanization; increased energy prices; and extremist ideology. Each of these issues has the potential to overwhelm the capacity of thinly staffed civilian bureaucracies and erode governmental legitimacy. Because of pre-existing tensions and pressures on the government from increasing population, ethnic and religious differences, and urban-rural economic discrepancies, none of these trends can be identified as the single cause of instability. However, they may serve as a multiplier effect, inflaming existing tensions into conflict or instability either within or between states.

Environmental security refers to situations where environmental issues may threaten or be used to promote national security or affect human security. Climate change is an environmental security issue that affects such variables as freshwater availability, soil fertility and productivity, disease, storm intensity and flooding–and directly affects governmental legitimacy. Environmental security issues and failed development schemes act as push factors that drive increased urbanization. Africa is rapidly urbanizing and is second only to South America in rate of urbanization. Uncontrolled migration to cities is swamping the social infrastructure, eroding government control of constantly expanding squatter camps rife with the drug trade, crime, and disease, and increasing food security problems (Cook, 2008). Dramatically higher energy costs is another problem, as they increase the outflow of scarce foreign exchange for fertilizer, fuel, and food imports, increase the cost of African exports, and limit development. These trends affect governmental legitimacy when a government is unable to satisfy demands placed upon the political system and may, thus, enhance the appeal of extremist ideology. Because these trends could threaten stability in strategically important mineral producing regions of Africa, they provide an opportunity for confidence building measures and multilateral cooperation on the part of industrial states seeking stability and long-term access to African resources. Astutely, China has already acted on this with alacrity.

China in Africa

China's interests in Africa are not new; China has long viewed itself as the leader of the developing world, and was involved in Africa as far back as the late 1960s and early 1970s, providing development aid to African socialist regimes, and supporting anti-colonial insurgencies. The crown jewel of this development assistance was the Tanzania – Zambia Railway (TAZARA), which ran intermittently from Dar es Salaam in Tanzania to the copper cobalt belt of Zambia. The Chinese sent 13,500 workers to Africa to build the line and provided a $412 million interest free construction loan (Moritz, 1982, p. 5). The TAZARA rail line was designed to carry 300,000 tons of copper from Zambia and Zaire and provide an alternative to depending on white governed, South African ports.

China's support of Robert Mugabe and Zimbabwe spans three decades. During Zimbabwe's Unilateral Declaration of Independence China provided logistical, training, arms and funding support to Mugabe's Zimbabwe Africa National Union (ZANU) liberation front. When Mugabe was elected he disbanded the rival political party and, with the support of China and the Shona speaking majority, has remained in power for over 25 years. While China retained many of its ties to Africa, it wasn't until the late 1980s that China began a renewed and focused presence on the continent, a presence driven by the need for resource access.

The major reason for China's renewed involvement in Africa is the need for access to Africa's natural resources, primarily energy and minerals. Since free market reforms were implemented in 1978, China's GDP has grown an average 9.9 percent a year (Hamlin, 2008). China is tapping into a variety of resource markets to feed their ever growing economy. The expense and extent of Chinese efforts to garner those resources is striking. China's intent is not to compete on the open market for natural resources, but to own them and their associated infrastructure to create a secure source of supply. In 2001, the Chinese Politburo set down its global *zou chuqu* ("go out") directive, instructing state-owned enterprises to seek long-term access to natural resources (Behar 2008). Varying levels of financial help have accompanied this push, with state-owned Chinese construction companies in Africa receiving incentives ranging from export credits to government guarantees for bank loans. At the same time, state-controlled banks have made inexpensive loans available to private Chinese companies that invest abroad. As Lucy Corkin, a China-Africa think tank expert from Stellenbosch University in South Africa, explains, "It's trickled down to your micro-entrepreneurs. It's a huge diversification and fragmentation of Chinese commercial actors coming out of China" (Behar 2008). The national security strategies of the George W. Bush administration are often characterized as having had three variables: diplomacy; development; and defense. China's efforts to come to grips with the diverse human and physical geography of Africa may be best examined through the lens of these three variables.

China's Mineral Diplomacy

"China's voracious appetite for resources, especially energy resources, is widely viewed as the primary motive for its expanding outreach to Africa" (Cooke 2008, p. 106).

The Chinese economy has been growing at between 7 and 10 percent per year since the 1980s and has doubled every decade. The Chinese Communist Party believes that

China must continue this level of growth if it is to maintain its control of the government, continue the shift from inefficient state controlled industries, and deal with the ever-increasing social unrest. Protests over the collapse of poorly constructed government built schools during the 2008 earthquake and a rash of food safety issues are but the latest in a growing wave of government criticism. In 1993 there were 8700 public protests in China; by 2005 that number had risen to 87,000 (CRS Report for Congress 2006). Dissent over issues such as employment, environmental degradation, social services, and government corruption grew 50 percent between 2004 and 2006 (CRS 2006). While such protests do not currently have the power to topple the government, China's population will increase by approximately 123 million by 2025 from a current population of 1.3 billion and the government fears that without sufficient economic growth social protest could grow to a level that would threaten the Chinese Communist Party control (United States Census Bureau 2008).

Continued economic growth in China requires access to foreign industrial and fuel minerals. In that regard, China is not unlike the U.S. in having a substantial natural resource base that has proven incapable of meeting the demands of an expanding domestic economy. Mineral imports are depended upon to supply the balance of industrial demand and the security of those mineral imports is of critical geo-strategic importance to both states. China is seeking many of its mineral supplies in Africa.

The Importance of Africa's Resources

At the height of the 1973 oil embargo, Soviet Premier Leonid Brezhnev clarified the Soviet Union's resource strategy to then Somalia President Siad Barre: "Our aim is to gain control of the two great treasure houses on which the West depends, the energy treasure house of the Persian Gulf and the mineral treasure house of Central and Southern Africa" (Nixon, 1980, p. 23).

During the Cold War, the Soviet Union supplied the West with chromium and manganese and used it to strategic advantage. In the wake of the Berlin blockade, the Soviets cut off supplies of these minerals. In 1978, the Soviet Union purchased a two year supply of cobalt immediately prior to the Cuban supported invasion of Zaire's (today, Democratic Republic of Congo's) copper cobalt producing Shaba province. Moreover, after the departure of the Portuguese, the Soviet Union stepped in and turned both Angola and Mozambique into Marxist client states with Soviet equipment and trained armies that created a strategic pincher movement on the mineral producing giant South Africa. The oil embargo further enlightened the U.S. about the geopolitical importance of the imbalance of supply and demand for strategically important resources, and the control of those resources by producing states or peer competitors. The Chinese have learned from this recent history and have developed a resource strategy aimed at ensuring adequate mineral imports to supply their rapacious economy. The most important aspect of China's resource strategy is its focus on establishing ownership or control of the mineral resource concession. Africa plays a significant role in that strategy.

The Soviet Union was autarkic, producing its industrial mineral supplies from domestic sources, except for small quantities of lateritic cobalt deposits imported from Cuba. Neither the U.S. nor its allies in Europe or Japan had sufficient domestic deposits of strategic minerals or petroleum. Vulnerable to a disruption of their mineral imports, the Western Allies focused clearly on the sources of petroleum and strategic minerals, and made resource access a salient tenet of their Cold War security strategy. Never was this clearer than when President Carter drew his line in the sand and declared the petroleum deposits of the Middle East vital to U.S. national security interests.

In the years since the end of the Cold War, however, the U.S. has sold off large portions of its strategic minerals stockpile, and now depends on the world market for most of its imports of petroleum and industrial materials. In the absence of a Soviet threat, the U.S. turned to the less costly free market strategy of purchasing mineral imports on the world market rather than concerning itself with the stability or alliances of mineral producing countries. If prices rose, the U.S. would simply outbid others for the minerals. For over fifteen years, the free market strategy has succeeded; however, the growth of the Chinese economy has outstripped its domestic supplies of critical industrial minerals and petroleum, created a rapacious new competitor for global resources, and substantially tightened the world commodity market. This is forcing the U.S. to examine its mineral import strategy and the national security implications of China's quest for mineral supplies.

Another trend is calling into question the free market strategy and its effects on U.S. national security. Mineral producing states that have been releasing their supplies to the world market are now constraining their availability based on political considerations. Venezuela and Russia are actively pursuing resource geopolitics as a way to promote a political agenda and further their national security interests. History has demonstrated that such policies discourage direct foreign investment in the mineral extraction industries, limit access to critical new technologies, and ultimately reduce mineral recovery. However, in the short term such policies may prove beneficial to the producing state. The U.S. geopolitical position is further eroded by the fact that most of the conventional oil production is concentrated in the critical Middle East and controlled by Muslim states, which have already demonstrated a willingness to embargo shipments to the West for political reasons. Although the U.S. has 700 million barrels of oil stored in the Strategic Petroleum Reserve (SPR), the recent Government Accounting Office report on the SPR stated that it would be inadequate for dealing with the cutoff of the 10 million barrels per day (B/D) of petroleum produced by Saudi Arabia, or the 17 million B/D of petroleum that flows out of the Persian Gulf (GAO 2006).

In light of these facts the importance of Africa's resources becomes clear. Although not a zero sum game, the international supply of minerals is tightening and China's demand for metals and petroleum is increasing almost exponentially and driving commodity prices to new levels. By 2004 China's economic growth had driven up global copper prices by 37 percent, oil by 33 percent and aluminum and zinc 25 percent. By 2007 copper prices were up 344 percent, nickel prices were up 760 percent, and zinc prices 218 percent (Coakley 2008). China's role in setting world prices reflects the volume of its consumption; in 2003 China consumed: 25 percent of global aluminum and steel production; 32 percent of iron ore and coal production: and 40 percent of the world's cement (Menzie 2006). Understanding, perhaps better than any other state, how its increasing demand and future expected consumption will further tighten world markets, China is taking action to create new reserves of these minerals and establish bilateral relationships that will ensure it of the new supply. The Chinese view the U.S. market strategy as being high risk and have taken a different path.

China's Import Dependence

China is the fastest growing energy consumer in the world; in 2003 China passed Japan to become the world's number two consumer of petroleum behind the U.S. (Wonacott, 2003). Once self-sufficient in petroleum production, China now imports 3.7 million barrels of oil per day of its daily consumption of 7.5 million barrels per day (Report to Congress, 2007). During the last five years, energy demand growth has been, on average, 13 percent per year (Report to Congress, 2007). This trend is likely to continue. Manufacturing accounts for 60 percent of energy consumption in China and 28 percent of that is from the fast growing iron and steel sector (Report to Congress, 2007). Lax environmental standards, government subsidies and its innate profitability will likely ensure little change of this consumption pattern. Moreover, affluence will drive an upsurge in transportation related petroleum consumption. Vehicle ownership in China is expected to reach 140 million by 2020, a significant increase from the 25 million vehicle owners in 2007. By 2025 as China's population increases another 123 million people, total oil consumption will be over 14 million barrels a day and China will likely import an additional 7.2 million barrels a day of foreign oil.

The source of China's oil imports is, therefore, of significant strategic importance and a focal point for China's state owned energy companies and its diplomatic corps. The politically unstable Middle East, led by Saudi Arabia, Iran and Oman, accounts for 44 percent of China's oil imports. Africa, led by Angola—the second largest single source of Chinese oil supply—the Sudan, and Nigeria, accounts for 32 percent of oil imports. Additionally, Russia supplies 11 percent of Chinese oil imports, via rail (International Energy Agency (IEA), 2007). Most of China's oil imports must transit the Malacca Strait and other key maritime choke points. The security of these choke points is guaranteed by the U.S. Navy; along with dependence on a U.S. dominated energy market, this is seen as a strategic vulnerability. China has a four concept strategy for minimizing this vulnerability: develop a blue water naval capability; develop a terrestrial, pipeline based petroleum import system from states such as Kazakhstan and Russia; create a strategic petroleum reserve of 100 million barrels to supplant 30 days of lost imports; and have Chinese oil companies purchase equity stakes in, explore for, and produce petroleum in foreign oil fields. While the equity stakes concept thus far accounts for only 600,000 barrels of oil imports per day, it is developing exploration, development, and negotiations skills within the state owned Chinese oil companies and making them a respected actor on the petroleum market stage (Morrison, 2008; IEA, 2007).

The bulk of the world's conventional oil reserves are located in the politically unstable Middle East. A distant second place is Europe and Eurasia, dominated by Russia, which is the largest oil-producing state. Close behind

Russia is Africa with over 120 billion barrels of petroleum reserves. Because of its debt, lack of infrastructure, and governmental capacity, and its extensive natural resource base, Africa is benefiting substantially from China's mineral import diplomacy. China's state enterprises identify states with significant natural resource reserves and work closely with Chinese diplomats to design an engagement program with apropos economic and diplomatic benefits.

As it was during the Cold War, Africa remains a major supplier of strategically important minerals. Essential industrial metals such as aluminum, bauxite, coltan, alumina, copper, iron ore, lead, nickel, zinc, and the industrial minerals of phosphate rock, coal, and uranium are all present in Africa in large quantities. Particularly important are the strategic minerals of chromium, cobalt, platinum group metals, and manganese. For their strategic applications in weapons systems and critical economic processes, there is generally no substitute for these minerals. The reserve bases of these minerals are highly concentrated geographically in South Africa, Democratic Republic of Congo (DRC), Zimbabwe, and Zambia, and not present in China or the U.S. in sufficient quantities to meet demand. For example, 33 percent of the world reserve base of chromium is found in the Republic of South Africa, and South Africa and Kazakhstan alone account for 95 percent of world chromium resources. Zambia and DRC have between them 52 percent of world cobalt reserves. South Africa has 77 percent of the world manganese reserve base and 88 percent of the reserve base for the platinum group metals (Minerals Commodity Summaries, 2008). The geographic concentration of these minerals and lack of alternative supplies or substitutes make them strategically important to China and other industrial states and contribute to China's intense interest in Africa.

China has moved aggressively to tie up mineral concessions in Africa. In 2008 China signed a long-term infrastructure development agreement with Democratic Republic of Congo worth over $9 billion (Whewell, 2008). At the same time, the DRC national mining company,

Gecamines, agreed to ease the major mining company, Katanga Mining Ltd., out of the two key copper deposits, Mashamba West and Dikuluwe in the copper-cobalt belt, paying Katanga the equivalent of $825 million and granting the concessions to a Chinese company. Interestingly, the deposits were not scheduled to produce copper until at least 2020, and China could not bring them into production for at least five years (Katanga, 2008). This is a good example of how minerals access is linked to development in China's Africa strategy.

Development

China's African Policy is rooted in development and "mutually beneficial cooperation" (People's Republic of China, 2006). A natural ally based on its long-term role as champion of the developing world, China can offer debt forgiveness, bilateral trade agreements, development packages, and grant aid. China often packages its diplomatic, defense, and development aid into synchronized and synergistic offerings. Chinese investment in Africa in its various forms is often directly attributable to the natural resources China is able to procure from that continent. Unlike the U.S., which ties its developmental aid to democratic reforms, fiscal transparency, and human rights, China insists only upon the isolation of Taiwan. The pursuit of this overriding objective is unambiguous and explicit: "The one China principle is the political foundation for the establishment of China's relations with African countries and regional organizations" (People's Republic of China, 2006).

China explains this One China concept as a respect for African states' autonomy in creating their own development programs, and a desire for their support in establishing a "new and rational economic order" (Cook 2008, p. 106). Differences in these development models are illustrated by the Chinese approach to the Sudan, which supplies 5-7 percent of China's oil. China supported the UN Security

Council Resolution 1769 creating a UN-African Union peacekeeping force for Darfur (UNAMID) and encouraged the Sudanese government to accept it. When President Hu Jintao visited the Sudan in 2007 he forgave debt totaling $80 million, announced the building of a new presidential palace with an interest free Chinese loan, and announced further infrastructure improvements, such as the building of a new railway, to complement the $2 billion Merowe Dam China is building, which could provide for Sudan's total electrical demand (Mallaby, 2007; Schihor, 2007; U.S. - China, 2007). China's African Policy document would characterize this as helping the Sudan "to develop and exploit rationally their resources" (People's Republic of China, 2006).

Colonial powers and the superpowers of the Cold War era were criticized for development efforts in Africa that left African countries as "hewers of wood and carriers of water". Besides Africa's strategic location and position astride major sea lines of communication, the chief interest of these two groups was African resources. China has now renewed its interest in Africa based upon a similar resource quest and is dedicating most of its development aid to natural resource rich states. Sudan, Algeria, Nigeria, Zambia, Zimbabwe, South Africa, Madagascar, and Angola have all received hundreds of millions of dollars in foreign direct investment (FDI), most of it dedicated to the exploration for, and exploitation and transport of resources. Gabon provides a good example. Chinese companies are targeting the Belinga iron ore reserves, which are located over 500 miles inland. To do so, China is investing several billion dollars to build a railway from the mine site to the coast and a deep water export terminal. Because electricity is unavailable, China will also build a hydroelectric scheme to provide power to mine the ore, process it, and transport it to the coast. China will have exclusive access to mine production (Amosu, 2007).

China is investing a great deal of money and resources rebuilding the infrastructure in its oil supplier Angola. China is providing $135 million in financing to rebuild Angola's electricity, water and road systems, expanding its stake in the oil-rich African state, Angola's state-run ANGOP news agency said recently (Simao, 2008). While the exact amount of the loan is unknown, it is estimated to range from $4 to $11 billion. In addition, China has agreed to help Angola establish a malaria prevention and treatment center in Angola's capital city of Luanda's General Hospital.

Trade between China and Angola is estimated to be approximately $5 billion per year. There is concern that the oil wealth will not be distributed among all regions of the state and will not reach the poverty stricken Angolans in the Ovumbundu regions, from which Jonas Savimbi fought the recently concluded civil war. Additionally, the thousands of jobs created by these huge construction projects are primarily going to Chinese workers and this is causing increased resentment by the local population. While the Angolan economy is growing at a rapid pace a majority of the population live in poverty; taking jobs that could be offered to the local population may exacerbate the situation (Geneticmemory.org, 2007).

The Chinese copper mining operation in Zambia is another example of China's investment. Because of its rich copper deposits, the Chinese government plans to make the Zambian Copper Belt Province one of a handful of "special economic zones" in Africa while investing a total of $800 million into a variety of improvement projects (Behar, 2008). Additionally, in efforts to form an export based "production chain," China plans on spending $220 million to build a new copper smelter in the region.

While Chinese mining companies employ local workers their reputation is coming under increasing scrutiny, particularly concerning their failure so far to offer competitive wages to those of the Indian, Canadian and Swiss mining companies also operating in the area (STRATFOR, 2008). In attempts to mitigate employee dissatisfaction and possible rioting, representatives from the Mineworkers Union of Zambia (MUZ) are accepting a salary increase offered by Chinese mine owners from $71-$114 per month to $85-$128 per month. However, research suggests this rate increase will not suffice as the salary rate at the Indian owned Konkola Copper Mines is $227-$284 per month, while workers at the Canadian-Swiss owned First Quantum Minerals mine receive $284-$426 per month (STRATFOR, 2008).

The Horn of Africa (HOA) is another region that has benefited from the Chinese incursion into the continent. Through its trade promotion and investment programs China has become one of the HOA's most important trading partners, providing low cost loans, debt relief and tariff considerations. Sudan and Eritrea have gained the most from these policies. By the first half of 2005, Chinese trade with the region topped $2 billion, compared to $2.8 billion for the entire year in 2004. China's investment in the HOA has been its most important contribution. In addition to road and housing construction projects, the Chinese have improved the bridging, power and water supply, irrigation, and telecommunications systems of the region. Examples of these projects include constructing: the Oratta Hospital in Asmara, Eritrea; Djibouti's Foreign Ministry; a highway system in Ethiopia's capital of Addis Ababa; and a hydroelectric power plant on Ethiopia's Tekeze River (Shinn, 2005).

Another and more longstanding aspect of Chinese assistance on the African continent comes in the form of medical assistance. Sometimes called "Health Diplomacy," teams of Chinese doctors have been rendering medical aid on the continent since 1964 to complement regular medical personnel exchanges and technical training for medical professionals. China's medical assistance to Africa has also produced a robust program for the prevention of infectious diseases to include malaria and HIV/AIDS. This assistance includes training seminars and conferences, and supplying entire medical units as part of their military contingent to UN peacekeeping operations on the continent.

The refurbishment of the dilapidated Benguela railway stretching from Angola to Democratic Republic of

Congo (DRC) is a prime example of Chinese investment in large infrastructure projects. The China International Fund Ltd, based in Hong Kong, is undertaking the $300 million rehabilitation project. The Benguela line was a significant transport link to the mineral rich Zaire and a vehicle for the export of manganese. The rail line has been neglected for a long period and was critically damaged during the Angolan civil war, which lasted from 1975 through 2002 (Emerging Minds, 2008; AsiaNews.it, 2006).

Mineral rich DRC provides an example of the assistance China will provide. China is not only acquiring natural resources itself, but also rebuilding critical infrastructure to ensure access. In addition, China recently signed a contract with DRC worth $6 billion to build approximately 3900 kilometers (2400 miles) of road, 3200 kilometers (2000 miles) of railway, 32 hospitals, 145 health centers and two universities (Whewell, 2008).

Chinese FDI in Africa was approximately $5 million annually in 1991, but by 1994 it was $25 million and in 1999, around $100 million. In 2006 China's FDI in Africa was $1.25 billion, and some sources, such as The People's Daily, believe that it exceeded $6 billion in 2007 (Amosu, 2007; Broadman 2008). Trade with China is growing with equally impressive speed. In the 1980s trade between China and Africa totaled $12 million per year. However by 2000, trade had grown to $10 billion (Amosu 2007). Growing at an annual rate of 40 percent, China-Africa bilateral trade reached $50 billion in 2006 (Caggeso, 2007).

China's trade with Africa is facilitated by a sophisticated Chinese investment scheme. In October 2007 the Industrial and Commercial Bank of China, by market value the largest in the world, purchased South Africa's Standard Bank Group Ltd. for $5.4 billion. Standard, operating in 18 African countries, leads all banks in African loans and has assets of nearly $120 billion (Caggeso, 2007). China complemented this purchase by acquiring a stake in the United Kingdom banking house of Barclays. Using the $200 billion assets of the China Investment Corp., China paid

$3 billion for a stake in the U.S. investment banking firm Blackstone. Blackstone then helped the China Development Bank acquire a $7 billion stake in Barclays Bank, the United Kingdom's leading African bank, with dominant positions in such resource powers as Nigeria, South Africa, Zambia, and Zimbabwe. These purchases guarantee Chinese access to powerful interests in the financial community of key African countries, and facilitate investment through non-bilateral government to government arrangements (Weidner, 2007; Preston, 2007; Barnett, 2007).

China's development miracle occurred in an authoritarian state where the demands on the political system are more easily managed. China's development model may not prove as successful in Africa. Africa is increasingly democratic and, as the recent election in Zambia demonstrates, the legitimacy of governments and popular support for their leaders will turn upon the leaders' capability to meet human security demands upon the political system.

Although the large scale development projects come with no strings, China's development assistance will cause social, economic and environmental changes in recipient states and regions. This should be part of China's calculus. If there is not "mutual benefit, reciprocity and common prosperity" (People's Republic of China 2006), China's economic and political objectives may not be realized; unintended consequences will occur.

In Zimbabwe the cholera outbreak that began in August 2008 and had killed 600 by year's end drew attention to failure of the Mugabe rule. This long-term and abysmal rule was abetted by China, as China's long term support encouraged President Mugabe to avoid necessary policy decisions. As a result Zimbabwe's major foreign exchange-earning mines closed, interest rates reached 9500 percent, inflation rocketed to 230 million percent, and the unpaid Army (and others) began looting banks (The Assay October, 2008).

Along the vital Nile River, the African riparian states created and their water ministers led the Nile Basin Initiative

(NBI). The objectives of this multi-lateral initiative are to "develop the Nile Basin water resources in a sustainable and equitable way to ensure prosperity, security and peace for all its peoples" (Nile Basin 2008). Boutros Boutros-Ghali, then Egypt's Minister of State for Foreign Affairs and later Secretary-General of the UN, famously stated in 1985 that wars of the future would be fought over water. The Sudan circumvented the NBI process by approaching China for support in building the Merowe Dam, which China agreed to do. Water experts consider this agreement to be de-stabilizing and an unhealthy action in terms of diminishing African multi-state solidarity.

China promoted its African Policy primarily through bilateral, government to government, secretive agreements, which have increasingly drawn public criticism. Beyond the expected criticism from former colonial powers and the West, African voices are now being heard. Then-South African President Thabo Mbeki cautioned China against dumping its low-cost textile and plastics products in Africa, thus denying Africans manufacturing jobs, and South Africa has placed a quota on imports of Chinese textiles (Cook 2008). In the recent Zambian presidential elections the opposition made a major issue of unsafe operating conditions in Chinese manufacturing plants and noncompetitive rates paid to Chinese metallurgical workers as a result of deals cut with the Zambian government. Concern in Africa that China is pursuing a neo-colonialist agenda is reinforced by the fact that the bulk of Chinese infrastructure development projects require 70 percent of workers to be Chinese with only 30 percent coming from the local African labor pool. An estimated 750,000 Chinese have relocated to Africa in the last 10 years (African Politics Portal, 2008). This African concern is causing China to review its trade approach.

China's Military Presence

China's military presence in Africa is limited but well focused. It has the potential to provide solid support to

China's African strategy, strengthening ties to the African Union while ensuring its access to strategically important minerals. China's military involvement has three significant areas: arms sales, training and capacity building, and peacekeeping operations.

At first glance Chinese weapons sales do not appear significant as the U.S., Russia, France, and Great Britain far outdistance China. From 2003 through 2006 the U.S. and Russia were among the leaders of weapons sales world-wide representing 37.6 percent and 16.9 percent respectively, while China supplied a paltry $1.3 billion worth of weapons representing only 2.9 percent of the total. However, for the same period China ranked third in weapons sales to the African continent. The sales are predominately small arms and ammunition. However, the Chinese have supplied some states with major end items such as armored fighting vehicles, wheeled vehicles of several types, artillery pieces, several types of jet fighters, and training and transport aircraft. One reason Chinese military products are so attractive to developing states in Africa is their low cost and simplicity, a prime example being the Chinese version of the Russian AK-47 Assault Rifle (Congressional Research Service, 2008).

China has been using military assistance as another vehicle to cement oil and trade agreements in Africa. For example, in 2005 Angola exported 17.5 million tons of crude oil to China, making it China's second largest oil supplier. In exchange China negotiated major housing contracts aimed at improving Angola's infrastructure. One contract included constructing the residences of many Angolan leaders. They have also provided the Angolan armed forces with eight Chinese built Su-27 SK fighter jets in addition to various types of small arms.

The resource rich African state exhibiting the greatest Chinese military influence is Sudan. Widely criticized for the genocide in Darfur, Sudan has purchased a variety of armaments from China. Its inventory of Chinese military equipment and weaponry includes cargo trucks, main battle tanks and fighter and transport aircraft. Other Chinese made weapons include mortars, field artillery pieces, rocket launchers and air defense weapons (Chang, 2007). In exchange, China receives more than 90 percent of Sudan's oil exports ($4.7 billion worth of oil in 2006) and 75 percent of their total exports (Human Rights First 2008). Moreover, China stations 4500 military personnel in the country to protect its multi-billion dollar oil infrastructure.

Zimbabwe also has a long history of cooperation with China to include military assistance. In the 1970s China became a staunch ally of Robert Mugabe, as it supplied his Zimbabwe African National Union (ZANU) guerrillas with arms and ammunition to fight the white rule in Rhodesia (Schaefer, 2008). Since then it has supplied mineral rich Zimbabwe with a variety of armaments ranging from small arms and ammunition, to a variety of armored fighting vehicles (Type 59 and Type 69 Tanks and Type 63 armored transport vehicles), and jet aircraft (FC-1 and J-7 fighters, and K-8 trainer aircraft). Additionally, China supplied the Mugabe regime with short wave radio jamming equipment, ostensibly to jam radio traffic from his political opposition as well as the Voice of America. Just prior to Mugabe's 2005 re-election, China also supplied Zimbabwe with riot equipment for the anticipated public protests (Bhola, 2007; Chang, 2007).

The Republic of Congo is one of China's largest sources of oil supplies and hardwoods. In 2005 it exported 5.5 million tons of crude oil to China, amounting for approximately 4.4 percent of China's total oil imports. Since there is still an international arms embargo on Congo, it is unlikely although not impossible for China to continue to sell military equipment to the troubled area. However, the Congo military forces are already armed with major Chinese end items: Type 59 tanks (30), Type 63 107-mm rocket launchers (30), Type 60 122-mm howitzers, and Type 59 130-mm cannons. Additionally, the Congolese own various types of Chinese mortars and an unknown amount of small arms and related ammunition (Chang, 2007).

Due in part to Egypt's oil reserves, it too has benefited from China's military assistance programs. The largest armaments transaction between the two has been for Egypt's production under a license agreement from China, of 80 K-8 trainer aircraft worth approximately $347 million. In 2005, Egypt ordered another 40 K-8 trainers making the total number 120 training aircraft with approximately 53 Chinese built J-7 fighter aircraft still in service in the Egyptian air force (Chang, 2007).

China's military influence is also notable in several other African states. For instance, in 2006 China sold Algeria a 5 million kilogram (5500 ton) training ship, and three 450,000 kilogram (500 ton) missile fast craft with C802 ship-to-ship missiles. In 2001 China delivered a 360,000 kilogram (400 ton) class patrol boat to the Mauritanian navy. Zambia and Namibia have also acquired Chinese K-8 training aircraft. Other weapons customers include Equatorial Guinea, Ethiopia, Eritrea, Burundi, Tanzania and Nigeria. In 2005 Nigeria spent $251 million buying Chinese jet aircraft, 12 F-7 NI and three FT-7 NI fighters. At the same time China and Nigeria reached a trade agreement in which Nigeria will supply China with 30,000 bpd of crude oil between 2005 and 2010 (Kolas, 2007). As part of their arms and equipment agreements, China's military influence extends to supplying "technical advisors" to its African clients and conducting educational and training courses. Chinese military influence is expanding with the growing number of Chinese defense attaché offices and increased participation in United Nations African Peacekeeping Operations. To date China maintains 14 attaché offices located in the states of Algeria, Democratic Republic of Congo, Egypt, Ethiopia, Liberia, Libya, Morocco, Mozambique, Nigeria, Namibia, Sudan, Tunisia, Zambia and Zimbabwe (Puska, 2007). Supplementing the work of their African attaché offices, the Chinese have conducted a number of military staff visits to Africa and have sponsored repeated security talks with South Africa. From 2001 to 2006 China conducted over 30 military staff visits to the African continent, with Egypt receiving 15 of those. The

Chinese Navy has occasionally visited African ports of call, but does not have a significant naval presence (Puska, 2007). Undoubtedly, the most important aspect of Chinese military presence has been their increased involvement in United Nations (UN) Peacekeeping Operations. Since 1990 the Chinese military has supplied UN Peacekeeping operations with police, military observers and organized military units. China's military supplies assets to 10 of 16 active UN Peacekeeping operations including six of seven operations in Africa; the Sudan; Darfur; Ivory Coast; Liberia; Congo and Western Sahara. In the Western Sahara operation, China provides military forces and the force commander, Major General Zhao Jingmin. The Chinese also support peacekeeping missions in Haiti, Timor Leste, Lebanon, and the Middle East (United Nations, 2008). Their support for UN and African Union Peace Operations is a politically wise decision that gains public support and good will at a time when they are being criticized for supporting African states with questionable human rights records.

Conclusion

It is important to put China's African presence in context. If the U.S. is uncertain how to approach China, as friend or foe, China is similarly ambivalent. The differences in the approaches of the Clinton and G.W. Bush administrations were substantial; China has many reasons to question U.S. intentions. China views the U.S. as the global hegemon and expects it to take actions to maintain that position. Given the U.S. history of a containment strategy against the former USSR, many in China see the current U.S. system of alliances with Japan, South Korea, Taiwan, Vietnam, Thailand, India, and most recently Central Asia as an effort to contain China. Although the Bush administration regularly condemned China's growing defense budget ($37.7B in 2005), the Chinese point to the annual U.S. defense budget of nearly $500 billion ($478B in 2005) (U.S.-China, 2007). China's limited domestic oil production makes it dependent upon Middle East oil for 44 percent of its oil imports, and some Chinese speculate on the geopolitical motivation behind the U.S. invasion of Iraq and efforts to sanction Iran, where China recently invested $100 billion in the oil and natural gas industry. Moreover, the Chinese view the commodity markets and international political and economic institutions as serving the interests of the West. The three Breton Woods institutions, the International Monetary Fund, the World Bank, and the World Trade Organization (formerly General Agreement on Tariffs and Trade) have traditionally favored developing states with a Western orientation. This perception was reinforced by the appointment in 2005 of former Deputy Secretary of Defense Paul Wolfowicz to head the World Bank (Ljacinto, 2008; Prensa-Latina, 2008). This view of U.S. intentions contributes to China's African Policy and its geopolitical focus on securing resource imports.

China's "go out" strategy has not yet guaranteed access to significant quantities of petroleum or minerals. It is too early to say for sure whether or not China's state owned companies will become major players in the oil and metals arena or if they will be overwhelmed and needlessly overpay for marginal concessions that fail to make a meaningful contribution to China's mineral import security. However, there is no doubt that China's quest for mineral security is providing substantial political influence with the beneficiaries of its African development strategy. At a time when U.S. foreign policy has been characterized by some states as unilateral and heavy-handed, with narrow restrictions that limit which states qualify for developmental assistance, the Chinese have been using their trade account surplus and sovereign wealth fund to support a new development model with, practically speaking, only one qualification—the One China Principle.

China's packaging of resource access agreements with a "no strings" development model and military training and hardware affects states that are strategically important to the U.S., such as Nigeria and Angola (Chang, 2007). Yet, China's presence in Africa is encountering problems and it appears that China and the U.S. both could benefit from cooperation dedicated to building capacity, sustaining governments, building capacity and promoting stability.

China's development focus on Africa is based on resource access and direct resource purchase agreements. Yet, its efforts to pursue resource based bilateral agreements are having mixed results. China receives only 600,000 barrels a day of petroleum from equity resource ownership while efforts to establish such ownership are creating a backlash of public criticism in Africa, where only two of China's trading partners, Angola and Sudan, have a positive trade balance with China. From Zambia, where China's relationship with the president became an embarrassment during the 2006 election campaign, to Zimbabwe, where the international community joined forces to stop Chinese weapons shipments to the oppressive Mugabe regime, China is recognizing the downside of its "no strings" developmental approach to Africa and its emphasis on resource ownership. The effort to control resources may in fact complicate China's other objectives of creating welcome markets for Chinese products and creating support for a new just and rational economic order.

Stable states with sound governance are considered a better investment risk than failing states beset with internal violence and dissent. It is worth considering that China has a vested interest in working with the U.S. and other donor states to create stability across Africa, where the resource-based economies of one state may depend upon the transport infrastructure, power grid and social stability of multiple neighbors. Moreover, cooperating in an effort to create greater stability on the African continent would create substantially more development—and therefore more African markets for China's goods—and also create greater potential for Africa to capitalize on its comparative advantage of cheap labor and, perhaps, become a future breadbasket for China.

Africa is resource rich and a potential market for Chinese manufactured goods, and China will gain influence through its investment and increase its access to industrial resources in a future resource constrained market. However, China's investment in Africa is targeted on resource rich states and is smaller than that of Western investors. It is unlikely that China will stage a takeover of the continent where centuries-old colonial economic and military ties offer significant influence without the unwelcome side effects. In fact as it is currently practiced, China's development strategy runs the risk of promoting corruption, creating environmental problems, stunting manufacturing development, and creating ill will from the dumping of low-cost Chinese consumer goods. Moreover, the slumping world economy may minimize China's investment in African mineral resource development for the near term. However, China will remain a growing challenge to U.S. regional influence and economic security. Cooperation would be particularly valuable in helping African states adapt to the effects of climate change, address fresh water availability issues, and develop local medical capabilities. These human security issues place demands upon fragile governments of limited capabilities and contribute to regional and state instability. Broadening China's developmental assistance, trade, and FDI objectives to include these human security and stability issues of sustainable development could complement the work of other donor organizations and states. It could, as China's support for African peacekeeping efforts demonstrates, be undertaken without undue focus on the differences between China and the West over conditionality of aid. Such an approach would serve as a confidence building measure between China and the U.S. at a time when the Obama presidency offers the opportunity to redefine the U.S.-China relationship and prevent China's resource quest in Africa from becoming a zero sum game.

Dr. Kent Hughes Butts is Professor and Director of the National Security Issues Group at the Center of Strategic Leadership, U.S. Army War College. A former U.S. Defense Attaché in Africa, his books include 'Geopolitics of Southern Africa: South Africa as

Regional Superpower' and 'Economics and National Security: the Case of China'.

Lieutenant Colonel (Retired) Brent Bankus is a member of the National Security Issues Group, U.S. Army War College. Mr. Bankus has worked in Eritrea and Benin and was previously Director of Joint Training and Exercises, U.S. Army Peacekeeping Institute, and has been widely published on peacekeeping, homeland security and homeland defense topics.

References

African Politics Portal. 2008. Top Ten Misconceptions about Chinese Investment in Africa. http://codrinarsene.com/2008/07/top-10-misconceptions-about-chinese-investment-in-africa/ (accessed December 5, 2008).

Amosu, Akwe. 2007. Foreign Policy in Focus. China in Africa: It's (Still) the Governance, Stupid. http://www.fpif.org/fpiftxt/4068 (accessed December 5, 2008).

AsiaNews.it. 2006. Angola is China's Main Oil Supplier. http://www.asianews.it/index.php?l=en&art=5821 (accessed December 5, 2008).

Baldauf, Scott, and Peter Ford. 2008. China Slammed For Arming Zimbabwe's Mugabe. http://majimbokenya.com/home/2008/04/23/china-slammed-for-arming-zimbabwes-mugabe/ (accessed December 5, 2008).

Barnett, Antony, and Christopher Thompson. 2007. Barclays' Millions Help Prop Up Mugabe Regime. http://www.guardian.co.uk/money/2007/jan/28/accounts.Zimbabwenews (accessed December 5, 2008).

BBC News. 2007. China in Africa, Developing Ties. http://news.bbc.co.uk/2/hi/africa/7086777.stm (accessed December 5, 2008).

BBC News. 2007. China in Africa, Friend or Foe. http://news.bbc.co.uk/2/low/africa/7086777.stm (accessed December 5, 2008).

BBC News. 2008. China Ships Food Aid to Zimbabwe. http://news.bbc.co.uk/2/hi/africa/7170374.stm (accessed December 5, 2008).

BBC News. 2008. Cholera Outbreak Strikes Zimbabwe. http://news.bbc.co.uk/2/hi/africa/7742762.stm (accessed December 5, 2008).

Behar, Richard. 2008. Mining Copper in Zambia. http://www.fastcompany.com/magazine/126/zambia-chinas-mineshaft.html?page=0%2C0 (accessed December 5, 2008).

Bhola, Gauarav. 2007. China and India Battle for Influence in Africa: Part 4. http://www.gimmiethescoop.com/china-and-india-battle-for-influence-in-africa-part-4 (accessed December 5, 2008).

Boutros Ghali, Boutros. http://www.allacademic.com/meta/p_mla_apa_research_citation/2/5 (accessed December 5, 2008).

Broadman, Harry G. 2008. New Trade Directions for Africa on Asia's Silk Road. The World Bank. http://web.worldbank.org/WBSITE/EXTERNAL/COUNTRIES/AFRICAEXT/0,,content MDK:21056305~pagePK:146736~piPK:146830~theSiteP K:258644,00.html (accessed December 5, 2008).

Caggeso, Mike. 2007. China Drills into Africa with $5.4 Billion Investment. Investment News: Money Morning. http://www.moneymorning.com/2007/12/04/china-drills-into-africa-with-54-billion-investment/ (accessed December 5, 2008).

Campos, Indira and Alex Vines. 2007. Angola and China, a Pragmatic Partnership. Paper Presented at a CSIS conference. Prospects for Improving U.S.-China-Africa Cooperation. http://www.csis.org/media/csis/pubs/080306_angolachina.pdf (accessed December 5, 2008).

Cheng, Eva. 2005. China: Protests Escalate. Green Left on Line. http://www.greenleft.org.au/2005/639/33964 (accessed December 5, 2008).

ChinaDaily.com.cn .2008. China's Economic Growth Cools to Slowest Since 2005. Bloomberg L.P. http://www.chinadaily.com.cn/china/2008-07/17/content_6857053.htm (accessed December 5, 2008).

Chang, Andrei. 2007. Chinese Arms and African Oil. Space Daily. http://www.spacedaily.com/reports/Analysis_Chinese_arms_and_African_oil_999.html (accessed December 5, 2008).

Chang, Andrei. 2008. China exports attack craft to Sudan. UPI Asia.com. http://www.upiasia.com/Security/2008/09/16/china_exports_attack_craft_to_sudan/4697/ (accessed December 5, 2008).

Christensen, Thomas J. and James Swan. 2008. U.S. Relations with the Peoples Republic of China. http://hongkong.usconsulate.gov/uscn_2008.html (accessed December 5, 2008).

Christensen, Thomas J. 2008. Shaping China's Global Choices Through Diplomacy. http://www.state.gov/p/eap/rls/rm/2008/03/102327.htm (accessed December 5, 2008).

Center for Naval Analyses. 2007. National Security and the Threat of Climate Change. http://securityandclimate.cna.org/report/ (accessed December 5, 2008).

Coakley, George. 2008. USGS. Coordinator Europe and Central Eurasia Programs International Programs Office U.S. Geological Survey, Address at U.S. Army War College Environmental Security Elective Class.

Collier, Paul. 2008. China's Investment in Africa. *China Digital Times.* http://chinadigitaltimes.net/2008/06/paul-collier-chinas-investment-in-africa/ (accessed December 5, 2008).

Cook, Nicolas. 2008. *China's Foreign Policy and "Soft Power" in South America, Asia, and Africa.* http://www.fas.org/irp/congress/2008_rpt/crs-china.pdf (accessed December 5, 2008).

Congressional Research Service Library of Congress. 2008. *China's Foreign Policy and "Soft Power" in South America, Asia and Africa.*

http://www.fas.org/irp/congress/2008_rpt/crs-china.pdf (accessed December 5, 2008).

Congressional Research Service (CRS) Report for Congress. 2006. *Social Unrest in China.* http://fas.org/sgp/crs/row/RL33416.pdf (accessed December 5, 2008).

Donnelly, John. 2005. China Scooping up deals in Africa as U.S. firms hesitate. *Boston Globe.* http://www.boston.com/news/world/asia/articles/2005/12/24/china_scooping_up_deals_in_africa_as_us_firms_hesitate/ (accessed December 5, 2008).

Emerging Minds, Organizing the Minds of the Future. 2008. China Plans to Construct Railway Across Sub-Saharan Africa. http://emergingminds.org/index.php?option=com_content&view=article&id=6078:China&catid=46:Top%20Black%20Business%20Story&Itemid=53 (accessed December 5, 2008).

Geneticmemory.org. 2007. China fund Rebuilding Angola. http://geneticmemory.org/joomla/index2.php?option=com_content&do_pdf=1&id=191 (accessed December 5, 2008).

Goodman, Leslie. 2008. Angola-China Relations, Sino Africa Virtual Institute. http://sinoafrica.org/2008/10/17/angola-china-relations/ (accessed December 5, 2008).

Government Accounting Office (GAO). 2008. Strategic Petroleum Reserve: Options to Improve the Cost-Effectiveness of Filling the Reserve. http://www.gao.gov/products/GAO-08-521T (accessed December 5, 2008).

Grobler, John. 2008. Rebuilding a Nation. *Mail and Guardian.* http://www.mg.co.za/article/2008-09-06-rebuilding-a-nation (accessed December 5, 2008).

Hamlin, Kevin and Li Yanpin. 2008. China's Economic Growth Cools to Slowest Since 2005. http://www.bloomberg.com/apps/news?pid=20601087&sid=a1wzyfR20ARs&refer=home (accessed December 5, 2008).

Hanson, Stephanie. 2008. China, Africa, and Oil. *Washington Post.* http://www.washingtonpost.com/wp-dyn/content/

article/2008/06/09/AR2008060900714.html   (accessed December 5, 2008).

Human Rights First. 2008. China's Arms Sales to Zimbabwe Fact Sheet. http://www.humanrightsfirst.info/pdf/080428-CAH-china-zimbab-arms-fs.pdf (accessed December 5, 2008).

Human Rights First. 2008. Arms Sales and other Support to Abusive Regimes: Sudan, Burma, Zimbabwe, Sri Lanka, North Korea.   http://www.stoparmstosudan.org/pages.asp?id=23 (accessed December 5, 2008).

International Energy Agency. 2007. http://www.uscc.gov/an-nual_report/2008/annual_report _full_08.pdf (accessed 5 December 2008).

Jamestown Foundation China Brief. 2005. China's Soft Power in Africa: From the Beijing Consensus to Health Diplomacy. http://www.jamestown.org/publications_details. php?volume_id=408&issue_id=3491&article_id=2370720 (accessed December 5, 2008).

Katanga Mining Unlimited. 2008. Katanga Announces Agreement of Transfer of Mashamba West and Dikuluwe Deposits. http://www.marketwire.com/press-release/Katanga-Mining-Limited-TSX-KAT-819163.html (accessed December 5, 2008).

Kolas, Ashild. 2007. China in African oil: Guilty as charged? Economists for Peace and Security. http://www.epsusa. org/publications/newsletter/june2007/kolas.htm (accessed December 5, 2008).

Ljacinto. 2008. Asian nations agree to reform international financial system. http://www.france.24.com/en (accessed December 5, 2008).

Makonese, E. M. 2008. Barclays Bank of Zimbabwe Limited Unaudited Financial Statements for the Half-Year Ended 30 June 2008 Old Currency. Barclays. http://www.barclays. com/africa/pdfs/half_year_results_zimbabwe_2008.pdf (accessed December 5, 2008).

Mallaby, Sebastian. 2007. A Palace for Sudan. *Washington Post.* http://www.washingtonpost.com/wp-   dyn/content/ article/2007/02/04/AR2007020401047.html   (accessed December 5, 2008).

Mineral Commodity Summaries. 2008. *U.S. Department of the Interior, U.S. Geological Survey.* http://minerals.usgs.gov/ minerals/pubs/mcs/2008/mcs2008.pdf (accessed December 5, 2008).

Morrison, J. Stephen 2008. Testimony before the U.S. Senate, Committee on Foreign Relations, Sub-committee on African Affairs. *Hearing on China in Africa; Implications for U.S. Policy.* June 4.

Moritz, F.A. 1982. Chinese Leaders Tour Africa With Few Gifts in Their Sack. Christian Science Monitor, http://www. csmonitor.com/1982/1222/122250.html (accessed December 5, 2008).

Nile Basin Initiative. 2008. NBI Background. Nile Basin Initiative. 2008. NBI Background. http://www.nilebasin.org/index. php?option=com_content&task=view&id=13&Itemid=42 (accessed December 5, 2008).

Nixon, Richard M. 1980. *The Real War.* New York: Warner Books.

People's Republic of China. 2006. *China's African Policy.* http:// www.gov.cn/misc/2006-01/12/content_156490.htm (accessed December 5, 2008).

Prensa Latina. 2008. Russia, China: Joint Efforts to Change Financial System, Havana, Cuba. *Latin American News Agency.* http://www.plenglish.com/article.asp (accessed December 5, 2008).

Preston, Robert. 2007. China Could Buy Stake in Barclays. *BBC News.*   http://news.bbc.co.uk/2/hi/business/6911138.stm (accessed December 5, 2008).

Puska, Susan. 2007. Military backs China's Africa adventure. Asia Times. http://www.atimes.com/atimes/china/if08ad02. html (accessed December 5, 2008).

Report to Congress, 2007, U.S. China Economic and Security Review Commission, One Hundred Tenth Congress, First Session, November 2007, http://www.uscc.gov

Reuters Alert Net. 2006. FACTBOX – Why is Africa Chasing African Oil. http://www.alertnet.org/thenews/newsdesk/ SP175749.htm (accessed December 5, 2008).

Schaefer, Brett D., and John J. Tkacik,. Jr. 2008. Zimbabwe's Enabler: How Chinese Arms Keep Mugabe in Power. *The Heritage Foundation.* http://www.heritage.org/Research/ africa/wm1997.cfm (accessed December 5, 2008).

Shinn, David. 2007. An opportunistic ally: China's increasing involvement in Africa.
All Business, A D&B Company. http://www.allbusiness. com/government/government-bodies-offices-government/5504463-1.html (accessed December 5, 2008).

Shinn, David, and Joshua Eisenman. 2005. Dueling Priorities for Beijing in the Horn of Africa. China Brief from the Jamestown Foundation. http://www.jamestown.org/publications_ details.php?volume_id=408&issue_id=3491&article_ id=2370720 (accessed December 5, 2008).

Shichor, Yitzhak. 2007. China's Darfur Policy. Association for Asian Research, May 1. http://www.asianresearch.org/ articles/3039.html (accessed December 5, 2008).

Simao, Paul. 2008. China expands credit line to oil-rich Angola. Reuters Alert Net Foundation. http://www.alertnet.org/ thenews/newsdesk/L0460226.htm (accessed December 5, 2008).

STRATFOR. 2008. Zambia: Copper, the Chinese and Electoral Strategy. http://www.stratfor.com/analysis/zambia_angry_ copper_miners_chinese_and_electoral_strategy (accessed December 5, 2008).

The Assay. 2008. A Bi-Monthly Compilation by the U.S. Mission. Pretoria. http://www.dpi.nsw.gov.au/__data/assets/pdf_file/0009/251469/ASSAY-47.pdf (accessed December 5, 2008).

United Nations.org. Welcome/Peace and Security/Peacekeeping/Current Operations. http://www.un.org/Depts/dpko/dpko/currentops.shtml#africa (accessed December 5, 2008). Wonacott, Peter; Jeanne Whalen; Bhushan Bahree, "China's Growing Thirst For Oil Is Reshaping Global Energy Market, "The Asian Wall Street Journal," December 3, 2003

United States Census Bureau. 2008. International Data Base, Country Summary: China. http://www.census.gov/ipc/www/idb/summaries.html (accessed December 5, 2008).

United States-China Economic and Security Review Commission (USCC). 2007. *China's Energy Consumption and Opportunities for U.S.-China Cooperation to Address the Effects of China's Energy Use.* 110th Cong., 1st sess. http://www.uscc.gov/hearings/2007hearings/transcripts/june_14_15/07_06_14_15_trans.pdf (accessed December 5, 2008).

U.S.-China Economic and Security Review Commission. *2007 Report to Congress.* 110th Cong., 2nd sess. http://www.uscc.gov/annual_report/2008/annual_report_full_08.pdf (accessed December 5, 2008).

Weidner, David. 2007. China leans on Blackstone for Barclays Deal. Market Watch. http://www.marketwatch.com/news/story/blackstone-does-matchmaking-barclays-china-deal/story.aspx?guid=%7B750F1FC3-1C02-4B1E-AF85-E15A4418CFE5%7D (accessed December 5, 2008).

Whewell, Tim. 2008. China to seal $9bn DR Congo deal. BBC News. http://news.bbc.co.uk/2/hi/programmes/newsnight/7343060.stm (accessed December 4,2008).

The Transformation of African Militaries

Thomas A. Dempsey

Key Points

- African militaries are undergoing a transformation that is professionalizing and internationalizing them.

- Despite their ongoing transformation, African militaries remain limited in capacity by their combat-heavy force structures and lack of necessary support "tail."

- Chronic underfunding of African militaries contributes to persistent problems with corruption.

- Some states on the continent are resisting both professionalization and internationalization, while some conflict zones threaten a return to state-versus-state warfare.

Generalizing about military organizations in an area as vast and diverse as Africa is risky at best. There are, however, features that are broadly characteristic of state-based militaries in the region. These features reveal emergent trends in the profession of arms in Africa that may have important consequences for state, subregional, and regional security. The purpose of this chapter is to identify those features and trends, and analyze their implications for human security in Africa.

African militaries have only recently emerged from a decades-long colonial and post-colonial interregnum, into a post-Cold War era of transformation. That transformation is building upon an ongoing professionalization and internationalization of African militaries that appears to be accelerating dramatically as we enter the 21st century. How this transformation will serve the interests of Africans themselves remains an open question. The one clear and discernable trend is that African militaries pursuing multilateral peace operations are becoming the central, and in some cases the dominant, stakeholders in African regional security.

African Militaries Prior to the End of the Cold War

The African militaries that emerged during the post-independence era lacked well-developed, genuinely national military traditions. This was in part a consequence of European systems of colonial rule imposed during the period surrounding the Berlin Conference of 1885. European colonial regimes systematically rooted out indigenous military traditions promoting and supporting resistance to colonial rule. They did so with armies that were trained and equipped along European lines, recruited (or conscripted) from indigenous African communities, and led by European officers and Non-Commissoned Officers (NCOs). These colonial-era militaries served the agendas of the colonial regimes, imposing the will of those regimes on restive African populations and sustaining regime authority in the face of local resistance to colonial rule. To the extent that these colonial-era militaries represented or shaped a military tradition themselves, it was a European tradition rather than an African tradition, rooted deeply in colonial systems of rule that lacked both local legitimacy and basic functionality (Crowder 1971; Saul and Royer 2001; Howe 2001; Edgerton 2002).

As colonial domination retreated in the wake of World War II, newly independent African states made creation of state-based militaries one of their first priorities. In most cases, the officer leadership and much of the rank-and-file in post-independence militaries were drawn directly from the ranks of the colonial era forces. Post-independence military individuals and institutions brought the baggage of their colonial roles and missions with them, including a focus on regime survival and a view of civil-

384

military relations that had been distorted by decades of colonial rule. These features of Africa's new state-based militaries were reinforced by what Herbert Howe calls the era of "authoritarian personal rule" (2001, 35). African militaries found themselves serving new African elites in post-colonial regimes that were themselves lacking in both legitimacy and functionality.

With weak rule of law frameworks and inadequately developed institutions of civil governance, post-independence African regimes witnessed a succession of military coups. As struggles for political power within African states became increasingly violent, the region witnessed the emergence of repressive, autocratic regimes, many of them run by military or former military leaders. During this period, African militaries came to be characterized by endemic corruption, systematic abuses of human rights, and the continuing focus on internal regime survival that have been ably documented by regional scholars (Jenkins and Kposowa 1992; Howe 2001; Edgerton 2002). To the extent that African militaries developed a tradition of military service, that tradition tended, at the individual level, to be a thin veneer of what might best be called pseudo-nationalism over a reality of personal aggrandizement, factional loyalty, and institutional power-seeking.

The military focus on internal mechanisms of regime survival undermined the professionalism and core competencies of the militaries themselves. Regime maintenance neither required nor rewarded most core military skills, leading to the atrophy of hard military capabilities at both the individual and institutional levels. Liberia under Doe, Sierra Leone under a succession of military juntas, Guinea under Lansana Conteh, Somalia under Barre, Democratic Republic of Congo under Mobutu, Uganda under Idi Amin, and Ethiopia under Mengistu and the Dergue, all illustrate the decline in professional and institutional military capacity that followed independence and that accelerated during, and in large part as a consequence of, the Cold War.

Foreign security assistance programs during the Cold War, whether from the West or the East, were intended more to reward client-ruling elites and to reinforce their internal hold on power than to promote military professionalism or core competencies. Civil-military relations rooted in rule of law and in civilian control of military institutions were viewed by the West as less important than maintaining client loyalty, and were regarded by the East as irrelevant if not antithetical to Soviet Block agendas. Client African militaries were regarded by Western and Eastern patrons as first and foremost, guarantors of regime security against internal threats, and only secondarily as defenders of the state against external threats. Even during the Cold War, most threats were internally generated. State versus state conflict was rare. What conflicts did occur between African states tended to be limited by Cold War sponsors who were wary of situations with the potential to escalate into open warfare between the super powers.

With the end of the Cold War, African military trends that had endured for more than a century suddenly found themselves upended by a wave of dramatic political, economic and social change. That change has led to a fundamental reappraisal of the military role in society by African states and by their partners in the international community. This reappraisal has not been driven by a changing or declining threat: the new post-Cold War world has not witnessed a decrease in conflict in Africa. If anything, conflict in the region has increased. The disappearance of the Cold War competition has removed, to some degree, the "governors" on conflict imposed by Soviet and American policy makers. Military grade weaponry, no longer limited by Cold War-era controls on arms sales, is swamping the region, lending greater lethality to local conflicts.

What has changed in the post-Cold War world is the nature of the response to conflict on the part of African regimes and their partners. This change, most evident in the evolution of conflict management mechanisms and collective security initiatives in regional African organizations like the

Economic Community of West African States (ECOWAS) is influencing African military institutions in profound ways. The change in the nature of the African response is being influenced in turn by political and economic change at the state level, as African states move to democratize and embrace fundamental reforms in governance and administration. These changes are contributing to transformative change within African military institutions.

The post-Cold War transformative change ongoing within African militaries has two primary components. State military forces in Africa are professionalizing at both the individual and institutional levels. Those same forces are becoming internationalized, shifting their operational context from post-colonial regime maintenance, traditional war fighting, and the struggle for black majority rule, to peace operations. These operations, under the control of sub-regional, regional and international organizations, are providing a new context for African military institutions and operations. Together, the professionalization and internationalization of African military forces are changing the institutional cultures of those forces in fundamental ways.

Post-Cold War Transformation: the Professionalization of African Militaries

The professionalization of African militaries is in part a consequence of the end of Cold War agendas among external stakeholders in African security. The U.S. and its bilateral partners have shifted their focus from the survival of client regimes to promoting stabilization, reconstruction, and governance among African states. As a result of this shift, post-Cold War bilateral security assistance programs are viewed through a much broader lens than before. Nested within policy initiatives that value fostering civil-military relations in a democratic context, professionalization of African militaries has emerged as a fundamental objective of American, French and British security assistance programs in the region.

The new generation of bilateral security assistance activities is not intended to reward political elites, but is focused instead on military and defense professionalization as a valued end in itself. These activities contain strong normative elements, endorsing civilian control of the military, promoting transparent accountability of military forces to democratic institutions, and encouraging compliance with broadly accepted international norms and standards in the planning and conduct of military operations. The Senior Leader Seminars conducted by the U.S. Africa Center for Strategic Studies (ACSS) are typical of this new direction in security assistance (Africa Center for Strategic Studies 2008). Similar programs have been initiated by other key bilateral security partners, most notably France and the United Kingdom, and are designed to strengthen professionalization among defense and military leaders at the strategic level.

Programs like the Senior Leaders Seminars have been complemented by bilateral capacity building initiatives at the institutional, organizational and individual levels. These include broadly focused "train and equip" programs like the British Military Advisory and Training Teams (BMATT), the French *Reinforcement des Capacites Africaines de la Paix* (RECAMP) and the U.S. African Crisis Response Initiative, now known as the Contingency Training and Assistance Program (ACOTA) (Kwiatkowski 2000). American, French, and British objectives in pursuing these programs have shifted from influencing African political leaders (dispensing diplomatic "carrots"), to building real African military capacity, underpinned by professionally competent forces and leaders. The transformation in foreign security assistance is clearly illustrated by the emergence of "security sector reform" as the organizing paradigm for security assistance by Europewan and U.S. agencies (Organization for Economic Cooperation and Development 2007; U.S. Army 2008). Emphasis by external partners on "train the trainer" approaches and on sustained engagement over time has sought to establish enduring improvements in the ability of African militaries to deploy capable, professional forces in support of regional security agendas.

Like the ACSS seminars, recent Western "train and equip" programs have had a significant normative component. Training programs routinely include substantial instruction on the law of land warfare, professional ethics, and standards of conduct. The recent U.S. restructuring of the armed forces of Liberia, for example, has incorporated classes for new recruits on ethics, on the Uniform Code of Military Justice, on civilian control of the military, and on civil-military relations in a democratic state.

Reinforcing the trend towards professionalization are political and military reforms among African states themselves. Democratic governance has become more prevalent across Africa since the end of the Cold War. With democratization have come institutional mechanisms for enforcing professional standards of behavior and for establishing the accountability of military forces to civil authority. The code of conduct adopted by the government of Mali for its armed forces in 1998 is an excellent example of this trend (Ayissi and Sangare 2006). The movement towards increased professionalization is being strengthened and supported by the emergence of more robust national institutions for training and educating military leaders in Africa. Senior Service Colleges are proliferating on the continent, as are national institutions for educating and training military leaders at the initial entry and intermediate levels of career development.

Transformation II: The Internationalization of African Militaries

The internationalization of African militaries refers to the growing prevalence of international peacekeeping missions as the operational context for African militaries, and the influence on institutional culture that those missions are exerting among African military organizations. The rise of collective security as the dominant paradigm among

African defense institutions is both a fundamental aspect of and a significant contributor to the internationalization process. Internationalization is changing how African professional soldiers regard themselves and how they pursue their professional responsibilities in ways that directly support and promote democratic governance, rule of law, and respect for human rights.

The process of internationalization really began in 1990 with the deployment of the ECOWAS Ceasefire Monitoring Group (ECOMOG) to Liberia following the collapse of the Liberian state. A purely West African military intervention, this operation was initiated with little external support beyond the resources and will of the ECOWAS member states that participated in it. The ECOWAS intervention in Liberia was followed by ECOWAS peace operations in Sierra Leone in 1998, in Guinea-Bissau in 1999 and in Cote D'Ivoire in 2003. Beyond West Africa, an African six-state "coalition of the willing" deployed a peacekeeping force to the Central African Republic in 1997, while the Southern African Development Community launched a sub-regional peace operation in Lesotho in 1998. The African Union entered the fray at the regional level with peace operations in Burundi in 2003 and Darfur in 2004.

In addition to participating in African regional and sub-regional peace operations missions, African militaries have furnished a growing share of United Nations Peacekeepers, both within and outside of Africa. This trend has been reinforced by the practice that emerged in the 1990s of transitioning African regional and sub-regional peacekeeping missions to UN operations, with African peacekeepers "reflagging" as UN peacekeepers. By 2006, four of the top ten UN troop contributing states were African: Nigeria, Ghana, Ethiopia, and Kenya (United Nations 2006). As of the summer of 2008, the vast majority of ongoing military operations in Africa were peacekeeping missions, and those missions provide the lion's share of operational experience for a growing proportion of African professional military leaders at every level.

The peace operations that have come to dominate African military operations since the end of the Cold War have several common features. Mission mandates typically focus on restoring order and on protecting civilian populations, rather than on garnering power for a particular faction or on the survival of a particular regime. At the tactical level, officers and noncommissioned officers find themselves tasked with responding to community needs, facilitating humanitarian assistance activities, supporting peace processes, and participating in post-conflict reconstruction efforts. Rules for the use of military force are shaped by this mission set, and are heavily influenced by UN peace operations doctrine that emphasizes respect for human rights and rule of law, support for the establishment of legitimate and effective governance, and the duty of military forces to protect civilians from the threat of physical violence (United Nations 2008).

At the operational and strategic levels, mission force commanders answer to civilian authorities in the form of sub-regional, regional, or international peace and security commissions or councils. African military members and organizations deployed in support of these missions find their agendas being shaped by instruments that incorporate explicit guidelines promoting the observance of international norms and standards of conduct. The ECOWAS mechanism for Conflict Management and Resolution furnishes a typical example, describing overarching objectives "to maintain or restore peace" that include humanitarian interventions, peace-building, and disarmament and demobilization activities. Military interventions under the auspices of the Mechanism are authorized in response to "serious and massive violations of human rights and the rule of law," and "in the event of an overthrow or attempted overthrow of a democratically elected government" (Economic Community of West African States 1999). Similar instruments have been adopted by SADC and by the African Union. With each successive peace operation, these instruments and the structures and organizations that they support are influencing civil-military relations within the African militaries that furnish the peacekeeping forces.

The internationalization of African militaries is diverting those militaries from the regime maintenance roles that proved so corrosive to military professionalism and civil-military relations in the colonial and post-colonial eras. Forces involved in peacekeeping and peace enforcement are, by the very nature of their missions, focused on human security needs within the mission area rather than on the survival of a particular regime. These forces function under the leadership of multinational, internationally sanctioned command structures, and are increasingly subjected to fairly robust accountability mechanisms designed to minimize (and sanction where necessary) misconduct or predatory behavior on the part of force members.

Internationalization has operated in tandem with the professionalization of African militaries and has contributed to the professionalizing process. The standards of conduct and normative framework articulated by UN peacekeeping doctrine are providing a common foundation for professional education and training within African military institutions. The proliferation of African peacekeeping centers as vehicles for professionalization of African military leaders is both a manifestation of this trend and a contributor to it. Institutions like the Kofi Annan International Peacekeeping Training Centre (KAIPTC) in Ghana reinforce normative frameworks based on respect for human rights, compliance with international humanitarian law and the law of land warfare, and acceptance of a broadly construed duty to protect civilians in military areas of operation. Together, these trends are establishing, for the first time in many cases, a solid foundation for legitimate, accountable, and functional civil-military relations within African militaries.

African Military Capabilities: Limiting Factors

At the same time that African militaries are experiencing transformative change, they continue to be characterized by structural and institutional weaknesses that limit their ability to fully exploit the benefits of that change. The most significant limitations derive from structural deficiencies affecting administration and support functions for land forces. Similar limitations characterize African air and naval capabilities, largely because of the extremely high "start-up" costs to establish these capabilities, and the equally expensive requirements to sustain them over time. Chronically inadequate funding levels and the problems with corruption that typically derive from funding shortfalls exacerbate these limitations.

The "tooth to tail" ratio is one of the best indicators of the ability to sustain military operations in field conditions and especially in combat. Tooth-to-tail expresses the ratio of combat forces — the "tooth" — to forces functioning in a non-combat role (administrative and logistics support echelons, for example) — the "tail" (McGrath 2007). At a state level, the measure can best be expressed by the ratio of total combat forces to the overall non-combat strength of the Army. This embraces the host state military infrastructure and personnel required to generate and sustain the deployment of forces over time — what the U.S. military refers to as the generating force. The lower the ratio, the more effectively the military can deploy, support, and sustain military operations in the field. Using the ratio of combat forces to total army strength, the U.S. tooth-to-tail ratio during World War II — still the gold standard for large-scale military operations — was about 1:5, or one combat soldier for every five non-combat soldiers in national service (McGrath 2007).

As a general rule, militaries with ratios below about 1:2 have significant problems sustaining even the most basic military operations in a field environment. This is especially true when that environment involves combat operations. Sustained combat dramatically increases the need for bulk logistics, medical services, and maintenance operations, as well as the replacement of combat losses in both equipment and personnel. The impact of higher tooth-to-tail ratios can be dramatic as the tempo of combat operations increases. Tooth-to-tail ratios in African militaries are among the highest in the world. Table 1, based on data from the 2008 *Military Balance*, shows tooth-to-tail ratios from a broadly representative cross section of African armies.

Table 1. Estimated Tooth-to-Tail Ratios for selected African Armies (derived from International Institute for Strategic Studies 2008)

State	Tooth to Tail Ratio	Army Size
South Africa	1:2.3	41.3K
Mali	1:2	7.3K
Ethiopia	1:2	135K
Kenya	1:1.6	20K
Nigeria	1:1.5	62K
Angola	1:1	100K
Botswana	1.4:1	8.5K
Ghana	3:1	20K
Burkina Faso	3.5:1	6.4K

Even those states in the region with some of the most sophisticated and highly developed support structures— South Africa, Mali, and Ethiopia—have marginal tooth-to-tail ratios. Much more representative are armies in the 1:1.5 or higher range: armies in which combat forces are almost equivalent in number to, or actually exceed, the support and force generation (recruitment, training, education, procurement) elements. As these numbers illustrate, African military institutions are "combat heavy" to a degree that sharply limits their capacity to function effectively when deployed without major assistance from external sources. The areas in which these limits are most problematic are strategic and tactical lift, sustainment, communications, and fire support. The implications of these limits for military operations dominated by African military forces are profound.

Absent significant external assistance, African military partners are frequently unable to deploy themselves to theater. Once in theater, those forces lack tactical mobility, are limited in their ability to engage in sustained combat, and suffer gradually increasing attrition from inadequate multifunctional logistics systems. Once in combat, the fragility of these forces becomes even more evident. Their inability to evacuate and treat casualties rapidly and effectively, poor maintenance and repair services, and limited to no replacement capacity (in terms of both personnel and equipment) result in rapidly escalating losses and sharply diminished combat effectiveness over time.

African military forces are especially weak in communications and fire support. This is in part a function of the higher dependency of these two functions on robust logistics systems, and in part on the high levels of training required to maintain functional proficiency within communications and fire support units. It is also due to the much higher costs associated with deploying large, relatively heavy fire support combat systems to theater, and of supplying those systems with the fuel and ammunition necessary to enable their effective employment. The tooth-to-tail problems that characterize African armies have a disproportionate negative impact on the communications and fire support functional areas.

Deficiencies in communications create a form of "reverse synergy" with fire support networks. Effective employment of fire support assets is dependent on maintaining reliable and continuous electronic communications between maneuver forces and fire support elements. When communications are unreliable, the ability to concentrate accurate fires in a timely manner suffers. In the worst cases, lack of effective electronic communications can lead to high levels of collateral damage and fratricide as frustrated fire support crews deliver fires based on map reconnaissance without reliable, timely targeting information from ground maneuver elements which would promote accuracy.

Shortfalls driven by high tooth-to-tail ratios can be effectively addressed by external support. Bilateral and multilateral partners have routinely provided strategic lift to move African military forces into theater. Where African military forces have fallen in on robust, externally provided support systems, African combat forces have demonstrated the ability to function effectively even in non-permissive environments. The comprehensive U.S.-led international assistance effort in support of ECOMOG in West Africa has demonstrated the utility of such partnerships.

The U.S.-led support effort in West Africa in the early nineties provided "cradle to grave" logistics and administrative support to ECOMOG forces in Liberia and subsequently in Sierra Leone. This support structure enabled combat forces from ECOWAS member states to deploy to and conduct sustained combat operations in the most remote areas of Liberia and Sierra Leone. When provided with robust multifunctional logistics support, reliable communications networks, and responsive tactical mobility (both wheeled vehicles and rotary wing aviation), ECOMOG combat elements proved highly effective on the ground in Liberia from 1996 until the ECOMOG withdrawal in 1999 (interviews with ECOMOG Officers 1998). The assistance provided by external partners in 1998 and early 1999 sustained the operations of Nigerian and Guinean combat maneuver forces during the heaviest fighting in Sierra Leone (Interviews with ECOMOG Officers 1999). The performance of those forces clearly demonstrated the ability of African forces to perform effectively in non-permissive environments when those forces are adequately supported. The successes of the ECOMOG partnership have been replicated elsewhere on the continent, and suggest that external partnership offers a workable solution to the African tooth-to-tail deficit.

The African military capability deficit also extends to the air and naval services. These services are the most expensive elements of the military instrument of power, both in terms of fiscal resources and the skilled manpower

396

necessary to raise, sustain, and operate them. Naval power, in particular, is cost-prohibitive. Economies of scale in establishing and maintaining a genuine, "blue-water" (ocean-going) naval capability make this element of the joint military force unaffordable to all but a handful of sub-Saharan states, most notably South Africa. Even in South Africa, the prohibitive costs of sustaining the South African surface combatants and submarine fleet have strained the national defense budget process. By 2000, only four of South Africa's twenty-four ships and submarines were still operational (Mbeki 2000).

Even where African militaries are able to procure and maintain significant air and naval forces, the costs of deploying and sustaining those forces beyond national borders is overwhelming. In this context, there is a nexus between tooth-to-tail shortfalls and naval and air capability deficits. Maintaining sophisticated air and naval systems in remote locations increases the stress on the military "tail" exponentially. The less than adequate support typically provided by African militaries can impact air and naval systems immediately and catastrophically, causing precipitous declines in operational readiness. External support packages are much less effective in addressing this deficit, because of the highly specialized nature of air and naval support requirements.

In practical terms, most air and naval capabilities required for operational missions in Africa will probably have to be provided by actors external to the African militaries themselves, at least in the immediate future. Some African militaries have demonstrated the ability to deploy limited air packages. The Nigerians maintained and operated Alpha jets as close air support platforms in Liberia and Sierra Leone throughout most of the 1990s, and South Africa has deployed and sustained air assets in support of missions in Burundi and Democratic Republic of Congo. These deployments were very limited in scale, however, and efforts to deploy naval assets by ECOWAS member states have been much less successful. Future military operations in the region are likely to continue past dependence on externally provided air and naval assets.

A final limiting factor in African military capability and capacity is a lack of adequate fiscal resources, exacerbated by lack of capacity to manage effectively the resources available. This is less a feature of military institutions than a characteristic of public administration in the region. African institutions of governance are chronically under-resourced, leading to deficits in administrative capacity and chronic underfunding of public goods and services, including security. Part of this underfunding extends to salaries and compensation, both in terms of levels and reliability of payment. African militaries suffer from the consequences as much as most other public agencies in their respective state governments. The impact on military capacity is both direct and indirect.

African military institutions experience the impact directly in their lack of public management capacity at senior levels. Service and defense force staffs are relatively small, poorly organized, and without robust procedures, regulations, and adequate statutory frameworks to govern their activities. The shortfall tends to be even more pronounced at the ministerial level. African ministries of national defense tend to be undermanned, poorly financed, and lacking robust administrative procedures and functional civil service regulations. Ministry civil servants frequently lack the highly specialized skills required to provide effective oversight and management of defense policy, acquisition, resource management, and budget implementation. All of these shortfalls impact directly on the ability of African states to generate and effectively direct military forces.

Less directly, underfunding of military institutions leads to setting compensation levels for long-service professionals (both officers and NCOs) that do not support adequate standards of living for themselves or their families. In more extreme cases, this is exacerbated by the inability of the state to guarantee the regular payment of full salaries to military members. The practical result of this is that military professionals in Africa—like their counterparts in African civil service positions—routinely maintain other employment in the private sector. At best, this secondary employment compromises the ability of military members to focus exclusively on their military duties. At worst, it institutionalizes conflicts of interest and encourages corruption as military officers try to balance the demands of their commercial activities with the ethical requirements of government service.

Thus, corruption is probably the most immediate obstacle to both professionalization and effective capacity building within African military institutions. The combination of low or uncertain compensation with weak public administration capacity creates both the motive and opportunity for endemic corruption among African military professionals and defense sector civil servants. Competing budget demands at the national level make this problem a very difficult one to address effectively.

Even where the political will exists to address funding and compensation shortfalls in state defense and military institutions, that process is impeded by the need to address similar problems throughout the public sector. Movement towards democratization and good governance has had a counterintuitive impact in this context. As public accountability improves and governments become more responsive to the popular will, advantaging military institutions over other institutions of governance becomes politically contentious. The sharp decline in funding for the Nigerian defense and military sector that followed the return to civilian democratic governance under President Obasanjo provides a compelling example of this dynamic. Addressing the problem of corruption in African defense communities under these circumstances is difficult, to say the least.

The trends and characteristics of African militaries identified in the previous discussion are in some ways contradictory. Professionalization is moving African militaries towards a new institutional culture that emphasizes professional norms and standards of conduct. That trend appears to conflict with the persistent corruption that has accompanied chronic underfunding of the defense and other public sectors by African governments.

Countervailing Trends

The trends and characteristics outlined above are a generalization, and like all generalizations, they admit important exceptions and countervailing trends. Professionalization is not proceeding in all African militaries. Internationalization and the collective security paradigm that supports it are countered by a return to state-versus-state warfare in some more recent African conflict zones. The capacity shortfall noted among African militaries is also countered by a small number of African states which are displaying the ability to project power beyond their own borders on a limited scale.

Several African militaries have resisted the professionalizing trends seen elsewhere on the continent. These militaries fall into three broad categories: militaries that have not effectively transitioned from Cold War-era institutional antecedents; "bush armies" that have emerged from periods of extended conflict; and militaries in collapsed states where state institutions have failed completely. Each category impedes professionalization of military institutions in slightly different ways.

Guinea, Equatorial Guinea, Zimbabwe, Cote D'Ivoire, Sudan, and Angola are examples of states whose militaries remain in the shadow of the Cold War. These militaries continue to be focused on supporting regime survival at an institutional level, and on personal aggrandizement at the individual level. The militaries in Zimbabwe and Angola are still heavily influenced by the political ideology of the struggle for black majority rule. They can be best described as "party armies," serving the interests of the Zimbabwe African National Union-Patriotic Front in Zimbabwe and the *Movimento Popular de Libertação de Angola* in Angola.

Efforts to professionalize these state militaries confront resistance from ruling elites who view them as the primary guarantors of regime control, and from military members for whom military service provides access to political power and opportunities for graft.

Extended, violent conflicts in Africa have led to the emergence of several national militaries with "bush armies" as their antecedents. Bush armies emerged as insurgent forces struggling against established state structures and the post-colonial militaries that supported them, or as one of several insurgent factions in post-colonial civil wars. These militaries, of which Ethiopia, Eritrea, Uganda, and Rwanda are most representative, lack the professional foundations of most post-independence African militaries. On the other hand, current officer and NCO leadership in these armies tends to be highly competent, a function of extensive experience in the very unforgiving school of hard combat. Most of these states are seeking to build a professional foundation for military service (Eritrea being the conspicuous exception), but constructing institutions literally from the ground up is both expensive and time consuming. Unless these militaries are successful in institutionalizing existing competence through professional training and education, their militaries are likely to lose effectiveness rapidly. This is especially true among units and individuals that do not continue to serve in active combat theaters.

A small number of African states have suffered complete collapse in the period since the end of the Cold War. Somalia, Liberia, Sierra Leone, and Democratic Republic of Congo (DRC) provide the principle examples of this genre. These states not only lack an established foundation for military professionalism, they also lack the necessary resources and functionality to acquire that foundation. Liberia and Sierra Leone, both examples of recovering collapsed states, are the sites of ongoing experiments in externally-provided professionalization led by the U.S. security sector reform (SSR) program in Liberia and the United Kingdom SSR program in Sierra Leone.

Neither Somalia nor DRC has witnessed any serious effort at professionalization, and the militaries in those two states are better described as factional fighters in uniform.

The peace operations and collective security paradigms driving the internationalization of African militaries are countered by a return to more traditional state-versus-state conflict in several parts of Africa. The most prominent example of this countervailing trend is found in the armed conflict between Ethiopia and Eritrea over the border area around Badme from 1998 to 2000. Reminiscent of the most violent battles of the two world wars, and fought on a scale unprecedented in the region, this conflict has generated devastating casualties on both sides. It appears to have been prompted more by the personal agendas of the two heads of state involved than by the human security issues that have shaped the mandates of multilateral peace operations missions in the region.

Like the conflict between Ethiopia and Eritrea, the war in DRC has all the hallmarks of traditional state-versus-state warfare. Initiated in 1996 by a Rwandan incursion into Eastern Congo in pursuit of Rwandan genocidaires, the conflict eventually witnessed large-scale warfare between the military forces of Zimbabwe, Rwanda, Uganda, Angola, and DRC. Motives ranged from security concerns with insurgent groups operating from DRC territory, to organized looting of the Congo's mineral wealth. Despite the deployment of the largest UN peacekeeping mission since the end of the Cold War, state-versus-state warfare has continued in DRC. The ongoing conflict now involves the presence of both trends, with various state military forces continuing to pursue narrow state agendas in the eastern areas, while a growing UN peacekeeping force attempts to protect civilians and limit the destructive fighting among local factions, the DRC Army, and external forces. The conflict in DRC, described by many observers as the "First African War," may constitute a bellwether of a continuance of African military institutions toward internationalization and regional collective security paradigms, or a return to more traditional forms of state-based warfare.

Limits to African military capacity also challenge countervailing trends. Several militaries in the region have demonstrated the ability to project sustained combat power on a limited scale, despite low tooth-to-tail ratios. Angolan operations in DRC in 1997, the deployment of Nigerian forces into Sierra Leone in late 1998 and early 1999, and more recent Ethiopian operations in Somalia, illustrate these capabilities. With sustained, substantial investment in strategic and tactical lift, multifunctional logistics, and military manpower systems, any of these three states could emerge as a truly continental military power.

More substantial air and naval capabilities are resident in a very small number of African states. Angola (90 combat aircraft), Nigeria (75 combat aircraft) and Ethiopia (48 combat aircraft) remain the only sub-Saharan African states with multi-role air forces capable of generating a full range of air missions on a substantial scale. Whether any of these states can currently deploy and sustain their air assets beyond the range of their own air bases is highly questionable. South Africa continues to maintain a highly effective air arm, but one that is limited in size (29 combat aircraft) (International Institute for Strategic Studies 2008).

In the area of naval forces, South Africa remains the only sub-Saharan African military capable of generating any significant blue water naval capability. Other states in the region show naval combatant vessels in their orders of battle, most notably Nigeria, but the post-Cold War collapse of external funding and assistance efforts necessary to maintain those vessels in operational status raises questions about how many of them are actually deployable. Current external maritime assistance programs focus on "brown water" (coastal and riverine) capabilities designed to patrol coastlines and inland waterways.

Conclusion: The Future of Transformation in African Militaries

The ongoing transformation of African militaries is a reflection in part of broader trends towards more representative and more accountable governance in Africa. As that movement accelerates, encouraged and supported by international partners with reform agendas, the internationalization and professionalization of African militaries can likewise be expected to continue and expand in scope. The new regionalism in Africa is also providing impetus to military transformation. As Grant and Soderbaum have argued, this new regionalism extends beyond state-centric intergovernmental organizations to encompass the broader human security agenda (2003). It is this human security agenda that is at the heart of military professionalization in Africa.

African military transformation can be expected to produce military institutions with a focus on broader human security agendas rather than on internal security and regime survival. Participation in multilateral peace operations that promote international norms and standards for military operations will continue to reinforce more direct efforts at professionalization by both African states and their bilateral military assistance providers. Both the internationalization and the professionalization of African militaries can be expected to shape the behavior of those militaries in ways that strengthen their legitimacy in the eyes of civilian populations.

The evolution towards more professional militaries, focused on multinational peace operations and collective security, will continue to be impeded by limited African military capacity. The need for non-military capacity building and development within African states will continue to compete with demands for more resources for military activities. Absent significant external support in building fully rounded African militaries with lower tooth-to-tail ratios, African military forces will continue to depend upon external actors to enable the deployment and operation of significant force packages. This is especially true where air and naval assets are concerned.

The diversion of African military organizations from internal security missions and regime survival agendas to international and regional peace operations raises issues that are not as benign as a simple lack of capacity. Even with the accelerating forces of globalization, governance and political accountability continue to reside at the state level in Africa and elsewhere. International peacekeeping missions, whether launched by the United Nations, the African Union, or sub-regional organizations like ECOWAS, do not provide the political accountability that accrues when military forces are deployed directly by and on behalf of their respective state sovereigns. It is unclear how this lack of accountability will influence civil-military relations at the state level in Africa, especially in view of a problematic lack of a strong indigenous military tradition and culture. The continuing influence of actors external to the region on African militaries is unsettling, to say the least, in this respect.

African states continue to depend upon foreign, and especially Western, states for training, education, organization and equipment of their military forces. Individual African officers are trained at foreign military institutions. Doctrine is typically borrowed from major bilateral security assistance partners. Even higher-level collective training is frequently designed and financed, if not actually administered, by external military assistance providers. While the influence exerted by the U.S. ACOTA, British BMATT and French RECAMP programs certainly contributes to the normative agendas of African professionalization, it also raises questions about the legitimacy of African military institutions themselves. When viewed in combination with the continuing lack of strong military traditions in African states, the role of external actors in shaping African militaries calls into question the extent to which those militaries are genuinely representative of or responsive to their parent state governments.

Complicating all of these issues is the problem of endemic corruption within African military organizations. Until African states provide adequate compensation for their military members, including salary levels for long-service professionals that support appropriate standards of living, secondary employment will remain an enduring feature of the military profession in the region. Weak institutions of civil governance and less than adequate civilian oversight and management mechanisms will continue to make such secondary employment highly corrosive to standards of conduct and ethical behavior among military professionals. It is this combination of inadequate compensation and weak governance that makes security sector reform so critical to sustaining the momentum of military transformation within African states.

Colonel (Retired) Thomas A. Dempsey is the Professor of Security Sector Reform at the U.S. Army Peacekeeping and Stability Operations Institute in Carlisle, Pennsylvania. Formerly an Army foreign area officer specializing in sub-Saharan Africa, he has served as the U.S. Defense Attaché in Liberia and Sierra Leone and was the Director of African Studies at the U.S. Army War College from 1999 to 2006. He holds graduate degrees in African Area Studies from UCLA and in Military Arts and Sciences from the School of Advanced Military Science at Fort Leavenworth, Kansas.

References

Africa Center for Strategic Studies. 2008. *ECOWAS Strategic Level Seminar Program Highlights, Bamako, Mali, 24-29 February, 2008.* http://www.africacenter.org/ (accessed January 6, 2009).

Ayissi, Anatolle and Nouhoum Sangare. 2006. Mali. In *Budgeting for the Military Sector in Africa: The Processes and Mechanisms of Control,* ed. Wuyi Omitoogun, and Eboe Hutchful. London: Oxford University Press.

Crowder, Michael, ed. 1971. *West African Resistance: the Military Response to Colonial Occupation*. New York: Africana Publishing Corporation.

Economic Community of West African States. 1999. Article 25: Conditions for Application. *Protocol Relating to the Mechanism for Conflict Prevention, Management, Resolution, Peace-keeping and Security*. Abuja: Economic Community of West African States.

Edgerton, Robert B. 2002. *Africa's Armies from Honor to Infamy: A History from 1791 to the Present*. Boulder, CO: Westview Press.

Grant, J. Andrew and Fredrik Soderbaum. 2003. Introduction: The New Regionalism in Africa. In *The New Regionalism in Africa*, ed. J. Andrew Grant and Fredrik Soderbaum. Burlington, VT: Ashgate Publishing Limited.

Howe, Herbert M. 2001. *Ambiguous Order: Military Forces in African States*. Boulder, CO: Lynne Rienner Publishers, Inc.

International Institute for Strategic Studies. 2008. Sub-Saharan Africa. *The Military Balance 2008*. London: Routledge.

Interviews with ECOMOG Officers. 1999. Interviews conducted by the author with officers serving with ECOMOG in Liberia and Sierra Leone, Freetown, Sierra Leone and Monrovia, Liberia.

Jenkins, J. Craig and Augustine J. Kposowa, 1992. The Political Origins of African Military Coups: Ethnic Competition, Military Centrality, and the Struggle over the Postcolonial State. *International Studies Quarterly* 36: 271-292.

Kwiatkowski, Karen U. 2000. *African Crisis Response Initiative (ACRI): Past, Present and Future?* Carlisle: U.S. Army Peacekeeping Institute.

Mbeki, Moeletsi. 2000. Preface. In *South Africa and Naval Power at the Millenium*, ed. Martin Edmonds and Gregg Mills.

Braamfontein, South Africa: South African Institute of International Affairs.

McGrath, John J. 2007. *The Other End of the Spear: The Tooth-to-tail Ratio (T3R) in Modern Military Operations Occasional Paper 23.* Leavenworth, KS: Combat Studies Institute Press.

Organization for Economic Co-operation and Development. 2007. *OECD DAC Handbook on Security System Reform.* Paris: OECD Development Assistance Committee.

Saul, Mahir and Patrick Royer. 2001. *West African Challenge to Empire: Culture and History in the Volta-Bani Anticolonial War.* Athens, OH: Ohio University Press.

United Nations. 2006. Secretary-General's Note on the Top Ten Providers of Military Troops and Police Personnel to UN Operations Based on Monthly Averages Over a Three Year Period. New York: The President of the General Assembly.

United Nations. 2008. *United Nations Peacekeeping Operations Principles and Guidelines.* New York: United Nations Department of Peacekeeping Operations Department of Field Support.

United States Army. 2008. *FM 3-07 Stability Operations.* Leavenworth, KS: U.S. Army Combined Arms Center.